KT-415-621

İstanbul

"All you've got to do is decide to go
and the hardest part is over.

So go!"

TONY WHEELER, COFOUNDER – LONELY PLANET

THIS EDITION WRITTEN AND RESEARCHED BY

Virginia Maxwell

Contents

Plan Your Trip   4

Explore İstanbul   40

Understand İstanbul   175

Survival Guide   197

İstanbul Maps   228

(left) **Grand Bazaar p85** Colourful lamps for sale

(above) **Beyoğlu p113** Traditional *meyhane* (Turkish tavern)

(right) **Aya Sofya p46** Colourful decoration inside

Welcome to İstanbul

This magical meeting place of East and West has more top-drawer attractions than it has minarets (and that's a lot).

Living History

İstanbul's strategic location has attracted many a marauding army over the centuries. The Greeks, Persians, Romans and Venetians took turns ruling before the Ottomans stormed into town and decided to stay – physical reminders of their various tenures are found littered across the city. And the fact that the city straddles two continents wasn't its only drawcard. This was the final stage on the legendary Silk Routes that linked Asia and Europe, and many of the merchants who came here liked it so much that they, too, decided to stay. In so doing, they endowed the city with a cultural diversity that it retains to this day.

Art & Architecture

The conquering armies of ancient times tended to ransack the city rather than endow it with artistic treasures, but all that changed with the Byzantines, who adorned their churches and palaces with mosaics and frescoes. Miraculously, many of these are still here to admire. Their successors, the Ottomans, were quick to launch an ambitious building program after their emphatic arrival. The magnificently decorated imperial mosques that followed are architectural triumphs that together form one of the world's great skylines.

Culinary Heritage

'But what about the food?' we hear you say. We're happy to report that the city's cuisine is as diverse as its heritage, and delicious to boot. Locals take their eating and drinking seriously – the restaurants here are the best in the country. You can eat edgy fusion creations, aromatic Asian dishes or Italian classics if you so choose, but most visitors prefer to sample the succulent kebaps, flavoursome mezes and freshly caught fish that are the city's signature dishes, washing them down with rakı, beer or a glass or two of locally produced and eminently quaffable wine.

Local Life

Some ancient cities are the sum of their monuments, but İstanbul factors a lot more into the equation. Chief among its manifold attractions are the locals, who have an infectious love of life and generosity of spirit. This vibrant, inclusive and expanding community is full of people who work and party hard, treasure family and friendships, and have no problem melding tradition and modernity in their everyday lives. Joining them in their favourite haunts – *çay bahcesis* (tea gardens), neighbourhood coffeehouses, *meyhanes* (Turkish taverns) and *kebapçıs* (kebap restaurants) – will be a highlight of your visit.

Why I Love İstanbul

By Virginia Maxwell, Author

Why do I love this city? Let me count the ways. I love the locals, who have an endless supply of hospitality, good humour and insightful conversation at their disposal. I love the fact that when I walk down a city street, layers of history unfold before me. I love listening to the sound of the *müezzins* duelling from their minarets and I love seeing the sun set over the world's most beautiful skyline. I love the restaurants, the bars and the tea gardens. But most of all, I love the fact that in İstanbul, an extraordinary cultural experience lies around every corner.

For more about our authors, see p248.

Top: Süleymaniye Mosque and the Eminönü docks

İstanbul's
Top 10

Aya Sofya (p46)

1 History resonates when you visit this majestic Byzantine basilica. Built by order of the Emperor Justinian in the sixth century AD, its soaring dome, huge nave and glittering gold mosaics contribute to its reputation as one of the world's most beautiful buildings, and its long and fascinating history as church, mosque and museum make it the city's most revealing time capsule. Looted by marauding Crusaders in the 13th century, stormed by Ottoman invaders during the Conquest in 1453 and visited by millions of tourists since becoming a museum, it is Turkey's greatest treasure.

◉ *Sultanahmet & Around*

Topkapı Palace (p53)

2 The secrets of the seraglio will be revealed during your visit to this opulent Ottoman palace complex occupying the promontory of İstanbul's Old City. A series of mad, sad and downright bad sultans lived here with their concubines and courtiers between 1465 and 1830, and extravagant relics of their centuries of folly, intrigue, excess, patronage, diplomacy and war are everywhere you look. Highlights include the huge Harem (private quarters), impressive Imperial Council Chamber, object-laden Imperial Treasury and picturesque Marble Terrace.

◉ *Sultanahmet & Around*

CHRIS HELLIER/CORBIS ©

Shopping in the Bazaars (p99)

3 The chaotic and colourful Grand Bazaar is the best-known shopping destination on the Historic Peninsula, but it certainly isn't the only one. After exploring its labyrinthine lanes and hidden caravanserais, follow the steady stream of local shoppers heading downhill into the busy shopping precinct of Tahtakale, which has at its hub the seductively scented Spice Bazaar. From there, head back up towards the Blue Mosque and its attached *arasta* (row of shops by a mosque), where you may well find a lasting memento of your trip. GRAND BAZAAR

🔒 *Bazaar District*

Bosphorus Ferry Trip (p150)

4 Climbing aboard one of the city's famous ferries is the quintessential İstanbul experience. The trip between Asia and Europe on a commuter ferry is hard to beat, but the Bosphorus tourist ferry that travels the length of the great strait from Eminönü to the mouth of the Black Sea is even better, offering passengers views of palaces, parks and ornate timber mansions on both the Asian and European shores. It doesn't matter whether you opt for a long or short cruise – either is sure to be memorable.

🚶 *Ferry Trips from İstanbul*

Süleymaniye Mosque (p88)

5 Dominating the Old City's skyline, Süleyman the Magnificent's most notable architectural legacy certainly lives up to its patron's name. The fourth imperial mosque built in İstanbul, the Süleymaniye was designed by Mimar Sinan, the most famous of all Ottoman architects, and was built between 1550 and 1557. Its extensive and largely intact *külliye* (mosque complex) buildings illustrate aspects of daily Ottoman life and are still used by the local community – making this a sight that truly lives up to the tag of 'living history'.

👁 *Bazaar District*

Basilica Cistern *(p68)*

6 When the Byzantine Emperors decided to build something, they certainly didn't cut corners! This extraordinary subterranean cistern located opposite Aya Sofya features a wildly atmospheric forest of columns (336 to be exact), vaulted brick ceilings, mysterious carved Medusa-head capitals and ghostly patrols of carp. A testament to the ambitious town planning and engineering expertise of the Byzantines, the cistern has played a starring role in innumerable motion pictures (remember *From Russia with Love?*) and is now one of the city's best-loved tourist attractions.

◉ *Sultanahmet & Around*

Kariye Museum *(p104)*

7 Tucked away in the shadow of Theodosius II's monumental land walls, Kariye Museum (Chora Church) is a tiny Byzantine building located in the little-visited Western Districts of the city. It's adorned with mosaics and frescoes that were created in the 14th century and illustrate the lives of Christ and the Virgin Mary. These are among the world's best examples of Byzantine art, rivalled only by mosaics adorning churches in Ravenna, Italy. Put simply, it's impossible to over-praise the exquisite interior here – visiting is sure to be a highlight of your trip. MOSAICS IN CHORA CHURCH

◉ *Western Districts*

7

8

Wining & Dining in Beyoğlu *(p124)*

8 Breathtaking views of the Bosphorus and Old City from the rooftop terraces of a constellation of glamorous bars are just one of the enticements on offer in bohemian Beyoğlu. Locals come here to carouse in traditional *meyhanes* (taverns), eat kebaps in *ocakbaşıs* (fireside kebap restaurants), sample Modern Turkish cuisine in sophisticated bistros and relax in casual European-style cafes and clubs. It's the eating and entertainment epicentre of the city – don't miss it.

✖ *Beyoğlu*

Blue Mosque (p64)

9 The city's signature building was the grand project of Sultan Ahmet I, who urged its architect and builders on in the construction process before his untimely death in 1617 aged only 27. The mosque's wonderfully curvaceous exterior features a cascade of domes and six tapering minarets. Inside, the huge space is encrusted with thousands of the blue İznik tiles that give the building its unofficial but commonly used name. Beloved by tourists and locals alike, it and Aya Sofya bookend Sultanahmet Park in a truly extraordinary fashion.

◉ *Sultanahmet & Around*

Visiting a Hamam (p38)

10 In life, there aren't too many opportunities to wander semi-naked through a 16th-century Ottoman monument. Unless you visit İstanbul, that is. The city's world-famous hamams offer a unique opportunity to immerse yourself in history, architecture, warm water and soap suds – all at the same time. A hamam treatment offers a relaxing finale to a day spent pounding the city's pavements, and gives a fascinating insight into the life and customs of Ottoman society. You can surrender to the steam at baths on both side of the Galata Bridge. CAĞALOĞLU HAMAMI

🛉 *Hamams & Spas*

What's New

Aya Sofya Restoration

They've taken 17 years to finish, so it's not surprising that the restoration works recently completed under the auspices of Unesco in the city's Byzantine basilica have been rapturously received. The atmospheric Ottoman-era chandeliers have been reinstated; a re-discovered and restored mosaic of a seraph (angel) has been unveiled; and the attached tombs of the Ottoman sultans have been restored and opened to the public (p46).

SALT Cultural Centres

Housed in cleverly adapted historic buildings, the SALT centres in Galata and Beyoğlu have joined the city's ever-growing portfolio of privately endowed contemporary art museums, and done so in style (p117 and p120).

Foodie Tours

Foodies have been clamouring to book a spot on the culinary walks around the Old City, Beyoğlu and 'Little Urfa' (Aksaray) offered by the dedicated food bloggers at Culinary Backstreets (p125).

Museum of Innocence

Is it a museum or a piece of conceptual art? Visit Orhan Pamuk's museum celebrating the novel of the same name to make up your mind (p121).

Ayasofya Hürrem Sultan Hamamı

Reopened with great fanfare after a three-year, US$13 million restoration, this 16th-century hamam is one of the city's most beautiful Ottoman-era buildings (p81).

Museum Pass İstanbul

Representing a possible saving of ₺36 on museum entries and allowing the holder to bypass admission queues, this discount pass is well worth considering (p69).

Pera Palace Hotel

İstanbul's most famous hotel has reopened after a €23 million renovation and features public spaces including a bar, patisserie, tea lounge and restaurant (p119).

Şakirin Mosque

This striking modern building in Üsküdar is a must-see for architecture buffs and contrasts fascinatingly with that suburb's profusion of Ottoman mosques (p148).

Turkish Coffee Workshop

Located in the Museum of Turkish & Islamic Arts, Müzenin Kahvesi offers a 30-minute 'coffee experience' that will see you brewing the perfect cup of Turkish coffee on your return home (p82).

Galata Mevlevi Museum

This 15th-century *tekke* (dervish lodge) in Galata has been renovated and now houses a fascinating museum focusing on Mevlevi (dervish) culture and history (p118).

Ottoman Cuisine in Sultanahmet

The city's infatuation with so-called 'Ottoman Palace Cuisine' continues unabated, and Sultanahmet is a first-time beneficiary courtesy of Matbah, a restaurant specialising in dishes created for the kitchens of Topkapı and Dolmabahçe (p76).

For more recommendations and reviews, see **lonelyplanet.com/ [Istanbul]**

Need to Know

Currency
Türk Lirası (Turkish Lira; ₺)

Language
Turkish

Visas
Not required for some European nationalities; most other nationalities can obtain a 90-day visa on arrival.

Money
ATMs widespread. Credit cards accepted at most shops, hotels and upmarket restaurants.

Mobile Phones
Most European and Australasian phones work here; some North American phones don't. Check with your provider. Pre-paid SIM cards must be registered when purchased.

Time
Eastern European time (UTC/GMT plus two hours November to March; plus three hours April to October).

Tourist Information
Tourist offices operate in Sultanahmet, Sirkeci, Karaköy and Atatürk International Airport. These offer free maps but are of little help otherwise.

Your Daily Budget
The following are average costs per day:

Budget under €60
➡ Dorm beds: €13–20
➡ Kebap or pide dinner: €9
➡ Beer at a neighbourhood bar: €4
➡ Tram, bus or ferry ride €0.90

Midrange €60-200
➡ Double room: from €70
➡ *Lokanta* lunch: €12
➡ *Meyhane* dinner with wine: €35
➡ Taxi from Sultanahmet to Beyoğlu: €15

Top End over €200
➡ Double room: from €180
➡ Restaurant dinner with wine: €45
➡ Cocktail in a rooftop bar: €10
➡ Hamam treatment: €70

Advance Planning

Three months before you go If you're travelling in spring, autumn or over Christmas, make your hotel booking as far in advance as possible.

Two months before you go İstanbul's big-ticket festivals and concerts sell out fast. Book your tickets online at Biletix (www.biletex.com).

Two weeks before you go Ask your hotel to make dinner reservations.

Useful Websites

➡ Lonely Planet (www.lonely planet.com) Check out the Thorn Tree bulletin board to find out what city discoveries are being made.

➡ Istanbul Beat (www.istanbul beatblog.com) Handy listings-based blog produced by the *Time Out İstanbul* crew

➡ Cornucopia (www.cornucopia .net) The online site of the glossy *Connoisseurs of Turkey* magazine has a handy arts diary as well as exhibitions listings and blogs.

➡ Hürriyet Daily News (www .hurriyetdailynews.com) English-language website of the secularist daily newspaper.

➡ Turkey Travel Planner (www .turkeytravelplanner.com) Useful travel info.

WHEN TO GO

Spring and autumn are the best times to visit, as the weather is good and festivals are in full swing. Summers can be unpleasantly hot and winters bone-chillingly cold.

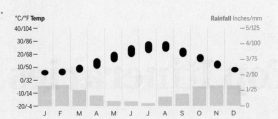

Arriving in İstanbul

Atatürk International Airport

Metro and tram to Sultanahmet (5.40am to 1.40am; ₺4).

Havataş bus to Taksim Meydanı (Taksim Sq; 4am to 1am; ₺10).

Taxis ₺40 to Sultanahmet, ₺50 to Taksim Meydanı.

Sabiha Gökçen International Airport

Havataş bus to Taksim Meydanı (5am to midnight with occasional shuttle services at other times; ₺12), from where a funicular (₺2) and tram (₺2) travel to Sultanahmet.

Taxis cost ₺120 to Sultanahmet and ₺90 to Taksim Meydanı.

For much more on **arrival** see p198

Getting Around

Rechargable İstanbulkarts (travelcards) save time and money.

➡ **Tram** Services run from Bağcılar, in the city's west, to Kabataş, near Taksim Meydanı in Beyoğlu, stopping at Zeytinburnu, Beyazıt-Grand Bazaar, Sultanahmet and Eminönü en route.

➡ **Ferry** Boats travel between the Asian and European shores, up and down the Golden Horn and Bosphorus, and over to the Princes' Islands.

➡ **Taxi** Inexpensive and plentiful.

➡ **Metro** One line connects Aksaray with the airport. Another connects Şişhane, near Tünel Meydanı in Beyoğlu, with Taksim Meydanı and the commercial and residential districts to its north.

➡ **Funicular** These make the trip from the tramline up to İstiklal Caddesi easy. One connects Karaköy with Tünel; the other connects Kabataş with Taksim Meydanı.

➡ **Bus** The lines following the Bosphorus shoreline are of most interest to travellers.

For much more on **getting around** see p200

Sleeping

Accommodation choices in İstanbul are as diverse, plentiful and expensive as in most major European cities. They're also in heavy demand during peak tourism periods such as spring, autumn and Christmas, so it's important to book ahead. At these times, prices spike. During winter and at the height of summer, prices can plummet. Most of the decent budget and midrange choices are in or around Sultanahmet; boutique and top-end options are clustered in Beyoğlu and along the Bosphorus.

In recent years there has been a proliferation of suite, apartment and boutique hotel openings. There's also been a huge growth in the number of apartment-rental services.

For much more on **sleeping** see p165

Top Itineraries

Day One

Sultanahmet & Around

 Head to Aya Sofya Meydanı (Square) and work out which of the museums and mosques in the immediate area will be on your visiting list. Don't miss **Aya Sofya**, the **Blue Mosque** and the **Basilica Cistern**.

> **Lunch** Cihannüma offers Ottoman dishes and stupendous views.

Sultanahmet & Around

Diverge from the tourist trail and visit some of Sultanahmet's hidden highlights. Source some souvenirs in the historic **Arasta Bazaar**, where you can browse in carpet, handicraft and bathwares shops.

> **Dinner** Hamdi serves delicious kebaps and has magnificent views.

Sultanahmet & Around

After enjoying an early dinner, make your way to Sirkeci, where you can watch dervishes whirl at **Hocapaşa Cultural Centre**, a converted 15th-century hamam. Alternatively, claim a table at **Derviş Aile Çay Bahçesi** or **Cafe Meşale**, where you can enjoy tea, nargile and a free (but very touristy) whirling-dervish performance.

Day Two

Bazaar District

 Get ready to explore the city's famous bazaar district. After exploring the labyrinthine lanes and hidden caravanserais of the world-famous **Grand Bazaar**, make your way to the most magnificent of all Ottoman mosques, the **Süleymaniye**.

> **Lunch** Eateries, including Bahar and Onur, surround the Grand Bazaar.

Bazaar District

After lunch, follow the steady stream of local shoppers making their way down the hill to the **Spice Bazaar**. While there, seek out the exquisite **Rüstem Paşa Mosque**, camouflaged in the midst of a busy produce market. As the sun starts to set, walk across the **Galata Bridge** towards the eating and entertainment district of Beyoğlu.

> **Dinner** *Meyhanes* (taverns) and restaurants aplenty in Beyoğlu.

Beyoğlu

Start with a pre-dinner drink in one of Beyoğlu's rooftop bars and then move on to dinner in a *meyhane* (tavern) or a stylish restaurant serving Modern Turkish cuisine. After dinner, kick on to a club or wind down at the **Tophane nargile cafes**.

Day Three

Sultanahmet & Around

 It's time to investigate the lifestyles of the sultans at **Topkapı Palace**. You'll need a half day to explore the palace Harem, marvel at the precious objects in the Treasury and wander through the pavilion-filled grounds.

> **Lunch** Matbah serves Ottoman food in a pleasant garden setting.

Western Districts

Take the Golden Horn (Haliç) ferry to Ayvansaray and then walk along the historic **land walls** to Edirnekapı so that you can admire the exquisite mosaics and frescoes that adorn almost every surface of **Kariye Museum**, a former Byzantine church. If you're keen to see more mosaics, the **Fethiye Museum** is a short walk away.

> **Dinner** Asmalımescit, in Beyoğlu, has bars and traditional *meyhanes*.

Sultanahmet & the Bazaar District

You've spent a full day sightseeing, so why not relax in the steamy surrounds of an Ottoman-era **hamam** (Turkish bath) after dinner? Afterwards, head back across the Galata Bridge to Beyoğlu so that you can sample more of its nightlife options.

Day Four

The Bosphorus

 Board the **Uzun Boğaz Turu** (Long Bosphorus Tour) to spend a full day exploring this culturally and architecturally rich waterway. After admiring the historic *yalıs* (waterside timber mansions) along its shores, alight from the ferry at Sarıyer and make your way back to town by bus, visiting museums and monuments along the way.

> **Lunch** MüzedeChanga – scenic terrace and Modern Turkish cuisine.

Beyoğlu

If you decided to take a 90-minute cruise on a Bosphorus excursion boat rather than the full-day trip, you can devote the afternoon to investigating Beyoğlu's exciting contemporary-art scene. Don't miss the **İstanbul Modern** museum and the **ARTER** and **SALT** cultural centres.

> **Dinner** Stylish Lokanta Maya showcases Modern Aegean cooking.

Beyoğlu

Wander the streets surrounding the **Galata Tower**, admiring the building stock, browsing in boutiques and perhaps enjoying an aperitif. Then move on to Lokanta Maya, a stylish showcase of Modern Aegean cooking in Karaköy, followed by a sweet finale at İstanbul's most famous baklava shop, **Karaköy Güllüoğlu**.

If You Like...

Contemporary Art

ARTER Four floors of cutting-edge visual art located on İstiklal Caddesi. (p120)

SALT Beyoğlu Nooks and crannies offer up challenging artworks in this recently opened cultural centre. (p120)

Galerist One of the many impressive commercial galleries in the city. (p120)

İstanbul Modern The city's pre-eminent art museum, with a huge permanent collection of Turkish artworks and world-class temporary exhibitions. (p116)

Ottoman Mosques

Süleymaniye Mosque Crowning the Old City's third hill, this magnificent and largely intact mosque complex is one of the city's major landmarks. (p88)

Blue Mosque Possesses more minarets and visual pizzazz than any mosque should rightly lay claim to. (p64)

Atik Valide Mosque A majestic structure sitting astride Üsküdar's highest hill, this is the most impressive of that suburb's many Ottoman mosques. (p148)

Mihrimah Sultan Mosque A tapering minaret and delicate stained-glass windows are just two of this mosque's elegant design features. (p108)

Museums

İstanbul Archaeology Museums Eclectic collection of artefacts from the imperial collections, including outstanding classical sculptures. (p66)

Museum of Turkish & Islamic Arts The world's most significant collection of antique carpets, plus exquisite calligraphy. (p71)

Şakirin Mosque by architect Hüsrev Tayla (p148)

Pera Museum A splendid collection of paintings featuring Turkish Orientalist themes plus a changing program of thematic exhibitions. (p120)

Sakıp Sabancı Museum Blockbuster international exhibitions in a scenic Bosphorus location. (p155)

Contemporary Architecture

Şakirin Mosque A wonderfully transparent building with stunning interior fitout. (p148)

SALT Galata This handsome 19th-century bank building has been sympathetically – and expensively – converted into a cutting-edge cultural centre. (p117)

Kanyon Shopping Mall Located in Levent, this modern take on the Grand Bazaar sports confident curves and tapering towers.

Atatürk Cultural Centre This landmark 1950s building on Taksim Square is currently undergoing what is hoped to be a stylish and sympathetic restoration. (p121)

Music

Babylon An İstanbul institution, with a diverse program of live music and an inclusive atmosphere. (p135)

Salon An intimate venue in the headquarters of the İstanbul Foundation for Culture & Arts (İKSV) building in Şişhane; great for jazz. (p135)

Hasnun Galip Sokak This Beyoğlu sidestreet is known for its concentration of *Türkü evlerı*, Kurdish-owned bars where musicians perform *halk meziği* (folk music). (p135)

Nardis Jazz Club The city's oldest and best-loved jazz venue is where afficionados congregate. (p135)

Ethnic Enclaves

Karaköy Home to Genoese traders in Byzantine times, this suburb was home to a wealthy Jewish community in the 19th century.

Fener A traditionally Greek suburb that has at its heart the symbolic headquarters of the Greek Orthodox church, the Ecumenical Patriarchate.

Arnavutköy Many members of the Greek community live in this pretty Bosphorus village.

Kuruçeşme The Armenian presence lives on in this suburb's still-functioning church of the Surp Haç (Holy Cross).

Ferry Trips

Crossing the Continents Flit between Europe and Asia in less than one hour on a ferry from Eminönü to Kadıköy or Üsküdar.

The Bosphorus One of the city's signature experiences, offering magnificent museums, mansions and meals along its length.

The Golden Horn Hop on and off the commuter ferry that services the city's western districts.

The Princes' Islands Escape the city and head towards these oases of calm in the Sea of Marmara.

For more top İstanbul spots, see the following:
⇒ Eating (p26)
⇒ Drinking & Nightlife (p31)
⇒ Shopping (p34)

PLAN YOUR TRIP IF YOU LIKE...

Views

Topkapı Terraces Sequestered in this palace complex, the Ottoman sultans must have loved the scenic viewpoints from its two panoramic terraces. (p53)

Galata Bridge Snapshots of local life and unbeatable 360-degree views await when you walk between Sultanahmet and Beyoğlu. (p91)

Rumeli Hisarı This majestic fortress commands views of the Bosphorus from its crumbling battlements. (p154)

Rooftop Bars Glamorous bars on rooftops across Beyoğlu offer sensational views from their outdoor terraces.

Byzantine History

Kariye Museum A concentration of Byzantine mosaics unrivalled here or perhaps anywhere in the world. (p104)

Aya Sofya 1500 years old and still going strong, this basilica has witnessed history unfold and its interior tells many stories. (p46)

İstanbul Archaeology Museums The city's largest collection of Byzantine artefacts is on display at this excellent museum. (p66)

Great Palace Mosaic Museum A remarkably intact and visually arresting remnant of the Great Palace of Byzantium. (p69)

Palaces

Topkapı Palace Home to the sultans for centuries, this cluster of ornately decorated pavilions houses treasures galore. (p53)

Dolmabahçe Palace This essay in decorative excess was built alongside the Bosphorus in the 19th century. (p141)

Beylerbeyi Palace Nestled under the Bosphorus Bridge, this 30-room imperial holiday shack is set in pretty gardens. (p152)

Yıldız Şale Originally an imperial hunting lodge, this oft-extended Ottoman guesthouse has hosted royalty galore. (p142)

Parks & Gardens

Yıldız Park The city's favourite urban retreat, with flowers and picnic possibilities galore. (p142)

Hıdiv Kasrı Art nouveau mansion and stunning woodland garden located above the Bosphorus suburb of Kanlıca. (p153)

Gülhane Park Escape the museum queues and tourist touts in the extensive grounds of what was once the sultan's private garden. (p73)

Markets

Grand Bazaar One of the world's oldest – and most atmospheric – shopping complexes. (p85)

Spice Bazaar Has been supplying locals with spices and sugary treats for nearly 400 years. (p90)

Kadıköy Pazarı The city's most enticing produce market is held in the streets surrounding the Kadıköy İskelesi (ferry dock).

Çarşamba Pazarı A bustling local street market held every Wednesday in the streets surrounding the Fatih Mosque. (p108)

Month by Month

March

It's cold at the start of the month, but as the weather improves, the tourists start to arrive and the festival season kicks off. Good hotel deals are on offer early in the month; high-season prices from Easter onwards.

☆ Akbank Short Film Festival

Beloved by the black-clad Beyoğlu bohemian set, this arty film-culture event is held at the Akbank Culture & Arts Centre (www.akbanksanat.com).

✳ Nevruz

Locals celebrate this ancient Middle Eastern spring festival on 21 March with jolly goings-on and jumping over bonfires.

April

Locals are well and truly into the springtime swing of things by April. Highlights include the blooming of tulips across the city and the arrival of fresh sea bass on restaurant menus.

☆ International İstanbul Film Festival

If you're keen to view the best in Turkish film, this is the event (http://film.iksv .org/en) to attend. Held early in the month in cinemas around town, it programs retrospectives and recent releases from Turkey and abroad.

☉ İstanbul Tulip Festival

The tulip *(lâle)* is one of İstanbul's traditional symbols, and the local government celebrates this fact by planting over 11 million of them annually. These bloom in early April, enveloping almost every street and park in vivid spring colours.

June

It's summertime and yes, the living is easy. There's an abundance of strawberries, cherries and plums in the produce markets and the open-air nightclubs on the Bosphorus start to hit their strides.

☆ İstanbul Music Festival

The city's premier arts festival (http://muzik.iksv.org /en) includes performances of opera, dance, orchestral concerts and chamber recitals. Acts are often internationally renowned and the action takes place in atmosphere-laden venues including Aya İrini, the İstanbul Archaeology Museums and İstanbul Modern.

July

It can be as hot as Hades at this time of year, so many locals decamp to beaches on the Mediterranean Coast. Those left in town keep the heat under control with a liberal dose of cool jazz.

☆ Efes Pilsen One Love

This two-day music festival (www.pozitif-ist.com) is organised by the major promoter of rock and pop concerts in Turkey, Pozitif, and is held at santralistanbul on the Golden Horn. International headline acts play everything from punk to pop, electro to disco.

☆ İstanbul Jazz Festival

This festival (http://caz.iksv .org/en) programs an exhilarating hybrid of conventional jazz, electronica, drum 'n' bass, world music and rock. Look out for Tünel Feast, its one-day 'festival within the festival', which stages free events around Tünel Meydanı (Tünel Square).

September

Autumn ushers in an influx of tourists with its cool breezes, and hotels revert to their high-season rates. Arty types are in seventh heaven when the

internationally acclaimed art biennial is launched.

◉ İstanbul Biennial

The city's major visual-arts shindig (http://bienal.iksv .org/en) takes place from early September to early November in odd-numbered years. An international curator or panel of curators nominates a theme and puts together a cutting-edge program that is then exhibited in a variety of venues around town.

☆ Efes Pilsen Blues Festival

The longest-running music festival in Turkey (www .pozitif-ist.com) tours nationally over September and October, leaving an echo of boogie-woogie, zydeco and 12-bar blues from Adana to Trabzon. It stops for a two-day program in İstanbul.

October

The year's final festivals take everyone's minds off the impending arrival of

winter. Fresh chestnuts are roasted on street braziers around town, and pomegranates come into season, making their ruby-red juice a popular treat.

☆ Akbank Jazz Festival

This older sister to the International İstanbul Jazz Festival is a boutique event (www.akbanksanat.com), with a program featuring traditional and avant-garde jazz. Venues are scattered around town.

◉ İstanbul Design Biennial

A new addition to the İKSV's stellar calendar of festivals, this event (http:// istanbuldesignbiennial.iksv .org/) sees the city's design community celebrating their profession and critically discussing its future. It's held in even-numbered years.

With Kids

İstanbul is perfect for a family-friendly break. Children might whinge at the number of mosques and museums on the itinerary, but they'll be appeased by the fantastic baklava, lokum (Turkish delight) and dondorma (ice cream), not to mention the castles, underground cisterns and parks.

For Toddlers

Playgrounds & Parks

There are good playgrounds in Gülhane Park and in the waterside park opposite the Fındıkı tram stop in Beyoğlu. Open areas such as the Hippodrome and Yıldız Park also offer loads of space for toddlers to expend energy.

Ferry Trips

Little kids love ferries, and İstanbul offers loads of opportunities to climb aboard.

For Bigger Kids

Rahmi M Koç Museum (p159)

Kids go crazy (in a good way) when they encounter all of the trains, planes, boats and automobiles on exhibit at this museum in Hasköy.

Rumeli Hisarı (p154)

This huge castle on the Bosphorus is a hit with kids. Just be sure that your junior knights and princesses are careful when they clamour up the battlements.

Princes' Islands (p162)

Your kids will love taking *fayton* (horse-drawn carriage) rides around the islands or hiring bicycles to get around under their own steam.

Basilica Cistern (p68)

It's creepy, and kids can explore the walkways suspended over the water. Way cool.

For Teenagers

Cooking Courses

Some teenagers see the kitchen as offering more than a refrigerator just waiting to be raided. Book yourself and your aspiring chef into a cooking class such as the one offered by Cooking Alaturka (p82) in Sultanahmet.

İstanbul Modern (p116)

The city's preeminent contemporary art gallery has plenty of exhibits – including lots of multimedia – that will amuse and engage.

Need to Know

➡ Kids under 12 receive free or discounted entry to most museums and monuments.

➡ Kids under seven travel free on public transport.

➡ Most pavements are cobbled, so strollers aren't very useful.

➡ Disposable nappies and formula are easy to purchase.

➡ Kids are almost inevitably made welcome in restaurants, although highchairs and kids' menus are the exception rather than the rule.

Like a Local

İstanbul's 14 million residents enjoy a lifestyle crammed with culture, backdropped by history and underpinned by family and faith. Head off the tourist trails to experience the city as they do.

Keyif

İstanbullus have perfected the art of *keyif* (quiet relaxation), and practice it at every possible opportunity. *Çay bahçesi* (tea gardens) and nargile cafes are *keyif* central, offering patrons pockets of tranquillity off the noisy and crowded streets. Games of *tavla* (backgammon), glasses of tea, nargiles (waterpipes) and quiet conversations are the only distractions on offer.

Produce Markets

Street vendors selling fruit and vegetables can be found working pavements around town, and most neighbourhoods have a produce market where stallholders hawk everything from pungent farmhouse cheese to plump olives and freshly caught fish, providing self-caterers with plenty of options.

The İskele

Traffic in İstanbul is nightmarish, so it's sensible to take to the waters rather than the roads wherever possible. The city's famous flotilla of ferries transports thousands of commuters every day. Many of these passengers spend time before or after their journey enjoying a glass of tea or a snack at the *iskele* (ferry dock), making these often ramshackle places wonderful pockets of local life.

The Mosque

İstanbul's magnificent Ottoman mosques may be popular tourist destinations, but their primary function is a religious one. Observe these rules when visiting:

➡ Remove your shoes before walking on the mosque's carpet; you can leave shoes on shelves near the mosque door.

➡ Women should always cover their heads and shoulders with a shawl or scarf; both women and men should dress modestly.

➡ Avoid visiting mosques at prayer times (within 30 minutes of when the *ezan*, or call to prayer, sounds from the mosque minaret) and also around Friday lunch, when weekly sermons and group prayers are held.

➡ Speak quietly and don't use flashes on your camera (and never photograph people praying).

For Free

The hippies and backpackers who flocked to İstanbul in the 1960s and 1970s would certainly blow their meagre budgets if they headed this way today. Fortunately, the ever-increasing price of hotel rooms, transport and meals is counterbalanced by an array of top-drawer sights that can be visited at no cost.

Mosques

Topping the seven hills of the Old City and adorning many of its streets, İstanbul's Ottoman mosques are jewels in the city's crown. Entry to these architectural wonders is open to everyone regardless of their religion.

Galleries

The recent trend for İstanbul's banks and business dynasties to endow private art galleries and cultural centres is the best thing to hit the city since the tulip bulb arrived. Most are on or near İstiklal Caddesi in Beyoğlu and charge no entry fees.

Parks & Gardens

Picnicking and promenading are two favourite local pastimes, so it's fortunate that there are so many wonderful parks and gardens open to the public. Particularly beautiful or historic examples include Gülhane Park (p73) and the Hippodrome (p70) in Sultanahmet; Yıldız Park (p142) in Beşiktaş; and Hıdiv Kasrı (p153) and Emirgan Woods on the Bosphorus.

Churches

There are a surprising number of still-functioning Christian churches in İstanbul, many of which are of great historical significance. The best known of these is the Patriarchal Church of St George (p107) in Fener, the symbolic headquarters of the Greek Orthodox church.

Byzantine Monuments

Many of the city's Byzantine churches were converted into mosques after the Conquest and still function as such. Other Byzantine monuments that can be visited at no charge include the beautifully restored cistern in the basement of the Nakkaş (p231) carpet store in Sultanahmet.

Tray of regional specialties

Eating

The locals love to eat. For them, food is much more than belly fuel, and meals are occasions to share and be celebrated. For most locals, the idea of eating in front of a TV or from a freezer is absolute anathema – theirs is a cuisine that is social, slow and seasonal.

What's on the Menu?

The local cuisine has been refined over centuries and is treated more reverently than any museum collection in the country. That's not to say it's fussy, because what differentiates Turkish food from other national noshes is its rustic and honest base. Here mezes are simple, kebaps uncomplicated, salads unstructured and seafood unsauced. Flavours explode in your mouth because ingredients are grown locally and are used when they are in season.

MARVELLOUS MEZES

Mezes aren't just a type of dish, they're a whole eating experience. In *meyhanes* (Turkish taverns) waiters heave around enormous trays full of cold meze dishes that customers can choose from – hot meze dishes are usually chosen from the menu.

Mezes are often vegetable-based, though seafood dishes also feature.

MEAT – THE TURKISH WAY

Overall, the Turks are huge meat eaters. Beef, lamb, mutton, liver and chicken are prepared in a number of ways and eaten at home, in *kebapçıs* (kebap restaurants) and in *köftecıs* (meatball restaurants).

The most famous meat dish is the kebap (*şiş* and *döner*) but *köfte*, *saç kavurma* (stir-fried cubed meat dishes) and *güveç* (meat and vegetable stews cooked in a terracotta pot) are just as common.

The most popular sausage in Turkey is the spicy beef *sucuk*. Garlicky *pastırma* (pressed beef preserved in spices) is regularly used as an accompaniment to egg dishes; it's occasionally served with warm hummus (chickpea, tahini and lemon dip) as a meze.

A few İstanbul restaurants serve the central Anatolian dish of *mantı* (Turkish ravioli stuffed with beef mince and topped with yoghurt, garlic tomato and butter).

FRESH FROM THE SEA
Fish is wonderful here, but can be pricey. In a *balık restoran* (fish restaurant) you should always choose your own fish from the display. The eyes should be clear and the flesh under the gill slits near the eyes should be bright red, not burgundy. After choosing, ask the approximate price. The fish will be weighed, and the price computed at the day's per-kilogram rate. Try to avoid eating *lüfer* when the fish are small (under 24cm in length), as overfishing is endangering the future of this much-loved local species.

VEGETABLES & SALADS
Turks love vegetables, eating them fresh in summer and pickling them for winter (pickled vegetables are called *turşu*). There are two particularly Turkish ways of preparing vegetables: the first is known as *zeytinyağlı* (sautéed in olive oil) and the second *dolma* (stuffed with rice or meat).

Simplicity is the key to a Turkish *salata* (salad), with crunchy fresh ingredients being eaten with gusto as a meze or as an accompaniment to a meat or fish main course. The most popular summer salad is *çoban salatası* (shepherd's salad), a colourful mix of chopped tomatoes, cucumber, onion and pepper.

SWEETS
Turks don't usually finish their meal with a dessert, preferring to serve fruit as a finale. Most of them love a mid-afternoon sugar hit, though, and will often pop into a *muhallebici* (milk pudding shop), *pastane* (cake shop) or *baklavacı* (baklava shop) for a piece of syrup-drenched baklava, a plate of chocolate-crowned profiteroles or a *fırın sütlaç* (rice pudding) tasting of milk, sugar and just a hint of exotic spices. Other Turkish sweet specialities worth sampling are *dondurma*, the local ice cream; *kadayıf*, dough soaked in syrup and topped with a layer of *kaymak* (clotted cream); and *künefe*, layers of *kadayıf* cemented together with sweet cheese, doused in syrup and served hot with a sprinkling of pistachio.

NEED TO KNOW

Price Ranges
The symbols below indicate the average cost of a main course in the reviewed restaurant or eatery:

€	less than ₺15
€€	₺15 to ₺25
€€€	more than ₺25

Opening Hours
Standard opening hours for restaurants and cafes:
➡ **Breakfast** 7.30am to 10.30am
➡ **Lunch** noon to 2.30pm
➡ **Dinner** 7.30pm to 10pm
Exceptions are noted in reviews.

Reservations
➡ We have included telephone numbers for those restaurants where it's advisable to book.
➡ Thursday, Friday and Saturday nights are busy at all popular restaurants – be sure to book a few days in advance.

Alcohol
Many simple eateries in İstanbul don't serve alcohol. In our reviews, we have indicated if a place is alcohol free.

Tipping
➡ In restaurants, bistros and *meyhanes*, a 10% tip is standard if you have been satisfied with the service.
➡ There's usually no expectation that customers will tip at cafes, *lokantas*, *kebapçıs*, *köftecis* and *pidecis*.

FAST FOOD
The nation's favourite fast food is undoubtedly döner kebap – lamb slow-cooked on an upright revolving skewer and then shaved off before being stuffed into bread or pide. Soggy cold French fries and green chillies are sometimes included; at other times garlicky yoghurt, salad and a sprinkling of slightly sour sumac are the accompaniments.

Coming a close second in the popularity stakes is *pide*, the Turkish version of

LOKANTAS

These casual eateries serve *hazır yemek* (ready-made food) kept warm in bain-maries, and usually offer a range of vegetable dishes alongside meat options. The etiquette when eating at one of these places is to check out what's in the bain-marie and tell the waiter or cook behind the counter what you would like to eat. You can order one portion (*bir porsyon*), a *yarım* (half) *porsyon* or a plate with a few different choices – you'll be charged by the portion.

pizza. It has a canoe-shaped base topped with *peynir* (cheese), *yumurta* (egg) or *kıymalı* (minced meat). A *karaşık* pide has a mixture of toppings. You can sit down to eat these in a *pideci* (Turkish pizza parlour) or ask for your pide *paket* (wrapped to go). *Lahmacun* (Arabic-style pizza) has a thinner crust than pide and is usually topped with chopped lamb, onion and tomato.

Börek (filled pastries) are usually eaten in the morning and are distinguished by their filling, cooking method and shape. They come in square, cigar or snail shapes and are filled with *peynir, ıspanaklı* (spinach), *patates* (potatoes) or *kıymalı*. Bun-shaped *poğaca* are glazed with sugar or stuffed with cheese and olives. *Su böreği*, a melt-in-the-mouth lasagne-like layered pastry laced with white cheese and parsley, is the most popular of all *börek* styles.

Gözleme (thin savoury crepes cooked with cheese, spinach or potato) are also great quick snacks.

STREET FOOD

Street vendors pound pavements across İstanbul, pushing carts laden with artfully arranged snacks to satisfy the appetites of commuters. You'll see these vendors next to ferry and bus stations, on busy streets and squares, even on the city's bridges.

Some of their snacks are innocuous – freshly baked *simits* (bread ring studded with sesame seeds), golden roasted *mısır* (corn on the cob), refreshing chilled and peeled *salatalık* (cucumber) – but others are more confrontational for non-Turkish palates. Those in the latter category include *midye dolma* (stuffed mussels), *çığ köfte* (raw spiced meatball) and *kokoreç* (seasoned lamb or mutton intestines wrapped around a skewer and grilled over charcoal).

VEGETARIANS & VEGANS

Though it's normal for Turks to eat a vegetarian (*vejeteryen*) meal, the concept of vegetarianism is quite foreign. Say you're a vegan and Turks will either look mystified or assume that you're 'fessing up to some strain of socially aberrant behaviour. There is a sprinkling of vegetarian restaurants in Beyoğlu, a couple of which serve some vegan meals, but the travelling vegetarian certainly can't rely on specialist restaurants.

The meze spread is usually vegetable-based, and meat-free salads, soups, pastas, omelettes and *böreks,* as well as hearty vegetable dishes, are all readily available. Ask '*Etsiz yemekler var mı?*' (Is there something to eat that has no meat?) to see what's on offer.

SELF-CATERING

İstanbul has many small supermarkets (DIA, Gima, Makro) sprinkled on the streets around Beyoğlu, with giant cousins (such as Migros) in the suburbs. These sell most of the items you will need if you plan to self-cater. Then there is the ubiquitous *bakkal* (corner shop), which stocks bread, milk, basic groceries and usually fruit and vegetables.

The best places to purchase fresh produce are undoubtedly the street markets. In Eminönü, the streets around the Spice Bazaar (Mısır Çarşısı) sell fish, meats, vegetables, fruit, spices, sweets and much more. In Beyoğlu, the Balık Pazarı (Fish Market) off İstiklal Caddesi is a great, if expensive, little market. As well as its many fish stalls, it has small shops selling freshly baked bread, greengrocers selling a wide range of fruit and vegetables, and delicatessens (*şarküteri*) selling cheeses, *pastırma,* pickled fish, olives, jams and preserves. Larger produce markets are found daily near the *iskele* in Kadıköy, in Fatih and Cankurtaran on Wednesdays, in Kadırga on Thursdays, in Beşiktaş on Saturdays and in Kasımpaşa (in Piyalepaşa Bulvarı) on Sundays.

Eating by Neighbourhood

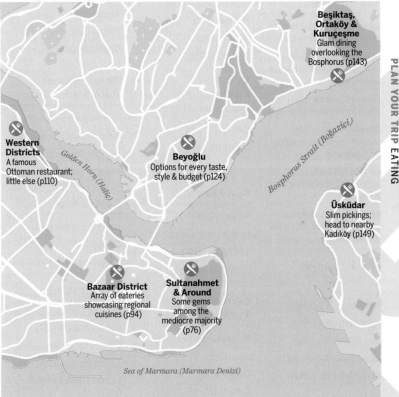

Beşiktaş, Ortaköy & Kuruçeşme
Glam dining overlooking the Bosphorus (p143)

Western Districts
A famous Ottoman restaurant; little else (p110)

Beyoğlu
Options for every taste, style & budget (p124)

Üsküdar
Slim pickings; head to nearby Kadıköy (p149)

Bazaar District
Array of eateries showcasing regional cuisines (p94)

Sultanahmet & Around
Some gems among the mediocre majority (p76)

Golden Horn (Haliç)

Bosphorus Strait (Boğaziçi)

Sea of Marmara (Marmara Denizi)

COOKING COURSES & TOURS

Ask İstanbullus what makes their city special, and the answer usually comes straight from their stomachs. The local cuisine has a fan club as numerous as it is vociferous, and its members enjoy nothing better than introducing visitors to the foods, eateries and providores of the city. In short, this is a dream destination for everyone who loves to eat, cook and shop for food, particularly as plenty of cooking courses and food-focused walking tours are on offer. These include the following:

Cooking Alaturka (p82) Runs popular classes suitable for all skill levels.

Culinary Backstreets (p125) Fantastic foodie walks.

Turkish Flavours (p124) Walking tours and excellent cooking classes held in an elegant Nişantaşı apartment. If requested, the course can focus on a Sephardic menu.

Istanbul Culinary Institute (p127) A wide range of themed cooking classes.

Lonely Planet's Top Choices

Asmalı Cavit (p126) The epitome of a traditional *meyhane*.

Lokanta Maya (p124) Stylish bistro serving modern takes on traditional dishes.

Zübeyir Ocakbaşı (p127) Succulent meats cooked over coals.

MüzedeChanga (p158) Sophisticated lunch venue on the Bosphorus.

Karaköy Güllüoğlu (p124) The perfect baklava stop at any time of day.

Heyamola Ada Lokantası (p164) Delicious mezes on the Princes' Islands.

Best by Budget

€

Fatih Damak Pide (p94)

Bahar Restaurant (p96)

Onur Et Lokantası (p96)

Asmalı Canım Ciğerim (p129)

Siirt Fatih Büryan (p94)

€€

Ahırkapı Balıkçısı (p76)

Paşazade (p78)

Sıdıka (p143)

Ca' d'Oro (p125)

€€€

Vogue (p143)

Zuma (p143)

Mikla (p129)

Changa (p129)

Best Lokantas

Hünkar (p124)

Karaköy Lokantası (p125)

Çiya Sofrası (p149)

Kömür Turk Mutfağı (p110)

Best Modern Turkish

Meze by Lemon Tree (p126)

Mikla (p129)

Changa (p129)

Kantın (p124)

Best Ottoman Food

Asitane (p110)

Matbah (p76)

Cihannüma (p76)

Best Regional Eateries

Akdenıs Hatay Sofrası (p93)

Hatay Has Kral Sofrası (p93)

Siirt Fatih Büryan (p94)

Antiochia (p127)

Best Kebaps

Hamdi Restaurant (p94)

Develi (p79)

Sur Ocakbaşı (p96)

Best Cooking Courses & Tours

Cooking Alaturka (p82)

Culinary Backstreets (p125)

Turkish Flavours (p124)

İstanbul Culinary Institute (p127)

Drinking & Nightlife

They may live in an officially Muslim country, but there are plenty of İstanbullus who enjoy nothing more than heading to a meyhane (tavern), bar or nightclub for a drink or two. Those who don't drink alcohol tend to gravitate to the city's rich array of çay bahçesis (tea gardens) and kahvehanes (coffee houses).

Popular Drinks

NONALCOHOLIC DRINKS

Drinking *çay* (tea) is the national pastime. Sugar cubes are the only accompaniment and they're needed to counter the effects of long brewing. No self-respecting Turk would dream of drinking *elma çay*, the sweet 'apple tea' offered to many tourists.

Surprisingly, *Türk kahve* (Turkish coffee) isn't widely consumed. A thick and powerful brew, it's drunk in a couple of short sips. If you order a cup, you will be asked how sweet you like it – *çok şekerli* means 'very sweet', *orta şekerli* 'middling', *az şekerli* 'slightly sweet' and *şekersiz* or *sade* 'not at all'.

Freshly squeezed *portakal suyu* (orange juice) and *nar suyu* (pomegranate juice) are extremely popular drinks. In *kebapçıs* (kebap restaurants) patrons often drink *ayran (*a refreshing yoghurt drink made by whipping yoghurt with water and salt) or *şalgam suyu* (sour turnip juice).

If you're here during winter, you should try delicious and unusual *sahlep*, a hot drink made from crushed tapioca-root extract.

ALCOHOLIC DRINKS

Turkey's most beloved tipple is rakı, a grape spirit infused with aniseed. Similar to Greek ouzo, it's served in long thin glasses and is drunk neat or with water, which turns the clear liquid chalky white; if you want to add ice (*buz*), do so after adding water, as dropping ice straight into rakı kills its flavour.

Bira (beer) is also popular. The local drop, Efes, is a perky pilsener that comes in bottles, in cans and on tap.

Turkey grows and bottles its own *şarap* (wine), which has greatly improved over the past decade but is quite expensive due to high government taxes. If you want red wine, ask for *kırmızı şarap*; for white ask for *beyaz şarap*. Labels to look out for include Sarafin (chardonnay, fumé blanc, sauvignon blanc, cabernet sauvignon, shiraz and merlot); Karma (cabernet sauvignon, shiraz and merlot); Kav Tuğra (narince, *kalecik karası* and

NARGILES

While in town, be sure to visit a *çay bahçesi*. These atmosphere-rich venues are frequented by locals who don't drink alcohol and are often redolent with apple-scented smoke from nargiles (waterpipes), their substitute indulgence.

When ordering a nargile, you'll need to specify what type of tobacco you would like. Most people opt for *elma* (when the tobacco has been soaked in apple juice, giving it a sweet flavour and scent), but it's possible to order it unadulterated (*tömbeki*). A nargile usually costs between ₺15 and ₺25 and can be shared (you'll be given individual plastic mouthpieces).

NEED TO KNOW

Business Hours

➡ Opening hours of cafes, *çay bahçesis*, bars and clubs vary wildly; we have included specific hours in our reviews.

➡ Clubs are busiest on Friday and Saturday nights, and the action doesn't really kick off until 1am. Cover charges are levied at many of the clubs on these nights.

➡ Many of the Beyoğlu clubs close from June or July until the end of September. Most of the Bosphorus clubs close over winter.

What's On

The monthly *Time Out* and *The Guide* magazines include useful listings sections. *Time Out* also produces the Istanbul Beat (p204) blog.

Entry Tips

➡ If you're keen to visit a Bosphorus club, you should consider booking to have dinner in its restaurant – otherwise you could be looking for a lucky break or a tip of at least ₺100 to get past the door staff.

➡ Long queues are ubiquitous at the popular Beyoğlu clubs after midnight on Fridays and Saturdays; some savvy clubbers arrive earlier to bypass these.

Dress Codes

When İstanbullus go out clubbing they dress to kill. If you don't do the same, you'll be unlikely to get past the door staff at the Bosphorus clubs or into the rooftop bar/clubs in Beyoğlu. Fortunately, what you're wearing won't affect entry at the live-music venues, *meyhanes* or grungier clubs.

öküzgözü); and DLC (most grape varieties). All are produced by **Doluca** (www.doluca.com). Its major competitor, **Kavaklidere** (www.kavaklidere.com), is known for the wines it puts out under the Pendore, Ancyra and Prestige labels (the Pendore *boğazkere* is particularly good), as well as its eminently quaffable Çankaya white blend.

Together, Doluca and Kavaklidere dominate the market, but producers such as **Vinkara** (www.vinkara.com) and **Kayra** (www.kayrasaraplari.com) are starting to build a reputation for themselves with wines such as Kayra's excellent Buzbağ. *Time Out* magazine and the Culinary Backstreets (p125) website publish regular reviews of new vintages.

Clubbing

The best nightclubs are in Beyoğlu and along the 'Golden Mile' between Ortaköy and Kuruçeşme on the Bosphorus.

The city's bohemian and student sets tend to gravitate to the bar and clubs in Beyoğlu's Cihangir, Asmalımescit and Nevizade enclaves or head over the water to grungy Kadife Sokak in the suburb of Kadıköy on the city's Asian side. This is known to everyone as Barlar Sokak (Bar Street).

Gay & Lesbian

Beyoğlu is the hub of the city's gay clubbing scene, and there are a number of venues to choose from. Most welcome both gay and straight clubbers, although the latter will feel vastly outnumbered. The monthly *Time Out İstanbul* magazine has Gay & Lesbian pages listing the top LGBTT venues in town.

Occasional police raids on gay venues occur (homosexuality has an ambiguous legal status – or lack thereof – in Turkey), but the general tenor in Beyoğlu is gay-friendly and inclusive.

Drinking & Nightlife by Neighbourhood

➡ **Sultanahmet & Around** (p79) A limited choice of cafes and *çay bahçesis* (tea gardens), but few bars worth considering.

➡ **Bazaar District** (p97) An atmospheric array of *çay bahçesis* and nargile cafes, but no nightlife to speak of.

➡ **Beyoğlu** (p131) The city's entertainment hub, with hundreds of bars, cafes and clubs to choose from.

➡ **Beşiktaş, Ortaköy & Kuruçeşme** (p144) A string of upmarket cafes, bars and nightclubs alongside the Bosphorus.

Lonely Planet's Top Choices

Babylon (p135) The best live-music venue in town.

MiniMüzikHol (p134) Hub of the avant-garde arts scene.

Mikla (p132) Spectacular views and a stylish clientele.

360 (p132) The city's most famous bar for good reason.

Tophane Nargile Cafes (p131) Alcohol-free but atmosphere-rich.

Best Çay Bahçesis

Erenler Çay Bahçesi (p98)

Lale Bahçesi (p98)

Pierre Loti Café (p112)

Hazzo Pulo Çay Bahçesi (p132)

Set Üstü Çay Bahçesi (p80)

Mistanbul Hancı Cafe (p149)

Best Turkish Coffee

Fazıl Bey (p149)

Manda Batmaz (p132)

Müzenin Kahvesi (p82)

Best Gay & Lesbian Venues

Love Dance Point (p133)

Tek Yön (p135)

Bigudi Cafe (p134)

Club 17 (p134)

Best Clubs

Indigo (p133)

Dogzstar (p133)

Sortie (p144)

Anjelique (p144)

Reina (p144)

Best Rooftop Bars

NuTeras (p133)

5 Kat (p134)

Leb-i Derya (p133)

Litera (p133)

X Bar (p132)

Best Boutique Bars

Baylo (p132)

Münferit (p133)

Le Fumoir (p132)

Best Bar/Club Combos

Kiki (p134)

Off Pera (p133)

Lucca (p159)

Best Neighbourhood Cafes

Mavra (p131)

Smyrna (p135)

Cafe Susam (p134)

Yeni Marmara (p80)

Grand Bazaar

Shopping

Over centuries, İstanbullus have perfected the practice of shopping. Trading is in their blood and they've turned making a sale or purchase into an art form. Go into any carpet shop and you'll see what we mean – there's etiquette to be followed, tea to be drunk, conversation to be had. And, of course, there's money to be spent and made.

What to Buy

ANTIQUES

The grand Ottoman-era houses of İstanbul are still surrendering treasures. Head to the antique shops of Çukurcuma or the Horhor Flea Market (p99) to find something to take home, but note that it is officially illegal to take anything over 100 years old out of the country. In reality, though, officials are only worried about objects from the Classical, Byzantine or early Ottoman eras.

BATHWARES

Attractive towels, *peştemals* (bath wraps) and bathrobes made on hand looms in southern Turkey are sold in designer bathwares shops around the city. Other popular purchases include olive-oil soaps and hamam sets with soap, shampoo, an exfoliation glove and a hamam bowl.

CARPETS & KILIMS

Asking locals for a recommendation when it comes to rug shops can be something of a knotty subject. This industry is rife with commissions, fakes and dodgy merchandise, so you need to be very careful when making a purchase. Don't fall for the shtick of touts on the street – these guys never, ever work for the truly reputable dealers.

Scam artists abound in the carpet trade. Be extremely wary in all of your negotiations and dealings.

CERAMICS

Turkish ceramics are beautiful and the standard fare fits within most budgets. Many of the tiles you see in the tourist shops have been painted using a silkscreen printing method and this is why they're cheap. Hand-painted bowls, plates and other pieces are more expensive – the best have original designs and are painted without the use of a carbon-paper pattern. Head to the Arasta Bazaar (p80) or Grand Bazaar (p85) to find good examples.

FASHION

The local fashion industry is thriving and there are plenty of chains, department stores and boutiques to investigate. Head to Serdar-ı Ekrem Sokak in Galata, to Cihangir and to Nişantaşı to find the most interesting boutiques.

GLASSWARE

İstanbul produces some unique glasswork, a legacy of the Ottoman Empire's affection for this delicate and intricate art. Paşabahçe (p137) shops around the city sell attractive glassware that is mass produced at its factory on the upper Bosphorus.

INLAID WOOD

Local artisans make jewellery boxes, furniture, and chess and backgammon boards that are inlaid with different-coloured woods, silver or mother-of-pearl. Make sure the piece really does feature inlay. These days, alarmingly accurate decals exist. Also, check the silver: is it really silver, or does it look like aluminium or pewter? And what about that mother-of-pearl – is it in fact 'daughter-of-polystyrene'?

JEWELLERY

İstanbul is a wonderful place to buy jewellery, especially pieces made by the city's growing number of artisans making contemporary pieces inspired by local culture. You'll find great examples around (but not inside) the Grand Bazaar, in Galata and in Nişantaşı.

TEXTILES

Turkey's southeast region is known for its textiles, and there are examples aplenty on show in the Grand Bazaar (p85). You can also find top-quality cotton, linen and silk there.

Collectors of antique textiles will be in seventh heaven when inspecting the decorative tribal textiles that have made their way here from Central Asia. These are often sold in carpet shops.

NEED TO KNOW

PLAN YOUR TRIP SHOPPING

Business Hours

The most common shopping hours are from 9am to 6pm Monday to Saturday, but this is by no means always the case. We have indicated specific hours in most reviews.

Taxes & Refunds

Turkey has a value-added tax (VAT) known as the *katma değer vergisi* (KDV). This means that a tax of between 1% and 60% is included in the price of most goods and services. Rates vary wildly – eg, alcohol is taxed at a mind-boggling 60%, whereas clothing is taxed at only 4%.

If you buy an item costing more than TL118 from a shop that participates in the national 'Global Refund: Tax Free Shopping' scheme, you are entitled to a refund of the KDV at your point of departure. At the airports, remember to have customs inspect your purchase(s) and stamp your tax-free form before you go through immigration; you can then collect your refund in the departure lounge.

TURKISH DELIGHT

Lokum (Turkish Delight) makes a great present for those left at home, but is even better to scoff on the spot. It's sold in speciality shops around the city and comes in flavours including *cevizli* (walnut), *fıstıklı* (pistachio), *bademli* (almond) and *roze* (rosewater). Ask for a *çeşitli* (assortment) if you want to sample the various types.

The Dying Art of Bargaining

The elaborate etiquette of the Ottoman Empire lingers in many day-to-day rituals still observed in its greatest creation, İstanbul. Until recently, the art of bargaining was one of these. Times have changed, though, and these days the non-negotiable price-tag reigns supreme in most of the city's retail outlets. Here, as in many former stops along the legendary Silk Route, the days of camel caravans have long gone, supplanted by multinational retailers, sleek supply-chain management and an increasingly homogeneous shopping experience.

Perhaps the only exception to this rule can be found in the city's carpet shops, particularly those located in the Grand

Bazaar (p85). Many of these still take pride in practising the ancient art of bargaining.

If you are visiting İstanbul and are keen to buy a carpet or rug in the bazaar, keep the following tips in mind:

→ The 'official' prices here have almost always been artificially inflated to allow for a bargaining margin – 20% to 30% is the rule of thumb.

→ Shopping here involves many aspects of Ottoman etiquette – you will drink tea, exchange polite greetings and size up how trustworthy the shopkeeper is. He, in turn, will drink tea, exchange polite greetings and size up how gullible you are.

→ Never feel pressured to buy something. Tea and polite conversation are gratis – if you accept them, you don't need to buy anything in exchange.

→ It's important to do your research. Always shop around to compare quality and pricing.

→ Before starting to bargain, decide how much you like the carpet or rug, and how much you are prepared to pay for it. It's important that you stick to this – the shopkeepers here are professional bargainers and have loads of practice in talking customers into purchases against their better judgement.

→ Your first offer should be around 60% of the initial asking price. The shopkeeper will laugh, look offended or profess to be puzzled – this is all part of the ritual.

→ He will then make a counter offer of 80–90%. You should look disappointed, explain that you have done your research and say that you are not prepared to pay that amount. Then you should offer around 70%.

→ By this stage you and the shopkeeper should have sized each other up. He will cite the price at which he is prepared to sell and if it corresponds with what you were initially happy to pay, you can agree to the deal. If not, you should smile, shake hands and walk away.

The same rules also apply in some textile, jewellery and antique shops in the bazaar, but they don't apply to all. The fashionable stores in Halıcılar Çarşışı Sokak started the trend toward set pricing here a number of years ago and many other shops have followed their lead.

Shopping by Neighbourhood

→ **Sultanahmet & Around** Top-notch ceramics, rug and bathware stores are found in and around the Arasta Bazaar.

→ **Bazaar District** Options galore in the Grand Bazaar, the Spice Bazaar and streets between the two.

→ **Beyoğlu** Galata, Cihangir and Çukurcuma are bursting with fashion boutiques, designer homewares stores and antique shops.

PLAN YOUR TRIP SHOPPING

Lonely Planet's Top Choices

Cocoon (p80) Striking textiles, rugs and handicrafts from Central Asia.

Dear East (p136) Designer homewares made by local and international artisans.

Haremlique (p145) Elegant Turkish-made bedlinen, bath-linen and throws.

Gönül Paksoy (p124) Ottoman-influenced ensembles featuring gorgeous fabrics.

Lokum (p145) Exquisitely packaged and totally delicious Turkish Delight.

Best for Homewares

Tulu (p81)

İroni (p136)

Paşabahçe (p137)

Best for Bathwares

Jennifer's Hamam (p80)

Abdulla Natural Products (p99)

Derviş (p99)

Hammam (p136)

Best for Carpets & Kilims

Mehmet Çetinkaya Gallery (p81)

Dhoku (p99)

Şişko Osman (p100)

A La Turca (p138)

Best for Jewellery

Sevan Bıçakçı (p100)

Selda Okutan (p136)

Serhat Geridönmez (p99)

Best for Textiles

Muhlis Günbatti (p99)

Yazmacı Necdet Danış (p99)

Mehmet Çetinkaya Gallery (p81)

Best for Handicrafts

Ak Gümüş (p99)

Beyoğlu Olgunlaşma Enstıtüsü (p137)

Lâl (p136)

Best for Art & Antiques

Khaftan (p80)

Sofa (p100)

Artrium (p137)

Best Fashion Boutiques

Bahar Korçan (p136)

Arzu Kaprol (p136)

Best for Lokum

Ali Muhıddin Hacı Bekir (p100)

Hafız Mustafa (p100)

Best for Books

Robinson Crusoe (p137)

Pandora (p137)

🏃 Hamams & Spas

Succumbing to a soapy scrub in a steamy hamam (bathhouse) is one of the city's quintessential experiences. Not everyone feels comfortable with baring all (or most) of their bodies in public, though. If you include yourself in this group, a number of the city's spas offer private hamam treatments.

Hamams

The concept of the steam bath was passed from the Romans to the Byzantines and then on to the Turks, who named it the hamam. They've even exported the concept throughout the world, hence the term 'Turkish bath'. Until recent decades, many homes in İstanbul didn't have bathroom facilities, and due to Islam's emphasis on personal cleanliness, the community relied on the hundreds of hamams throughout the city, often as part of the *külliye* (mosque complex) of a mosque. Now that most people have bathrooms in İstanbul, hamams are nowhere near as popular, but some carry on due to their roles as local meeting places. Others have become successful tourist attractions.

The city's hamams vary enormously. Some are dank dives where you may come out dirtier than you went in (note: Turks call cockroaches 'hamam insects'); others are plain and clean, servicing a predominantly local clientele. A small number have built a reputation as gay meeting places (we're talking truly steamy here), and an increasing number are geared exclusively towards tourists. A few hotels in Sultanahmet have hamams that customers can use free of charge. These include the Sirkeci Konak (p168) and Neorion Hotel (p169).

We haven't reviewed any gay hamams in this book, as the current socio-political climate makes their legal status ambiguous.

BATH PROCEDURE

Upon entry you are shown to a *camekan* (entrance hall or space) where you will be allocated a dressing cubicle (*halvet*) or locker and given a *peştemal* (bath wrap) and *plastik çarıklar* (plastic sandals) or *takunya* (wooden clogs). Store your clothes and don the *peştemal* and footware. An attendant will then lead you through the *soğukluk* (intermediate section) to the *hararet* (steam room), where you sit and sweat for a while, relaxing and loosening up, perhaps on the *göbektaşı* (central, raised platform atop the heating source).

Soon you will be half-asleep and as soft as putty from the steamy heat. The cheapest bath is the one you do yourself, having brought your own soap, shampoo and towel. But the real Turkish bath experience is to have an attendant wash, scrub and massage you.

If you have opted for the latter, an attendant douses you with warm water and lathers you with a sudsy sponge. Next you are scrubbed with a *kese* (coarse cloth mitten), loosening dirt you never suspected you had. After a massage (these yo-yo between being enjoyable, limp-wristed or mortally dangerous) comes a shampoo and another dousing with warm water, followed by one with cool water.

When the scrubbing is over, relax in the *hararet* or head to the *camekan*, where you can get dressed or have a rest; at some hamams you can order something to eat or drink. The average hamam experience takes around one hour.

Spas

Most of İstanbul's five-star hotels have spas where a hamam exists alongside facilities such as saunas, steam-rooms, plunge pools and rain-shower rooms. Hamam treatments in these spas are private, and often incorporate added extras such as facials, foot massages, hair treatments and body wraps. Some also offer remedial massages.

Lonely Planet's Top Choices

Four Seasons Istanbul at the Bosphorus (p145) The best of the luxury spas.

Ambassador Spa (p82) An expert masseur makes this modest place worth considering.

Ayasofya Hürrem Sultan Hamamı (p81) Built by order of Süleyman the Magnificent, and recently restored.

Cağaloğlu Hamamı (p82) The most beautiful of the city's Ottoman hamams.

Çemberlitaş Hamamı (p101) Another architecturally splendid Ottoman hamam.

Gedikpaşa Hamamı (p101) A neighbourhood hamam dating from Ottoman times.

Ağa Hamamı (p138) Mixed bathing in Beyoğlu.

NEED TO KNOW

Business Hours

Most of the tourist hamams and hotel spas are open from 8am to 11pm or midnight. Local hamams with only one bath have one set of hours for females and another for males; generally they close earlier than the tourist hamams.

Practicalities

Soap, shampoo and towels are provided at all of the hamams we've reviewed. If you're only having a bath, you'll need to pay for the soap and shampoo separately; it's always included in the cost of full treatments. You'll get drenched, so make sure you take a comb, toiletries, make-up and (if you choose to wear underwear during the massage) a dry pair of replacement underpants. There are usually hair-dryers available for customer use.

Modesty

Traditional Turkish baths have separate sections for men and women, or have only one set of facilities and admit men or women at different times.

Bath etiquette requires that men remain covered with a *peştemal* at all times. Women either bare all or wear a bikini or a pair of knickers. During the bathing, everyone washes their private parts themselves, without removing the bath-wrap or underclothes.

In tourist areas, there are a couple of hamams with only one bath area that allow foreign men and women to bathe together. In these cases, women should wear a bikini.

Tipping

This is discretionary. Don't feel obliged to tip if your treatment was cursory or sub-standard.

Explore
İstanbul

İSTANBUL'S TOP SIGHTS

Neighbourhoods at a Glance

1 Sultanahmet & Around (p44)

Many visitors to İstanbul never make it out of Sultanahmet. And while this is a shame, it's hardly surprising. After all, not many cities have such a concentration of historic sights, shopping precincts, hotels and eateries within easy walking distance. Ideally suited to exploration by foot, the neighbourhood is a showcase of the city's glorious past, crammed with mosques, palaces, churches and houses dating from the Roman, Byzantine and Ottoman periods.

2 Bazaar District (p83)

This beguiling district is home to the Grand Bazaar and Spice Bazaar. A&mid the thousands of shops that surround these centu-

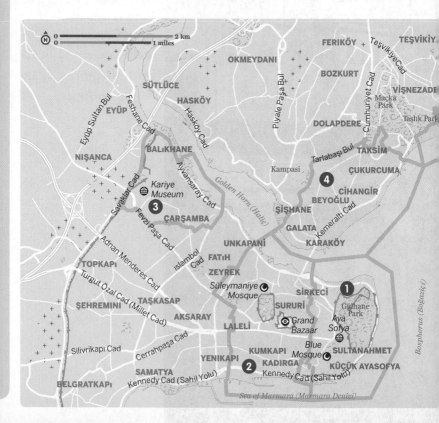

ries-old marketplaces are magnificent Ottoman mosques, historic hamams and atmospheric *çay bahçesis* (tea gardens) where locals smoke nargiles (water pipes) and play games of *tavla* (backgammon). The streets between the bazaars are a popular stamping ground for İstanbullus, and seem to crackle with a good-humoured and infectious energy.

③ Western Districts (p102)

A showcase of İstanbul's ethnically diverse and endlessly fascinating history, this neighbourhood to the west of the Historic Peninsula contains synogogues built by the Jews in Balat and churches constructed by the Greeks in Fener. In recent times, migrants from the east of Turkey have settled here, attracted by the vibrant Wednesday street market in Fatih and the presence of two important Islamic pilgrimage sites: the tombs of Mehmet the Conqueror and Ebu Eyüp el-Ensari.

④ Beyoğlu (p113)

The high-octane hub of eating, drinking and entertainment in the city, Beyoğlu is where visitors and locals come in search of good restaurants, glamorous rooftop bars, live-music venues, hip hotels and edgy boutiques. Built around the major boulevard of İstiklal Caddesi, it incorporates a mix of bohemian residential districts such as Çukurcuma and Cihangir, bustling entertainment enclaves such as Asmalımescit and historically rich pockets such as Galata and Karaköy.

⑤ Beşiktaş, Ortaköy & Kuruçeşme (p139)

Nineteenth-century French writer Pierre Loti described the stretch of the Bosphorus shore between Beşiktaş and Ortaköy as featuring '...a line of palaces white as snow, placed at the edge of the sea on marble docks'. Fortunately, his description remains as accurate as it is evocative. North of this palace precinct is the famous 'Golden Mile', a string of upmarket nightclubs running between the waterside suburbs of Ortaköy and Kuruçeşme, once humble fishing villages and now pockets of prime real estate.

⑥ Üsküdar (p146)

Seen from the ferry, the hilly terrain of this residential suburb on the Asian shore is studded with minarets, indicating the number of mosques that were built here by order of Ottoman nobility. Today, it's a conservative neighbourhood that has an authentically Anatolian, rather than European, flavour.

Sultanahmet & Around

SULTANAHMET | KÜÇÜK AYASOFYA | GÜLHANE | SİRKECİ | EMİNÖNÜ

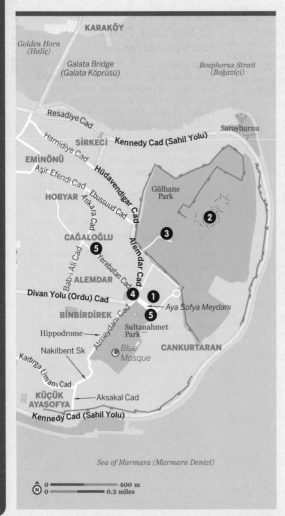

Neighbourhood Top Five

1 Standing beneath the magnificent dome of **Aya Sofya** (p46) and imagining what it would have been like to attend a candlelit service in this, the greatest of all Byzantine churches

2 Uncovering the secrets of the seraglio in opulent **Topkapı Palace** (p53).

3 Learning about the fascinating history of the city in the **İstanbul Archaeology Museums** (p66).

4 Exploring the watery depths of the atmospheric **Basilica Cistern** (p68).

5 Surrendering to the steam and admiring the historic surrounds in an Ottoman-era **hamam**.

For more detail of this area see, Map p230 and p232 ➡

Explore: Sultanahmet

The fact that there are so many significant monuments and museums in this area means that setting an itinerary is important. To do the neighbourhood justice, you'll need at least three days (four or five would be better).

Plan to visit one of the major museums (Aya Sofya, Topkapı, the İstanbul Archaeology Museums) each day and then add the less time-intensive sights into your daily itineraries. For instance, it makes sense to visit the Archaeology Museums and Gülhane Park together on one day and Aya Sofya, the Blue Mosque and the Basilica Cistern on another. Topkapı deserves a day to itself.

The ever-present battalions of tour groups tend to visit the museums first thing in the morning or after lunch – you will find that queues are shorter and exhibits less crowded if you visit during lunchtime or later in the afternoon.

Local Life

➡ **Produce Markets** There are weekly street markets in Cankurtaran on Wednesday and in nearby Kadırga on Thursday.

➡ **Backgammon** Head to Yeni Marmara (p80), Derviş Aile Çay Bahçesi (p79) or Cafe Meşale (p79) to join locals in smoking nargiles (water pipes), drinking tea and playing backgammon.

➡ **Promenade** On weekends, follow the local families who promenade through the Hippodrome (p70) and picnic in Gülhane Park (p73).

Getting There & Away

➡ **Tram** An efficient tram service runs between Bağcılar in the city's west and Kabataş near Taksim Meydanı (Taksim Square) in Beyoğlu. Trams stop at the Grand Bazaar, Sultanahmet and Eminönü en route. Get off the tram at the Sultanahmet stop to visit most of the sights in this chapter.

Lonely Planet's Top Tip

If you are spending a full three days in the city and plan to visit the major museums in Sultanahmet, the Museum Pass İstanbul will save you money and enable you to jump queues.

Best Places to Eat

➡ Cihannüma (p76)
➡ Ahırkapı Balıkçısı (p76)
➡ Cooking Alaturka (p76)
➡ Matbah (p76)
➡ Hocapaşa Sokak (p78)

For reviews, see p76

Best Places to Shop

➡ Cocoon (p80)
➡ Arasta Bazaar (p80)
➡ Khaftan (p80)
➡ Mehmet Çetinkaya Gallery (p81)
➡ Tulu (p81)

For reviews, see p80 ➡

Best Museums

➡ Aya Sofya (p46)
➡ Topkapı Palace (p53)
➡ İstanbul Archaeology Museums (p66)
➡ Museum of Turkish & Islamic Arts (p71)

For reviews, see p69 ➡

TOP SIGHTS
AYA SOFYA

There are many important monuments in İstanbul, but this venerable structure – commissioned by the great Byzantine emperor Justinian, consecrated as a church in 537, converted to a mosque by Mehmet the Conqueror in 1453 and declared a museum by Atatürk in 1935 – surpasses the rest due to its innovative architectural form, rich history, religious importance and extraordinary beauty.

Known as Hagia Sophia in Greek, Sancta Sophia in Latin and the Church of the Divine Wisdom in English, Aya Sofya has a history as long as it is fascinating. It was constructed on the site of Byzantium's acropolis, which had also been the site of two earlier churches of the same name, one destroyed by fire and another during the Nika riots of 532.

On entering his commission for the first time, Justinian exclaimed, 'Glory to God that I have been judged worthy of such a work. Oh Solomon! I have outdone you!' Entering the building today, his hubris is understandable. The exterior may be visually underwhelming, but the recently restored interior with its magnificent domed roof soaring heavenward is so sublimely beautiful that many seeing it for the first time are quite literally stunned into silence.

In Justinian's time, a street led uphill from the west straight to the main door. Today the entrance is off Aya Sofya Meydanı. Enter the building and walk straight ahead through the outer and inner narthexes to reach the **Imperial Door**, which is crowned with a striking mosaic of **Christ as Pantocrator (Ruler of All)**. Christ holds a book that carries the inscription 'Peace be With You. I am the Light of the World.' At his feet an emperor (probably Leo VI) prostrates

DON'T MISS...

➡ Christ as Pantocrator
➡ Virgin and Christ Child
➡ Deesis
➡ Virgin Mary, Emperor John Comnenus II and Empress Eirene
➡ Constantine the Great, the Virgin Mary and the Emperor Justinian

PRACTICALITIES

➡ Hagia Sophia
➡ Map p230
➡ www.ayasofya muzesi.gov.tr
➡ Aya Sofya Meydanı 1
➡ adult/under 12yr ₺25/free
➡ ⊙9am-6pm Tue-Sun mid-Apr–Sep, to 4pm Oct–mid-Apr
➡ 🚇Sultanahmet

himself. The Virgin Mary is on Christ's left and to his right is the Archangel Gabriel.

Through the Imperial Door you will find the building's main space, which is famous for its dome, huge nave and gold mosaics.

Nave

Made 'transparent' by its profusion of windows and columned arcades, Aya Sofya's nave is as visually arresting as it is enormous.

The **chandeliers** hanging low above the floor are Ottoman additions. In Byzantine times, rows of glass oil lamps lined the balustrades of the gallery and the walkway at the base of the dome.

The focal point at this level is the **apse**, with its magnificent 9th-century mosaic of the **Virgin and Christ Child**. The *mimber* (pulpit) and the *mihrab* (prayer niche indicating the direction of Mecca) were added during the Ottoman period. The mosaics above the apse once depicted the archangels Gabriel and Michael; today only fragments remain.

The Byzantine emperors were crowned while seated in a throne placed within the omphalion, the section of inlaid marble in the main floor.

The large 19th-century **medallions** inscribed with gilt Arabic letters are the work of master calligrapher Mustafa İzzet Efendi, and give the names of God (Allah), Mohammed and the early caliphs Ali and Abu Bakr. Though impressive works of art in their own right, they seem out of place here, detracting from the austere magnificence of the building's interior.

The curious elevated kiosk screened from public view is the imperial loge *(hünkar mahfili)*. Sultan Abdül Mecit I had this built in 1848 so he could enter, pray and leave unseen, preserving the imperial mystique. The ornate library behind the omphalion was built by Sultan Mahmut I in 1739.

Looking up towards the northeast (to your left if you are facing the apse), you will see three mosaics at the base of the northern tympanum (semicircle) beneath the dome. These are 9th-century portraits of **St Ignatius the Younger**, **St John Chrysostom** and **St Ignatius Theodorus of Antioch**. To their right, on one of the pendentives (concave triangular segments below the dome), is a 14th-century mosaic of the face of a **seraph** (six-winged angel charged with the caretaking of God's throne).

In the side aisle to the northeast of the Imperial Door is a column with a worn copper facing pierced by a hole. Known as the **Weeping Column**, legend has it that the pillar was blessed by St Gregory the Miracle Worker and that putting one's finger into the hole can lead to ailments being healed if the finger emerges moist.

MOSAICS

In Justinian's day, the great dome, the semi-domes, the north and south tympana and the vaults of the narthexes, aisles and galleries were covered in gold mosaics. Remnants exist, but one can only imagine what the interior looked like when overlaid with glittering and gleaming tesserae (small glass tiles incorporating gold leaf). There were no figurative mosaics at this time – these date from after the Iconoclastic period, which ended in the early 9th century. When the church was converted into a mosque, the mosaics were considered inappropriate; fortunately most were covered with plaster and not destroyed. Some were uncovered and restored during building works in the mid-19th century, and though once again covered (by paint), they were left in good condition for a final unveiling after the mosque was deconsecrated.

Vikings are said to have left the 'Eric woz here'–type graffiti that is carved into the balustrade in the upstairs south gallery. You'll find it near the Deesis mosaic.

TIMELINE

537 Emperor Justinian, depicted in one of the church's most famous mosaics **1**, presides over the consecration of Byzantium's new basilica, Hagia Sophia (Church of the Holy Wisdom).

557 The huge dome **2**, damaged during an earthquake, collapses and is rebuilt.

843 The second Byzantine Iconoclastic period ends and figurative mosaics begin to be added to the interior. These include a depiction of the Empress Zoe and her third husband, Emperor Constantine IX Monomakhos **3**.

1204 Soldiers of the Fourth Crusade led by the Doge of Venice, Enrico Dandolo, conquer and ransack Constantinople. Dandolo's tomb **4** is eventually erected in the church whose desecration he presided over.

1453 The city falls to the Ottomans; Mehmet II orders that Hagia Sophia be converted into a mosque and renamed Aya Sofya.

1577 Sultan Selim II is buried in a specially designed tomb, which sits alongside the tombs of four other Ottoman Sultans **5** in Aya Sofya's grounds.

1847–49 Sultan Abdül Mecit I orders that the building be restored and redecorated; the huge Ottoman Medallions **6** in the nave are added.

1935 The mosque is converted into a museum by order of Mustafa Kemal Atatürk, president of the new Turkish Republic.

2009 The face of one of the four seraphs **7** beneath the dome is uncovered during major restoration works in the nave.

2012 Restoration of the exterior walls and western upper gallery commences.

TOP TIPS

➡ Bring binoculars if you want to properly view the mosaic portraits in the apse and under the dome.

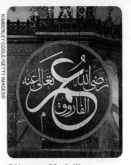

KIMBERLEY COOLE/GETTY IMAGES ©

Ottoman Medallions
These huge medallions are inscribed with gilt Arabic letters giving the names of God (Allah), Mohammed and the early caliphs Ali and Abu Bakr.

Imperial Loge

Omphalion

Imperial Door

Seraph Figures
The four huge seraphs at the base of the dome were originally mosaics, but two (on the western side) were recreated as frescoes after being damaged during the Latin occupation (1204–61).

EYE UBIQUITOUS/ALAMY ©

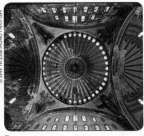

Dome
Soaring 56m from ground level, the dome was originally covered in gold mosaics but was decorated with calligraphy during the 1847–49 restoration works overseen by Swiss-born architects Gaspard and Giuseppe Fossati.

Ottoman Tombs
The tombs of five Ottoman sultans and their families are located in Aya Sofya's southern corner and can be accessed via Kabasakal Caddesi. One of these occupies the church's original Baptistry.

Christ Enthroned with Empress Zoe and Constantine IX Monomakhos
This mosaic portrait in the upper gallery depicts Zoe, one of only three Byzantine women to rule as empress in their own right.

Aya Sofya Tombs

Former Baptistry

Astronomer's House & Workshop

Grave of Enrico Dandolo
The Venetian doge died in 1205, only one year after he and his Crusaders had stormed the city. A 19th-century marker in the upper gallery indicates the probable location of his grave.

Main Entrance

Exit

Ablutions Fountain

Primary School

Constantine the Great, the Virgin Mary and the Emperor Justinian
This 11th-century mosaic shows Constantine (right) offering the Virgin Mary the city of Constantinople. Justinian (left) is offering her Hagia Sophia.

AYA SOFYA - Ground Floor & Upstairs Galleries

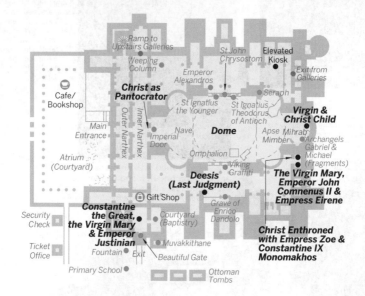

Dome

Aya Sofya's dome is 30m in diameter and 56m in height. It's supported by 40 massive ribs constructed of special hollow bricks made in Rhodes from a unique light and porous clay, and these ribs rest on four huge pillars concealed in the interior walls. On its completion, the Byzantine historian Procopius described it as being 'hung from heaven on a golden chain', and it's easy to see why. The great Ottoman architect Mimar Sinan, who spent his entire professional life trying to design a mosque to match the magnificence and beauty of Aya Sofya, used the same trick of concealing pillars and 'floating' the dome when designing the Süleymaniye Mosque almost 1000 years later.

Upstairs Galleries

To access the galleries, walk up the switchback ramp at the northern end of the inner narthex. When you reach the top, you'll find a large circle of green marble marking the spot where the throne of the empress once stood. The view over the main space towards the apse from this vantage point is quite spectacular.

In the south gallery (straight ahead and then left) are the remnants of a magnificent **Deesis** (Last Judgement). This 13th-century mosaic depicts Christ with the Virgin Mary on his left and John the Baptist on his right.

Close by is the **Tomb of Enrico Dandolo**.

Further on, at the eastern (apse) end of the gallery, is an 11th-century mosaic depicting **Christ Enthroned with Empress Zoe and Constantine IX Monomakhos**. When this portrait was started, Zoe (r 1042) was 50 years old and newly married (for the first time) to the aged Romanus III Argyrus. Upon Romanus' death in 1034, she had his face excised from the mosaic and replaced it with that of her virile new husband and consort, Michael IV. Eight years later, with Michael dead from an illness contracted on a military campaign, Zoe, helped by her sister

Colourful mosaics inside Aya Sofya

THE BUTTRESSES

The original building form designed by Aya Sofya's architects, Anthemios of Tralles and Isidoros of Miletus, has been compromised by the addition of 24 buttresses, added to reinforce the building and its enormous dome. Some date from Byzantine times, others from the Ottoman period; seven buttresses are on the eastern side of the building, four on the southern, four on the northern and five on the western. The remaining four support the structure as weight towers.

Theodora, ruled as empress in her own right, but did it so badly that it was clear she would have to marry again. At the age of 64, she wed an eminent senator, Constantine IX Monomakhos (r 1028–55), whose portrait was added here and remains only because he outlived the empress.

To the right of Zoe and Constantine is a 12th-century mosaic depicting the **Virgin Mary, Emperor John Comnenus II and Empress Eirene**. The emperor, who was known as 'John the Good', is on the Virgin's left and the empress, who was known for her charitable works, is to her right. Their son **Alexius**, who died soon after the portrait was made, is depicted next to Eirene.

In the north gallery, look for the 10th-century mosaic portrait of **Emperor Alexandros**.

Outbuildings

Exit through the **Beautiful Gate**, a magnificent bronze gate dating from the second century BC. This originally adorned a pagan temple in Tarsus and was brought to İstanbul by Emperor Theophilos in 838.

As you leave the building, be sure to look back to admire the 10th-century mosaic of **Constantine the Great, the Virgin Mary and the Emperor Justinian** on the lunette of the inner doorway. Constantine (right) is offering the Virgin, who holds the Christ Child, the city of İstanbul; Justinian (left) is offering her Aya Sofya.

The last Byzantine Emperor, Constantine XI, prayed in Aya Sofya just before midnight on 28 May 1453. Hours later he was killed while defending the city walls from the attack being staged by the army of Mehmet II. The city fell to the Ottomans on the 29th, and Mehmet's first act of victory was to make his way to Aya Sofya and declare that it should immediately be converted to a mosque.

Just before you exit the building, there is a doorway to your left. This leads into a small courtyard that was once part of a 6th-century **Baptistry**. In the 17th century the Baptistry was converted into a tomb for Sultans Mustafa I and İbrahim I. The huge stone basin displayed in the courtyard is the original **font**.

To the right of the exit is a recently restored rococo-style *şadırvan* (ablutions fountain) dating from 1740. Next to it is a small primary school also dating from 1740. The small structure next to the gate is the *muvakkithane* (house and workshop of the mosque astronomer), which was built between 1847 and 1849.

The first of Aya Sofya's minarets was added by order of Mehmet the Conqueror. Sinan designed the other three between 1574 and 1576.

After exiting the museum grounds, walk east (left) and then turn left again on Kabasakal Caddesi to visit the Aya Sofya Tombs (p69).

TOP SIGHTS
AYA SOFYA

IZZET KERIBAR/GETTY IMAGES ©

TOPKAPI PALACE

Topkapı (Topkapı Sarayı) is the subject of more colourful stories than most of the world's museums put together. Libidinous sultans, ambitious courtiers, beautiful concubines and scheming eunuchs lived and worked here between the 15th and 19th centuries when it was the court of the Ottoman empire. Visiting the palace's opulent pavilions, jewel-filled Imperial Treasury and sprawling Harem gives a fascinating glimpse into their lives.

Mehmet the Conqueror built the first stage of the palace shortly after the Conquest in 1453, and lived here until his death in 1481. Subsequent sultans lived in this rarefied environment until the 19th century, when they moved to ostentatious European-style palaces such as Dolmabahçe, Çırağan and Yıldız that they built on the shores of the Bosphorus.

Buy your tickets to the palace at the main ticket office just outside the gate to the Second Court. Guides for the palace congregate next to the main ticket office. A one-hour tour costs a hefty €100 per small group, so many visitors choose instead to hire an audio guide with rudimentary commentary about the palace for ₺10. These are available at the audio booth just inside the turnstile entrance to the Second Court.

First Court

Before you enter the **Imperial Gate** (Map p230) (Bab-ı Hümayun) of Topkapı, take a look at the ornate structure in the cobbled square just outside. This is the rococo-style **Fountain of Sultan Ahmet III** (Map p230), built in 1728 by the

DON'T MISS...

➡ Imperial Council Chamber
➡ Outer Treasury
➡ Harem
➡ Audience Chamber
➡ Imperial Treasury
➡ Marble Terrace

PRACTICALITIES

➡ Topkapı Sarayı
➡ Map p230
➡ www.topkapisarayi
.gov.tr
➡ Babıhümayun Caddesi
➡ palace ₺25, Harem ₺15
➡ ⊙9am-6pm Wed-Mon mid-Apr–Sep, to 4pm Oct–mid-Apr, Harem closes 4.30pm Apr-Oct, 3.30pm Nov-Mar
➡ 🚋Sultanahmet

DAILY LIFE IN THE IMPERIAL COURT

A visit to this opulent palace compound, with its courtyards, harem and pavilions, offers a fascinating glimpse into the lives of the Ottoman sultans. During its heyday, royal wives and children, concubines, eunuchs and servants were among the 4000 people living within Topkapı's walls.

The sultans and their families rarely left the palace grounds, relying on courtiers and diplomats to bring them news of the outside world. Most visitors would go straight to the magnificent Imperial Council Chamber **1**, where the sultan's Grand Vizier and Dîvân (Council) regularly met to discuss affairs of state and receive foreign dignitaries. Many of these visitors brought lavish gifts and tributes to embellish the Imperial Treasury **2**.

After receiving any guests and meeting with the Dîvân, the Grand Vizier would make his way through the ornate Gate of Felicity **3** into the Third Court, the palace's residential quarter. Here, he would brief the sultan on the Dîvân's deliberations and decisions in the ornate Audience Chamber **4**.

Meanwhile, day-to-day domestic chores and intrigues would be underway in the Harem **5** and servants would be preparing feasts in the massive Palace Kitchens **6**. Amid all this activity, the Marble Terrace **7** was a tranquil retreat where the sultan would come to relax, look out over the city and perhaps regret his sequestered lifestyle.

DON'T MISS

➡ There are spectacular views from the terrace behind the Imperial Treasury and from the Marble Terrace in the Fourth Court.

Harem
The sultan, his mother and the crown prince had sumptuously decorated private apartments in the harem. The most beautiful of these are the Twin Kiosks (pictured), which were used by the crown prince.

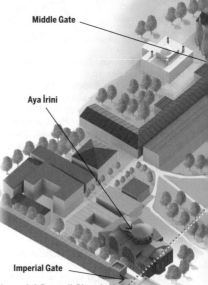

Harem Ticket Office

Middle Gate

Aya İrini

Imperial Gate

Imperial Council Chamber
This is where the Dîvân (Council) made laws, citizens presented petitions and foreign dignitaries were presented to the court. The sultan sometimes eavesdropped on proceedings through the window with the golden grill.

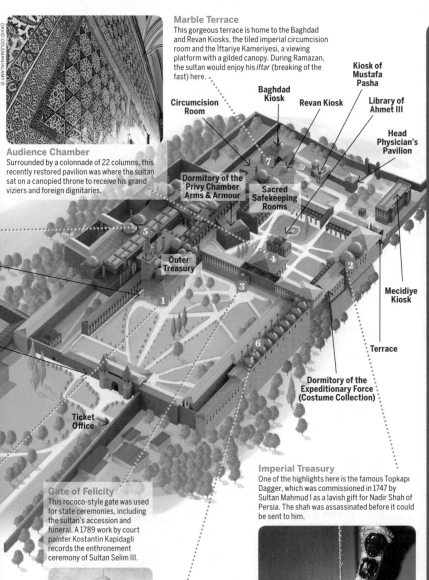

Marble Terrace
This gorgeous terrace is home to the Baghdad and Revan Kiosks, the tiled imperial circumcision room and the İftariye Kameriyesi, a viewing platform with a gilded canopy. During Ramazan, the sultan would enjoy his *iftar* (breaking of the fast) here.

Audience Chamber
Surrounded by a colonnade of 22 columns, this recently restored pavilion was where the sultan sat on a canopied throne to receive his grand viziers and foreign dignitaries.

Circumcision Room

Baghdad Kiosk

Revan Kiosk

Kiosk of Mustafa Pasha

Library of Ahmet III

Head Physician's Pavilion

Dormitory of the Privy Chamber Arms & Armour

Sacred Safekeeping Rooms

Outer Treasury

Mecidiye Kiosk

Terrace

Dormitory of the Expeditionary Force (Costume Collection)

Ticket Office

Gate of Felicity
This rococo-style gate was used for state ceremonies, including the sultan's accession and funeral. A 1789 work by court painter Kostantin Kapidagli records the enthronement ceremony of Sultan Selim III.

Palace Kitchens
Keeping the palace's 4000 residents fed was a huge task. Topkapı's kitchens occupied 10 domed buildings with 20 huge chimneys, and were workplace and home for 800 members of staff.

Imperial Treasury
One of the highlights here is the famous Topkapı Dagger, which was commissioned in 1747 by Sultan Mahmud I as a lavish gift for Nadir Shah of Persia. The shah was assassinated before it could be sent to him.

sultan who so favoured tulips. As you pass through the Imperial Gate, you enter the First Court, known as the Court of the Janissaries or the Parade Court. On your left is the Byzantine church of Hagia Eirene, more commonly known as Aya İrini (p71).

Second Court

The **Middle Gate** (Ortakapı or Bab-üs Selâm) led to the palace's Second Court, used for the business of running the empire. Only the sultan and the *valide sultan* (mother of the sultan) were allowed through the Middle Gate on horseback. Everyone else, including the grand vizier, had to dismount. To the right after you enter are imperial carriages made in Paris, Turin and Vienna for the sultan and his family.

Like the First Court, the Second Court has an attractive parklike setting. Unlike typical European palaces, which feature one large building with outlying gardens, Topkapı is a series of pavilions, kitchens, barracks, audience chambers, kiosks and sleeping quarters built around a central enclosure.

The great **Palace Kitchens** on your right currently hold a small portion of Topkapı's vast collection of Chinese celadon porcelain, valued by the sultans for its beauty but also because it was reputed to change colour if touched by poisoned food.

On the left (west) side of the Second Court is the ornate **Imperial Council Chamber**. The Imperial Divan (council) met in the chamber to discuss matters of state, and the sultan sometimes eavesdropped through the gold grille high in the wall.

North of the Imperial Council Chamber is the **Outer Treasury**, where an impressive collection of Ottoman and European arms and armour is displayed.

Harem

The entrance to the Harem is beneath the Tower of Justice on the western side of the Second Court. If you decide to visit – and we highly recommend that you do – you'll need to buy a dedicated ticket from the Harem ticket office.

As popular belief would have it, the Harem was a place where the sultan could engage in debauchery at will. In more prosaic reality, these were the imperial family quarters, and every detail of Harem life was governed by tradition, obligation and ceremony. The word 'harem' literally means 'forbidden' or 'private'.

The sultans supported as many as 300 concubines in the Harem, although numbers were usually lower than this. Upon entering the Harem, the girls would be schooled in Islam and in Turkish culture and language, as well as the arts of make-up, dress,

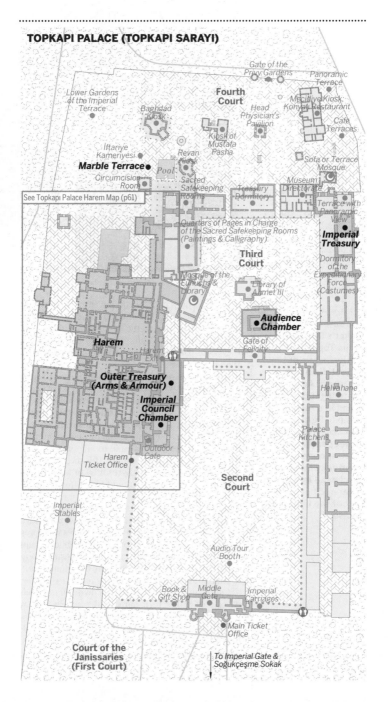

TOPKAPI PALACE (TOPKAPI SARAYI)

Gate of the Privy Gardens

Panoramic Terrace

Lower Gardens of the Imperial Terrace

Fourth Court

Baghdad Kiosk

Head Physician's Pavilion

Mecidiye Kiosk; Konyalı Restaurant

Cafe Terraces

Iftariye Kameriyesi

Revan Kiosk

Kiosk of Mustafa Pasha

Marble Terrace

Pool

Sofa or Terrace Mosque

Circumcision Room

Sacred Safekeeping Rooms

Treasury Dormitory

Museum Directorate

See Topkapı Palace Harem Map (p61)

Terrace with Panoramic View

Quarters of Pages in Charge of the Sacred Safekeeping Rooms (Paintings & Calligraphy)

Imperial Treasury

Third Court

Dormitory of the Expeditionary Force (Costumes)

Mosque of the Eunuchs & Library

Library of Ahmet III

Harem

Audience Chamber

Harem Exit

Gate of Felicity

Outer Treasury (Arms & Armour)

Helvahane

Imperial Council Chamber

Palace Kitchens

Outdoor Cafe

Harem Ticket Office

Second Court

Imperial Stables

Audio Tour Booth

Book & Gift Shop

Middle Gate

Imperial Carriages

Main Ticket Office

Court of the Janissaries (First Court)

To Imperial Gate & Soğukçeşme Sokak

POMP & CIRCUMSTANCE

During the great days of the empire, foreign ambassadors were received at Topkapı on days when the janissaries (the sultan's personal bodyguard) were scheduled to receive their pay. Huge sacks of silver coins were brought to the Imperial Council Chamber in the Second Court and court officers would dispense the coins to long lines of the tough, impeccably costumed and faultlessly disciplined troops as the ambassadors looked on in admiration.

The so-called Spoonmaker's Diamond in the Topkapı collection is one of the largest diamonds in the world. According to legend, it was found in a rubbish dump in Eğrıkapı and purchased by a wily street peddler for three spoons before eventually being purchased by a grand vizier and becoming part of the Imperial Treasury.

Entrance to the Imperial Council Chamber of Topkapı Palace

comportment, music, reading, writing, embroidery and dancing. They then entered a meritocracy, first as ladies-in-waiting to the sultan's concubines and children, then to the sultan's mother and finally – if they were particularly attractive and talented – to the sultan himself.

The sultan was allowed by Islamic law to have four legitimate wives, who received the title of *kadın* (wife). If a wife bore him a son she was called *haseki sultan*; *haseki kadın* if it was a daughter. The Ottoman dynasty did not observe primogeniture (the right of the first-born son to the throne), so in principle the throne was available to any imperial son. In the early years of the empire, this meant that the death of a sultan regularly resulted in a fratricidal bloodbath as his sons – often from different mothers – battled it out among themselves for the throne. Later sultans imprisoned their brothers in the Harem, beginning the tradition of *kafes hayatı* (cage life). This house arrest meant that princes were prey to the intrigues of the women and eunuchs, kept ignorant of war and statecraft, and thus usually rendered unfit to rule if and when the occasion arose.

Ruling the Harem was the *valide sultan* (mother of the reigning sultan), who often owned large landed estates in her own name and controlled them through black eunuch servants. Able to give orders directly to the grand vizier, her influence on the sultan, on the selection of his wives and concubines, and on matters of state was often profound.

The earliest of the 300-odd rooms in the Harem were constructed during the reign of Murat III (r 1574–95); the harems of previous sultans were at the Eski Saray (Old Palace), near current-day Beyazıt Meydanı.

The Harem complex has six floors, but only one of these can be visited. This is approached via the **Carriage Gate**. Inside the gate is the Dome with Cupboards. Beyond it is a room where the Harem's eunuch guards were stationed. This is decorated with fine Kütahya tiles from the 17th century.

Beyond this room is the narrow **Courtyard of the Black Eunuchs**, also decorated with Kütahya tiles. Behind the marble colonnade on the left are the Black Eunuchs' Dormitories. In the early days white eunuchs were used, but black eunuchs sent as presents by the Ottoman governor of Egypt later took control. As many as 200 lived here, guarding the doors and waiting on the women of the Harem.

At the far end of the courtyard is the Main Gate into the Harem, as well as a guard room featuring two gigantic gilded mirrors. From this, a corridor on the left leads to the **Courtyard of the Women Servants and Consorts**. This is surrounded by baths, a laundry fountain, a laundry, dormitories and private apartments.

Further on is **Sultan Ahmet's Kiosk**, decorated with a tiled chimney, followed by the **Apartments of the Valide Sultan**, the centre of power in the Harem. From these ornate rooms the *valide sultan* oversaw and controlled her huge 'family'. Of particular note is the **Salon of the Valide** with its lovely 19th-century murals featuring bucolic views of İstanbul.

Past the adjoining **Courtyard of the Valide Sultan** is a splendid reception room with a large fireplace that leads to a vestibule covered in Kütahya and İznik tiles dating from the 17th century. This is where the princes, *valide sultan* and senior concubines waited before entering the handsome **Imperial Hall** for an audience with the sultan. Built during the reign of Murat III, it was redecorated in baroque style by order of Osman III (r 1754–57).

Nearby is the **Privy Chamber of Murat III**, one of the most sumptuous rooms in the palace. Dating from 1578, virtually all of its decoration is original and is thought to be the work of Sinan. The three-tiered marble fountain was designed to give the sound of cascading water and to make it difficult to eavesdrop on the sultan's conversations. The gilded canopied seating areas are later 18th-century additions.

Take the left door in the Privy Chamber of Murat III to access the **Privy Chamber of Ahmet III** and an adjoining dining room built in 1705. This exquisite space is lined with wooden panels decorated with images of flowers and fruits painted in lacquer.

Northeast (through the door to the right) of the Privy Chamber of Murat III are two of the most beautiful rooms in the Harem – the **Twin Kiosk/Apartments of the Crown Prince**. These two rooms date from around 1600; note the painted canvas dome in the first room and the fine İznik tile panels above the fireplace in the second. The stained glass is also noteworthy.

To the east of the Twin Kiosk is the **Courtyard of the Favourites**. Over the edge of the courtyard (really a terrace) you'll see a large pool. Just past the courtyard (but on the floor above) are the many small dark rooms that comprised the *kafes* where brothers or sons of the sultan were imprisoned.

From here, a corridor leads east to a passage known as the Golden Road and then out into the palace's Third Court.

Note that the visitor route through the Harem changes when rooms are closed for restoration or stabilisation, so some of the areas mentioned here may not be open during your visit.

SULTANAHMET & AROUND TOPKAPI PALACE

LIFE IN THE CAGE

In the early centuries of the empire, Ottoman princes were schooled as youths in combat and statecraft by direct experience. But as the Ottoman dynasty did not observe primogeniture (succession of the firstborn), the death of the sultan regularly resulted in a fratricidal bloodbath as his sons – often from different mothers – battled among themselves for the throne. This changed when Sultan Ahmet I (r 1603–20) couldn't bring himself to murder his brother Mustafa and decided instead to keep him imprisoned in Topkapı's Harem, so beginning the tradition of *kafes hayatı* (cage life). This house arrest, adopted in place of fratricide by succeeding sultans, meant that princes were kept ignorant of war and statecraft and usually rendered unfit to rule when the occasion arose. This contributed to the decline of the Empire's power and that of succeeding sultans, even though in later years the dynasty observed the custom of primogeniture.

Sultan Murat III (r 1574–95) had 112 children.

Third Court

The Third Court is entered through the **Gate of Felicity**. The sultan's private domain, it was staffed and guarded by white eunuchs. Inside is the **Audience Chamber**, constructed in the 16th century but refurbished in the 18th century. Important officials and foreign ambassadors were brought to this little kiosk to conduct the high business of state. The sultan, seated on divans with cushions embroidered with over 15,000 seed pearls, inspected the ambassador's gifts and offerings as they were passed through the small doorway on the left.

Right behind the Audience Chamber is the pretty **Library of Ahmet III**, built in 1719. Light-filled, it has comfortable reading areas and stunning inlaid woodwork.

On the eastern edge of the Third Court is the **Dormitory of the Expeditionary Force**, which now houses a rich collection of imperial robes, kaftans and uniforms worked in silver and gold thread. Also here is a fascinating collection of talismanic shirts, which were believed to protect the wearer from enemies and misfortunes of all kinds. Textile design reached its highest point during the reign of Süleyman the Magnificent, when the imperial workshops produced cloth of exquisite design and weave. Don't miss Süleyman's gorgeous silk kaftan with its appliquéd tulip design.

On the other side of the Third Court are the **Sacred Safekeeping Rooms**. These rooms, sumptuously decorated with İznik tiles, house many relics of the Prophet. When the sultans lived here, the rooms were opened only once a year so that the imperial family could pay homage to the memory of the Prophet on the 15th day of the holy month of Ramazan.

Next to the sacred Safekeeping Rooms is the **Dormitory of the Privy Chamber**, which houses portraits of 36 sultans. It includes a copy of Gentile Bellini's portrait of Mehmet the Conqueror (the original is in London's National Gallery) and a wonderful painting of the **Enthronement Ceremony of Sultan Selim III** (1789).

Imperial Treasury

Located on the eastern edge of the Third Court, Topkapı's Treasury features an incredible collection of objects made from or decorated with gold, silver, rubies, emeralds, jade, pearls and diamonds. The building itself was constructed during Mehmet the Conqueror's reign in 1460 and was used originally as reception rooms.

In the first room, look for the jewel-encrusted Sword of Süleyman the Magnificent and the Throne

61

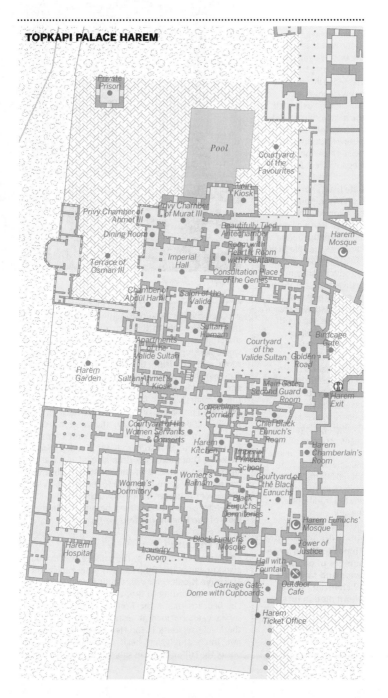

TOPKAPI PALACE HAREM

TULIP SULTAN

When he ascended to the throne aged 29, Sultan Ahmet III (r 1703–30) introduced many changes at Topkapı. He extended the palace Harem and ordered that a number of new structures be built. These include the elegant street fountain outside the Imperial Gate that is named in his honour. Ahmet is best known, however, as the sultan who presided over the period known as the Lâle Devri (Tulip Period). He even introduced an annual festival to celebrate the blooming of this prized flower. Held over the three days surrounding the first full moon in April, this fete was staged in the gardens of the palace's Fourth Court, which was specially decorated with vases of tulips and tiny coloured glass lamps. Trilling nightingales in cages provided entertainment, as did palace musicians. Today the annual İstanbul Tulip Festival in April continues the tradition across the city.

Ahmet III had a large number of concubines and fathered 52 children, 34 of whom died in infancy.

Topkapı Palace interior

of Ahmet I, which is inlaid with mother-of-pearl and was designed by Sedefhar Mehmet Ağa, architect of the Blue Mosque. In the second room, the tiny Indian figures, mainly made from seed pearls, are well worth seeking out. After passing through the third room and admiring the 16th-century gold-plated Ottoman helmet encrusted with turquoises, rubies and emeralds, you will come to a fourth room and the Treasury's most famous exhibit: the **Topkapı Dagger**. The object of the criminal heist in Jules Dassin's 1964 film *Topkapi*, the dagger features three enormous emeralds on the hilt and a watch set into the pommel. Also here is the **Kasıkçı (Spoonmaker's) Diamond**, a teardrop-shaped 86-carat rock surrounded by dozens of smaller stones. First worn by Mehmet IV at his accession to the throne in 1648, it's one of the largest diamonds in the world.

Before leaving the Treasury, be sure to admire the **view of the Bosphorus** from its terrace.

Fourth Court

Pleasure pavilions occupy the palace's Fourth Court, also known as the Tulip Garden. These include the **Mecidiye Kiosk**, which was built by Abdül Mecit (r 1839–61) according to 19th-century European models. Beneath this is the Konyalı restaurant, which serves cafeteria food at restaurant prices. West of the Mecidiye Kiosk is the **Head Physician's Pavilion**. Interestingly, the head physician was always one of the sultan's Jewish subjects. Nearby, you'll see the **Kiosk of Mustafa Pasha**, sometimes called the Sofa Köşkü. During the reign of Ahmet III, the Tulip Garden outside the kiosk was filled with the latest varieties of the flower.

Up the stairs at the end of the Tulip Garden is the **Marble Terrace**, a platform with a decorative pool, three pavilions and the whimsical **İftariye Kameriyesi**, a small structure commissioned by İbrahim the Crazy in 1640 as a picturesque place to break the fast of Ramazan.

Murat IV built the **Revan Kiosk** in 1636 after reclaiming the city of Yerevan (now in Armenia) from Persia. In 1639 he constructed the **Baghdad Kiosk**, one of the last examples of classical palace architecture, to commemorate his victory over that city. Notice its superb İznik tiles, painted ceiling and mother-of-pearl and tortoiseshell inlay. The small **Circumcision Room** (Sünnet Odası) was used for the ritual that admits Muslim boys to manhood. Built by İbrahim in 1640, the outer walls of the chamber are graced by particularly beautiful tile panels.

İstanbul's most photogenic building was the grand project of Sultan Ahmet I (r 1603–17), whose *türbe* (tomb) is located on the north side of the site facing Sultanahmet Park. The mosque's wonderfully curvaceous exterior features a cascade of domes and six slender minarets. Blue İznik tiles adorn the interior and give the building its unofficial but commonly used name.

Ahmet set out to build a monument that would rival and even surpass the nearby Aya Sofya in grandeur and beauty. So enthusiastic was the young sultan about the project that he is said to have worked with the labourers and crafts-men on site, pushing them along and rewarding extra ef-fort. Ahmet did in fact come close to his goal of rivalling Aya Sofya, and in so doing achieved the added benefit of making future generations of hotel owners in Sultanahmet happy – a 'Blue Mosque view' from the roof terrace being the number-one selling point of the fleet of hotels in the area.

With the mosque's exterior, architect Sedefhar Mehmet Ağa managed to orchestrate the visual wham-bam effect that Aya Sofya achieved with its interior. Its curves are vo-luptuous, it has more minarets than any other İstanbul mosque (in fact, there was concern at the time of its construction that the sultan was being irreverent in specifying six mina-rets – the only equivalent being in Mecca) and the courtyard is the biggest of all the Otto-man mosques. The interior is conceived on a similarly grand scale: the İznik tiles number in the tens of thousands, there are 260 windows and the central prayer space is huge.

In order to fully appreciate the mosque's design you should approach it via the mid-dle of the Hippodrome rather than entering from Sultanahmet Park. When inside the courtyard, which is the same size as the mosque's interior, you'll be able to appreciate

DON'T MISS...

➡ The approach from the Hippodrome
➡ İznik tiles
➡ Mimber

PRACTICALITIES

➡ Sultan Ahmet Camii
➡ Map p232
➡ Hippodrome
➡ ⊙9am-12.15pm, 2-4.30pm & 5.30-6.30pm Sat-Thu, 9-11.15am, 2.30-4.30pm & 5.30-6.30pm Fri
➡ 🚇Sultanahmet

the perfect proportions of the building. Walk towards the mosque through the gate in the peripheral wall, noting on the way the small dome atop the gate: this is the motif Sedefhar Mehmet Ağa uses to lift your eyes to heaven. As you walk through the gate, your eyes follow a flight of stairs up to another gate topped by another dome; through this gate is yet another dome, that of the ablutions fountain in the centre of the mosque courtyard. As you ascend the stairs, semidomes come into view: first the one over the mosque's main door, then the one above it, and another, and another. Finally the main dome crowns the whole, and your attention is drawn to the sides, where forests of smaller domes reinforce the effect, completed by the minarets, which lift your eyes heavenward.

The mosque is such a popular tourist sight that admission is controlled so as to preserve its sacred atmosphere. Only worshippers are admitted through the main door; tourists must use the north door (follow the signs). Shoes must be taken off and women who haven't brought their own headscarf or are too scantily dressed will be loaned a headscarf and/or robe.

Inside, the **stained-glass windows** and **İznik tiles** immediately attract attention. Though the windows are replacements, they still create the luminous effects of the originals, which came from Venice. Tiles line the walls, particularly in the gallery (which is not open to the public); those downstairs are especially fine.

Once inside, it's easy to see that the mosque, which was constructed between 1606 and 1616 – over 1000 years after Aya Sofya, is not as architecturally daring as its predecessor. Four massive pillars hold up the less ambitious dome, a sturdier solution lacking the innovation and grace of the 'floating' dome in Justinian's cathedral.

The semidomes and the dome are painted with graceful **arabesques**. Of note in the main space are the **imperial loge**, covered with marble latticework, which is to the left of the *mihrab*; the **mihrab** itself, which features a piece of the sacred Black Stone from the Kaaba in Mecca; and the high, elaborate **mahfil** (chair) from which the imam gives the sermon on Friday. The beautifully carved white marble **mimber** with its curtained doorway at floor level features a flight of steps and a small kiosk topped by a spire.

SULTAN AHMET I

The Tomb of Sultan Ahmet I is on the north side of the mosque facing Sultanahmet Park. Ahmet, who had ascended to the imperial throne aged 13, died one year after the mosque was constructed, aged only 27. Buried with him are his wife, Kösem, who was strangled to death in the Topkapı Harem, and his sons, Sultan Osman II (r 1618–22), Sultan Murat IV (r 1623–40) and Prince Beyazıt (murdered by Murat). Like the mosque, the *türbe* features fine İznik tiles.

Mosques built by the great and powerful usually included numerous public-service institutions, including hospitals, soup kitchens and schools. Here, a large *medrese* (Islamic school of higher studies) on the northwestern side of the complex (closed to the public) and an *arasta* (row of shops by a mosque; now the Arasta Bazaar) remain. The rent from shops in the *arasta* has always supported the upkeep of the mosque.

TOP SIGHTS
BLUE MOSQUE

İSTANBUL ARCHAEOLOGY MUSEUMS

This superb complex of museums has archaeological and artistic treasures from the Topkapı collections. Housed in three buildings, its exhibits include ancient artefacts, classical statuary and objects showcasing Anatolian history. There are many highlights, but the 'İstanbul Through the Ages' exhibition, which focuses on the city's Byzantine past, is particularly satisfying.

The complex has three main parts: the Archaeology Museum (Arkeoloji Müzesi), the Museum of the Ancient Orient (Eski Şark Eserler Müzesi) and the Tiled Pavilion (Çinili Köşk). These museums house the palace collections formed during the late 19th century by museum director, artist and archaeologist Osman Hamdi Bey. The complex can be easily reached by walking down the slope from Topkapı's First Court, or by walking up the hill from the main gate of Gülhane Park.

Museum of the Ancient Orient

Immediately on the left after you enter the complex, this 1883 building has a collection of pre-Islamic items collected from the expanse of the Ottoman Empire. Highlights include a series of large blue-and-yellow glazed-brick panels that once lined the processional street and the Ishtar gate of ancient Babylon. The panels depict real and mythical animals such as lions, dragons and bulls.

Archaeology Museum

On the opposite side of the courtyard is this imposing neoclassical building housing an extensive collection of classical statuary and sarcophagi plus a sprawling exhibit documenting İstanbul's history.

DON'T MISS

➡ Glazed panels from the processional street and Ishtar gate of ancient Babylon
➡ Alexander Sarcophagus
➡ Mourning Women Sarcophagus
➡ Columned Sarcophagi of Anatolia
➡ Statuary Galleries
➡ İstanbul Through the Ages exhibition

PRACTICALITIES

➡ Map p230
➡ www.istanbul arkeologi.gov.tr
➡ Osman Hamdi Bey Yokuşu, Gülhane
➡ admission ₺10
➡ ⊘9am-6pm Tue-Sun mid-Apr–Sep, to 4pm Oct–mid-Apr
➡ 🚇Gülhane

A Roman statue of Bes, an impish half-god of inexhaustible power who was thought to protect against evil, greets visitors as they enter the museum's main entrance. To its left, past the museum shop, cloakroom and small cafe, are two dimly lit rooms where the museum's major treasures – sarcophagi from the Royal Necropolis of Sidon and surrounding area – are displayed. These sarcophagi were unearthed in 1887 by Osman Hamdi Bey in Sidon (Side in modern-day Lebanon).

In the next room is an impressive collection of ancient grave-cult sarcophagi from Syria, Lebanon, Thessalonica and Ephesus. Beyond that is a room called **Columned Sarcophagi of Anatolia**, filled with amazingly detailed sarcophagi dating from between 140 and 270 AD. Many of these look like tiny temples or residential buildings; don't miss the **Sidamara Sarcophagus** from Konya.

Further rooms contain Lycian monuments and examples of Anatolian architecture from antiquity.

Back towards the statue of Bes is a staircase leading up to the underwhelming 'Anatolia and Troy Through the Ages' and 'Neighbouring Cultures of Anatolia, Cyprus, Syria and Palestine' exhibitions.

On the other side of Bes are the museum's famed **Statuary Galleries**, which were closed for renovation when this book went to print.

On the floor above the Statuary Galleries (accessed behind the cloakroom) is a fascinating exhibition called **İstanbul Through the Ages** that traces the city's history through its neighbourhoods during different periods: Archaic, Hellenistic, Roman, Byzantine and Ottoman. The exhibition continues downstairs, where there is an impressive gallery showcasing Byzantine artefacts.

Tiled Pavilion

The last of the complex's museum buildings is this handsome pavilion, constructed in 1472 by order of Mehmet the Conqueror. The portico, with its 14 marble columns, was constructed during the reign of Sultan Abdül Hamit I (1774–89) after the original one burned down in 1737.

On display here is the best collection of Seljuk, Anatolian and Ottoman tiles and ceramics in the country; these date from the end of the 12th century to the beginning of the 20th century. The collection includes İznik tiles from the period between the mid-14th and 17th centuries when that city produced the finest coloured tiles in the world. When you enter the central room you can't miss the stunning *mihrab* from the İbrahim Bey İmâret in Karaman, built in 1432.

THE ALEXANDER SARCOPHAGUS

The Royal Necropolis of Sidon room in the Archaeology Museuem showcases this famous piece of classical sculpture – so named not because it belonged to the Macedonian general, but because it depicts him among his army battling the Persians, who were led by King Abdalonymos (whose sarcophagus it is). Truly exquisite, the sarcophagus is carved out of Pentelic marble and dates from the last quarter of the 4th century BC. Alexander, on horseback, has a lion's head as a headdress. Remarkably, the sculpture retains remnants of its original red-and-yellow paintwork.

The Tiled Pavilion in the museum compound was originally an outer pavilion of Topkapı Palace. The sultan used it to watch sporting events being staged in the palace grounds below (now Gülhane Park).

TOP SIGHTS
BASILICA CISTERN

This subterranean structure was commissioned by Emperor Justinian and built in 532. The largest surviving Byzantine cistern in İstanbul, it was constructed using 336 columns, many of which were salvaged from ruined temples and feature fine carved capitals. Its symmetry and sheer grandeur of conception are quite breathtaking, and its cavernous depths make a great retreat on summer days.

The cistern was originally known as the Basilica Cistern because it lay underneath the Stoa Basilica, one of the great squares on the first hill. Designed to service the Great Palace and surrounding buildings, it was able to store up to 80,000 cu metres of water delivered via 20km of aqueducts from a reservoir near the Black Sea, but was closed when the Byzantine emperors relocated from the Great Palace. Forgotten by the city authorities some time before the Conquest, it wasn't rediscovered until 1545, when scholar Petrus Gyllius was researching Byzantine antiquities in the city and was told by local residents that they were able to obtain water by lowering buckets into a dark space below their basement floors. Some were even catching fish this way. Intrigued, Gyllius explored before finally accessing the cistern through one of the basements. Even after his discovery, the Ottomans (who referred to the cistern as Yerebatan Saray) didn't treat the so-called 'Underground Palace' with the respect it deserved – it became a dumping ground for all sorts of junk, as well as corpses.

The cistern was cleaned and renovated in 1985 by the İstanbul Metropolitan Municipality and opened to the public in 1987. It's now one of the city's most popular tourist attractions. Walking along its raised wooden platforms, you'll feel the water dripping from the vaulted ceiling and see schools of ghostly carp patrolling the water – it certainly has bucketloads of atmosphere.

DON'T MISS...

➡ Upside-down head of Medusa used as a column base
➡ Teardrop column

PRACTICALITIES

➡ Yerebatan Sarnıçı
➡ Map p230
➡ www.yerebatan.com
➡ Yerebatan Caddesi 13
➡ admission ₺10
➡ ⏱9am-6.30pm
➡ 🚇Sultanahmet

⊙ SIGHTS

⊙ Sultanahmet

TOPKAPI PALACE   PALACE
See p53.

AYA SOFYA   MUSEUM
See p46.

BLUE MOSQUE   MOSQUE
See p64.

**İSTANBUL ARCHAEOLOGY
MUSEUMS**   MUSEUM
See p66.

BASILICA CISTERN   CISTERN
See p68.

FREE **AYA SOFYA TOMBS**   TOMBS

Map p232 (Aya Sofya Müzesi Padişah Türbeleri; Kabasakal Caddesi; ⊙9am-5pm; ♿Sultanahmet) Part of the Aya Sofya complex but entered via Kabasakal Caddesi, these tombs are the final resting places of five sultans – Mehmet III, Selim II, Murad III, İbrahim I and Mustafa I – most of whom are buried with members of their families. The ornate interior decoration in the tombs features the very best Ottoman tilework, calligraphy and decorative paintwork.

Mehmet III's tomb dates from 1608 and Murad III's from 1599; both are adorned with particularly beautiful İznik tiles. Next to Murad's tomb is that of his five children; this was designed by Sinan and has simple but superb painted decoration.

Selim II's tomb, which was designed by Sinan and built in 1577, is particularly poignant, as it houses the graves of five of his sons, murdered on the same night in December 1574 to ensure the peaceful succession of the oldest, Murad III. It also houses the graves of 19 of Murad's sons, murdered in January 1595 to facilitate Mehmet III's succession. They were the last of the royal princes to be murdered by their siblings – after this, the younger brothers of succeeding sultans were confined to the *kafes* (cage) in Topkapı Palace instead.

The fifth tomb is Aya Sofya's original Baptistry, converted to a mausoleum for sultans İbrahim I and Mustafa I during the 17th century.

**GREAT PALACE MOSAIC
MUSEUM**   MUSEUM

Map p232 (Torun Sokak; admission ₺8; ⊙9am-6.30pm Tue-Sun Apr-Oct, to 4.30pm Nov-Mar; ♿Sultanahmet) When archaeologists from the University of Ankara and the University of St Andrews (Scotland) excavated around the Arasta Bazaar at the rear of the Blue Mosque in the mid-1950s, they uncovered a stunning mosaic pavement featuring hunting and mythological scenes. Dating from

---

ℹ️ MUSEUM PASS İSTANBUL

Most visitors spend at least three days in İstanbul and cram as many museum visits as possible into their stay, so the recent introduction of this **discount pass** (www .muze.gov.tr/museum_pass) is most welcome. Valid for 72 hours from your first museum entrance, it costs ₺72 and allows entrance to Topkapı Palace and Harem, Aya Sofya, the Kariye Museum (Chora Church), the İstanbul Archaeology Museums, the Museum of Turkish and Islamic Arts and the Great Palace Mosaics Museum. Purchased individually, admission fees to these sights will cost ₺108, so the pass represents a saving of ₺36. Its biggest benefit is that it allows you to bypass ticket queues and make your way straight into the museums – something that is particularly useful when visiting ever-crowded Aya Sofya.

As well as providing entry to these government-operated museums, the pass gives a 20% discount on entry to the privately run Rahmi M Koç Industrial Museum (p159) on the Golden Horn and a 30% discount on entry to the Sakıp Sabancı Museum (p155) on the Bosphorus, which is operated by the university of the same name.

The pass can be purchased from some hotels and also from the ticket offices at Aya Sofya, the Kariye Museum, Topkapı Palace and the İstanbul Archaeology Museums.

early Byzantine times, it was restored from 1983 to 1997 and is now preserved in this museum.

Thought to have been added by Justinian to the Great Palace of Byzantium, the pavement is estimated to have measured from 3500 to 4000 sq m in its original form. The 250 sq m that is preserved here is the largest discovered remnant – the rest has been destroyed or remains buried underneath the Blue Mosque and surrounding shops and hotels.

The pavement is filled with bucolic imagery and has a gorgeous ribbon border with heart-shaped leaves. In the westernmost room is the most colourful and dramatic picture, that of two men in leggings carrying spears and holding off a raging tiger.

The museum has informative panels documenting the floor's rescue and renovation.

HIPPODROME PARK

Map p232 (Atmeydanı; ⊠Sultanahmet) The Byzantine emperors loved nothing more than an afternoon at the chariot races, and this rectangular arena was their venue of choice. In its heyday, it was decorated by obelisks and statues, some of which remain in place today. Recently relandscaped, it is one of the city's most popular meeting places and promenades.

Originally the arena consisted of two levels of galleries, a central spine, starting boxes and the semicircular southern end known as the **Sphendone** (Map p232), parts of which still stand. The level of galleries that once topped this stone structure was damaged during the Fourth Crusade and ended up being totally dismantled in the Ottoman period – many of the original columns were used in construction of the Süleymaniye Mosque.

The Hippodrome was the centre of Byzantium's life for 1000 years and of Ottoman life for another 400 years and has been the scene of countless political dramas. In Byzantine times, the rival chariot teams of 'Greens' and 'Blues' had separate sectarian connections. Support for a team was akin to membership of a political party and a team victory had important effects on policy. Occasionally Greens and Blues joined forces against the emperor, as was the case in 532 BC when a chariot race was disturbed by protests against Justinian's high tax regime – this escalated into the Nika riots (so called after the protesters'

cry of Nika!, or Victory!), which led to tens of thousands of protesters being massacred in the Hippodrome by imperial forces. Not unsurprisingly, chariot races were banned for some time afterwards.

Ottoman sultans also kept an eye on activities in the Hippodrome. If things were going badly in the empire, a surly crowd gathering here could signal the start of a disturbance, then a riot, then a revolution. In 1826 the slaughter of the corrupt janissary corps (the sultan's personal bodyguards) was carried out here by the reformer Sultan Mahmut II. In 1909 there were riots here that caused the downfall of Abdül Hamit II.

Despite the ever-present threat of the Hippodrome being the scene of their downfall, emperors and sultans sought to outdo one another in beautifying it, adorning the centre with statues from the far reaches of their empire. Unfortunately, many priceless statues carved by ancient masters have disappeared from their original homes here. Chief among the villains responsible for such thefts were the soldiers of the Fourth Crusade, who invaded Constantinople, a Christian-ally city, in 1204. After sacking Aya Sofya, they tore all the plates from the **Rough-Stone Obelisk** (Map p232) at the Hippodrome's southern end in the mistaken belief that they were solid gold (in fact, they were gold-covered bronze). The crusaders also stole the famous quadriga, or team of four horses cast in bronze, a copy of which now sits atop the main door of the Basilica di San Marco in Venice (the original is inside the basilica).

Near the northern end of the Hippodrome, the little gazebo with beautiful stonework is known as **Kaiser Wilhelm's Fountain** (Map p232). The German emperor paid a state visit to Sultan Abdül Hamit II in 1901 and presented this fountain to the sultan and his people as a token of friendship. The monograms in the stonework are those of Abdül Hamit II and Wilhelm II, and represent their political union.

The immaculately preserved pink granite **Obelisk of Theodosius** (Map p232) in the centre was carved in Egypt during the reign of Thutmose III (r 1549–1503 BC) and erected in the Amon-Re temple at Karnak. Theodosius the Great (r 379–95) had it brought from Egypt to Constantinople in AD 390. On the marble billboards below the obelisk, look for the carvings of Theodosius, his wife, sons, state officials and bodyguards watching the chariot-race action from the *kathisma* (imperial box).

South of the obelisk is a strange column coming up out of a hole in the ground. Known as the **Spiral Column** (Map p232), it was once much taller and was topped by three serpents' heads. Originally cast to commemorate a victory of the Hellenic confederation over the Persians in the battle of Plataea, it stood in front of the temple of Apollo at Delphi from 478 BC until Constantine the Great had it brought to his new capital city around AD 330. Though badly damaged in Byzantine times, the serpents' heads survived until the early 18th century. Now all that remains of them is one upper jaw, housed in the İstanbul Archaeology Museums (p66).

FREE MARMARA UNIVERSITY
REPUBLICAN MUSEUM   MUSEUM
Map p232 (◷10am-6pm Tue-Sun; 🚇Sultanahmet) Located at the southern end of the Hippodrome, this museum is housed in a handsome example of Ottoman Revivalism, a homegrown architectural style popular in the late 19th century. The university's collection of original prints by Turkish artists is displayed here.

TOP CHOICE MUSEUM OF TURKISH & ISLAMIC ARTS   MUSEUM
Map p232 (Türk ve Islam Eserleri Müzesi; www.tiem.gov.tr; Atmeydanı Caddesi 46; admission ₺10; ◷9am-6.30pm Tue-Sun Apr-Oct, to 4.30pm Nov-Mar; 🚇Sultanahmet) This Ottoman palace on the western edge of the Hippodrome was built in 1524 for İbrahim Paşa, childhood friend, brother-in-law and grand vizier of Süleyman the Magnificent. It's now home to a magnificent collection of artefacts, including exquisite examples of calligraphy and a collection of antique carpets that is generally held to be the best in the world.

Born in Greece, İbrahim Paşa was captured in that country as a child and sold as a slave into the imperial household in İstanbul. He worked as a page in Topkapı, where he became friendly with Süleyman, who was the same age. When his friend became sultan, İbrahim was made in turn chief falconer, chief of the royal bedchamber and grand vizier. This palace was bestowed on him by Süleyman the year before he was given the hand of Süleyman's sister, Hadice,

in marriage. Alas, the fairy tale was not to last for poor İbrahim. His wealth, power and influence on the monarch became so great that others wishing to influence the sultan became envious, chief among them Süleyman's powerful wife, Haseki Hürrem Sultan (Roxelana). After a rival accused İbrahim of disloyalty, Roxelana convinced her husband that İbrahim was a threat and Süleyman had him strangled in 1536.

The museum's exhibits date from the 8th and 9th centuries up to the 19th century. Highlights include the superb calligraphy exhibits, with *müknames* (scrolls outlining an imperial decree) featuring the sultan's *tuğra* (monogram). Look out for the exquisite Iranian book binding from the Safavid period (1501–1786). And whatever you do, don't miss the extraordinary collection of carpets displayed in the *divanhane* (ceremonial hall) – it includes Holbein, Lotto, Konya, Uşhak, Iran and Caucasia examples. The lower floor of the museum houses ethnographic exhibits. Labels are in Turkish and English throughout.

While here, be sure to enjoy an expertly prepared Turkish coffee at Müzenin Kahvesi (p82) in the courtyard.

AYA İRINI   CHURCH
Map p230 (Hagia Eirene, Church of the Divine Peace; 1st Court, Topkapı Palace; 🚇Sultanahmet) Commissioned by Justinian in the 540s, this Byzantine church is almost exactly as old as its close neighbour, Aya Sofya. When Mehmet the Conqueror began building Topkapı, the building was within the grounds and was most fortunately retained. Used as an arsenal for centuries, it now functions as an atmospheric concert venue during the İstanbul International Music Festival.

The serenely beautiful interior and superb acoustics mean that tickets to events here are usually the most sought-after in town (they're also the only way to see the building's interior, as it is usually closed to the public). During the festival there is a temporary box office located outside the church; tickets can also be booked online at Biletix.

There is talk of the church being used as a museum of Byzantium in the future, but the first priority identified by heritage authorities is to undertake stabilisation and restoration work, as the structure is in a relatively serious state of disrepair.

GREAT PALACE OF BYZANTIUM

Constantine the Great built the Great Palace soon after he founded Constantinople in AD 324. Successive Byzantine leaders left their mark by adding to it, and the complex eventually consisted of hundreds of buildings enclosed by walls and set in terraced parklands stretching from the Hippodrome over to Aya Sofya (Hagia Sofia) and down the slope, ending at the sea walls on the Sea of Marmara. The palace was finally abandoned after the Fourth Crusade sacked the city in 1204, and its ruins were pillaged and filled in after the Conquest, becoming mere foundations of much of Sultanahmet and Cankurtaran.

Various pieces of the Great Palace have been uncovered – many by budding hotelier 'archaeologists'. The mosaics in the Great Palace Mosaic Museum (p69) once graced the floor of the complex, and excavations at the Sultanahmet Archaeological Park in Kabasakal Caddesi, near Aya Sofya, have uncovered other parts of the palace. Controversially, some of these excavations are being subsumed into a new extension of the neighbouring luxury Four Seasons Hotel.

For more information, check out www.byzantium1200.com, which has 3D images that bring ancient Byzantium to life, or purchase a copy of the lavishly illustrated guidebook *Walking Through Byzantium: Great Palace Region*, which was also produced as part of the Byzantium 1200 project. You'll find it in shops around Sultanahmet.

SOĞUKÇEŞME SOKAK   HISTORIC AREA

Map p230 (🏛Sultanahmet, Gülhane) Running between the Topkapı Palace walls and Aya Sofya, this cobbled street is named after the Soğuk Çeşme (Cold Fountain) at its southern end. It is home to a row of faux-Ottoman houses functioning as a hotel as well as an undoubtedly authentic restored Byzantine cistern that now operates as the hotel restaurant.

In the 1980s the Turkish Touring & Auto-mobile Association (Turing) acquired a row of buildings on this street and decided to demolish most of them to build nine re-creations of the prim Ottoman-style houses that had occupied the site in the previous two centuries. What ensued was a vitriolic battle played out on the pages of İstanbul's newspapers, with some experts arguing that the city would be left with a Disney-style architectural theme park rather than a legitimate exercise in conservation architecture. Turing eventually got the go-ahead (after the intervention of the Turkish president no less) and in time opened all of the re-created buildings as Ayasofya Konakları, one of the first boutique heritage hotels in the city. Conservation theory aside, the street is particularly picturesque and worth a view.

FREE CAFERAĞA
MEDRESESI   HISTORIC BUILDING

Map p230 (www.tkhv.org; Soğukkuyu Çıkmazı 5, off Caferiye Sokak; ☺8.30am-5pm; 🏛Sultanahmet) This lovely little building tucked away in the shadows of Aya Sofya was designed by Sinan on the orders of Cafer Ağa, Süleyman the Magnificent's chief black eunuch. Built in 1560 as a school, it is now home to a cultural organisation teaching and promoting traditional Turkish handicrafts. It has a pleasant *lokanta* (eatery serving ready0made food; p78) and *çay bahçesi* (tea garden).

⊙ Küçük Ayasofya

FREE LITTLE AYA SOFYA   MOSQUE

Map p232 (Küçük Aya Sofya Camii, SS Sergius & Bacchus Church; Küçük Ayasofya Caddesi; 🏛Sultanahmet, Çemberlitaş) Justinian and his wife Theodora built this little church sometime between 527 and 536, just before Justinian built Aya Sofya. You can still see their monogram worked into some of the frilly white capitals. Recently restored, the building is one of the most beautiful Byzantine structures in the city.

Named after Sergius and Bacchus, the two patron saints of Christians in the Roman army, it has been known as Little (*Küçük* in Turkish) Aya Sofya for much of its existence. The building's dome is architecturally noteworthy and its plan – an irregular octagon – is quite unusual. Like Aya Sofya, its interior was originally decorated with gold mosaics and featured columns made from fine green and red marble. The mosaics are long gone, but the impressive columns remain. The church was converted into a mosque by the chief white eunuch Hüseyin Ağa around 1500; his tomb is to the north of the building. The minaret and *medrese* date from this time.

The *medrese* cells, arranged around the mosque's forecourt, are now used by second-hand booksellers and bookbinders. In the leafy forecourt there is a tranquil *çay bahçesi* where you can relax over a glass of tea.

SOKOLLU ŞEHİT MEHMET PAŞA MOSQUE

MOSQUE

Map p232 (Sokollu Mehmet Paşa Camii; cnr Şehit Çeşmesi & Katip Sinan Camii Sokaks, Kadırga; Sultanahmet, Çemberlitaş) Sinan designed this mosque in 1571, at the height of his architectural career. Besides its architectural harmony, the mosque is unusual because the *medrese* is not a separate building but actually part of the mosque structure, built around the forecourt. The interior is decorated with spectacular red-and-blue İznik tiles – some of the best ever made.

Though named after the grand vizier of the time, the mosque was actually sponsored by his wife Esmahan, daughter of Sultan Selim II. Inside are four fragments from the sacred Black Stone in the Kaaba at Mecca: one above the entrance framed in gold, two in the *mimber* and one in the *mihrab*.

If the mosque isn't open, wait for the guardian to appear; he may offer photos for sale and will certainly appreciate a tip.

⊙ Gülhane, Sirkeci & Eminönü

GÜLHANE PARK

PARK

Map p230 (Gülhane Parkı; Gülhane) Gülhane Park was once the outer garden of Topkapı Palace, accessed only by the royal court. These days, crowds of locals come here to picnic under the many trees, promenade past the formally planted flowerbeds and enjoy wonderful views over the Golden Horn and Sea of Marmara from the Set Üstü Çay Bahçesi on the park's northeastern edge.

Recent beautification works have seen improvements to walkways and amenities, and have included the opening of a new museum, the İstanbul Museum of the History of Science & Technology in Islam (p76).

Next to the southern entrance is a bulbous little kiosk built into the park wall. Known as the **Alay Köşkü** (Map p230; Parade Kiosk), this is where the sultan would sit and watch the periodic parades of troops and trade guilds that commemorated great holidays and military victories. It is now the İstanbul headquarters of the Ministry of Culture and Tourism.

Across the street and 100m northwest of the park's main gate is an outrageously curvaceous rococo gate leading into the precincts of what was once the grand vizierate, or Ottoman prime ministry, known in

---

HIPPIE HIPPIE SHAKE

Plenty of monuments in Sultanahmet evoke the city's Byzantine and Ottoman past, but there are few traces of an equally colourful but much more recent period in the city's history – the hippie era of the 1960s and 1970s. Back then, the first wave of Intrepids (young travellers following the overland trail from Europe to Asia) descended upon İstanbul and can be said to have played a significant role in the Europeanisation of Turkey. The Intrepids didn't travel with itineraries, tour guides or North Face travel gear – their baggage embodied a rejection of materialism, a fervent belief in the power of love and a commitment to the journey rather than the destination. All that was leavened with liberal doses of drugs, sex and protest music, of course.

Sultanahmet had three central hippie hang-outs in those days: the Gülhane Hostel (now closed); a cafe run by Sitki Yener, the 'King of the Hippies' (now a leather shop on İncriçavuş Sokak); and the still-operating **Lâle Pastanesi** (Map p232; 522 2970; Divan Yolu Caddesi 6; 7am-11pm; Sultanahmet) on Divan Yolu, known to hippies the world over as the Pudding Shop. Sadly, this retains few if any echoes of its counter-culture past these days, substituting bland food in place of its former menu of psychedelic music and chillums of hash.

To evoke those days, we highly recommend Rory Maclean's *Magic Bus: On the Hippie Trail from Istanbul to India*, a thought-provoking and wonderfully written history/travelogue.

SULTANAHMET & AROUND SIGHTS

JOHN SONES SINGING BOWL MEDIA/GETTY IMAGES ©

1. İstanbul Archaeology Museums (p66)
Close up with ancient sculptures

2. Grand Bazaar (p85)
Colourful lamps for sale

3. Topkapı Palace (p53)
Wandering through the main gate

4. Sultanahmet Park, Sultanahmet (p44)
Fountain and views to surrounding mosques

the West as the **Sublime Porte** (Map p230). Today the buildings beyond the gate hold various offices of the İstanbul provincial government (the Vilayeti).

İSTANBUL MUSEUM OF THE HISTORY OF SCIENCE & TECHNOLOGY IN ISLAM
MUSEUM

Map p230 (Gülhane Park; admission ₺5; ⊘9am-5pm Wed-Mon; ⊡Gülhane) Of interest to science buffs, the didactic exhibition in this museum argues that Islamic advances in science and technology preceded and greatly influenced those in Europe. Most of the exhibits are reconstructions of historical instruments and tools.

✗ EATING

It's a shame the food served up in Sultanahmet eateries is largely mediocre. Too often lovely settings and great views are accompanied by disappointing meals. That said, we've eaten our way through the neighbourhood and there are some gems amid the rubble. (Note that places close early around here.) If you're in the Sirkeci neighbourhood at lunchtime, join the locals in Hocapaşa Sokak, a pedestrianised street lined with cheap eateries. Here, *lokantas* offer *hazır yemek* (ready-made dishes), *köftecis* dish out flavoursome meatballs, *kebapçis* grill meat to order and the Hocapaşa Pidecisi serves pides straight from the oven. For more about eating ın Sirkeci, check http://sirkecirestaurants.com.

✗ Sultanahmet

TOP CHOICE CIHANNÜMA
TURKISH $$$

Map p230 (☑212-520 7676; www.cihannuma istanbul.com; And Hotel, Yerebatan Caddesi 18; mezes ₺5-19, mains ₺27-47; ⊡Sultanahmet) The view from the top-floor restaurant of this modest hotel is probably the best in the Old City. The Blue Mosque, Aya Sofya, Topkapı Palace, Galata Tower, Dolmabahçe Palace and the Bosphorus Bridge provide a stunning backdrop to a menu showcasing good kebaps (we recommend the the *kuzu şiş*), interesting Ottoman-influenced stews and a few vegetarian dishes.

TOP CHOICE AHIRKAPI BALIKÇISI
SEAFOOD $$

Map p232 (☑212-518 4988; Keresteci Hakkı Sokak 46, Cankurtaran; mezes ₺5-25, fish ₺15-70; ⊘4-11pm; ⊡Sultanahmet) For years we've been promising locals not to list this neighbourhood fish restaurant in our book. We sympathised with their desire to retain the place's low profile, particularly as it's tiny and relatively cheap. However, the food here is so good and the eating alternatives in this area so bad that we've finally decided to share the secret. Book ahead.

COOKING ALATURKA
TURKISH $$

Map p232 (☑212-458 5919; www.cookingalaturka .com; Akbıyık Caddesi 72a, Cankurtaran; set lunch or dinner ₺50; ⊘lunch Mon-Sat & dinner by reservation Mon-Sat; ⊡Sultanahmet) Dutch-born owner/chef Eveline Zoutendijk and her Turkish colleague Fehzi Yıldırım serve a set four-course menu of simple Anatolian dishes at this tranquil restaurant near the Blue Mosque. The menu makes the most of fresh seasonal produce, and can be tailored to suit vegetarians or those with food allergies (call ahead). No children under six at dinner and no credit cards.

MATBAH
OTTOMAN $$$

Map p230 (☑212-514 6151; www.matbah restaurant.com; Ottoman Imperial Hotel, Caferiye Sokak 6/1; mezes ₺10-22, mains ₺28-48; ⊘lunch & dinner; ⊡Sultanahmet) This recent addition to the city's growing number of restaurants specialising in so-called 'Ottoman Palace Cuisine' is well worth a visit. The chef has sourced 375 recipes from the imperial archives and offers an array of dishes, some of which are more successful than others. The surrounds are attractive and live Ottoman music is performed on Friday and Saturday nights.

BALIKÇI SABAHATTİN
SEAFOOD $$$

Map p232 (☑212-458 1824; www.balikcisabahattin .com; Seyit Hasan Koyu Sokak 1, Cankurtaran; mezes ₺10-30, fish ₺30-60; ⊘noon-midnight; ⊡Sultanahmet) The limos outside Balıkçı Sabahattın pay testament to its enduring popularity with the city's establishment, who join cashed-up tourists in enjoying its limited menu of meze and fish. The food here is excellent, though the service is often harried. You'll dine in a wooden Ottoman house or under a leafy canopy in the garden.

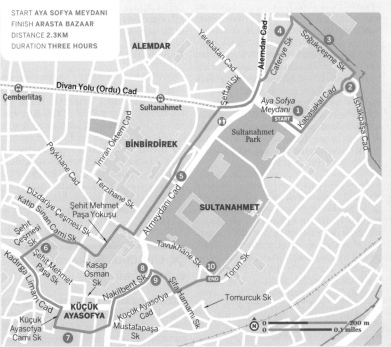

START **AYA SOFYA MEYDANI**
FINISH **ARASTA BAZAAR**
DISTANCE **2.3KM**
DURATION **THREE HOURS**

SULTANAHMET & AROUND NEIGHBOURHOOD WALK

Neighbourhood Walk
Sultanahmet Saunter

Set off from Aya Sofya Meydanı and turn left into Kabaskal Caddesi to visit the ① **Aya Sofya Tombs**. After admiring their splendid interior decoration, head towards the ② **Fountain of Sultan Ahmet III** outside Topkapı Palace. This kiosk once dispensed cold drinks of water or şerbet (sherbet) to thirsty Ottoman travellers.

Veer left into cobbled ③ **Soğukçeşme Sokak** and then turn left into Caferiye Sokak to visit the ④ **Caferağa Medresesi**, where you can enjoy a glass of tea after admiring the elegant, Sinan-designed building. Back on Caferiye Sk, continue until you reach the busy thoroughfare of Alemdar Caddesi and then head to the ⑤ **Hippodrome**, where horse-drawn chariots stormed around the perimeter in Byzantine times.

Walk down Şehit Mehmet Paşa Yokuşu and continue down Katip Sinan Cami Sokak. You will soon arrive at the ⑥ **Sokollu Şehit Mehmet Paşa Mosque** on the left-hand side of the street.

After admiring its İznik tiles, veer left down Şehit Çeşmesi Sk into the residential neighborhood of Küçük Ayasofya. You will come to a busy but narrow road called Kadırga Limanı Caddesi. Veer left here and follow the road until you arrive at Küçük Ayasofya Camii Sk. Turn right and you will see ⑦ **Little Aya Sofya**, one of the most beautiful Byzantine buildings in the city.

Continue east along Küçük Ayasofya Caddesi and walk left up the hill at Aksakal Caddesi. At the crest is the ⑧ **Sphendone**, originally part of the Hippodrome's southern stadium. Opposite is a huge carpet shop called ⑨ **Nakkaş**. Pop in here and ask a staff member to show you the restored Byzantine cistern in its basement.

From here, continue along Nakilbent Sk and then veer right, walking down Şifa Hamamı Sk, turning left into Küçük Ayasofya Caddesi and continuing straight ahead to visit the ⑩ **Arasta Bazaar**, Sultanahmet's pre-eminent shopping precinct.

TERAS RESTAURANT TURKISH $$$

Map p232 (☎212-455 4455; www.armada hotel.com.tr/pg_en/terrace.asp; Hotel Armada, Ahırkapı Sokak 24, Cankurtaran; mezes ₺7-15, mains ₺22-39; ☺lunch & dinner ; ⓂSultanahmet) The terrace restaurant at this upmarket hotel offers good food, a killer view of the Blue Mosque, Aya Sofya and Sea of Marmara, an excellent (and affordable) wine list and very comfortable seating – a compelling combination indeed. Added extras come courtesy of a kids' menu (₺12 to ₺14) and decent coffee. We recommend starting with a meze tray to share (₺26 to ₺29).

SEFA RESTAURANT TURKISH $

Map p230 (Nuruosmaniye Caddesi 17; portions ₺7-12, kebaps ₺12-18; ☺7am-5pm; ☑; ⓂSultanahmet) Locals rate this place near the bazaar highly. It describes its cuisine as Ottoman, but what's really on offer here are *hazır yemek* (ready-made) dishes and kebaps at extremely reasonable prices. You can order from an English menu or choose daily specials from the bain-marie. Try to arrive earlyish for lunch because many of the dishes run out by 1.30pm. No alcohol.

KARADENIZ AILE PIDE VE KEBAP SALONU PIDE, KEBAP $

Map p232 (Biçki Yurdu Sokak, off Divan Yolu Caddesi; pides ₺8-12; ☺11am-11pm; ⓂSultanahmet) This long-timer off Divan Yolu serves a delicious *mercimek* (lentil soup) and decent pides. You can claim a table in the utilitarian interior, but in warm weather most people prefer those on the cobbled lane. No alcohol.

CAFERAĞA MEDRESESİ LOKANTA & ÇAY BAHÇESİ TURKISH $

Map p230 (Soğukkuyu Çıkmazı 5, off Caferiye Sokak; soup ₺4, portions ₺10; ☺8.30am-4pm; ⓂSultanahmet) In Sultanahmet, it's rare to eat in stylish surrounds without being lavishly charged for the privilege. That's why the small *lokanta* in the gorgeous courtyard of this Sinan-designed *medrese* near Topkapı Palace is such a find. The food isn't anything to write home about, but it's fresh and inexpensive. You can enjoy a tea break here, but it's an alcohol-free zone.

ÇIĞDEM PASTANESİ CAFE $

Map p232 (Divan Yolu Caddesi 62a; cappuccino ₺5, tea ₺2, pastries ₺1-4; ☺8am-11pm; ⓂSultanahmet) Strategically located on the main drag between Aya Sofya Meydanı and the Grand Bazaar, Çiğdem has been serving locals since 1961 and is still going strong. Pop in for a quick cup of tea or coffee accompanied by a cake, *börek* (filled pastry) or *acma* (Turkish-style bagel).

KARAKOL RESTAURANT INTERNATIONAL $$$

Map p230 (www.karakolrestaurant.com; First Court, Topkapı Palace; sandwiches ₺19-22, salads ₺20-26, mains ₺20-35; ☺10am-6pm year-round, to 10pm summer; ⓂSultanahmet) It goes against the grain for us to recommend a place that is so outrageously overpriced (₺7 for a glass of tea!), but we do so because Karakol's location in Topkapı Palace's First Court is wonderful. The menu features international and Turkish dishes, but we recommend sticking to a simple sandwich or salad.

✖ Gülhane, Sirkeci & Eminönü

ᴛᴏᴘ ᴄʜᴏɪᴄᴇ HAFIZ MUSTAFA SWEETS $

Map p230 (www.hafizmustafa.com; Muradiye Caddesi 51, Sirkeci; börek ₺5, baklava ₺6-7.50, puddings ₺6; ☺7am-2am; ⓂSirkeci) Making locals happy since 1864, this *şekerlemeleri* (sweets shop) sells delicious *lokum* (Turkish Delight), baklava, milk puddings, pastries and *börek*. Put your sweet tooth to good use in the upstairs cafe, or choose a selection of indulgences to take home. There's a second branch in the Kıraathanesi Foundation of Turkish Literature on **Divan Yolu** (Map p232; Divan Yolu Caddesi 14, Sultanahmet; ⓂSultanahmet) and a third on Hamidiye Caddesi (p100) close to the Spice Bazaar.

HOCAPAŞA PİDECİSİ PIDE $

Map p230 (www.hocapasa.com.tr; Hocapaşa Sokak 19, Sirkeci; pides ₺8-14; ☺10am-10pm Mon-Sat; ⓂSirkeci) This much-loved place has been serving piping-hot pides straight from its oven since 1964. Accompanied by pickles, they can be eaten at one of the outdoor tables or ordered *paket* (to go).

PAŞAZADE TURKISH $$

Map p230 (☎212-513 3750; www.pasazade .com; İbn-i Kemal Caddesi 5a, Sirkeci; mezes ₺7-18, mains ₺18-28; ☺lunch & dinner; ⓂGülhane) Advertising itself as an *Osmanlı mutfağı* (Ottoman kitchen), Paşazade has long garnered rave reviews from tourists staying in the hotels around Sirkeci. Well-priced

KING OF KEBAPS

Turkey's signature dish is undoubtedly the kebap. Turks will tuck into anything cooked on a stick with gusto, and if asked where they would like to celebrate a special event, they will often nominate **Develi** (☎212-529 0833; www.develikebap.com; Gümüşyüzük Sokak 7, Samatya; mains ₺15-35; ☻noon-midnight; ⓜKoca Mustafa Paşa), a restaurant that opened its first branch in İstanbul in 1912. If you are staying in Sultanahmet, the closest branch is in Samatya, next to Theodosius' Great Wall.

The succulent kebaps here come in many guises and often reflect the season – the keme kebabı (truffle kebab) is only served for a few weeks each year, for instance. The most popular menu item is the fıstıklı (pistachio) kebap, which Develi claims to have invented. Prices here are extremely reasonable for the quality of food on offer and the place is enormous, so it's always possible to score a table – in summer, request one on the roof terrace, which has great sea views. To get here from Sultanahmet, take a taxi (approximately ₺15).

dishes are served in the streetside restaurant or on the rooftop terrace (summer only). Portions are large, the food is tasty and service is attentive. Top marks go to the traditional meze platter (₺17).

KONYALI LOKANTASI TURKISH $
Map p230 (Mimar Kemalettin Caddesi 5; soups ₺5-10, portions ₺5.50-16.50, sweets ₺6-7.50; ☻closed Sun; ⓜSirkeci) The bustle of the Eminönü docks is replicated inside this popular lokanta every lunchtime, when crowds of shoppers, workers and commuters pop in here to choose from the huge range of soups, böreks, kebaps and stews on offer. This isn't a place where lingering over one's meal is encouraged (it's far too busy for that), but you can move on to the next-door pastanesi for a glass of tea and a delicious pastry if you so choose.

FASULİ LOKANTALARI ANATOLIAN $
Map p230 (www.fasuli.com.tr; Muradiye Caddesi 35-37, Sirkeci; beans & rice ₺13; ⓜSirkeci) A branch of the popular Black Sea–style fasulye (bean) restaurant based in Tophane.

🍷 DRINKING & NIGHTLIFE

Sadly, there are few pleasant bars in Sultanahmet. The joints along Akbıyık Caddesi are suited to backpackers and unthinkable for everyone else. Don't despair, though. Why not substitute tobacco or caffeine for alcohol and visit one of the many atmospheric çay bahçesis dotted around the neighbourhood?

🍷 Sultanahmet

HOTEL NOMADE TERRACE BAR BAR
Map p232 (www.hotelnomade.com; Ticarethane Sokak 15, Alemdar; ☻noon-11pm; ⓜSultanahmet) The intimate terrace of this boutique hotel overlooks Aya Sofya and the Blue Mosque. Settle down in a comfortable chair to enjoy a glass of wine, beer or freshly squeezed fruit juice. The only music that will disturb your evening reverie is the Old City's signature sound of the call to prayer.

YEŞİL EV BAR, CAFE
Map p232 (Kabasakal Caddesi 5; ☻noon-10.30pm; ⓜSultanahmet) The elegant rear courtyard of this Ottoman-style hotel is a true oasis for those wanting to enjoy a quiet drink. In spring, flowers and blossoms fill every corner; in summer the fountain and trees keep the temperature down. You can order a sandwich, salad or cheese platter if you're peckish.

CAFE MEŞALE NARGILE CAFE
Map p232 (Arasta Bazaar, Utangaç Sokak, Cankurtaran; ☻24hr; ⓜSultanahmet) Located in a sunken courtyard behind the Blue Mosque, Meşale is a tourist trap par excellence, but still has loads of charm. Generations of backpackers have joined locals in claiming one of its cushioned benches and enjoying a tea and nargile. It has sporadic live Turkish music and a bustling vibe in the evening.

DERVİŞ AİLE ÇAY BAHÇESİ TEA GARDEN
Map p232 (Mimar Mehmet Ağa Caddesi; ☻9am-11pm Apr-Oct; ⓜSultanahmet) Superbly located directly opposite the Blue Mosque, the

Derviş beckons patrons with its comfortable cane chairs and shady trees. Efficient service, reasonable prices and peerless people-watching opportunities make it a great place for a leisurely tea, nargile and game of backgammon.

DENIZEN COFFEE   CAFE
Map p232 (Şehit Mehmet Paşa Yokuşu 8; ⊙8.30am-10pm Mon-Sat; ⊠Sultanahmet) Ken Weimar and Earl Everett opened this American-style coffeeshop in 2011 and describe it simply ('for us, it's all about the coffee'). Come here for espresso, decaf, hot chocolate and hot white chocolate served in a welcoming space decorated with Ken's photos of Sultanahamet and Beyoğlu. Pastries, panini, salads and mezes are available.

KYBELE CAFE   BAR, CAFE
Map p230 (www.kybelehotel.com; Yerebatan Caddesi 35; ⊙7.30am-11.30pm; ⊠Sultanahmet) The lounge bar/cafe at this charmingly eccentric hotel close to the Basilica Cistern is chock-full of antique furniture, richly coloured rugs and old etchings and prints, but its signature style comes courtesy of the hundreds of colourful glass lights hanging from the ceiling.

📍 Küçük Ayasofya

YENİ MARMARA   NARGILE CAFE
Map p232 (Çayıroğlu Sokak, Küçük Ayasofya; ⊙10am-1am; ⊠Sultanahmet) This is the genuine article: a neighbourhood teahouse frequented by backgammon-playing regulars who slurp tea and puff on nargiles. The place has loads of character, featuring rugs, wall hangings and *fasıl* music on the CD player. In winter a wood stove keeps the place cosy; in summer patrons sit on the rear terrace, which overlooks the Sea of Marmara.

📍 Gülhane, Sirkeci & Eminönü

SET ÜSTÜ ÇAY BAHÇESİ   TEA GARDEN
Map p230 (Gülhane Park, Sultanahmet; ⊙9am-10.30pm; ⊠Gülhane) Come to this terraced tea garden to watch the ferries ply the route from Europe to Asia while at the same time enjoying an excellent pot of tea accompanied by hot water (such a relief after the usual fiendishly strong Turkish brew). Add

a cheap *tost* (toasted cheese sandwich) and you'll be able to make a lunch of it.

☆ ENTERTAINMENT

HOCAPAŞA CULTURE CENTRE   PERFORMING ARTS
Map p230 (Hodjapasha Culture Centre; ☎212-511 4626; www.hodjapasha.com; Hocapaşa Hamamı Sokak 3b, Sirkeci; adult/child under 12yr whirling dervish show ₺50/30, Turkish dance show ₺60/40; ⊠Sirkeci) Occupying a beautifully converted 550-year-old hamam near Eminönü, this cultural centre stages a one-hour whirling dervish perfromance for tourists on Friday, Saturday, Sunday, Monday and Wednesday evenings at 7.30pm, and a 1½-hour Turkish dance show on Tuesday and Thursday at 8pm and Saturday and Sunday at 9pm. Note that children under seven are not admitted to the whirling dervish performance.

🛍 SHOPPING

The best shopping in Sultanahmet is found in and around the Arasta Bazaar. This historic arcade of shops was once part of the *külliye* (mosque complex) of the Blue Mosque and rents still go towards the mosque's upkeep. Some of Turkey's best-known rug and ceramic dealers have shops in the surrounding streets.

TOP CHOICE COCOON   CARPETS, TEXTILES
Map p232 (www.cocoontr.com; Küçük Aya Sofya Caddesi 13; ⊙8.30am-7.30pm; ⊠Sultanahmet) There are so many rug and textile shops in İstanbul that choosing individual shops to recommend is incredibly difficult. We had no problem whatsoever in singling this one out, though. Felt hats, antique costumes and textiles from central Asia are artfully displayed in one store, while rugs from Persia, Central Asia, the Caucasus and Anatolia adorn the other. There's a another shop in the Arasta Bazaar and a third in the Grand Bazaar.

KHAFTAN   ART, ANTIQUES
Map p232 (www.khaftan.com; Nakilbent Sokak 33; ⊙9am-8pm; ⊠Sultanahmet) Owner Adnan Cakariz sells antique Kütahya and İznik ceramics to collectors and museums here and

overseas, so you can be sure that the pieces he sells in his own establishment are top-notch. Gleaming Russian icons, delicate calligraphy (old and new), ceramics, Karagöz puppets and contemporary paintings are all on show in this gorgeous shop.

MEHMET ÇETİNKAYA GALLERY
CARPETS, TEXTILES

Map p232 (www.cetinkayagallery.com; Tavukhane Sokak 7; ⊙9.30am-7.30pm; 🚇Sultanahmet) Mehmet Çetinkaya is known as one of the country's foremost experts on antique oriental carpets and kilims. His flagship store-cum-gallery stocks items that have artistic and ethnographic significance, and is full of treasures. There's a second shop selling rugs, textiles and objects in the Arasta Bazaar.

TULU
HOMEWARES

Map p232 (www.tulutextiles.com; Üçler Sokak 7; 🚇Sultanahmet) One of the new breed of contemporary homeware stores taking İstanbul by storm, Tulu is owned by American Elizabeth Hewitt, a textile collector and designer who produces a stylish range of cushions, bedding and accessories inspired by textiles from Central Asia. These are sold alongside an array of furniture, textiles and objects sourced in countries including Uzbekistan, India, Japan and Indonesia.

YİLMAZ IPEKÇİLİK
TEXTILES

Map p232 (www.yilmazipekcilik.com/en; İshakpaşa Caddesi 36; ⊙9am-9pm Mon-Sat, to 7pm in winter; 🚇Sultanahmet) Well-priced, hand-loomed silk textiles made in Antakya are on sale in this slightly out-of-the-way shop. Family-run, the business has been operating since 1950 and specialises in producing good-quality scarves, shawls and *peştemals*.

JENNIFER'S HAMAM
BATHWARE

Map p232 (www.jennifershamam.com; 43 & 135 Arasta Bazaar; ⊙9am-10.30pm Apr-Sep, 9am-7.30pm Oct-Mar; 🚇Sultanahmet) Owned by Canadian Jennifer Gaudet, the two Arasta Bazaar branches of this shop stock top-quality hamam items including towels, robes and *peştemals* (bath wraps) produced on old-style hand-shuttled looms. It also sells natural soaps and *keses* (coarse cloth mittens used for exfoliation).

İZNİK CLASSICS & TILES
CERAMICS

Map p232 (www.iznikclassics.com; Arasta Bazaar 67, 73 & 161; ⊙9am-8pm; 🚇Sultanahmet) İznik Classics is one of the best places in town to source hand-painted collector-item ceramics made with real quartz and using metal oxides for pigments. Admire the range in the two shops and gallery in the Arasta Bazaar, in the Grand Bazaar store or in the shop at 17 Utangaç Sokak.

GALERİ KAYSERİ
BOOKS

Map p232 (www.galerikayseri.com; Divan Yolu Caddesi 11 & 58; ⊙9am-9pm; 🚇Sultanahmet) These twin shops near the Sultanahmet tram stop offer a modest range of English-language fiction and a more impressive selection of books about İstanbul and Turkey. The second, smaller, shop is on the opposite side of the road half a block closer to Aya Sofya.

🏃 ACTIVITIES

TOP CHOICE İSTANBUL WALKS
WALKING & CULTURAL TOURS

Map p232 (☎212-516 6300; www.istanbulwalks.net; 2nd fl, Şifa Hamamı Sokak 1; walking tours €25-75, child under 6yr free; 🚇Sultanahmet) Specialising in cultural tourism, this small company is run by a group of history buffs and offers a large range of guided walking tours conducted by knowledgeable English-speaking guides. Tours concentrate on İstanbul's various neighbourhoods, but there are also tours to major monuments including Topkapı Palace, the İstanbul Archaeology Museums and Dolmabahçe Palace. Student discounts are available.

AYASOFYA HÜRREM SULTAN HAMAMI
HAMAM

Map p232 (☎212-517 3535; www.ayasofyahamami.com; Aya Sofya Meydanı; massages €40-75, bath treatments €70-165, ⊙8am-11pm; 🚇Sultanahmet) Reopened in 2011 after a meticulous restoration, this twin hamam is now offering the most luxurious traditional bath experience in the Old City. Designed by Sinan between 1556 and 1557, it was built just across the road from Aya Sofya by order of Süleyman the Magnificent and named in honour of his wife Hürrem Sultan, commonly known as Roxelana.

The building's three-year, US$13 million restoration was closely monitored by heritage authorities and the end result is wonderful, retaining Sinan's austere design but endowing it with an understated modern luxury. There are separate baths for males and females, both with a handsome *soğukluk* (entrance vestibule) surrounded by wooden change cubicles. Though relatively expensive, treatments are expert and the surrounds are exceptionally clean. The basic 35-minute treatment costs €70 and includes a scrub and soap massage; olive-oil soap and your personal *kese* (coarse cloth mitten) are included in the price. In warm weather, a cafe and restaurant operate on the outdoor terrace .

TOP CHOICE COOKING ALATURKA COOKING COURSE
(☑0536 338 0896; www.cookingalaturka.com; Akbıyık Caddesi 72a, Cankurtaran; cooking class per person €60; ⧉Sultanahmet) Dutch-born Eveline Zoutendijk opened the first English-language Turkish cooking school in İstanbul in 2003 and since then has built a solid reputation for her hands-on classes, which offer a great introduction to Turkish cuisine and are suitable for both novices and experienced cooks. The delicious results are enjoyed over a five-course meal in the school's restaurant (p76).

MÜZENİN KAHVESİ COFFEE
Map p232 (☑212-517 4580; Museum of Turkish & Islamic Arts, Atmeydanı Caddesi 46; ⧖9am-6.30pm Tue-Sun Apr-Oct, to 4.30pm Nov-Mar; ⧉Sultanahmet) Head to the stylish cafe/laboratory in the courtyard of the Museum of Turkish & Islamic Arts (p71) for the best Turkish coffee on the Historic Peninsula. Afficionados can sign up for a 30-minute 'Treasures of Turkey' coffee experience (₺20) that demonstrates roasting, grinding, brewing and service techniques and includes – naturally – a cup of the stuff in question. Bookings essential.

AMBASSADOR SPA HAMAM
Map p232 (☑212-512 0002; www.istanbul ambassadorhotel.com; Ticarethane Sokak 19; Turkish bath treatments €40-60, remedial & aromatherapy massage €25-90; ⧖9am-10pm; ⧉Sultanahmet) There's no Ottoman ambience on offer at the shabby spa centre of this hotel just off Divan Yolu, but all treatments are private, meaning that you get the

small hamam all to yourself. Best of all is the fact that the signature 60- or 75-minute 'Oriental Massage' package includes both a hamam treatment and an expert 30-minute oil massage.

The spa's massage therapist Zeki Ulusoy is trained in sports, remedial and aromatherapy massage and he really knows his stuff – you'll float out of here at the end of a session. The 'Oriental Massage' treatment costs between €50-60; a 50-minute 'Back to Traditions' package comprises a 20-minute body scrub and a 30-minute foam massage and costs €40.

CAĞALOĞLU HAMAMI HAMAM
Map p230 (☑212-522 2424; www.cagaloglu hamami.com.tr; Yerebatan Caddesi 34; bath, scrub & massage packages €50-110; ⧖8am-10pm; ⧉Sultanahmet) This is undoubtedly the most beautiful of the city's hamams. Built in 1741 by order of Sultan Mahmut I, it offers separate baths for men and women and a range of bath services that are – alas – overpriced considering how quick and rudimentary the wash, scrub and massage treatments are. Consider signing up for the self-service treatment (€30) only.

URBAN ADVENTURES WALKING & CULTURAL TOURS
Map p232 (☑212-512 7144; www.urbanadven tures.com; 1st fl, Ticarethane Sokak 11; all tours ₺50; ⧖8.30am-5.30pm; ⧉Sultanahmet) The international tour company Intrepid offers a program of city tours including a popular four-hour guided walk around Sultanahmet and the Bazaar District. Also on offer is the 'Home Cooked İstanbul' tour, which includes a no-frills dinner with a local family in their home plus a visit to a neighbourhood teahouse for tea, a nargile and a game of backgammon.

LES ARTS TURCS CULTURAL TOUR
Map p232 (☑212-527 6859; www.lesartsturcs .com; 3rd fl, İncili Çavuş Sokak 19; workshops ₺100-150, tours from ₺150, dervish ceremony ₺60; ⧉Sultanahmet) This small cultural tourism company organises a range of tours and workshops, including visits to Sufi *tekke*s where the whirling dervish ceremony is held, *ebru* (paper marbling) and calligraphy workshops, belly-dancing lessons, tours of synagogues in the Western districts and photography tours.

Bazaar District

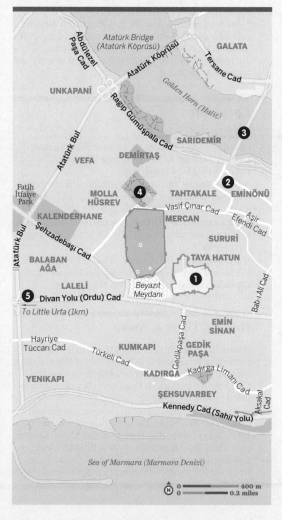

Neighbourhood Top Five

1 Enjoying getting lost in the labyrinthine laneways of the world's oldest shopping mall, the glorious **Grand Bazaar** (p85).

2 Shopping in and around the seductively scented **Spice Bazaar** (p90).

3 Viewing the Old City's skyline while walking across the **Galata Bridge** (p91) at sunset.

4 Visiting the remarkably intact *külliye* of the **Süleymaniye Mosque** (p88), the greatest of İstanbul's Ottoman monuments.

5 Embarking on a foodie adventure in Aksaray's **Little Urfa** (p93) district.

For more detail of this area, see, Map p87 and p234 ➡

Lonely Planet's Top Tip

If you are walking to the Grand Bazaar from Sultanhamet, you can avoid the traffic and touts along Divan Yolu Caddesi by instead heading up Yerebatan Caddesi, left into Nuruosmaniye Caddesi, across Cağaloğlu Meydanı, along pedestrianised Nuruosmaniye Caddesi and across Vezir Han Caddesi towards the Nuruosmaniye Mosque.

✕ Best Places to Eat

➡ Fatih Damak Pide (p94)

➡ Little Urfa (p93)

➡ Hamdi Restaurant (p94)

➡ Siirt Fatih Büryan (p94)

For reviews, see p94 ➡

☕ Best Places to Drink

➡ Zeyrekhane (p98)

➡ Erenler Çay Bahçesi (p98)

➡ Lale Bahçesi (p98)

➡ Türk Ocaği Kültür ve Sanat Merkezi İktisadi İşletmesi Çay Bahçesi (p98)

➡ Ethem Tezçakar Kahveci (p98)

For reviews, see p97 ➡

◉ Best Mosque Architecture

➡ Süleymaniye Mosque (p88)

➡ Rüstem Paşa Mosque (p92)

➡ Şehzade Mehmet Mosque (p93)

For reviews, see p91 ➡

Explore: Bazaar District

There's loads to see in this district so you'll need to plan your time to make the most of it. Ideally you should dedicate a full day to the bazaars, starting at the Grand Bazaar in the morning, having lunch and then walking down Mahmputpaşa Yokuşu to the Spice Bazaar and Eminönü.

Another day could be spent following our Mosques & Monastery walking tour. On this you'll visit two important Ottoman mosques, get a taste of local life while lunching at a regional eatery in the Kadın Pazarı (Women's Market) near the Aqueduct of Valens, and see one of the most important Byzantine monuments in the city: the Monastery of Christ Pantokrator.

Nothing much is open in this district on Sundays – visit Monday to Saturday only. And try to avoid the mosques at prayer times and from late morning to early afternoon on Friday, when weekly group prayers and sermons are held.

Local Life

➡ **Tahtakale** Locals shop in the streets between the Grand and Spice Bazaars rather than in the bazaars themselves. Head to Mahmputpaşa Yokuşu and Hasırcılar Caddesi to join them.

➡ **Kadın Pazarı** This atmospheric square in the Zeyrek neighbourhood is full of regional eateries and produce shops.

➡ **Fish sandwiches** The city's signature fast-food treat is best enjoyed with crowds of locals at the Eminönü ferry docks.

➡ **Nargile** Follow the evocative scent of apple tobacco to discover busy nargile (water pipe) cafes underneath the Galata Bridge or along Divan Yolu Caddesi.

Getting There & Away

➡ **Bus** To get here from Taksim Meydanı (Taksim Square), take bus 46H or 61B. Both travel along Atatürk Bulvarı, stopping at the corner of Ordu Caddesi and then continuing through Laleli on to Beyazıt Meydanı next to the Grand Bazaar.

➡ **Tram** The neighbourhood is sliced into north and south by Ordu Caddesi, the western continuation of Divan Yolu Caddesi. The tram from Bağcılar to Kabataş runs along this major road, passing through Aksaray, past the Grand Bazaar, across Sultanahmet and then down the hill to Eminönü, where the Spice Bazaar is located.

TOP SIGHTS
GRAND BAZAAR

This colourful and chaotic bazaar is the heart of the Old City and has been so for centuries. Starting as a small vaulted *bedesten* (warehouse) built on the order of Mehmet the Conqueror in 1461, it grew to cover a vast area as laneways between the *bedesten*, neighbouring shops and *hans* (caravanserais) were roofed and the market assumed the sprawling, labyrinthine form that it retains today.

When here, be sure to peep through doorways to discover hidden *hans*, veer down narrow laneways to watch artisans at work and wander the main thoroughfares to differentiate treasures from tourist tat. It's obligatory to drink lots of tea, compare price after price and try your hand at the art of bargaining. Allow at least three hours for your visit; some travellers spend three days!

Check out our tips (p35) on how to bargain in the bazaar.

A Tour of the Bazaar

There are thousands of shops in the bazaar, and this can be overwhelming for the first-time visitor. By following this suggested itinerary, you should be able to develop an understanding of the bazaar's history, its layout and its important position as the hub of the surrounding retail precinct.

Start at the tram stop next to the tall column known as Çemberlitaş (p91). From here, walk down Vezir Han Caddesi and you will soon come to the entrance of the Vezir Han, a caravanserai built between 1659 and 1660 by the Köprülüs, one of the Ottoman Empire's most distinguished families. Five of its members served as Grand Vizier (Vezir) to the sultan, hence its name. In Ottoman times, this *han* would have offered travelling merchants accommodation and a place to do business. Though gold manufacturers still work here, the *han* is in a sadly dilapidated state, as are the many

DON'T MISS...

➡ Cevahir (Jewellery) Bedesteni
➡ Halıcılar Çarşısı Sokak
➡ Kuyumcular Caddesi
➡ Takkeciler Sokak
➡ Sandal Bedesteni

PRACTICALITIES

➡ Kapalı Çarşı, Covered Market
➡ Map p234
➡ www.kapalicarsi .org.tr
➡ 🕙9am-7pm Mon-Sat
➡ 🚃Beyazıt-Kapalı Çarşı

MAHMUTPAŞA YOKUŞU

This busy thoroughfare links the Grand Bazaar with the Spice Bazaar at Eminönü. Locals come here to buy everything from wedding dresses to woollen socks, coffee cups to circumcision outfits. From the Grand Bazaar, leave the Mahmutpaşa Kapısı (Mahmutpaşa Gate, Gate 18) and walk downhill. Along the way you will pass one of the oldest hamams in the city: the **Mahmutpaşa Hamamı** (Map p234, now a shopping centre). If you veer left onto Tarakçılar Caddesi before coming to the *hamam* and walk all the way to Çakmakçılar Yokuşu, you will see the historic **Büyük Valide Han** (Map p234), a huge and sadly dilapidated caravanserai built by order of Murad IV's mother in 1651. It once accommodated up to 3000 travelling merchants and their animals every night.

Over the bazaar's history, most silversmiths who have worked here have been of Armenian descent and most goldsmiths have been of Arabic or Aramaic descent – this is still true today.

(some experts say hundreds) of similar buildings dotted throughout the district. Look for the *tuğra* (crest) of the sultan over the main gateway.

Continue walking down Vezir Han Caddesi until you come to a cobbled pedestrianised street on your left. Walk along this until you come to the Nuruosmaniye Mosque (p92). In front of you is one of the major entrances to the Grand Bazaar, the Nuruosmaniye Kapısı (Nuruosmaniye Gate, Gate 1), adorned by another *tuğra*.

The brightly lit street in front of you is **Kalpakçılar Caddesi**, the busiest street in the bazaar. Originally named after the makers of *kalpakçılars* (fur hats) who had their stores here, it's now full of jewellers, who pay up to US$80,000 per year in rent for this high-profile location. Start walking down the street and then turn right and take the marble stairs down to the **Sandal Bedestenı**, a stone warehouse featuring 20 small domes. This warehouse has always been used for the storage and sale of fabric, although the current range of cheap textiles on sale couldn't be more different from the fine *sandal* (fabric woven with silk) that was sold here in the past.

Exit the Sandal Bedestenı on its west (left) side, turning right into Sandal Bedestenı Sokak and then left into Ağa Sokak, which takes you into the oldest part of the bazaar, the **Cevahir (Jewellery) Bedesten**, also known as the Eski (Old) or İç (Inner) Bedesten. This has always been an area where precious items are stored and sold, and these days it's where most of the bazaar's antique stores are located. Slave auctions were held here until the mid-19th century.

Exiting the *bedesten* from its south door, walk down to the first cross-street, **Halıcılar Çarşışı Sokak**, where popular shops including Abdulla Natural Products (p99), **Cocoon** (Map p234; www .cocoontr.com; Halıcılar Çarşışı Sokak 38, Grand Bazaar; 9am-7pm Mon-Sat; Beyazıt-Kapalı Çarşı) and Derviş (p99) are located. Also here is a good spot for a tea or coffee, Ethem Tezçakar Kahveci (p98).

Walking east (right) you will come to a major cross-street, **Kuyumcular Caddesi** (Street of the Jewellers). Turn left and walk past the little kiosk in the middle of the street. Built in the 19th century and known as the **Oriental Kiosk**, this now houses a jewellery store but was once home to the most famous *muhallebici* (milk-pudding shop) in the district. A little way further down, on the right-hand side of the street, is the entrance to the pretty **Zincirli (Chain) Han**, home to one of the bazaar's best-known carpet merchants: Şişko Osman. Returning to Kuyumcular Caddesi, turn sharp left into Perdahçılar Sokak (Street of the Polishers). Walk until you reach **Takkeçiler Sokak**, where

GRAND BAZAAR

Örücüler Hamamı Sk · Örücüler Kapısı · Tığcılar Sk · ⊕ N · 0 · 100 m · Terakçılar Cad

Küçük Safran Han · Safran Han · Astarcı Han · Mercan Kızlar · Bezciler Sk · Mahmutpaşa Yokuşu

Çuku Han · Ağası Hanı · İmameli Han

Kara Mehmet · Yazmacı · Neddet Danış · Muhlis Kapısı · Mercan Kapısı · Zincirli Han

İç Cebeci Han · Cebeci Hanı · Günbattı · Burç · Perdahçılar Sk · Şişko Osman

Ocakbaşı · Takkeciler Sk · Mahmutpaşa Kapısı

Haliciler Çarşısı Sk · Yağlıkçılar Cad · Oriental Kiosk · Aynacılar Sk · Çuhacı Han

Kavaflar Sk · Derviş · Ethem Tezçakar Kahveci · Ağa Sk

Ak Gümüş · Cocoon · Fes Cafe · Kılıççılar Sk

Abdulla Natural Products · Serhat Geridönmez

Sahaflar Çarşısı · Yorgancılar · Şark Kahvesi · EthniCon · Şerifağa Sk · Kuyumcular Cad · SANDAL BEDESTENİ · Nuruosmaniye Mosque

Havuzlu Restaurant · Dhoku · Derviş · Kesericiler Cad

Bodrum Han · Sipahi Sk · Kazaslar Sk · Divrikli Sk · Terziler Cad · Silk & Cashmere · Yağcı Han · Nuruosmaniye Kapısı

Haliciler Sk · Fesçiler Cad · Serpuşçular Sokağı · Kalpakçılar Cad · Kebabçı Han · Bahar Restaurant

Beyazıt Meydanı · Çarşı Kapısı · CEVAHIR (JEWELLERY) BEDESTENİ · Kürkçüler Kapısı · Tavuk Pazarı Sk

(Map labels, left-to-right margin: BAZAAR DISTRICT GRAND BAZAAR)

you should turn left. This charming street is known for its marble *sebils* (public drinking fountains) and shops selling kilims (pileless woven rugs). Turn right into Zenneciler Sokak (Street of the Clothing Sellers) and you will soon come to a junction with another of the bazaar's major thoroughfares: Sipahi Sokak (Avenue of the Cavalry Soldiers). Şark Kahvesi (p98), a traditional coffee house, is right on the corner. Sipahi Sokak becomes Yağlıkçılar Caddesi to the north (right) and Feraçeciler Sokak to the south (left).

Take a left into Sipahi Sokak and walk until you return to Kalpakçılar Caddesi. Turn right and exit the bazaar from the Beyazıt Kapısı (Beyazit Gate, Gate 7). Turn right again and walk past the market stalls to the first passage on the left to arrıve at the **Sahaflar Çarşısı** (Old Book Bazaar; Map p234; Çadırcılar Caddesi, btwn Grand Bazaar & Beyazıt Mosque), which has operated as a book and paper market since Byzantine times. At the centre of its shady courtyard is a bust of İbrahim Müteferrika (1674–1745), who printed the first book in Turkey in 1732.

The Süleymaniye crowns one of İstanbul's seven hills and dominates the Golden Horn (Haliç), providing a landmark for the entire city. Though it's not the largest of the Ottoman mosques, it is certainly one of the grandest and it is unusual in that many of its original *külliye* (mosque complex) buildings have been retained and sympathetically adapted for reuse.

Commissioned by Süleyman I, known as 'The Magnificent', the Süleymaniye was the fourth imperial mosque built in İstanbul and it certainly lives up to its patron's nickname. The mosque and its surrounding buildings were designed by Mimar Sinan, the most famous and talented of all imperial architects.

The Mosque

The mosque was built between 1550 and 1557. Though it's seen some hard times, having been damaged by fire in 1660 and then having its wonderful columns covered by cement and oil paint at some point after this, restorations in 1956 and 2010 mean that it's now in great shape. It's also one of the most popular mosques in the city, with worshippers rivalling the Blue and New Mosques in number.

The building's setting and plan are particularly pleasing, featuring gardens and a three-sided forecourt with a central domed ablutions fountain. The four **minarets** with their 10 beautiful *şerefes* (balconies) are said to represent the fact that Süleyman was the fourth of the Osmanlı sultans to rule the city and the 10th sultan after the establishment of the empire.

In the garden behind the mosque is a **terrace** offering lovely views of the Golden Horn. The street underneath once housed the *külliye's arasta* (row of shops), which was built into the retaining wall of the terrace. Close by was a five-level *mülazim* (preparatory school).

DON'T MISS

➡ Mosque
➡ *Türbes* (tombs)
➡ *Külliye* (mosque complex)
➡ View from terrace

PRACTICALITIES

➡ Map p234
➡ Prof Sıddık Sami Onar Caddesi
➡ ⧉Beyazıt-Kapalı Çarşı

Inside, the building is breathtaking in its size and pleasing in its simplicity. Sinan incorporated the four buttresses into the walls of the building – the result is wonderfully 'transparent' (ie open and airy) and highly reminiscent of Aya Sofya, especially as the dome is nearly as large as the one that crowns the Byzantine basilica.

There is little interior decoration other than some very fine İznik tiles in the *mihrab* (niche in a minaret indicating the direction of Mecca), window shutters inlaid with mother-of-pearl, gorgeous stained glass windows done by one İbrahim the Drunkard, and four massive columns – one from Baalbek in modern-day Lebanon, one from Alexandria and two from Byzantine palaces in İstanbul. The painted arabesques on the dome are 19th-century additions.

The Külliye

Süleyman specified that his mosque should have the full complement of public services: *imaret* (soup kitchen), *medrese* (Islamic school of higher studies), hamam, caravanserai, *darüşşifa* (hospital) etc. Today the **imaret**, with its charming garden courtyard, houses the Dârüzziyafe Restaurant and is a lovely place to enjoy a çay. On its right-hand side (north) is a **caravanserai** that was being restored at the time of writing. On its left-hand side (south) is Lale Bahçesi, a tea garden set in a sunken courtyard where the the hospital was once located. This is an atmospheric venue for çay and nargile.

The main entrance to the mosque is accessed via Prof Sıddık Sami Onar Caddesi, formerly known as **Tiryaki Çarşışı** (Market of the Addicts). The buildings here once housed three *medreses* and a primary school; they're now home to the Süleymaniye Library and a raft of popular streetside *fasülye* (bean) restaurants that were formerly teahouses selling opium (hence the street's former name).

The still-functioning **Süleymaniye Hamamı** is on the eastern side of the mosque.

Türbes

To the right (southeast) of the main entrance is the cemetery, home to the **tombs** of Süleyman and his wife Haseki Hürrem Sultan (Roxelana). The tilework in both is superb. In Süleyman's tomb, little jewel-like lights in the dome are surrogate stars. In Roxelana's tomb, the many tile panels of flowers and the delicate stained glass produce a serene effect.

SU
STRE

The streets ...ing the mosque ...home to what may ...be the most extensive concentration of Ottoman timber houses on the historic peninsula, many of which are currently being restored as part of an urban regeneration project. To see some of these, head down Felva Yokuşu (between the caravanserai and Sinan's tomb) and then veer right into Namahrem Sokak and into Ayrancı Sokak. One of the many Ottoman-era houses here was once occupied by Mimar Sinan; it now houses a cafe. To see other timber houses in the area, take a walk around the area.

Although Sinan described the smaller Selimiye Mosque in Edirne as his best work, he chose to be buried here in the Süleymaniye complex, probably knowing that this would be the achievement that he would be best remembered for. His *türbe* is just outside the mosque's walled garden, next to a disused *medrese* building.

TOP SIGHTS
SPICE BAZAAR

Vividly coloured spices are displayed alongside jewel-like *lokum* (Turkish delight) at this Ottoman-era marketplace, providing eye candy for the thousands of tourists and locals who make their way here every day. As well as spices and *lokum*, stalls sell dried herbs, caviar, nuts, honey in the comb, dried fruits and *pestil* (fruit pressed into sheets and dried). The number of stalls selling tourist trinkets increases annually, yet this remains a great place to stock up on edible souvenirs, share a few jokes with the vendors and marvel at the well-preserved building. It's also home to one of the city's oldest restaurants, Pandeli (p98).

The market was constructed in the 1660s as part of the New Mosque (p92); rent from the shops supported the upkeep of the mosque as well as its charitable activities, which included a school, hamam and hospital. The name Mısır Çarşısı (Egyptian Market) comes from the fact that the building was initially endowed with taxes levied on goods imported from Egypt. In its heyday, the bazaar was the last stop for the camel caravans that travelled the Silk Routes from China, India and Persia.

On the west side of the market there are outdoor produce stalls selling fresh foodstuff from all over Anatolia, including a wonderful selection of cheeses. Also here is the most famous coffee supplier in İstanbul, Kurukahveci Mehmet Efendi (p100), established over 100 years ago. This is located on the corner of Hasırcılar Caddesi, which is full of shops selling foodstuffs and kitchenware.

At the time of writing, the bazaar was opening on Sundays from 9am to 6pm, but this is subject to change.

DID YOU KNOW?

➡ Leeches are still used for traditional medical treatments in Turkey. You'll see them being offered for sale in the outdoor market on the eastern side of the Spice Bazaar, alongside poultry and other small animals.

PRACTICALITIES

➡ Mısır Çarşısı, Egyptian Market

➡ Map p234

➡ ⏰8am-6pm Mon-Sat, 9am-6pm Sun

➡ 🚇Eminönü

◉ SIGHTS

GRAND BAZAAR   MARKET
See p85.

SÜLEYMANİYE MOSQUE   MOSQUE
See p88.

SPICE BAZAAR   MARKET
See p90.

GALATA BRIDGE   BRIDGE
Map p234 (Galata Köprüsü; 🚇Eminönü, Karaköy)
To experience İstanbul at its most magical, walk across the Galata Bridge at sunset. At this time, the historic Galata Tower is surrounded by shrieking seagulls, the mosques atop the seven hills of the city are silhouetted against a soft red-pink sky, and the evocative scent of apple tobacco wafts out of the nargile cafes under the bridge.

During the day, the bridge carries a constant flow of İstanbullus crossing to and from Beyoğlu and Eminönü, a handful or two of hopeful anglers trailing their lines into the waters below, and a constantly changing procession of street vendors hawking everything from fresh-baked *simits* (sesame-encrusted bread rings) to Rolex rip-offs. Underneath, restaurants and cafes serve drinks and food all day and night. Come here to enjoy a beer and nargile while watching the ferries making their way to the Eminönü and Karaköy ferry docks.

The present, quite ugly, bridge was built in 1992 to replace an iron structure dating from 1909 to 1912, which in turn had replaced two earlier structures. The iron bridge was famous for the ramshackle fish restaurants, teahouses and nargile joints that occupied the dark recesses beneath its roadway, but it had a major flaw: it floated on pontoons that blocked the natural flow of water and kept the Golden Horn from flushing itself free of pollution. In the late 1980s the municipality started to draw up plans to replace it with a new bridge that would allow the water to flow. A fire expedited these plans in the early 1990s and the new bridge was built a short time afterwards. The remains of the old, much-loved bridge were moved further up the Golden Horn near Hasköy.

ÇEMBERLİTAŞ   MONUMENT
Map p234 (Divan Yolu Caddesi; 🚇Çemberlitaş)
Next to the Çemberlitaş tram stop, in a plaza packed with pigeons, you'll find one of the city's most ancient monuments: a column known as the Çemberlitaş (Hooped Column) that was erected by Constantine to celebrate the dedication of Constantinople as capital of the Roman Empire in 330.

The column was placed in what was the grand Forum of Constantine and was topped by a statue of the great emperor himself in the guise of Apollo. It lost its crowning statue of Constantine in 1106 and was damaged in the 1779 fire that ravaged the nearby Grand Bazaar. Recently restored, it is a strange-looking remnant of the city's early Byzantine past.

Also in this vicinity is the historic Çemberlitaş Hamamı (p101).

BEYAZIT MEYDANI   SQUARE
Map p234 (Beyazıt Meydanı; 🚇Beyazıt, 🚇Beyazıt-Kapalı Çarşı) Beyazıt Meydanı is officially called Hürriyet Meydanı (Freedom Square), though everyone knows it simply as Beyazıt. In Byzantine times it was called the Forum of Theodosius. Today the square is home to street vendors, students from **İstanbul University** (Map p234) and plenty of pigeons, as well as a few policemen who like to keep an eye on student activities.

The square is backed by the impressive portal of İstanbul University. After the Conquest, Mehmet the Conqueror built his first palace here, a wooden structure called the Eski Sarayı (Old Seraglio). After Topkapı was built, the Eski Sarayı became home to women when they were pensioned out of the main palace – this was where *valide sultans* came when their sultan sons died and they lost their powerful position as head of the Harem. The original building was demolished in the 19th century to make way for a grandiose Ministry of War complex designed by Auguste Bourgeois; this now houses the university. The 85m-tall **Beyazıt Tower** (Map p234) in its grounds sits on top of one of the seven hills on which Constantine the Great built the city, following the model of Rome. Commissioned by Mahmut II, the stone tower was designed by Senekerim Balyan and built in 1828 in the same location as a previous wooden tower. The tower was used by the İstanbul Fire Department to spot fires until 1993. Both the university and tower are off limits to travellers.

BEYAZIT MOSQUE   MOSQUE
Map p234 (Beyazıt Camii, Mosque of Sultan Beyazıt II; Beyazıt Meydanı, Beyazıt; 🚇Beyazıt-Kapalı Çarşı) The second imperial mosque

built in İstanbul (after the Fatih Camii), Beyazıt Camii was built between 1501 and 1506 by order of Beyazıt II, son of Mehmet the Conqueror. Architecturally, it links Aya Sofya, which obviously inspired its design, with great mosques such as the Süleymaniye, which are realisations of Aya Sofya's design fully adapted to Muslim worship.

The mosque's exceptional use of fine stone is noteworthy, with marble, porphyry, verd antique and rare granite featuring. The *mihrab* is simple, except for the rich stone columns framing it. The courtyard features 24 small domes and a central ablutions fountain.

Of the original *külliye* buildings, the *imaret* has been turned into a library. Unfortunately the once-splendid hamam has been closed for many years. Beyazıt's *türbe* is behind the mosque.

NURUOSMANİYE MOSQUE   MOSQUE

Map p234 (Nuruosmaniye Camii, Light of Osman Mosque; Vezir Han Caddesi, Beyazıt; ⓜÇemberlıtaş) Facing Nuruosmaniye Kapısı, one of several gateways into the Grand Bazaar, this mosque was built in Ottoman-baroque style between 1748 and 1755. Construction was started by order of Mahmut I and finished by his successor Osman III.

Though it was meant to exhibit the sultans' 'modern' taste, the baroque building has very strong echoes of Aya Sofya, specifically the broad, lofty dome, colonnaded mezzanine galleries, windows topped with Roman arches and the broad band of calligraphy around the interior. Despite its prominent position on the busy pedestrian route from Cağaloğlu Meydanı and Nuruosmaniye Caddesi to the bazaar, it is surprisingly peaceful and contemplative inside.

The mosque was undergoing a major renovation at the time of writing.

RÜSTEM PAŞA MOSQUE   MOSQUE

Map p234 (Rüstem Paşa Camii; Hasırcılar Caddesi, Rüstem Paşa; ⓜEminönü) Nestled in the middle of the busy Tahtakale shopping district, this diminutive mosque is a gem. Dating from 1560, it was designed by Sinan for Rüstem Paşa, son-in-law and grand vizier of Süleyman the Magnificent. A showpiece of the best Ottoman architecture and tilework, it is thought to have been the prototype for Sinan's greatest work, the Selimiye in Edirne.

At the top of the two sets of entry steps there is a terrace and the mosque's colonnaded porch. You'll immediately notice the panels of İznik tiles set into the mosque's facade. The interior is covered in more tiles and features a lovely dome, supported by four tiled pillars.

The preponderance of tiles was Rüstem Paşa's way of signalling his wealth and influence – İznik tiles being particularly expensive and desirable. It may not have assisted his passage into the higher realm, though, because by all accounts he was a loathsome character. His contemporaries dubbed him Kehle-i-Ikbal (the Louse of Fortune) because he was found to be infected with lice on the eve of his marriage to Mihrimah, Süleyman's favourite daughter. He is best remembered for plotting with Roxelana to turn Süleyman against his favourite son, Mustafa. They were successful and Mustafa was strangled in 1553 on his father's orders.

The mosque is easy to miss because it's not at street level. There's a set of access stairs on Hasırcılar Caddesi and another on the small street that runs right (north) off Hasırcılar Caddesi towards the Golden Horn.

NEW MOSQUE   MOSQUE

Map p234 (Yeni Camii; Yenicamii Meydanı Sokak, Eminönü; ⓜEminönü) Only in İstanbul would a 400-year-old mosque be called 'New'. Dating from 1597, its design references both the Blue Mosque and the Süleymaniye Mosque, with a large forecourt and a square sanctuary surmounted by a series of semidomes crowned by a grand dome. The interior is richly decorated with gold leaf, coloured İznik tiles and carved marble.

Originally commissioned by Valide Sultan Safiye, mother of Sultan Mehmet III, it was completed six sultans later in 1663 by order of Valide Sultan Turhan Hadice, mother of Sultan Mehmet IV.

The site had earlier been occupied by a community of Karaite Jews, radical dissenters from Orthodox Judaism. When the *valide sultan* decided to build her grand mosque here, the Karaites were moved to Hasköy, a district further up the Golden Horn that still bears traces of their presence.

The mosque was created after Ottoman architecture had reached its peak. Consequently, even its tiles are slightly inferior products, the late 17th century having seen a diminution in the quality of the products coming out of the İznik workshops. You will see this if you compare these tiles with the exquisite examples found in the nearby Rüstem Paşa Mosque, which are from the high period of İznik tilework. Nonetheless, it is a popular working mosque and a much-loved adornment to the city skyline.

Across the road from the mosque you will find the tomb of Valide Sultan Turhan Hadice, who completed construction of the New Mosque. Buried with her are no fewer than six sultans, including her son Mehmet IV, plus dozens of imperial princes and princesses.

ŞEHZADE MEHMET MOSQUE   MOSQUE

Map p234 (Şehzade Mehmet Camii, Mosque of the Prince; Şehzadebaşı Caddesi, Kalenderhane; 🚇Ak-saray) Süleyman the Magnificent built this mosque between 1543 and 1548 as a memorial to his son, Mehmet, who died of smallpox in 1543 at the age of 22. It was the first important mosque to be designed by Mimar Sinan. Although not one of his best works, it has a lovely setting, two beautiful minarets and attractive exterior decoration.

Among the many important people buried in tile-encrusted tombs here are Prince Mehmet, his brothers and sisters, and Süleyman's grand viziers, Rüstem Paşa and İbrahim Paşa.

AQUEDUCT OF VALENS   LANDMARK

Map p234 (Atatürk Bulvarı, Zeyrek; 🚇Aksaray) Rising majestically over the traffic on busy Atatürk Bulvarı, this limestone aqueduct is one of the city's most distinctive landmarks. Commissioned by the Emperor Valens and completed in AD 378, it linked the third and fourth hills and carried water to a cistern at Beyazıt Meydanı before finally ending up at the Great Palace of Byzantium (p72).

The aqueduct was part of an elaborate system sourcing water from the north of the city and linking more than 250km of water channels, some 30 bridges and over 100 cisterns within the city walls, making it one of the greatest hydraulic engineering achievements of ancient times. After the Conquest it supplied the Eski (Old) and Topkapı Palaces with water.

BAZAAR DISTRICT SIGHTS

WORTH A DETOUR

LITTLE URFA

In recent decades, the Laleli and Aksaray neighbourhoods west of the Bazaar District have developed a reputation as being the centre of İstanbul's main red-light district, home to seedy nightclubs, petty crims and prostitutes from Eastern Europe. A sad fate for areas where *valide sultans* (mothers of reigning sultans) once commissioned ornate imperial mosques and Ottoman merchants built huge *hans* (caravanserais), and mansions to flaunt their wealth to the world.

There is, however, another claim to fame that this area possesses. For decades, Aksaray has been home to a large concentration of immigrants from the southeast of Turkey. Many of these residents have opened food stands and restaurants serving dishes popular in the southeast, and the streets immediately north of the Aksaray metro station have become known as 'Little Urfa' after the city on the Turkish–Syrian border.

Every adventurous foodie should be sure to eat here at least once during their time in the city. Head to the streets around Sofular Caddesi and enjoy a sit-down Syrian-influenced feast at **Hatay Has Kral Sofrası** (📞210-534 9707; www.hatayhaskralsofrasi. com; Ragıb Bey Sokak 25; 🚇Aksaray) or at **Akdeniz Hatay Sofrası** (📞212-444 7247; www .akdenizhataysofrasi.com.tr; Ahmediye Caddesi 44; 🚇Aksaray). Alternatively, pop into **Şanlı Urfa Zaman** (Simitçi Şakir Sokak 38; 🚇Aksaray) for a *ciğer* (liver) kebap; **Ehli Kebap** (Simitçi Şakır Sokak 32; 🚇Aksaray) for a delicious and filling bowl of *bayran çorbası* (thick lamb-based soup); **Tarihi Onbaşı Kebap & Lahmacun Salonu** (Sofular Caddesi 5a; 🚇Aksaray) for a crispy and spicy *içli köfte* (bulgur shell filled with mincemeat and spices); or the small traditional bakery on Ragıb Bey Sokak for crispy *lahmacun* (thin pizza) straight from the oven.

Alternatively sign up for the evening 'Kebap Krawl' run by the passionate and knowledgeable foodies who put together Culinary Backstreets (p125), a fantastic blog that covers eating in the city.

MONASTERY OF CHRIST PANTOKRATOR
MONASTERY

(Zeyrek Camii; İbadethane Sokak, Zeyrek; ⓐAksaray) This Byzantine monastery originally comprised two churches, a library, a cistern, a hospital and a chapel, but only one church and a cistern remain. The church was dedicated to Islam after the Conquest. One of the finest examples of Byzantine religious architecture in İstanbul, it is the second-largest surviving Byzantine religious structure in the city after Aya Sofya.

The monastery was commissioned in 1118 by Empress Eirene (she features in a mosaic at Aya Sofya with her husband Emperor John II Comnenus), who wanted to give succour to 'poor, sick, and suffering souls'. Building works were completed after her death. The north and south churches, dedicated to Christ Pantokrator and the Archangel St Michael, were connected by an imperial chapel, used as a mausoleum for the Komnenos and Palaiologos dynasties.

The mosque was named after Molla Zeyrek, a well-known scholar who lived during the reign of Sultan Mehmed II.

Until recently the building was included on the World Monument Fund's (WMF) list of the world's 100 most endangered cultural heritage sites. It is now undergoing a slow restoration that was instigated and initially funded by the WMF.

When visiting, be sure to admire the view of the Golden Horn from the garden terrace of the adjacent cafe-restaurant, Zeyrekhane (p98).

✖ EATING

Generations of shoppers have worked up an appetite around the Grand Bazaar. Fortunately there have always been eateries to meet this need, including a range of good *lokantas* (eateries serving ready-made food) such as Bahar Restaurant and Onur Et Lokantası. Down near the water there aren't too many choices – a fish sandwich on the quay at Eminönü or a tasty kebap at Hamdi Restaurant are your best bets.

⌂TOP⌂ FATİH DAMAK PİDE
PIDE $

(Büyük Karaman Caddesi 48, Zeyrek; pide ₺8-12; ☺11am-11pm; ⓐAksaray) It's worth making the trek to this *pideçi* (pizza place) overlooking the İtfaiye Yanı Park Karşısı (Fire Station Park) near the Aqueduct of Valens, as its reputation for making the best Black Sea (Karadeniz)–style pide on the Historic Peninsula is well deserved. Toppings are pretty well standard (the *sucuklu-peynirli* option is particularly tasty), but there's also an unusual *bafra pidesi* (rolled-up pitta-style pizza) on offer, and an organic buffet brunch on weekends costing a mere ₺12.50 per person. The free pots of tea served with meals are a nice touch. No alcohol. Great pide, great staff, great choice!

⌂TOP⌂ HAMDİ RESTAURANT
KEBAP $$

Map p234 (☎212-528 8011; www.hamdirestorant.com.tr; Kalçın Sokak 17, Eminönü; mezes ₺7-15, kebaps ₺20-28, desserts ₺7-15; ⓐEminönü) Hamdi Arpacı arrived in İstanbul in the 1960s and almost immediately established a street stand near the Spice Bazaar where he grilled and sold tasty kebaps made according to recipes from his hometown Urfa, in Turkey's southeast. His kebaps became so popular with locals that he soon acquired this nearby building, which has phenomenal views from its top-floor terrace.

A meal here offers views of the Old City, Golden Horn and Galata, as well as tasty food and a bustling atmosphere. Try the *yoğurtlu şakşuka* (yoghurt meze with fried aubergine, peppers and potato), the *içli köfte* (meatballs rolled in bulgur) and the *lahmacun* (thin, meat-topped pizza) followed by any of the kebaps and you'll leave replete and happy – extremely replete if you finish with the house-made baklava or *künefe* (see Sweets, p27). Any place this good is always going to be busy, so make sure you book, and don't forget to request a rooftop table with a view (outside if the weather is hot). If you arrive early, you might be able to score one of these without booking.

One slight caveat: staff work hard and are clearly encouraged to turn tables over as fast as possible. Don't expect much in terms of personal service, and be prepared for little time between courses.

The restaurant is accessed via elevators in the ground-floor baklava shop.

⌂TOP⌂ SİİRT FATİH BÜRYAN
TURKISH $

(İtfaiye Caddesi 20a, Zeyrek; büryan ₺11, perde pilavi ₺10; ⓐAksaray) Those who enjoy investigating regional cuisines should head to this eatery in the Kadın Pazarı near the Aque-

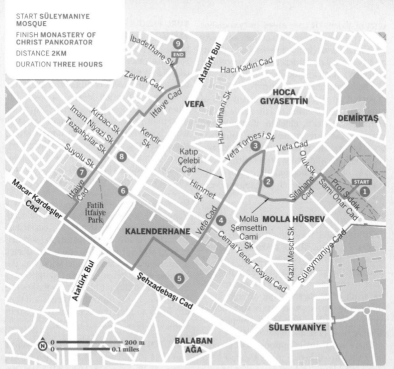

Neighbourhood Walk
Mosques & Monastery

Start at the magnificent ❶ **Süley-maniye Mosque**. From here, follow Şifahane and Molla Şemsettin Cami Sokaks down into the residential streets of the Molla Hüsrev district, currently undergoing heavy restoration as part of the Süley-maniye Urban Regeneration Project. Veer right (west) when you reach the small, sadly decrepit ❷ **Molla Gürani Mosque**. Built in the 12th century, this was known as the Church of the Virgin Mary of Vefa before the Conquest. Opposite is a small Ottoman cemetery.

Continue downhill past the cemetery until you hit Vefa Caddesi. Turning left, you will pass the recently restored ❸ **Library of Atıf Efendı** (built 1741–42 and now occupied by one of İstanbul University's Alumni Associations) and the famous ❹ **Vefa Bozacısı** – consider sampling a glass of its *boza* drink. Continue straight ahead into the rundown alley and enter through the rear gate of the

pretty ❺ **Şehzade Mehmet Mosque**. If the gate is closed you will need to backtrack and make your way down Dede Efedi Caddesi to the main entrance on Şehzadebaşı Caddesi.

After visiting the mosque, head west; you'll see remnants of the majestic Byzantine ❻ **Aqueduct of Valens** to your right. Cross Atatürk Bulvarı and then head towards the aqueduct through the scruffy park.

Passing a handsome Ottoman Revivalist building housing the ❼ **Fatih İtfaiye (Fire Station)** on your left, head under the aqueduct and into the ❽ **Kadın Pazarı (Women's Bazaar)** on İtfaiye Caddesi, a vibrant local local shopping precinct. If you are here around lunchtime, consider making a stop at Fatih Damak Pide, Siirt Fatih Büryan or Sur Ocakbaşı. Finally continue up the hill to reach the Byzantine ❾ **Monastery of Christ Pantokrator**.

duct of Valens. It specialises in two dishes that are a specialty of the southeastern city of Siirt: *büryan* (lamb slow-cooked in a pit) and *perde pilavi* (chicken and rice cooked in pastry). Both are totally delicious.

The *büryan* here is meltingly tender and is served on flat bread with crispy bits of lamb fat and a dusting of salt. *Perde pilavi* is made with rice, chicken, almonds and currants that are encased in a thin pastry shell and then baked until the exterior turns golden and flaky. Order either with a glass of frothy homemade *ayran* (salty yoghurt drink) and you'll be happy indeed. No alcohol.

SUR OCAKBAŞI   KEBAP $$

(☎212-533 8088; www.surocakbasi.com; İtfaiye Caddesi 27; kebaps ₺11-20; ⓜAksaray) Indulge in some peerless people-watching while enjoying the grilled meats at this popular place in the Kadın Pazarı. The square is always full of locals shopping or enjoying a gossip, and tourists were a rare sight before Anthony Bourdain filmed a segment of *No Reservations* here and blew Sur's cover.

There are plenty of options on offer: consider the mixed kebap plate, the *içli köfte* (deep-fried lamb and onion meatballs with a bulgur coating) and the *çiğ köfte* (meat pounded with spices and eaten raw). No alcohol, but there's homemade *ayran*.

BAHAR RESTAURANT   TURKISH $

Map p234 (Yağcı Han 13, off Nuruosmaniye Sokak, Nuruosmaniye; soup ₺4, dishes ₺9-15; ⊙11am-4pm Mon-Sat; ⓩ; ⓜÇemberlitaş) Our favourite eatery in the Grand Bazaar precinct, tiny Bahar (Spring) is popular with local shopkeepers and is always full, so arrive early to score a table. Dishes change daily and with the season – try the delicious lentil soup, tasty *hünkar beğendi* (lamb and aubergine stew) or creamy macaroni. The latter is made only once per week. No alcohol.

ONUR ET LOKANTASI   TURKISH, KEBAP $

Map p234 (Shop 7, Ali Baba Türbe Sokak 21, Nuruosmaniye; dishes ₺9-16; ⊙8am-4pm Mon-Sat; ⓜÇemberlitaş) Another excellent neighbourhood eatery. Onur grills succulent kebaps to order and displays an array of daily dishes in its bain-marie. Of these, the aubergine dishes are particularly tasty. No alcohol.

KURU FASÜLYECİ ERZİNCANLİ
ALİ BABA   TURKISH $

Map p234 (www.kurufasulyeci.com; Prof Sıddık Sami Onar Caddesi 11, Süleymaniye; beans with pilaf & pickles ₺10; ⊙7am-7pm; ⓩ; ⓜLaleli Üniversite) Join the crowds of hungry locals at this long-time institution located opposite the Süleymaniye Mosque. It's been dishing up its signature *kuru fasulye* (Anatolian-style white beans cooked in a spicy tomato sauce) since 1924 and it's delicious when accompanied by pilaf (rice) and pickles. Next-door **Kanaat Fasülyeci** (Map p234) is nearly as old and serves up more of the same. No alcohol.

DÖNERCİ ŞAHİN USTA   KEBAP $

Map p234 (Kılıççılar Sokak 7, Nuruosmaniye; döner kebap ₺10; ⊙10am-3pm Mon-Sat; ⓜÇemberlitaş) Turks take family, football and food seriously. And when it comes to food, few dishes are sampled and assessed as widely as the humble döner kebap. Ask any shopkeepers in the Grand Bazaar about who makes the best döner in the immediate area, and they are likely to give the same answer: 'Şahin Usta, of course!'. Takeaway only.

HAVUZLU RESTAURANT   TURKISH $$

Map p234 (Gani Çelebi Sokak 3, Grand Bazaar; dishes ₺8-18, kebaps ₺17-20; ⊙11.30am-5pm Mon-Sat; ⓩ; ⓜBeyazıt-Kapalı Çarşı) After a morning spent in the Grand Bazaar, many visitors choose to park their shopping bags at this well-known *lokanta*. A lovely space with a vaulted ceiling, Havuzlu (named after the small fountain at its entrance) serves up simple but tasty fare to hungry hordes of tourists and shopkeepers – go early when the food is freshest.

The restaurant also has a clean toilet, something quite rare in the bazaar. No alcohol, though.

FES CAFE   CAFE $$

Map p234 (www.fescafe.com; Ali Baba Türbe Sokak 25, Nuruosmaniye; sandwiches ₺12-19, salads ₺16-18, pasta ₺17-19; ⊙closed Sun; ⓩ; ⓜÇemberlitaş) After a morning spent trading repartee with the touts in the Grand Bazaar, you'll be in need of a respite. Fortunately, this stylish cafe just outside the Nuruosmaniye Gate is an excellent place to relax over lunch or a coffee. Popular choices include Turkish coffee (served with a piece of *lokum*), homemade lemonade and generously proportioned bowls of pasta.

The cafe has a second **branch** (Map p234; ☎212-527 3684; Halicilar Caddesi 62, Grand Bazaar; ⊙9.30am-6.30pm Mon-Sat; 🚇Beyazıt-Kapalı Çarşı) inside the Grand Bazaar.

BURÇ OCAKBAŞI
KEBAP $

Map p234 (off Yağlıkçılar Caddesi, Grand Bazaar; kebaps ₺7-25; ⊙9am-6pm Mon-Sat; 🚇Beyazıt-Kapalı Çarşı) The *üsta* (master chef) at this simple place presides over a charcoal grill where choice cuts of southeastern-style meats are cooked. You can claim a stool or ask for a *dürüm* (meat wrapped in bread) kebap to go.

Another place to source good, similarly priced kebaps in the bazaar is **Kara Mehmet** (Map p234; İç Cebeci Han 92, Grand Bazaar) in the Cebeci Han.

NAMLI
DELI $

Map p234 (www.namlipastirma.com.tr; Hasırcılar Caddesi 14-16; ⊙6.30am-7pm Mon-Sat; 🖊; 🚇Eminönü) Namlı's mouth-watering selection of cheeses, *pastırma* (air-dried beef) and meze are known throughout the city. Fight your way to the counter and order a tasty fried *pastırma* roll or a takeaway container of meze. You can also grab a tasty light lunch in the upstairs cafeteria. There's another branch (p126) in Karaköy.

İMREN LOKANTASI
TURKISH $

Map p234 (Kadırga Meydanı 143; dishes ₺5-10, kebaps ₺8-12; ⊙7am-10pm Mon-Sat; 🚇Çemberlitaş) Well and truly off the tourist trail, İmren is a tiny neighbourhood *lokanta* with extremely friendly staff. It serves decent, dirt-cheap dishes such as peppery lamb *guveç* (stew) and *musakka* (baked aubergine and mincemeat). Go for lunch rather than dinner. No alcohol.

NAR LOKANTASI
TURKISH $$$

Map p234 (www.narlokantasi.com; Nuruosmaniye Caddesi 65, Nuruosmaniye; meze ₺8-27, pide ₺14-22, mains ₺16-43; ⊙noon-11pm Mon-Sat; 🖊; 🚇Çemberlitaş) We were in two minds as to whether we should list this restaurant on the 5th floor of the frighteningly expensive Armaggan store near the Grand Bazaar. We do so for two reasons: it has a convenient location and it is one of the few eateries in this area where patrons can enjoy wine or beer with their meal.

Opened in 2012, the restaurant-*lokanta* is a project of Vedat Başaran, the energy behind the admirable NAR Gourmet, an

FISH SANDWICHES

The city's favourite fast-food treat is undoubtedly the *balık ekmek* (fish sandwich), and the most atmospheric place to try one of these is at the Eminönü end of the Galata Bridge. Here, in front of fishing boats tied to the quay, are a number of stands where mackerel fillets are grilled, crammed into fresh bread and served with salad; a generous squeeze of bottled lemon is optional but recommended. A sandwich will set you back a mere ₺5 or so, and is delicious accompanied by a glass of the *şalgam* (sour turnip juice) sold by nearby pickle vendors.

There are plenty of other places around town to try a *balık ekmek* – head to any *iskele* (ferry dock) and there's bound to be a stand nearby. Alternatively, **Fürreyya Galata Balıkçısı** (Map p240), a tiny place opposite the Galata Tower, serves an excellent version for ₺7.

organisation that describes itself as being 'devoted to the principle of natural eating inspired by Turkey's diverse provincial food cultures'. Unfortunately we have found that the pricey food on offer here ranges from adequate to inedible. If you decide to give it a go, come at lunch and make your choice from the bain-marie at the rear of the restaurant – don't order from the menu unless you decide to limit yourself to mezes or pide.

The dining space itself has large, well-spaced tables but lacks character. Service is attentive, but this doesn't adequately compensate for the disappointing food and the fact that the wine list is outrageously overpriced (glass of wine ₺26).

🍷 DRINKING

Like most parts of the Old City, the area around the Grand Bazaar is conservative and there are few places serving alcohol. There are a number of *çay bahçesi* (tea garden) that are worth checking out though, as well as a *kahvehanesi* (coffee house) or two.

TOP CHOICE ZEYREKHANE
CAFE

(www.zeyrekhane.com; İbadethane Arkası Sokak 10, Zeyrek; ⊙9.30am-10pm Tue-Sun; 🚇Aksaray) This lovely cafe opposite the Byzantine Monastery of Christ Pantokrator has a dining space filled with antique handicrafts, as well as a garden terrace offering magnificent views of the Golden Horn and Süleymaniye Mosque. Though the menu includes choices such as sandwiches and *köfte*, we recommend coming here to enjoy the view over a coffee or sunset aperitif.

TOP CHOICE ERENLER ÇAY BAHÇESİ
TEA GARDEN

Map p234 (Yeniçeriler Caddesi 35, Beyazıt; ⊙7am-midnight; 🚇Beyazıt-Kapalı Çarşı) Set in the vine-covered courtyard of the Çorlulu Ali Paşa Medrese, this nargile cafe near the Grand Bazaar is a favourite with students from nearby İstanbul University.

TOP CHOICE LALE BAHÇESİ
TEA GARDEN

Map p234 (Şifahane Caddesi, Süleymaniye; ⊙9am-11pm; 🚇Laleli-Üniversite) In a sunken courtyard that was once part of the Süleymaniye *külliye*, this charming outdoor teahouse is always full of students from the nearby theological college and İstanbul University, who come here to sit on cushioned seats under trees and relax while watching the pretty fountain. It's one of the cheapest places in the area to enjoy a çay and nargile.

TOP CHOICE TÜRK OCAĞI KÜLTÜR VE SANAT MERKEZİ İKTİSADİ İŞLETMESİ ÇAY BAHÇESİ
TEA GARDEN

Map p234 (cnr Divan Yolu & Bab-ı Ali Caddesi; ⊙8am-midnight; 🚇Çemberlitaş) Tucked into the rear right-hand corner of a shady courtyard filled with Ottoman tombs, this enormously popular tea garden is a perfect place to escape the crowds and relax over a çay and nargile. You can even score a cheap and tasty *gözleme* (Turkish crêpe filled with cheese, spinach or potato) here.

TOP CHOICE ETHEM TEZÇAKAR KAHVECİ
CAFE

Map p234 (Halıcılar Çarşışı Sokak, Grand Bazaar; ⊙8.30am-7pm Mon-Sat; 🚇Beyazıt-Kapalı Çarşı) Bekir Tezçakar's family has been at the helm of this tiny coffee shop for four generations. Smack bang in the middle of the bazaar's most glamorous retail strip, its traditional brass-tray tables and wooden stools stand in stark contrast to the Western-style Fes Cafe, opposite.

ŞARK KAHVESİ
CAFE

Map p234 (Oriental Coffeeshop; Yağlıkçılar Caddesi 134, Grand Bazaar; ⊙8.30am-7pm Mon-Sat; 🚇Beyazıt-Kapalı Çarşı) The Şark's arched ceiling betrays its former existence as part of a bazaar street; years ago some enterprising *kahveci* (coffeehouse owner) walled up several sides and turned it into a cafe. Located on one of the bazaar's major thoroughfares, it's popular with both stallholders and tourists.

PANDELİ
CAFE

Map p234 (www.pandeli.com.tr; Spice Bazaar, Eminönü; ⊙noon-4pm Mon-Sat; 🚇Eminönü) Pandeli's three salons are encrusted with stunning turqoise-coloured İznik tiles and furnished with chandeliers and richly upholstered banquettes. Though its location above the main entrance to the Spice Bazaar makes it a popular lunch spot for tourists (locals wouldn't dream of eating here), we suggest visiting for a tea or coffee after the main lunch service instead.

KAHVE DÜNYASI
CAFE

Map p234 (Nuruosmaniye Caddesi 79; ⊙7.30am-9.30pm) The name means 'Coffee World', and this coffee chain has the local world at its feet. The secret of its success lies in the huge coffee menu, reasonable prices, delicious chocolate spoons (yes, you read that correctly), comfortable seating and free wi-fi. The filter coffee is better than its espresso-based alternatives.

There's another **branch** (Map p234; Kızıhan Sokak 18, Eminönü; 🚇Eminönü) near the Spice Bazaar.

VEFA BOZACISI
BOZA BAR

Map p234 (www.vefa.com.tr; cnr Vefa & Katip Çelebi Caddesis, Molla Hüsrev; boza ₺2.50; ⊙8am-midnight; 🚇Laleli-Üniversite) This famous *boza* bar was established in 1875 and locals still flock here to drink the viscous tonic, which is made from water, sugar and fermented barley. The mucous-coloured beverage has a reputation for building up strength and virility – it won't be to everyone's taste, but the bar's pretty interior is worth a visit in its own right.

If the *boza* is too confrontational for you, the bar also serves *şıra*, a fermented grape juice.

ANTIQUES, ANYONE?

Those seeking out authentic Ottoman souvenirs should visit the **Horhor Flea Market** (Horhor Bit Pazarı; Kırık Talumba Sokak, Aksaray), a decrepit building in Aksaray that is home to five floors of shops selling antiques, curios and bric-a-brac of every possible description, quality and condition.

To get there, catch the tram to Aksaray, cross Ataturk Bulvarı, pass the Valide Sultan Mosque and veer right when the main road divides. Horhor Caddesi is to your right, going up the hill. The market is on Kırık Talumba Sokak, on the right-hand side near the top of the hill.

Note that the market is closed on Sundays.

🔒 SHOPPING

In the Bazaar District you'll find the city's two most famous marketplaces: the Grand and Spice Bazaars. In between the two is the vibrant local shopping neighbourhood of Tahtakale.

ABDULLA NATURAL PRODUCTS   TEXTILES, BATHWARE

Map p234 (Halıcılar Çarşışı Sokak 62, Grand Bazaar; ⊘9am-7pm Mon-Sat; 🚇Beyazıt-Kapalı Çarşı) The first of the Western-style designer stores to appear in this ancient marketplace, Abdulla sells top-quality cotton bed linen and towels, handspun woollen throws from eastern Turkey, cotton *peştemals* (bath wraps) and pure olive-oil soap. There's another **branch** (Map p234; Ali Baba Türbe Sokak 25, Nuruosmaniye) in the Fes Cafe in Nuruosmaniye.

DERVİŞ   TEXTILES, BATHWARE

Map p234 (www.dervis.com; Keseciler Caddesi 33-35, Grand Bazaar; ⊘9am-7pm Mon-Sat; 🚇Beyazıt-Kapalı Çarşı) Gorgeous raw cotton and silk *peştemals* share shelf space here with traditional Turkish dowry vests and engagement dresses. If these don't take your fancy, the pure olive-oil soaps and old hamam bowls are sure to step into the breach. There's another **branch** (Map p234; Halıcılar Çarşışı Caddesi 51), also in the bazaar.

MUHLİS GÜNBATTI   TEXTILES

Map p234 (www.muhlisgunbatti.net; Perdahçılar Sokak 48, Grand Bazaar; ⊘9am-7pm Mon-Sat; 🚇Beyazıt-Kapalı Çarşı) One of the most famous stores in the bazaar, Muhlis Günbattı specialises in *suzani* fabrics from Uzbekistan. These beautiful bedspreads, table cloths and wall hangings are made from fine cotton embroidered with silk. As well as the textiles, it stocks top-quality carpets, brightly coloured kilims and a small range of antique Ottoman fabrics richly embroidered with gold. Its **second shop** (Tevkifhane Sokak 12; 🚇Sultanahmet) in Sultanahmet sells a wider range of costumes at stratospheric prices.

AK GÜMÜŞ   HANDICRAFTS

Map p234 (Gani Çelebi Sokak 8, Grand Bazaar; ⊘9am-7pm Mon-Sat; 🚇Beyazıt-Kapalı Çarşı) Specialising in Central Asian tribal arts, this delightful store stocks an array of felt toys and hats, as well as jewellery and other objects made using coins and beads.

YAZMACI NECDET DANIŞ   TEXTILES

Map p234 (Yağlıkçılar Caddesi 57, Grand Bazaar; ⊘9am-7pm Mon-Sat; 🚇Beyazıt-Kapalı Çarşı) Fashion designers and buyers from every corner of the globe know that when in İstanbul, this is where to come to source top-quality textiles. It's crammed with bolts of fabric of every description – shiny, simple, sheer and sophisticated – as well as *peştemals,* scarves and clothes. Murat Danış next door is part of the same operation.

SERHAT GERİDÖNMEZ   JEWELLERY

Map p234 (Şerifağa Sokak 69, Grand Bazaar; ⊘9am-7pm Mon-Sat; 🚇Beyazıt-Kapalı Çarşı) There are plenty of jewellers in the Grand Bazaar, but few sell objects as gorgeous as the expertly crafted copies of Hellinistic, Roman and Byzantine pieces on offer at this tiny store.

KOÇ DERİ LEATHER   CLOTHING

Map p234 (Kürkçüler Çarşışı 22-46, Grand Bazaar; ⊘9am-7pm; 🚇Beyazıt-Kapalı Çarşı) If you fancy a leather jacket or coat, Koç is bound to have something that suits. It's one of the bazaar's busiest stores and certainly the most stylish of the leather outlets here.

DHOKU   CARPETS

Map p234 (www.dhoku.com; Takkeçiler Sokak 58-60, Grand Bazaar; ⊘9am-7pm Mon-Sat; 🚇Beyazıt-Kapalı Çarşı) One of the new generation of rug stores opening in the bazaar, Dhoku (meaning 'texture') sells artfully designed wool kilims in resolutely modernist designs. Its sister store, **EthniCon** (Map p234; www.ethnicon.com; Takkeçiler Sokak, Grand Bazaar), opposite this store, sells similarly stylish rugs in vivid colours and can be said to have started the current craze in contemporary kilims.

ŞİŞKO OSMAN CARPETS

Map p234 (Fatty Osman; www.siskoosman.com. tr; Zincirli Han 15, Grand Bazaar; ⊘9am-7pm Mon-Sat; 🚇Beyazıt-Kapalı Çarşı) The Osmans have been in the rug business for four generations and are rated by many as the best dealers in the bazaar. Certainly, their stock is a cut above many of their competitors. Most of the rugs on sale are dowry pieces and all have been hand woven and coloured with vegetable dyes.

SEVAN BIÇAKÇI JEWELLERY

Map p234 (www.sevanbicakci.com; Gazi Sinan Paşa Sokak 16, Nuruosmaniye; ⊘10am-6pm Mon-Sat; 🚇Çemberlitaş) Inspired by the monuments and history of his much-loved İstanbul, flamboyant jeweller Sevan Bıçakçı creates wearable art that aims to impress. His flagship store is in the Kutlu Han near the Grand Bazaar's Nuruosmaniye Gate.

SOFA ART, JEWELLERY

Map p234 (www.kashifsofa.com; Nuruosmaniye Caddesi 53, Nuruosmaniye; ⊘9.30am-7pm Mon-Sat; 🚇Çemberlitaş) Investigation of Sofa's artfully arranged clutter reveals an eclectic range of pricey jewellery, prints, textiles, calligraphy, Ottoman miniatures and contemporary Turkish art.

SILK & CASHMERE CLOTHING

Map p234 (www.silkcashmere.com; Nuruosmaniye Caddesi 69, Nuruosmaniye; ⊘9.30am-7pm Mon-Sat; 🚇Çemberlitaş) Nuruosmaniye branch of this popular chain selling cashmere and silk-cashmere-blend cardigans, jumpers, tops and shawls. All are remarkably well priced considering their quality. There's another, smaller **store** (Map p234; Kalpakçılar Caddesi 74) inside the Grand Bazaar.

ALİ MUHIDDIN HACI BEKİR FOOD

Map p234 (www.hacibekir.com.tr/eng; Hamidiye Caddesi 83, Eminönü; ⊘8am-8pm Mon-Sat; 🚇Eminönü) It's obligatory to sample *lokum* while in İstanbul, and one of the best places

to do so is at this historic shop, which has been operated by members of the same family for over 200 years. Buy it *sade* (plain), or made with *cevizli* (walnut), *fıstıklı* (pistachio), *badem* (almond) or *roze* (rose water). There's another store (p137) in Beyoğlu.

HAFIZ MUSTAFA FOOD

Map p234 (🖀212-526 5627; Hamidiye Caddesi 84-86, Eminönü; ⊘8am-8pm Mon-Sat, 9am-8pm Sun; 🚇Eminönü) Located opposite Ali Muhiddin Hacı Bekir, Hafız Mustafa also sells excellent Turkish delight. You can buy a small bag of freshly made treats to sample, plus gift boxes to take home. Best of all, they're happy to let you taste before buying (within reason, of course). There are other branches in Sirkeci (p78) and Sultanahmet (p78).

VAKKO İNDİRİM CLOTHING, ACCESSORIES

Map p234 (Vakko Sale Store; Yeni Camii Caddesi 13; ⊘9.30am-6pm Mon-Sat; 🚇Eminönü) This remainder outlet of İstanbul's famous fashion store should be on the itinerary of all bargain hunters. Top-quality men's and women's clothing – often stuff that's been designed and made in Italy – is sold here for a fraction of its original price.

ARMİNE CLOTHING

Map p234 (www.armine.com; Mahmutpaşa Yokuşu 181, Eminönü; ⊘10am-6pm Mon-Sat; 🚇Eminönü) İstanbul is a fashionable city with a highly idiosyncratic style. In Bebek and Beyoğlu the fashion might be for tight jeans, revealing jackets and chunky jewellery, but in the city's conservative neighbourhoods, there's little make-up and even less flesh on show. Wildly popular Armine is where Zara style meets the headscarf, and it's an exemplar of affordable Islamic chic.

KURUKAHVECİ MEHMET EFENDİ COFFEE

Map p234 (www.mehmetefendi.com/eng; cnr Tahmis Sokak & Hasırcılar Caddesi; ⊘9am-6pm Mon-Sat; 🚇Eminönü) Caffeine addicts are regularly spotted queuing outside this, the flagship store of İstanbul's most famous coffee purveyor. You can join them in getting a fix of the freshest beans in town, and also purchase cute coffee sets to take home.

UCUZCULAR BAHARAT SPICES

Map p234 (www.ucuzcular.com.tr; Spice Bazaar 51; ⊘8am-6.30pm, 9am-6pm Sun high season; 🚇Eminönü) Showcasing the colour and fragrance of hundreds of spices, Ucuzcular concocts its own spice blends and will vacuum pack these for those travellers who are keen to add them to their luggage.

MEHMET KALMAZ BAHARAT   BEAUTY

Map p234 (Spice Bazaar 41; ⊗8am-6.30pm Mon-Sat, 9am-6pm Sun high season; ☐Eminönü) One of the few shops in the Spice Bazaar that specialises in potions and lotions, this antiquated place sells remedies to make women younger, others to make men stronger, and a royal love potion that, we guess, is supposed to combine the two. It also stocks spices, bath accessories, teas and medicinal herbs.

MALATYA PAZARI   FOOD

Map p234 (www.malatya-pazari.com; Spice Bazaar 20-44, Eminönü; ⊗8am-6.30pm Mon-Sat, 9am-6pm Sun high season; ☐Eminönü) The city of Malatya in central-eastern Turkey is famous for its apricots, and this shop with three branches near the Spice Bazaar's Tahmis Caddesi doorway stocks the cream of the crop, dried both naturally and chemically. Its other quality dried fruit and nuts eclipse all others in this bazaar.

🏃 ACTIVITIES

ÇEMBERLİTAŞ HAMAMI   HAMAM

Map p234 (☑212-522 7974; Vezir Han Caddesi 8; bath, scrub & soap massage €29; ⊗6am-midnight; ☐Çemberlitaş) There won't be too many times in your life when you'll get the opportunity to have a Turkish bath in a building dating back to 1584, so now might well be the time to do it – particularly as this twin hamam was designed by the great architect Sinan and is among the most beautiful in the city.

The building was commissioned by Nurbanu Sultan, wife of Selim II and mother of Murat III. Both of its bath chambers have a huge marble *sıcaklık* (circular marble heat platform) and a gorgeous dome with glass apertures. The *camekan* (entrance hall) for men is original, but the women's version is new.

It costs an extra €20 to add an oil massage to the standard bath package, but all massages and treatments here are perfunctory so we'd suggest giving this a miss. Tips are meant to be covered in the treatment price and there's a 20% discount for International Student Identity Card holders.

GEDİKPAŞA HAMAMI   HAMAM

Map p234 (☑212-517 8956; www.gedikpasa hamami.com; Emin Sinan Hamamı Sokak 61, Gedikpaşa; bath, scrub & soap massage ₺55; ⊗men 6am-midnight, women 9am-11pm; ☐Çemberlitaş) This Ottoman-era hamam has been operating since 1475. Its interior isn't as beautiful as those at Çemberlitaş, but services are slightly cheaper and there are separate hamams, small dipping pools and saunas for both sexes. The operators will sometimes transport guests to and from Sultanahmet hotels at no charge; ask your hotel to investigate this option.

BAZAAR DISTRICT ACTIVITIES

Western Districts

Neighbourhood Top Five

1 Admiring the exquisite mosaics and frescos adorning the interior of one of İstanbul's great Byzantine treasures, the **Kariye Museum** (p104; Chora Church).

2 Walking on or along the **historic land walls** (p109) that once protected Constantinople from foreign invaders.

3 Visiting the Greek Orthodox **Patriarchal Church of St George** (p107), one of Turkey's major pilgrimage destinations.

4 Sipping tea and enjoying the Golden Horn view at the **Pierre Loti Café** (p112) in Eyüp.

5 Spotting landmarks on the shore when arriving at Ayvansaray İskelesi on the **Golden Horn ferry**.

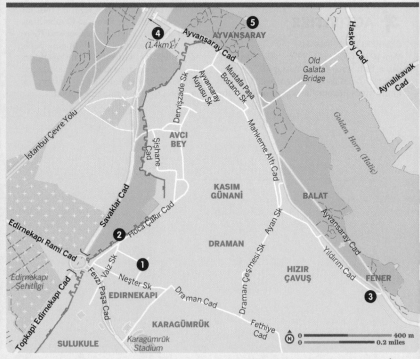

For more detail of this area, see Map p244

Explore: Western Districts

It's a great shame that so few visitors head to this fascinating part of town. Try to dedicate at least one day of your stay to exploring the area; two would be better.

Spend the first of these taking the Golden Horn (Haliç) ferry trip from Eminönü, alighting at Ayvansaray and then following our Walk Along the Walls tour. Make sure that you allow enough time to admire the Byzantine mosaics and frescos at the Kariye Museum (Chora Church).

If you are able to spend a second day here, we highly recommend that you start your day following our Mosque & Monastery walking tour in the Bazaar District (p93) and then continue uphill towards the Fatih Mosque. Sites such as the Fethiye Museum and the Sultan Selim Mosque are only a short walk away.

Note that these districts are deathly quiet at night and on Sundays, so you're best off exploring during the day on weekdays or Saturday.

Local Life

➡ **Produce shopping** Locals shop along Fevzi Paşa Caddesi in Fatih, on Murat Molla Caddesi in Çarşamba, along Vodina Caddesi in Balat and at the Çarşamba Pazarı (Wednesday Market) in Fatih.

➡ **Gathering spots** Popular local gathering spots include the terrace of the Sultan Selim Mosque (p109) and the forecourts of the Eyüp Sultan Mosque (p110) and Fatih Mosque (p107).

➡ **Ferry hopping** Regular commuters enjoy catching up with friends and neighbours over a glass of tea on the Golden Horn ferry.

Getting There & Away

➡ **Ferry** The most enjoyable way to access these suburbs is aboard the Golden Horn ferry from Eminönü, which stops at Ayvansaray near Edirnekapı.

➡ **Bus** Regular services travel from Eminönü along Mürsel Paşa Caddesi (at various points also called Abdülezel Paşa Caddesi and Sadrazam Ali Paşa Caddesi), which follows the shore of the Golden Horn through Balat, Fener and Avansaray and on to Eyüp. From Eminönü there are also regular services to Fatih and Edirenkapı along Fevzi Paşa Caddesi (the continuation of Macar Kardeşler and Şehzadebaşı Caddesis). We have provided information about relevant bus routes in our reviews.

Lonely Planet's Top Tip

If you plan to visit Fatih, try to do so on Wednesdays, when the Çarşamba Pazarı (Wednesday Market) is held in the streets around the Fatih Mosque.

Best Places to Eat & Drink

➡ Asitane (p110)
➡ Kömür Turk Mutfağı (p110)
➡ Pierre Loti Café (p112)

For reviews, see p110 ➡

Best Churches

➡ Patriarchal Church of St George (p107)
➡ Church of St Stephen of the Bulgars (p109)
➡ Church of St Mary of the Mongols (p107)

For reviews, see p107 ➡

Best Byzantine Sites

➡ Kariye Museum (p104)
➡ Fethiye Museum (p107)
➡ Historic Land Walls (p109)

For reviews, see p104 ➡

WESTERN DISTRICTS

TOP SIGHTS
KARİYE MUSEUM (CHORA CHURCH)

İstanbul has more than its fair share of Byzantine monuments, but few are as drop-dead gorgeous as this mosaic-laden church. Nestled in the shadow of Theodosius II's monumental land walls and now a museum overseen by the Aya Sofya curators, it receives a fraction of the visitor numbers that its big sister attracts but offers an equally fascinating insight into Byzantine art.

The building was originally known as the Church of the Holy Saviour Outside the Walls (Chora literally means 'country'), reflecting the fact that when it was first built it was located outside the original city walls built by Constantine the Great. Within a century the church and the monastery complex in which it was located were engulfed by Byzantine urban sprawl and enclosed within a new set of walls built by Emperor Theodosius II. Around AD 500, the Emperor Anastasius and his court moved from the Great Palace of Byzantium in Sultanahmet to the Palace of Blachernae, a new complex built close to the point where Theodosius' land walls met the old sea walls on the Golden Horn. Its proximity to the Chora Monastery led to the monastery expanding and being rebuilt in 536 during the rule of Justinian.

What you see today isn't Justinian's church, though. That building was destroyed during the Iconoclastic period (711–843) and reconstructed at least five times, most significantly in the 11th, 12th and 14th centuries. Today, the Chora consists of five main architectural units: the nave, the two-storied structure (annex) added to the north, the inner and the outer narthexes, and the chapel for tombs (parecclesion) to the south.

DON'T MISS...

→ Khalke Jesus
→ Genealogy of Christ
→ Mary and the Baby Jesus
→ Frescos in parecclesion

PRACTICALITIES

→ Kariye Müzesi
→ Map p160
→ kariye.muze.gov.tr
→ Kariye Camii Sokak, Edirnekapı
→ admission ₺15
→ ◷9am-7pm Thu-Tue Apr-Oct, to 4.30pm Nov-Mar
→ 🚌31E, 32, 36K, 38E from Eminönü, 87 from Taksim

Virtually all of the interior decoration – the famous mosaics and the less renowned but equally striking frescos – dates from 1312 and was funded by Theodore Metochites. One of the museum's most wonderful mosaics (item 48), found above the door to the nave in the inner narthex, depicts Theodore offering the church to Christ.

Metochites also established a very large and rich library inside the monastery; unfortunately, no traces of this or the other monastery buildings have survived.

The structure and environs of the church weren't the only thing to change over the years – after centuries of use as a church, the building became a mosque during the reign of Beyazıt II (1481–1512) and a museum in 1945.

Mosaics

Most of the interior is covered with mosaics depicting the lives of Christ and the Virgin Mary. Look out for the **Khalke Jesus** (item 33), which shows Christ and Mary with two donors – Prince Isaac Comnenos and Melane, daughter of Mikhael Palaiologos VIII. This is under the right dome in the inner narthex. On the dome itself is a stunning depiction of **Jesus and his ancestors** (the **Genealogy of Christ**; item 27). On the narthex's left dome is a serenely beautiful mosaic of **Mary and the Baby Jesus surrounded by her ancestors** (item 34).

In the nave are three mosaics: of **Christ** (item 50c), of **Mary and the Baby Jesus** (item 50b) and of the **Dormition of the Blessed Virgin** (Assumption; item 50a) – turn around to see this, as it's over the main door you just entered. The 'infant' being held by Jesus is actually Mary's soul.

Frescos

To the right of the nave is the pareeclesion, a side chapel built to hold the tombs of the church's founder and his relatives, close friends and associates. This is decorated with frescos that deal with the themes of death and resurrection, depicting scenes taken from the Old Testament. The striking painting in the apse known as the **Anastasis** (item 51) shows a powerful Christ raising Adam and Eve out of their sarcophagi, with saints and kings in attendance. The gates of Hell are shown under Christ's feet. Less majestic but no less beautiful are the **frescos adorning the dome** (item 65), which show Mary and 12 attendant angels.

Though no one knows for certain, it is thought that the frescos were painted by the same masters who created the mosaics. Theirs is an extraordinary

THE CHORA'S PATRON

Theodore Metochites was born in Constantinople in 1270 the son of a senior official in the court of Michael VIII Palaiologos. In 1290, he was accepted into the court of Andronikos II and was appointed logothetes, the official responsible for the treasury. This made him the highest Byzantine official after the emperor. In 1316 Metochites was appointed by the emperor as *ktetor* (donor) for the restoration of the Chora Monastery. When the restoration of the monastery was completed in 1321 he was granted the title of grand logothetes. Metochites lost his position as grand logothetes in 1328 when Emperor Andronikos II was dethroned, and was banished from Constantinople. He was allowed to return in 1330 and chose to become a priest in the monastery that he had so generously endowed. He died in 1332 and is buried in a grave niche in the pareeclesion.

After visiting the museum, consider sampling the Ottoman dishes o n offer at the Asitane restaurant, which is in the basement of the Kariye Oteli next door.

accomplishment, as the paintings, with their sophisticated use of perspective and exquisitely portrayed facial expressions, are reminiscent of those painted by the Italian master Giotto, the painter who more than any other ushered in the Italian Renaissance.

Marble

The nave and the narthexes feature very fine, multicoloured marblework. The marble door in the north axis of the nave is an imitation of the bronze-and-wood doors of the 6th century, and is one of the few surviving examples of its kind.

Restoration

Between 1947 and 1958 the church's interior decoration was carefully restored under the auspices of the Byzantine Society of America. Plaster and whitewash covering the mosaics and frescos was removed and the works were cleaned.

Despite signs clearly prohibiting the use of camera flashes in the museum, many visitors wilfully ignore this rule, endangering these wonderful mosaics and frescos. Please don't be one of them.

⊙ SIGHTS

KARİYE MUSEUM
(CHORA CHURCH)   MUSEUM
See p104.

FETHİYE MUSEUM   MUSEUM
Map p244 (Fethiye Müzesi, Church of Pammaka-ristos; Fethiye Caddesi, Çarşamba; admission ₺5; ⊙9am-4.30pm Thu-Tue; ☐33ES, 90, 44B, 36C, 399B&C from Eminönü, 55T from Taksim) Not long after the Conquest, Mehmet the Con-queror visited this 13th-century church to discuss theological questions with the Patriarch of the Orthodox Church. They talked in the southern side chapel known as the **parecclesion**, which is now open as a small museum. The chapel was added to the church in the 14th century and is deco-rated with gold mosaics.

The most impressive of the mosaics are the **Pantokrator and 12 Prophets** adorn-ing the dome, and the **Deesis (Christ with the Virgin and St John the Baptist)** in the apse.

The building itself was extended several times over the centuries before being convert-ed to a mosque in 1573. It was named Fethiye (Conquest) to commemorate Sultan Murat III's victories in Georgia and Azerbaijan.

PATRIARCHAL CHURCH OF
ST GEORGE   CHURCH
Map p244 (St George in the Phanar; www.ec-patr .org; Sadrazam Ali Paşa Caddesi, Fener; ⊙8.30am-4.30pm; ☐33ES, 90, 44B, 36C, 399B&C from Em-inönü, 55T from Taksim) Dating from 1836, this church is part of the Greek Patriarchate, a compound of buildings nestled behind the historic sea walls fronting the Golden Horn. Inside are artefacts including Byzan-tine mosaics, religious relics and a wood-and-inlay patriarchal throne. The most eye-catching feature is an ornately carved wooden iconostasis (screen of icons) that was restored and lavishly gilded in 1994.

The patriarchal throne is in the middle of the nave. Made of walnut inlaid with ivory, mother-of-pearl and coloured wood, it is thought to date from the last years of Byzantium.

Other treasures include the 11th-century mosaic icon that is on the south wall to the right of the iconostasis. This shows the Virgin Mary holding and pointing to the Christ Child, and was originally created for the Byzantine church of Pammakaristos (now the Fethiye Museum).

Look for the Column of Christ's Flagella-tion in the southern corner of the nave. The church claims that this is a portion of the column to which Jesus Christ was bound and whipped by Roman soldiers before the Crucifixion. It was supposedly brought to Constantinople by St Helen, mother of the first Christian emperor, Constantine.

Note that the church is closed between 9.15am and 12.20pm for Sunday service when the Patriarch is in residence (usually once per month).

CHURCH OF ST MARY OF
THE MONGOLS   CHURCH
Map p244 (Church of Theotokos Panaghiotissa, Kanlı Kilise; Tevkii Cafer Mektebi Sokak, Fener; ⊙9am-5pm Sat & Sun; ☐33ES, 90, 44B, 36C, 399B&C from Eminönü, 55T from Taksim) Conse-crated in the 13th century and saved from conversion into a mosque by the personal decree of Mehmet the Conqueror, this is the only church in İstanbul to remain in Greek hands ever since Byzantine times. It was named after Princess Maria Paleologina, an illegitimate daughter of Emperor Michael VIII Paleologos.

Maria was sent from Byzantium to mar-ry Hulagu, the Great Khan of the Mongols, in 1265. By the time she arrived in his king-dom he had died (we guess it was a very long trip), so she was forced to marry his son Abagu instead. On Abagu's death she returned to Byzantium and retired to a con-vent attached to this church.

The church is usually open on weekends. If the doors aren't open, ring the bell on the outside gate to attract the attention of the caretaker.

FATİH MOSQUE   MOSQUE
(Fatih Camii, Mosque of the Conqueror; Fevzi Paşa Caddesi, Fatih; ☐31E, 32, 336E, 36KE, 38E from Eminönü, 87 from Taksim) The Fatih was the first great imperial mosque built in İstanbul following the Conquest. Mehmet the Conqueror chose to locate it on the hill-top site of the ruined Church of the Apos-tles, burial place of Constantine and other Byzantine emperors. Mehmet decided to be buried here as well – his tomb is behind the mosque and is inevitably filled with worshippers.

The original *külliye* (mosque complex), finished in 1470, was enormous. Set in extensive grounds, it included 15 chari-table establishments such as *medreses*

WESTERN DISTRICTS SIGHTS

THE ECUMENICAL PATRIARCHATE

The Ecumenical Patriarchate of Constantinople (Rum Ortodoks Patrikhanesi) is the symbolic headquarters of the Greek Orthodox church, the 'Mother Church' of Eastern Orthodox Christianity. It has been led by 270 Ecumenical Patriarchs since its establishment in AD 330.

To the Turkish government, the Ecumenical Patriarch is a Turkish citizen of Greek descent nominated by the church and appointed by the government as an official in the Directorate of Religious Affairs. In this capacity he is the religious leader of the country's Orthodox citizens and is known officially as the Greek Patriarch of Fener (Fener Rum Patriği).

The Patriarchate has been based in a series of churches over its history, including Aya İrini (Hagia Eirene, 272–398), Aya Sofya (Hagia Sofya, 398–1453) and the Church of Pammakaristos (Fethiye Museum, 1456–1587). It moved to its current location in Fener in 1601.

The relationship between the Patriarchate and the wider Turkish community has been strained in the past, no more so than when Patriarch Gregory V was hanged for treason after inciting Greeks to overthrow Ottoman rule at the start of the Greek War of Independence (1821–32).

Current tensions are focused on the Turkish government's refusal to allow the the Patriarchate to reopen the Orthodox Theological School of Halki, located on Heybeliada in the Princes Islands. Opened in 1844, the school was closed by government order in 1971.

(Islamic schools of higher studies), a hospice for travellers and a caravanserai. Many of these still stand – the most interesting is the multidomed *tabhane* (dervish inn) to the southeast of the mosque. Its columns are said to have been originally used in the Church of the Apostles.

Unfortunately the mosque you see today is not the one Mehmet built. The original stood for nearly 300 years before toppling in an earthquake in 1766. The current mosque was constructed between 1767 and 1771.

The front courtyard of the mosque is a favourite place for locals to congregate. On Wednesday the streets behind and to the north of the mosque host the **Çarşamba Pazarı** (Fatih Pazarı, Wednesday Market), a busy weekly market selling food, clothing and household goods.

MİHRİMAH SULTAN MOSQUE   MOSQUE
Map p244 (Mihrimah Sultan Camii; Ali Kuşçu Sokak, Edirnekapı; 🚌31E, 32, 36K, 38E from Eminönü, 87 from Taksim) The great architect Mimar Sinan put his stamp on the entire city, and this mosque, constructed in the 1560s next to the Edirnekapı section of the historic land walls, is one of his best works. Commissioned by Süleyman the Magnificent's favourite daughter, Mihrimah, it features a wonderfully light and airy interior

with delicate stained-glass windows and an unusual 'bird cage' chandelier.

Occupying the highest point in the city, the mosque's dome and one slender minaret are major adornments to the city skyline; they are particularly prominent on the road from Edirne. Remnants of the *külliye* include a still-functioning **hamam** (Map p244; Ali Kuşçu Sokak, Edirnekapı) on the corner of Ali Kuşçu and Eroğlu Sokaks.

PALACE OF CONSTANTİNE
PORPHYROGENİTUS   HISTORIC BUILDING
Map p244 (Palace of the Sovereign, Tekfur Sarayı; Hoca Çakır Caddesi, Edirnekapı; 🚌31E, 32, 36K 38E from Eminönü, 87 from Taksim) Though only a shell these days, the remnants of this Byzantine palace give a good idea of how it would have looked in its heyday. Built in the late 13th or early 14th century, the large three-storied structure may have been an annex of the nearby imperial Palace of Blachernae, of which few traces exist today.

The building's later uses were not so regal: after the Conquest it functioned in turn as a menagerie for exotic wild animals, a brothel, a poorhouse for destitute Jews and a pottery.

The structure was undergoing restoration works at the time of writing. When these are completed an entry fee may be levied.

GÜL MOSQUE
MOSQUE

(Gül Camii; cnr Gül Camii & Şerefiye Sokaks, Fener; 🚌33ES, 90, 44B, 36C, 399B&C from Eminönü, 55T from Taksim) This mosque started life as the 11th-century Church of St Theodosia. Legend has it that one day before the Conquest, worshippers filled the church with rose petals in St Theodosia's honour and prayed for her intervention against the Ottomans. Their prayers went unanswered, but the invaders renamed the building Gül (Rose) Mosque after the petals they found on entering.

But legends, however evocative, are rarely true. In reality, the building was used as a shipyard warehouse after the Conquest and wasn't converted into a mosque until the reign of Beyazıt II (r 1481–1512). The central, extremely high, dome is an Ottoman addition and the pretty minaret dates from the rule of Selim II (r 1512–20).

CHURCH OF ST STEPHEN OF THE BULGARS
CHURCH

Map p160 (Sveti Stefan Church; 🕿212-521 1121; Mürsel Paşa Caddesi 85, Fener; 🚌33ES, 90, 44B, 36C, 399B&C from Eminönü, 55T from Taksim) These days we're accustomed to kit homes and assemble-yourself furniture from Ikea, but back in 1871, when this Gothic Revival-style church was constructed from cast-iron pieces shipped down the Danube and across the Black Sea from Vienna on 100 barges, the idea was extremely novel.

The building's interior features screens, a balcony and columns all cast from iron; it is extremely beautiful, with the gilded iron glinting in the hazy light that filters in through stained-glass windows.

The congregation are members of the Bulgarian Orthodox Exarchate (Bulgarian Orthodox Church), which broke away from the Greek Ecumenical Orthodox Patriarchate in 1872. This is the church's İstanbul base.

The building was closed for restoration at the time of writing.

SULTAN SELİM MOSQUE
MOSQUE

Map p244 (Sultan Selim Camii, Mosque of Yavuz Selim; Yavuz Selim Caddesi, Çarşamba; 🚌90 from Eminönü) The sultan to whom this mosque was dedicated (Süleyman the Magnificent's father, Selim I, known as 'the Grim') was by all accounts a nasty piece of work. He is famous for having killed his father, two of his brothers, six of his nephews and three of his own sons. Odd, then, that İstanbullus love his mosque so much.

The reason becomes clear when a visit reveals the mosque's position on a terrace with spectacular views of the Golden Horn – picnic spots don't come much better than this.

Topping one of İstanbul's six hills, the mosque is located in the fascinating Çarşamba district, one of the city's most conservative enclaves. Women in black chadors and men with long beards and traditional clothing are seen everywhere, often hurrying to prayers at the İsmail Ağa Mosque, headquarters of the Nakşibendi Tarikatı, a Sufi sect.

The building itself, constructed in 1522, has a simple but elegant design and was

---

MAŞALLAH!

If you visit Eyüp on a Friday, Sunday or holy day, you will see young boys in white suits being carried by their proud fathers and followed by a circle of relatives. These apprehensive yet excited young chaps are about to undergo one of the most important Muslim rites – *sünnet* (circumcision). Their white suit is supplemented with a spangled hat and red satin sash emblazoned with the word *Maşallah* (May God Protect Him).

Circumcision is performed on a Turkish Muslim boy when he is between five and 11 years old (odd-numbered years are thought to be luckier), and marks his formal admission into the faith.

On the day of the operation the boy is dressed in the special suit, visits relatives and friends, and leads a parade – formerly on horseback, now in cars – around his neighbourhood or city, attended by musicians and merrymakers.

The operation, performed in a hospital or in a clinic during the afternoon, is followed by a celebration with music and feasting. The newly circumcised boy attends, resting in bed, as his friends and relatives bring him special gifts and congratulate him on having entered manhood.

nearing the end of a major renovation at the time of writing. Inside, its tilework and painted woodwork provide the most distinctive features.

EYÜP SULTAN MOSQUE
MOSQUE

Map p160 (Eyüp Sultan Camii, Mosque of the Great Eyüp; Camii Kebir Sokak, Eyüp; ⊙tomb 9.30am-4.30pm; ☐36CE, 44B, 99 from Eminönü, ⛴Eyüp) This important complex marks the supposed burial place of Ebu Eyüp el-Ensari, a friend of the Prophet's who fell in battle outside the walls of Constantinople while carrying the banner of Islam during the Arab assault and siege of the city from 674 to 678. His tomb is İstanbul's most important Islamic shrine.

Eyüp's grave was identified in a location outside the city walls Immediately after the Conquest, and Sultan Mehmet II decided to build a grand tomb to mark its location. The mosque complex that he commissioned became the place where the Ottoman princes came for the Turkish equivalent of a coronation ceremony: girding the Sword of Osman to signify their power and their title as *padişah* (king of kings), or sultan. In 1766 Mehmet's building was levelled by an earthquake; a new mosque was built on the site by Sultan Selim III in 1800.

If you arrive by ferry, cross the road from the ferry stop and walk up İskele Caddesi, until you reach the mosque complex. From the plaza outside the complex, enter the great doorway to a courtyard shaded by a huge plane tree; the mosque is to your right and the tomb, rich with silver, gold and crystal chandeliers and coloured İznik tiles, is to your left. Even though women pray in a separate room to the right of the mosque, females can usually enter the mosque itself and stand at the rear if they are properly covered.

Be careful to observe the Islamic proprieties when visiting, as this is an extremely sacred place for Muslims, ranking fourth after the big three: Mecca, Medina and Jerusalem. It's always busy on Fridays and religious holidays.

During your visit you may see boys dressed up in white suits with spangled caps and red satin sashes emblazoned with the word 'Maşallah'. These lads are on the way to their circumcision and have made a stop beforehand at this holy place.

EATING & DRINKING

ASİTANE
OTTOMAN $$$

Map p244 (☎212-635 7997; www.asitane restaurant.com; Kariye Oteli, Kariye Camii Sokak 6, Edirnekapı; starters ₺12-18, mains ₺26-42; ⊙11am-midnight; 🖋; ☐31E, 32, 36K, 38E from Eminönü, 87 from Taksim) This elegant restaurant next to the Kariye Museum (Chora Church) serves Ottoman dishes devised for the palace kitchens at Topkapı, Edirne and Dolmabahçe. Its chefs have been tracking down historic recipes for years, and the menu is full of versions that will tempt most modern palates. There's a comfortable indoor space and an outdoor courtyard for summer dining.

KÖMÜR TURK MUTFAĞI
TURKISH $

(www.komurturkmutfagi.com; Fevzi Paşa Caddesi 18, Fatih; veg dishes ₺6-7, meat dishes ₺9-13, grills ₺10-18; ⊙lunch; 🖋; ☐31E, 32, 336E, 36KE, 38E from Eminönü, 87 from Taksim) Located amid the wedding-dress shops on Fatih's main drag is this five-floor *Türk mutfağı* (Turkish kitchen) where brides-to-be join businessmen and worshippers from the nearby Fatih Mosque for lunch. The gleaming ground-floor space has a huge counter where ready-made dishes are displayed and where fresh meat and fish can be cooked to order.

KÖFTECİ ARNAVUT
KÖFTE $

Map p160 (☎212-531 6652; Mürsel Paşa Caddesi 139, Balat; köfte ₺8, piyaz ₺5; ⊙8am-4pm; ☐33ES, 90, 44B, 36C, 399B&C from Eminönü, 55T from Taksim) Unsigned and unassuming, this famous *köfteci* (*köfte* restraurant) first opened in 1947 and is a safe spot to scoff *köfte* (meatballs) served with *piyaz* (white beans). It's to the left of the ferry stop on the opposite side of the main road.

TARİHİ HALİÇ İŞKEMBECİSİ
TURKISH $

Map p160 (☎212-534 9414; www.haliciskem becisi.com; Abdülezel Paşa Caddesi 315, Fener; soup ₺10.50; ⊙24hr; ☐33ES, 90, 44B, 36C, 399B&C from Eminönü, 55T from Taksim) Locals swear by the hangover-fighting properties of *işkembe* (tripe soup) and often make late-night pilgrimages to this, the most famous *işkembecisi* (tripe soup venue) in the city. It's on the main road opposite the ferry stop.

START **AYVANSARAY İSKELESİ**

FINISH **MIHRIMAH SULTAN MOSQUE**

DISTANCE **2KM**

DURATION **TWO HOURS**

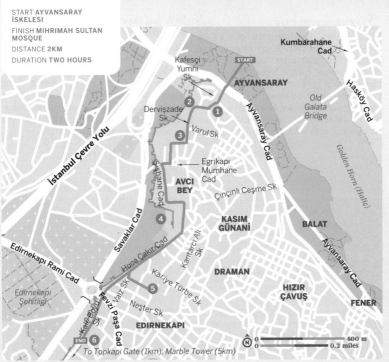

Neighbourhood Walk

A Walk Along the Walls

Take the Golden Horn ferry from Eminönü to Ayvansaray. Disembark and you will see remnants of Theodosius II's land walls in front of you. Cross busy Ayvansaray Caddesi, enter the gate punched into the walls and walk uphill into Ayvansaray Kuyusu Sokak. Veer right into Dervişzade Sokak (Street of the Dervis' Son). On your left is the ❶ **Emir Buhari Tekkesi**, a dervish lodge built in 1513.

Opposite the *tekke* are the remains of the vast ❷ **Anemas Zindanları** (Anemas Dungeons), once part of the Blachernae Palace built by the Emperor Anastasius (491–518). A number of deposed emperors were imprisoned, tortured and even murdered in this prison.

The diminutive ❸ **İvaz Efendi Mosque** further up the hill was built in the shadow of the walls in the 1580s. Its *mihrab* (niche facing Mecca) is decorated with fine İznik tiles.

Continue following the walls until you reach the ruins of the Byzantine ❹ **Palace of Constantine Porphyrogenitus** on the corner of Sişhane and Hoca Çakır Caddesis. Then veer left into Vaiz Sokak and Kariye Camii Sokak to arrive at the mosaic-adorned ❺ **Kariye Museum**. The cafe opposite is a lovely spot for a glass of tea.

Backtrack to Hoca Çakır Caddesi. This stretch of the walls has been restored, so you can climb up and enjoy a magnificent view. Continue uphill to busy Fevzi Paşa Caddesi and cross the road to reach the Edirnekapı (Edirne Gate), built on the summit of the city's sixth hill. Nearby is the lovely ❻ **Mihrimah Sultan Mosque**.

From here you will be you will be able to view the monumental progress of the walls towards Topkapı Gate, which was famously breached by the Ottomans during the seige of 1453. If you have time (and sturdy shoes), it's possible to continue walking from Edirnekapı past the gate all the way to the ruins of the Marble Tower on the shore of the Sea of Marmara, part of an imperial sea pavilion in Byzantine times. This will add about three hours to your walk.

TOP
CHOICE PIERRE LOTI CAFÉ   CAFE

Map p160 (Gümüşsuyu Balmumcu Sokak 1, Eyüp; ⊗8am-midnight; ⊠Eyüp) Many visitors head to this hilltop cafe after visiting the Eyüp Sultan Mosque (p110). Named for the famous French novelist who is said to have come here for inspiration, it offers lovely views across the Golden Horn and is a popular weekend destination for locals, who relax over tea, coffee, ice cream and nargiles.

To find the cafe, walk out of the mosque's main gate and turn right. Walk around the complex (keeping it to your right) until you see a set of stairs and a cobbled path going uphill into the Eyüp Sultan Mezarlığı (Cemetery of the Great Eyüp), where many important Ottomans are buried. It's a 15-minute walk up the steep hill. Alternatively, take the cable car that links the waterfront with the top of the hill.

Beyoğlu

GALATA | TOPHANE | KARAKÖY | İSTİKLAL & AROUND | ÇUKURCUMA | CİHANGİR | GALATA | TOPHANE | ÇUKURÇUMA | CİHANGİR

Neighbourhood Top Five

❶ Visiting cultural centres such as **İstanbul Modern** (p116), **SALT Beyoğlu** (p120), **ARTER** (p120) and **SALT Galata** (p117) to see why international artists, collectors and critics think that İstanbul has one of the world's most exciting visual-art scenes.

❷ Sampling the sights, smells and flavours in the historic **Balık Pazarı** (p120).

❸ Seeing dervishes whirl in a 15th-century *semahane* (whirling-dervish hall) at the **Galata Mevlevi Museum** (p118).

❹ Investigating the convivial cafe, bar and restaurant scenes in **Cihangir** (p127) and **Asmalımescit** (p130).

❺ Joining the locals promenading along **İstiklal Caddesi** (p115).

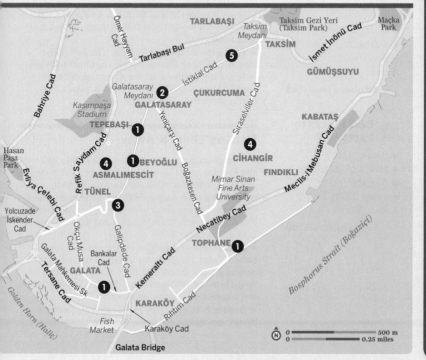

For more detail of this area, see Map p236 and p240 ➡

Lonely Planet's Top Tip

The neighbourhoods within Beyoğlu all have distinct and fascinating characters. Be sure to veer off İstiklal Caddesi and explore districts such as Cihangir, Çukurcuma, Asmalımescit and Galata.

✕ Best Places to Eat

➡ Asmalı Cavit (p126)

➡ Karaköy Güllüoğlu (p124)

➡ Lokanta Maya (p124)

➡ Meze by Lemon Tree (p126)

➡ Zübeyir Ocakbaşı (p127)

For reviews, see p124 ➡

🍷 Best Places to Drink

➡ Tophane Nargile Cafes (p131)

➡ Mikla (p132)

➡ 360 (p132)

➡ Baylo (p132)

➡ 5 Kat (p134)

For reviews, see p131 ➡

☆ Best Places to Party

➡ Babylon (p135)

➡ MiniMüzikHol (p134)

➡ Dogzstar (p133)

➡ Indigo (p133)

➡ Kiki (p134)

For reviews, see p133 ➡

BEYOĞLU

Explore: Beyoğlu

If you have the time, it makes sense to spread your exploration of this neighbourhood over two days. The first day could be spent in Galata, Tophane and Tünel, visiting sights such as the İstanbul Modern and wandering around the fascinating streets. The second day could be spent walking from Taksim Meydanı (Taksim Square) along İstiklal Caddesi, veering off into the districts of Cihangir, Çukurcuma, Asmalımescit and Tepebaşı.

If you only have one day, start in Taksim Meydanı and work your way down İstiklal, exploring the Balık Pazarı, heading into Tepebaşı to visit the Pera Müzesi and then backtracking to İstiklal Caddesi to start our walking tour.

Even if you are staying in another neighbourhood, it makes sense to follow the lead of locals and head here every night for dinner, bar-hopping and clubbing.

Local Life

➡ **Streetside cafes** Take a break and enjoy a glass of tea at old-fashioned outdoor cafes such as Hazzo Pulo Çay Bahçesi (p132) off İstiklal Caddesi, Kardeşler Cafe in Cihangir and Cafe Gündoğdu in the square below Galata Tower.

➡ **Football & nargile** If you're in town when a Süper Lig or UEFA match is being played, head to one of the Tophane Nargile Cafes to drink tea, smoke a nargile (water pipe) and join the fans in making your team allegiances clear.

➡ **Tea by the Bosphorus** To enjoy a million-dollar view with a cheap glass of tea, try the ramshackle *çay bahçesi* at the edge of the Bosphorus opposite the Fındıklı tram stop. There's even a kids' playground nearby to make toddlers happy.

Getting There & Away

➡ **Tram** A tram runs between Bağcılar in the city's west and Kabataş near Taksim Meydanı in Beyoğlu, stopping at Sultanahmet, Eminönü and Karaköy en route.

➡ **Funicular** It's a steep uphill walk from all tram stops to İstiklal, so most commuters use the funiculars that link Karaköy with Tünel Meydanı and Kabataş with Taksim Meydanı.

➡ **Metro** A modern metro system travels between Şişhane (near Tünel Meydanı) and Taksim, where commuters can transfer to the funicular or to another metro heading to Nişantaşı and the ritzy residential and commercial suburbs to its north.

➡ **Bus** Buses to every part of the city leave from the chaotic bus station at Taksim Meydanı.

TOP SIGHTS
İSTİKLAL CADDESİ

Once called the Grand Rue de Pera but renamed İstiklal (Independence) in the early years of the Republic, Beyoğlu's premier boulevard is a perfect metaphor for 21st-century Turkey. A long pedestrianised strip cluttered with shops, cafes, cinemas and cultural centres, it showcases İstanbul's Janus-like personality, embracing modernity one minute and happily bowing to tradition the next.

At its northern end is frantically busy Taksim Meydanı, the symbolic heart of the modern city. Here, a constant stream of locals arrive by car, bus, funicular and metro to shop, eat and be entertained. At its southern end is the relatively tranquil district of Galata, home to crooked cobble-stone lanes and traces of a fortified settlement built by Genoese merchants in the 13th century.

In the 19th century, traders and diplomats from Europe brought new ideas to Ottoman daily life and the streets of Pera (as Beyoğlu was originally called). The Europeans who lived here imported new fashions, machines, arts and manners to the city. This part of town had telephones, the world's second-oldest underground train (the Tünel), tramways (one still functioning), electric light and a modern municipal government. There were even European-style patisseries and shopping arcades, a number of which remain. In contrast, the Historic Peninsula (Old Stamboul) on the opposite side of the Golden Horn kept its oriental bazaars, great mosques, draughty palaces, narrow streets and traditional values.

Today, promenading along the length of İstiklal is the most popular activity in town, and huge crowds of İstanbullus head here in the early evening and at weekends to browse in boutiques and bookshops, see exhibitions at galleries including SALT Beyoğlu and ARTER, listen to the street buskers, drink coffee in chain cafes and party in *meyhanes* (taverns). We highly recommend that you join them.

DON'T MISS...

➡ Çiçek Pasajı
➡ Balık Pazarı
➡ SALT Beyoğlu
➡ ARTER

PRACTICALITIES

➡ Independence Ave
➡ Map p236

İSTANBUL MODERN

In recent years İstanbul's contemporary-art scene has boomed. Facilitated by the active cultural philanthropy of the country's industrial dynasties (many of which have built extraordinary art collections), museum buildings are opening nearly as often as art exhibitions. İstanbul Modern, funded by the Eczcıbaşı family, is the big daddy of them all. Opened with great fanfare in 2005, this huge converted shipping terminal has a stunning location right on the shores of the Bosphorus at Tophane and is easily accessed by tram from Sultanahmet.

The museum's curatorial program is twofold: the 1st floor highlights the Eczcıbaşı family's collection of Turkish 20th-century and contemporary art using a thematic approach; the downstairs spaces host temporary exhibitions from local and international artists. Look for works by Şekere Ahmet Ali Paşa (1841–1907), Orhan Peker (1926–78), İsmet Doğan (1957–), Ömer Kaleşi (1932–), Cihat Burak (1915–94), Tayfun Erdoğmuş (1958–), İhsan Cemal Karaburçak (1897–1970), Avni Arbaş (1919–2003), Selma Gürbüz (1960–), Alaaddin Aksoy (1942–), Fahreinissa Zeid (1901–91), Nurullah Berk (1906–82) and Adnan Çoker (1927–), plus the temporary exhibitions and permanent installations.

Of the permanent works on display, don't miss *False Ceiling* (installation; Richard Wentworth; 1995–2005) downstairs and *The Road to Tate Modern* (video; Erkan Özgen and Şener Özmen; 2003), an ironic reworking of Cervantes' *Don Quixote*, in the upstairs projection room.

Also of note are the museum's cafe (p125) and gift shop (p136).

DON'T MISS...

➡ Shows in the main temporary gallery

➡ *False Ceiling*

➡ *The Road to Tate Modern*

PRACTICALITIES

➡ İstanbul Modern Sanat Müzesi

➡ Map p240

➡ www.istanbul modern.org

➡ Meclis-i Mebusan Caddesi, Tophane

➡ adult/student/ under 12yr ₺15/8/free

➡ ⊘10am-6pm Tue, Wed & Fri-Sun, to 8pm Thu

➡ 🚋Tophane

◉ SIGHTS

◉ Galata, Tophane & Karaköy

İSTANBUL MODERN MUSEUM
See p116.

JEWISH MUSEUM OF TURKEY MUSEUM
Map p240 (500 Yil Vakfi Türk Musevileri, The Quincentennial Foundation Museum of Turkish Jews; www.muze500.com; Perçemli Sokak, Karaköy; admission ₺10; ☺10am-4pm Mon-Thu, to 2pm Fri & Sun; ⓜKaraköy) Housed in the ornate 19th-century Zullfaris synagogue near the Galata Bridge, this museum was established in 2001 to commemorate the 500th anniversary of the arrival of the Sephardic Jews in the Ottoman Empire. Its modest but extremely well-intentioned collection comprises photographs, papers and objects that document the mostly harmonious co-existence between Jews and the Muslim majority in this country.

The history of the Jews in Turkey is as long as it is fascinating. In the late 15th century, Isaac Sarfati, Chief Rabbi of Edirne, wrote the following to brethren in Germany: 'Brothers and teachers, friends and acquaintances! I, Isaac Sarfati, proclaim to you that Turkey is a land wherein nothing is lacking, and where, if you will, all shall yet be well with you...Here, every man may dwell at peace under his own vine and fig tree.' At around the same time, Sultan Beyazıt II proclaimed '...the Jews of Spain should not be refused, but rather be welcomed with warm feelings'. Alas, this enlightened state didn't last through the centuries, and Jewish Turks were made to feel considerably less welcome when racially motivated 'wealth taxes' were introduced in 1942 and violence against Jews and other minorities was unleashed in 1955, prompting many families to flee the country. More recently Islamist terrorists have bombed synagogues on a number of occasions. Despite these recent events, the museum chooses to focus on the positive rather than the negative.

Approximately 23,000 Jews currently live in Turkey, with most residing in İstanbul. Sephardic Jews make up approximately 96% of this number, while the rest are primarily Ashkenazic. Today there are a total of 16 synagogues in İstanbul, all of which are Sephardic except for one. For a list of these see www.jewish-europe.net/turkey/en/synagogue.

ARAB MOSQUE MOSQUE
Map p240 (Arap Camıı; Galata Mahkemesi Sokak, Galata; ⓜKaraköy) Built by the Genoese in 1337, this mosque was the largest of İstanbul's Latin churches. It was converted to a mosque after the Conquest and given to the recently arrived community of Spanish Muslims after their expulsion from Spain and arrival in İstanbul in the late 15th century. Notable features include the impressive stone exterior and a magnificent wooden ceiling.

SALT GALATA CULTURAL CENTRE
Map p240 (www.saltonline.org/en; Bankalar Caddesi 11, Karaköy; ☺noon-8pm Tue-Sat, 10.30am-6pm Sun; ⓜKaraköy) The descriptor 'cultural centre' is used a lot in İstanbul, but is often a misnomer. Here at SALT Galata it really does apply. Housed in a magnificent 1892 bank building designed by Alexandre Vallaury and cleverly adapted by local architectural firm Mimarlar Tasarım, this cutting-edge institution offers an exhibition space, auditorium, arts research library, cafe and glamorous rooftop restaurant.

Funded by the Garanti Bank, SALT aims to be a centre of learning and debate in the city and hosts regular conferences, lectures and workshops. The building also houses a small Ottoman Bank Museum.

KASA GALERİ GALLERY
Map p240 (http://kasagaleri.sabanciuniv.edu; Bankalar Caddesi 2, Karaköy; ☺9am-5pm Mon-Sat; ⓜKaraköy) Kasa Galeri is located in the basement vault of the Minerva Han, a splendid Islamic Revival–style building that was built as the Greek-owned Bank of Athens in the early 20th century. Funded by Sabaci University, it supports and exhibits collaborative international art projects that are experimental in nature. It also offers residencies and shows to emerging Turkish artists.

SCHNEİDERTEMPEL ART CENTER GALLERY
Map p240 (Schneidertempel Sanat Merkezi; www.schneidertempel.com; Felek Sokak 1, Galata; ☺10.30am-5pm Mon-Fri, noon-4pm Sun; ⓜKaraköy) Housed in an old synagogue, the Schneidertempel exhibits work by local Jewish artists, as well as frequent exhibitions from abroad. Quality varies, but we've seen some excellent photographic exhibitions here.

GALATA TOWER
LANDMARK

Map p240 (Galata Kulesi; www.galatatower.net; Galata Meydanı, Galata; admission ₺12; ⊙9am-8pm; 🚇Karaköy) The cylindrical Galata Tower stands sentry over the approach to 'new' İstanbul. Constructed in 1348, it was the tallest structure in the city for centuries, and it still dominates the skyline north of the Golden Horn. Its vertiginous upper balcony offers 360-degree views of the city, but we're not convinced that the view (though spectacular) justifies the steep admission cost.

CHRIST CHURCH
CHURCH

Map p240 (Crimean Memorial Church; ☑0555 810 1010; Serdar-i Ekrem Sokak 52, Galata; ⊙services 10am Sunday; 🚇Karaköy, then funicular to Tünel) The cornerstone of this Gothic-style Anglican church was laid in 1858 by Lord Stratford de Redcliffe, known as 'The Great Elchi' (elçi meaning ambassador) because of his paramount influence in mid-19th-century Ottoman affairs. The largest of the city's Protestant churches, it was dedicated in 1868 as the Crimean Memorial Church and restored and renamed in the mid-1990s.

Inside, there is a painted rood screen by Scottish artist Mungo McCosh that depicts notable İstanbul residents (mainly expats). The church's chaplain and congregation are actively involved in refugee welfare within the city.

To visit, attend the Sunday service or SMS the chaplain to organise a convenient time.

DEPO
CULTURAL CENTRE

Map p240 (www.depoistanbul.net; Lüleci Hendek Caddesi 12, Tophane; ⊙11am-7pm Tue-Sun; 🚇Tophane) Occupying a former tobacco warehouse, this alternative space is operated by **Anadolu Kültür** (www.anadolukultur .org), a not-for-profit organisation that facilitates artistic collaboration, promotes cultural exchange and stimulates debates on social and political issues relevant to Turkey, the South Caucasus, the Middle East and the Balkans. It hosts talks, exhibitions and film screenings. The **Rodeo** (www.rodeo gallery.com) commercial contemporary-art gallery is also located here.

GALATA MEVLEVİ MUSEUM
MUSEUM

Map p240 (Galata Mevlevihanesi Müzesi; www .mekder.org; Galipdede Caddesi 15, Tünel; admission ₺5; ⊙9am-4.30pm Tue-Sun; 🚇Karaköy,

then funicular to Tünel) The semahane at the centre of this tekke (dervish lodge) was erected in 1491 and renovated in 1608 and 2009. It is part of a complex including a meydan-ı şerif (courtyard), çeşme (drinking fountain), türbesi (tomb) and hamuşan (cemetery). The oldest of six historic Mevlevihaneleri (Mevlevi tekkes) remaining in İstanbul, the complex was converted into a museum in 1946.

The Mevlevi tarika (order), founded in the central Anatolian city of Konya during the 13th century, flourished throughout the Ottoman Empire. Like several other orders, the Mevlevis stressed the unity of humankind before God regardless of creed.

Taking their name from the great Sufi mystic and poet Celaleddin Rumi (1207–73), called Mevlana (Our Leader) by his disciples, Mevlevis seek to achieve mystical communion with God through a sema (ceremony) involving chants, prayers, music and a whirling dance. This tekke's first şeyh (sheikh) was Şemaî Mehmed Çelebi, a grandson of the great Mevlana.

Dervish orders were banned in the early days of the Turkish republic because of their ultraconservative religious politics. Although the ban has been lifted, only a handful of functioning tekkes remain in İstanbul, including this one. Konya remains the heart of the Mevlevi order.

Beneath the semahane is a fascinating exhibit that includes displays of Mevlevi clothing, turbans and accessories. The mahfiller (upstairs floor) houses the tekke's collection of traditional musical instruments, calligraphy and ebru (paper marbling).

The hamuşan is full of stones with graceful Ottoman inscriptions, including the tomb of Galip Dede, the 17th-century Sufi poet whom the street is named after. The shapes atop the stones reflect the headgear of the deceased, each hat denoting a different religious rank.

For more on the whirling dervish ceremonies see the boxed text.

◉ İstiklal & Around

PATISSERIE LEBON
HISTORIC BUILDING

Map p240 (İstiklal Caddesi 360-362; 🚇Karaköy, then funicular to Tünel) In Pera's heyday, there was no more-glamorous spot to see and be

SEEING THE DERVISHES WHIRL

If you thought the Hare Krishnas or the Harlem congregations were the only religious orders to celebrate their faith through music and movement, think again. Those sultans of spiritual spin known as the 'whirling dervishes' have been twirling their way to a higher plane ever since the 13th century and show no sign of slowing down.

There are a number of opportunities to see dervishes whirling in İstanbul. Probably the best of these is the weekly ceremony held in the *semahane* (hall) in the Galata Mevlevi Museum (p135) in Tünel.

Another good option is to attend one of the *semas* (ceremonies) held most Monday nights at a *tekke* (dervish lodge) in Karagumruk in the Fatih District and Thursday nights at a *tekke* in Silivrikapi, also in Fatih. These are the real deal, not performances put on for tourists. Note, though, that chanting – rather than whirling – is the main event. The easiest way to attend is to go with Les Arts Turcs (p82), a cultural tourism company that charges ₺60 per person to give you a briefing about the meaning of the ceremony, take you to the *tekkes* from its office near Aya Sofya and bring you back after the ceremony.

For a more touristy experience, the Hocapaşa Culture Centre (p80), housed in a beautifully converted 15th-century hamam near Eminönü, presents whirling dervish performances four evenings per week throughout the year.

Remember that the ceremony is a religious one – by whirling, the adherents believe that they are attaining a higher union with God – so don't talk, leave your seat or take flash photographs while the dervishes are spinning or chanting.

BEYOĞLU SIGHTS

seen than Patisserie Lebon. Its gorgeous art nouveau interior featured chandeliers, a decorative tiled floor and large tiled wall panels designed by Alexandre Vallaury, the architect of the Pera Palace Hotel (p119). Though now sadly functioning as a fast-food joint, much of its interior has been retained.

The patisserie is one of the best-loved buildings in Beyoğlu, as much for its history as for its interior design. After decades as the Lebon, the business was taken over by Avedis Çakır in 1940 and renamed Patisserie Markiz. It continued to trade until the 1960s, when Pera's decline and a lack of customers led to its closure. Fortunately, closure didn't mean destruction – the building was boarded up and left just as it had been, fittings and all. In the 1970s local artists and writers lobbied the authorities to have the patisserie and adjoining shopping arcade added to the country's register of historical buildings; this occurred in 1977, ensuring the entire building's preservation.

In late 2003 the magnificently restored patisserie re-opened to great acclaim. It had a short-lived and much-lamented second life as an upmarket patisserie, but has recently been reinvented as Yemek Kulübü, a cafe serving cheap coffee and food. Still, the glorious interior means that a stop here remains well worthwhile.

PERA PALACE HOTEL HISTORIC BUILDING
Map p236 (Pera Palas Oteli; www.perapalace.com; Meşrutiyet Caddesi 52, Tepebaşı; 🚊Karaköy, then funicular to Tünel) The Pera Palas was a project of Georges Nagelmackers, the Belgian entrepreneur who linked Paris and Constantinople with his famous Orient Express train service. The 1892 building has undergone a €23-million restoration in recent years and claims to have regained its position as İstanbul's most glamorous hotel. Its bar, patisserie, tea lounge and restaurant are open to the public.

Nagelmackers founded the Compagnie Internationale des Wagons-Lits et Grands Express Européens in 1868. The Orient Express service first operated in 1883 and Nagelmackers soon realised that İstanbul had no suitably luxurious hotels where his esteemed passengers could stay. His solution was to build one himself, and he commissioned the fashionable İstanbul-born but French-trained architect Alexandre Vallaury to design it.

On opening, the hotel advertised itself as having 'a thoroughly healthy situation, being high up and isolated on all four sides', and 'overlooking the Golden Horn and the whole panorama of Stamboul'. Its guests included Agatha Christie, who supposedly wrote *Murder on the Orient Express* in Room 411; Mata Hari, who no doubt frequented the elegant bar with its lovely stained-glass windows and excellent eaves-dropping opportunities; and Greta Garbo, who probably enjoyed her own company in one of the spacious suites.

PERA MUSEUM
MUSEUM

Map p236 (Pera Müzesi; www.peramuzesi.org.tr; Meşrutiyet Caddesi 65, Tepebaşı; adult/student/child under 12yr ₺10/7/free; ⊙10am-7pm Tue-Sat, noon-6pm Sun; ⛴Karaköy, then funicular to Tünel) Head to this museum to admire works from Suna and İnan Kıraç's splendid collection of paintings featuring Turkish Orientalist themes. A changing program of thematic exhibitions provide fascinating glimpses into the Ottoman world from the 17th to the early 20th century. Some works are realistic, others highly romanticised – all are historically fascinating.

The most beloved painting in the Turkish canon – Osman Hamdı Bey's *The Tortoise Trainer* (1906) – is the stand-out work in the collection, but there's plenty more to see, including a permanent exhibit of Kütahya tiles and ceramics, and a somewhat esoteric collection of Anatolian weights and measures.

SALT BEYOĞLU
CULTURAL CENTRE

Map p236 (www.saltonline.org/en; İstiklal Caddesi 136; ⊙noon-8pm Tue-Sat, 10.30am-6pm Sun; ⛴Karaköy, then funicular to Tünel) Its three floors of exhibition space, bookshop, walk-in cinema and cafe make SALT Beyoğlu nearly as impressive as its Galata-based sibling. Occupying a former apartment building dating from the 1850s, it shows the work of both high-profile and emerging international and local artists.

GALERIST
GALLERY

Map p236 (www.galerist.com.tr; 1st fl, Meşrutiyet Caddesi 67, Tepebaşı; ⊙11am-7pm Tue-Sat; ⛴Karaköy, then funicular to Tünel) The most fashionable of the city's commercial galleries and the only one with a strong international profile, Galerist is owned by architect Melkan Gürsel Tabanlıoğlu and serious (ie megamoneyed) art collector Taha Tatlıcı. It shows Turkish artists working in a variety of media. The gallery's second space is located in the rapidly gentrifying suburb of Hasköy on the Golden Horn.

ARTER
GALLERY

Map p236 (www.arter.org.tr; İstiklal Caddesi 211; ⊙11am-7pm Tue-Thu, noon-8pm Fri-Sun; ⛴Karaköy, then funicular to Tünel) Funded by the Vehbi Koç Foundation, this four-floor contemporary-arts space has been neck-and-neck with the Garanti Bank's SALT cultural centres in the race for the accolade of most exciting new arts venue in the city. In our view, the result is a tie. Come here to see shows by Turkish and international artists of the calibre of Mona Hatoum.

GALERI NEV
GALLERY

Map p236 (www.galerinevistanbul.com; 4th & 5th fl, Mısır Apt, İstiklal Caddesi 163; ⊙11am-6.30pm Tue-Sat; ⛴Karaköy, then funicular to Tünel) One of the city's oldest and most impressive commercial galleries, Nev counts many of the country's best-known modernists among its stable of artists.

ÇİÇEK PASAJI
HISTORIC BUILDING

Map p236 (Flower Passage; İstiklal Caddesi; ⛴Kabataş, then funicular to Taksim) Back when promenading down the Grand Rue de Pera (now İstiklal Caddesi) was the height of fashion, the Cité de Pera building was İstanbul's most glamorous address. Built in 1876 and decorated in Second Empire style, it housed a shopping arcade and apartments. The arcade is now known as the Çiçek Pasajı (Flower Passage) and is full of boisterous *meyhanes*.

As Pera declined in the mid-20th century, so too did this building. Its once-stylish shops gave way to rough *meyhanes* where beer barrels were rolled out onto the pavement, marble slabs were balanced on top, wooden stools were arranged and enthusiastic revellers caroused the night away. It continued in this vein until the late 1970s, when parts of the building collapsed. When it was reconstructed, the arcade acquired a glass canopy to protect pedestrians from bad weather, its makeshift barrels and stools were replaced with solid wooden tables and benches, and its broken pavement was covered with smooth tiles. These days its raffish charm is nearly gone and most locals bypass the touts and the mediocre food on offer here and instead make their way behind the passage to the *meyhanes* on or around Nevizade Sokak.

BALIK PAZARI
MARKET

Map p236 (Fish Market; Şahne Sokak off İstiklal Caddesi, Galatasaray; ⛴Kabataş, then funicular to Taksim) Next to the Çiçek Pasajı. Full of small stands selling *midye tava* (skewered mussels fried in hot oil), *kokoreç* (seasoned lamb or mutton intestines wrapped around a skewer and grilled over charcoal) and other snacks. You'll also find shops selling fish, caviar, fruit, vegetables and other produce; most of these are in Duduodaları Sokak on the left (southern) side of the market.

Many of the shops have been here for close on a century and have extremely loyal clientele – check out **Sütte Şarküteri** (Map p236; ☑212-293 9292; Duduodatarı Sokak 13, Balık Pazarı, Galatasaray; ☺8am-10pm; 🚇Kabataş, then funicular to Taksim) for its delicious charcuterie, *kaymak* (clotted cream) and take-away sandwiches; **Tarihi Beyoğlu Ekmek Fırını** (Map p236; Duduodaları Sokak 5, Balık Pazarı, Galatasaray; 🚇Kabataş, then funicular to Taksim) for fresh bread; **Üç Yıldız Şekerleme** (Map p236; ☑212-293 8170; www.ucyildizsekerleme.com; Duduodaları Sokak 7, Balık Pazarı, Galatasaray; ☺7am-8.30pm Mon-Sat, 9am-6pm Sun; 🚇Kabataş, then funicular to Taksim) for jams, *lokum* (Turkish Delight) and sweets; **Petek Turşuları** (Map p236; Duduodaları Sokak 6, Balık Pazarı, Galatasaray; 🚇Kabataş, then funicular to Taksim) for pickles; and **Reşat Balık Market** (Map p236; ☑212-293 6091; Sahne Sokak 30, Balık Pazarı, Galatasaray; 🚇Kabataş, then funicular to Taksim) for caviar and the city's best *lakerda* (strongly flavored salted kingfish).

At 24a, look for the gigantic black doors to the courtyard of the Üç Horan Ermeni Kilisesi (Armenian Church of Three Altars), which dates from 1838. Visitors can enter the church providing the doors are open. On the opposite side of the street is the neoclassical **Avrupa Pasajı** (European Passage; Map p236), an attractive arcade full of shops that once sold antiques but now seem to stock little except tourist tat.

GALERI APEL   GALLERY

Map p236 (www.galleryapel.com; Hayriye Caddesi 5a, Galatasaray; ☺11.30am-6.30pm Tue-Sat, closed Aug; 🚇Kabataş, then funicular to Taksim) This long-established commercial gallery behind the Galatasaray Lycée has a large stable of Turkish artists working in a number of media. Its shows are always worth a visit.

MUSEUM OF INNOCENCE   MUSEUM

Map p240 (www.masumiyetmuzesi.org; Dalgıç Çıkmazı 2, off Çukurcuma Caddesi, Çukurcuma; admission ₺25; ☺10am-6pm Tue-Sun, to 9pm Fri; 🚇Tophane) His status as a Nobel laureate deserves respect, but we feel obliged to say that we think Orhan Pamuk is a bit cheeky to charge a whopping ₺25 for entrance to his new museum. That said, this long-anticipated museum/piece of conceptual art is worth a visit, particularly if you have read and admired the novel it celebrates.

The museum is set in a 19th-century house and seeks to evoke and re-create aspects of Pamuk's 1988 novel *The Museum of Innocence* by displaying found objects in traditional museum-style glass cases. It also includes strangely beautiful installations such as a wall displaying the 4213 cigarette butts supposedly smoked by the book's heroine Füsun. In all, the exhibits are successful in evoking what Pamuk has described as 'the melancholy of the period' in which he grew up and in which the novel is set.

AKBANK ART CENTRE   CULTURAL CENTRE

Map p236 (Akbank Sanat; www.akbanksanat.com; cnr İstiklal Caddesi & Zambak Sokak; ☺10.30am-7.30pm Tue-Sat; 🚇Kabataş, then funicular to Taksim Meydanı) Turkey's big banks and philanthropic trusts vie with each other to be seen as the greatest sponsor of the arts. İstiklal is a showcase for their generosity, and with this venue Akbank joins SALT Beyoğlu and ARTER in offering a showcase for the city's thriving arts scene. It has an art gallery, performance hall, dance studio, music-listening studio and arts library.

The centre is the venue for the Akbank-sponsored İstanbul Jazz and Short Film Festivals as well as for performances by the Akbank Chamber Orchestra.

TAKSİM MEYDANI   SQUARE

Map p236 (🚇Kabataş, then funicular to Taksim) Named after the 18th-century stone *taksim* (water storage unit) on its western side, this busy square is the symbolic heart of modern İstanbul. Hardly a triumph of urban design, it is home to a chaotic bus terminus, a cultural centre, the upmarket Marmara Hotel and an often-overlooked monument to the founding of the Republic.

The Atatürk Cultural Centre was designed by Hayati Tabanlıoğlu in 1956–57 and appears to best advantage at night, when its elegant steel mesh is illuminated. It is currently undergoing long-overdue restoration works.

The **Republic Monument** (Cumhuriyet Anıtı Map p236) was created by Canonica, an Italian sculptor, in 1928. This features Atatürk, his assistant and successor, İsmet İnönü, and other revolutionary leaders.

GEORGE TSAFOS/GETTY IMAGES ©

IZZET KERIBAR ©

1. Galata Tower (p118)
Once the tallest structure in the city

2. Outdoor life in Beyoğlu (p124)
Traditional *meyhane* (Turkish tavern)

3. Leb-i Derya, İstiklal (p133)
Food and drinks come with views of the Old City

4. Camondo Stairs (p128)
To be seen on a walking tour of Galata

IZZET KERIBAR ©

When this book went to print, İstanbul's newspapers were full of heated debate about the future of the square after the mayor of Beyoğlu, Ahmet Misbah Demircan, announced plans to redevelop the public park behind the bus terminal on the northeast side of the square as a shopping mall. Local activists cited it as one of many current instances of public space being sold off to private developers without proper public consultation or approval. The site, which has been a park since the early 1940s, was previousy occupied by an Ottoman military barracks.

✖ EATING

A recent local-government ban on outdoor drinking in Beyoğlu has had a sorry impact on this neighbourhood's restaurant and bar scene, sending some venues with streetside seating broke and causing the interior dining spaces of others to become unpleasantly crowded. We, like many locals, can only hope that good sense prevails and that the ban is rescinded in the near future. The only enclave to escape the ban was Nevizade Sokak behind the Balık Pazarı, which continues to host boisterous crowds on weekend evenings. The food in the restaurants here is adequate rather than memorable, but the atmosphere is always fun.

✖ Galata, Tophane & Karaköy

TOP CHOICE **KARAKÖY GÜLLÜOĞLU** SWEETS, BÖREK $
Map p240 (www.karakoygulluoglu.com; Kemankeş Caddesi, Karaköy; baklava ₺4-7, börek ₺6; ⊙8am-11pm; ⊠Karaköy) This Karaköy institution has been making customers deliriously happy and dentists obscenely rich since 1947. Head to the register and order a *porsiyon* (portion) of whatever baklava takes your fancy (*fıstıklı* is pistachio, *cevizli* walnut and *sade* plain), preferably with a glass of tea. Then hand your ticket over to the servers. The *börek* (filled pastry) here is good, too.

TOP CHOICE **LOKANTA MAYA** MODERN TURKISH $$
Map p240 (✆212-252 6884; www.lokantamaya .com; Kemankeş Caddesi 35a, Karaköy; mezes ₺11-28, mains ₺26-35; ⊙lunch Mon-Sat, dinner Tue-Sat, brunch Sun; ✈; ⊠Karaköy) Critics and

---

WORTH A DETOUR

NİŞANTAŞI

If you're a dab hand at air-kissing and striking a pose over a caffe latte, you'll feel totally at home in Nişantaşı. Serious shoppers, visiting celebs, PR professionals and the city's gilded youth gravitate towards this upmarket enclave, which is located about 2km north of Taksim Meydanı and is accessed via the metro (Osmanbey stop). Bars, restaurants, boutique hotels and international fashion and design shops are found in the streets surrounding the main artery, Teşvikiye Caddesi, prompting some locals to refer to that area as Teşvikiye.

If you decide to spend a day or half-day shopping here, consider taking a break and eating at **Hünkar** (✆212-225 4665; www.hunkar1950.com; Mim Kemal Öke Caddesi 21; portions ₺14-22; ⊙noon-10.30pm; ⊠Osmanbey), one of the best *lokantas* (restaurants serving ready made food) in the city; **Borsa** (✆212-232 4201; www.borsarestaurant.com; Lütfi Kırdar Congress Centre, Harbiye; starters ₺9-38, mains ₺35-48; ⊙lunch & dinner), an upmarket restaurant with an outdoor terrace; or Slow Food–favourite **Kantın** (✆212-219 3114; www.kantin.biz; Akkavak Sokağı 30; salads ₺10-18, mains ₺16-30; ⊙11.30am-9pm Mon-Sat; ⊠Osmanbey), one of the city's best bistros.

Those keen to acquire some of the culinary excellence that Nişantaşı is known for should consider signing up for a cooking class or foodie walk with Selin Rozanes' **Turkish Flavours** (✆0532 218 0653; www.turkishflavours.com; Apt 3, Vali Konağı Caddesi 14; cooking classes US$100, per person tours US$100-145).

Nişantaşı is the fashion hub of the city, and the queen of the local industry is undoubtedly **Gönül Paksoy** (✆212-261 9081; Atiye Sokak 6a; ⊙10am-7pm Mon-Sat; Osmanbey), who creates and sells pieces that transcend fashion and step into art.

İSTANBUL'S FOOD CULTURE

Ansel Mullins and Yigal Schleifer produce **Culinary Backstreets** (www.culinaryback streets.com), an excellent blog that investigates the traditional food culture of the city. Here, they recommend some of their favourite shopping, eating and drinking destinations:

Favourite Produce Market in İstanbul

The Kastamonu market held in Piyalepaşa Bulvarı in Kasimpaşa early on Sunday mornings.

Favourite Produce Shops

➡ Online shopping at **İpek Hanım Çiftliği** (www.ipekhanim.com; İpek Hanım's Farm).

➡ Titiz Manav (Titez Greengrocer) in Beyoglu's Balık Pazarı (p120).

Best Foodie Strip

The side streets of the Kadıköy Produce Market.

Most Exciting Food Trend

Chefs focusing on local, traditional cuisine rather than the latest international fad.

Worst Food Trend

Local fast-food chains. On the one hand, it's better to see a *cığ köfte* (raw spiced meatball) chain than another McDonald's, but these local fast-food chains threaten the livelihood of *ustas* (real craftsmen).

Foodie Institutions That Have Stood the Test of Time

➡ Manda Batmaz (p132) for a Turkish coffee.

➡ Cıya Sofrası (p149) for some of the best and most diverse Anatolian cooking in the city.

➡ Asmalı Cavit (p126), where the classic *meyhane* (tavern) tradition is protected.

Most Romantic Eating Destination

A sunset dinner on the edge of the Bosphorus at **Kandilli Suna'nin Yeri** (☎216-332 3241; Kandilli İskele Cad 4-17, Kandilli; ☺daily), a casual fish restaurant on the Asian side of town.

chowhounds alike are raving about the dishes created by chef Didem Şenol at her stylish restaurant near the Karaköy docks. The author of a successful cookbook focusing on Aegean cuisine, Didem's food is light, flavoursome, occasionally quirky and always assured – everyone eats well here. You'll need to book for dinner; lunch is cheaper and more casual.

KARAKÖY LOKANTASI   MEYHANE, LOKANTA **$$**
Map p240 (☎212-292 4455; Kemankeş Caddesi 37a, Karaköy; mezes ₺6-10, portions ₺7-12, grills ₺11-16; ☺dinner daily, lunch Mon-Sat; ☑; ⊟Karaköy) Known for its gorgeous tiled interior, genial owner and bustling vibe, Karaköy Lokantası serves tasty and well-priced food to its loyal local clientele. It functions as a *lokanta* during the day, but at night it morphs into a *meyhane*, with slightly higher prices. Bookings are essential for dinner.

CA' D'ORO   ITALIAN **$$**
Map p240 (☎212-243 8292; www.istanbuldoors .com; Bankalar Caddesi 11, Galata; starters ₺10-29, pizzas ₺15-21, mains ₺18-55; ☺lunch & dinner Tue-Sun; ☑; ⊟Karaköy) The glamorous rooftop restaurant at the SALT Galata cultural centre serves *molto buono* Italian staples such as pasta, pizza and risotto, but is most memorable for its extraordinary view over the Golden Horn to the Historic Peninsula. Vegetarians will appreciate the generous array of suitable options on the menu.

İSTANBUL MODERN
CAFE/RESTAURANT   INTERNATIONAL **$$$**
Map p240 (☎212-292 2612; Meclis-i Mebusan Caddesi, Tophane; pizzas ₺19-28, pasta ₺19-33, mains ₺28-55; ☺10am-midnight ; ☑; ⊟Tophane) The cafe-restaurant at İstanbul's preeminent contemporary-art museum offers an 'industrial arty' vibe and great views over

the Bosphorus when there are no cruise ships moored in front. The pasta is home-made, pizzas are Italian-style and service is slick – all of which makes for a happy lunch experience. For a table on the terrace you'll need to book ahead.

GALATA HOUSE
GEORGIAN $$

Map p240 (Galata Evi; 212-245 1861; www .thegalatahouse.com; Galata Kulesi Sokak 61; starters ₺14-16, mains ₺18-25, desserts ₺10-12; noon-midnight Tue-Sun; Karaköy) This would have to be one of the most eccentric restaurants in town. Run by the charming husband-and-wife team of Nadire and Mete Göktuğ, it is housed in the Old British Jail, just down from Galata Tower. Nadire uses recipes handed down from her Georgian mother to concoct simple comfort food and also plays the piano and sings for guests.

The jail functioned from 1904 to 1919, and has been sympathetically but comfortably restored by Mete, who is one of İstanbul's most prominent heritage architects.

KİVA HAN
ANATOLIAN $$

Map p240 (www.galatakivahan.com; Galata Kulesı Meydanı 4, Galata; soup ₺5, veg portions ₺10-15, meat portions ₺10-20; 11am-11pm; Karaköy) Located in the shadow of Galata Tower, this *lokanta* specialises in seasonal dishes from the different regions of Turkey. Inspect the ready-made food on display before choosing, as we have found that not all dishes are successful here. The mezes tend to be more impressive than the mains.

FASULİ LOKANTALARI
ANATOLIAN $

Map p240 (www.fasuli.com.tr; Tophane İskele Caddesi 10-12, Tophane; beans & rice ₺13; Tophane) There are two types of *fasulye* (bean dishes) served in Turkey: Erzincan-style beans cooked in a spicy tomato sauce, and Black Sea–style beans cooked in a red gravy full of butter and meat. This *lokanta* next to the nargile joints in Tophane serves its beans Black Sea–style, and they are truly delicious. There's another branch in Sirkeci (p79).

GÜNEY RESTAURANT
TURKISH $$

Map p240 (www.guneyrestaurant.com.tr; Kuledibi Şah Kapısı 6, Galata; portions ₺10-20, grills ₺12-24; 7am-midnight Mon-Sat; Karaköy) You'll be lucky if you can fight your way through the crowds of hungry locals to claim a lunch-time table at this bustling eatery directly opposite Galata Tower. Friendly waiters will set you up with a basket of fresh bread and point you towards the array of mezes and hot dishes on display.

NAMLI
DELI $

Map p240 (www.namligida.com.tr; Rıhtım Caddesi 1, Karaköy; 7am-10pm; ; Karaköy) As well as being one of the best delicatessens in the city, Namlı stocks hard-to-find Asian ingredients, imported tea and other treats. Take away your choice from the impressive salad and meze selection, or grab one of the tables at the front and eat in. There's another branch (p97) on Harıcılar Caddesi next to the Spice Market in Eminönü.

GALATA KONAK PATISSERIE CAFE
CAFE $$

Map p240 (www.galatakonakcafe.com; Hacı Ali Sokak 2, Galata; 10am-10pm; Karaköy) After checking out the pastries and cakes on sale in the ground-floor patisserie, make your way up the stairs to the rooftop terrace cafe, where you can order anything that has taken your fancy downstairs and enjoy it with a tea or coffee. The view from the terrace encompasses the Sultanahmet skyline, the Bosphorus and the Golden Horn.

İstiklal & Around

TOP CHOICE ASMALI CAVİT
MEYHANE $$

Map p240 (Asmalı Meyhane; 212-292 4950; Asmalımescit Sokak 16, Asmalımescit; mezes ₺6-20, mains ₺18-24; Karaköy, then funicular to Tünel) Cavit Saatcı's place is quite possibly the best *meyhane* in the city. The old-fashioned interior gives no clue as to the excellence of the food on offer. Stand-out dishes include *yaprak ciğer* (liver fried with onions), *patlıcan salatası* (eggplant salad), *muska boreği* (filo stuffed with beef and onion) and *kalamar tava* (fried calamari). Bookings essential.

TOP CHOICE MEZE BY LEMON TREE
MODERN TURKISH $$$

Map p236 (212-252 8302; www.mezze.com.tr; Meşrutiyet Caddesi 83b, Tepebaşı; mezes ₺8-25, mains ₺26-36; Karaköy, then funicular to Tünel) Chef Gençay Üçok creates some of the most interesting – and delicious – modern Turkish food seen in the city. Come to his small restaurant opposite the Pera Palace Hotel to sample triumphs such as the

CAFE CHAINS

In recent years, the city's fashionable streets and shopping malls have been colonised by an ever-proliferating colony of concept cafes. With designer interiors, strong visual branding, international menus and reasonable prices, these chains have been embraced by young İstanbullus with alacrity, and are great places to spend an hour or so people-watching over a coffee, drink or meal. Look out for branches of the following:

➡ **The House Cafe** The most glamorous of them all, with interiors by the uber-fashionable Autoban architectural group, menus by Australian/UK-trained chef Coşkun Uysal and prominent locations, including İstiklal Caddesi, Teşvikiye Caddesi in **Nişantası** (Teşvikiye Caddesi 146, Teşvikiye; Ⓜ Osmanbey), Sofyalı Sokak in **Asmalımescit** (Map p240; www.thehousecafe.com.tr; Sofyalı Sokak; Ⓕ Karaköy, then funicular to Taksim), Cevdet Paşa Caddesi in Bebek, and Ortaköy Meydanı on the Bosphorus. Best branch: **Ortaköy Meydanı** (Map p242; İskele Meydanı 42; breakfast platters ₺24, sandwiches ₺15-26, pizzas ₺17.50-27.50, mains ₺16.50-29.50; ⊙ 9am-1am Mon-Thu, to 2am Fri & Sat, to 10.30pm Sun; Ⓕ Kabataş Lisesi) – go for the Sunday brunch.

➡ **Kitchenette** House-baked bread and pastries are the hallmarks of these popular outfits, which are found in locations such as **Taksim** (Map p236; www.kitchenette.com.tr; Tak-ı Zafer Caddesi 3; Ⓕ Kabataş, then funicular to Taksim) and **Ortaköy** (Map p242; Eski Vapur İselesi ve Sağlık Sk 4). Best branch: **Bebek**, which occupies all three floors of a stunning art deco building opposite the Bebek ferry dock.

➡ **Midpoint** A laid-back West Coast American feel is evident here, with sleek but anonymous interiors and huge menus, featuring wraps, salads, crêpes, burgers and quesadillas. Best branch: **İstiklal Caddesi** (Map p236; www.midpoint.com.tr; İstiklal Caddesi 187; Ⓕ Karaköy, then funicular Tünel), which has a terrace complete with Bosphorus view.

monkfish casserole or grilled lamb sirloin with baked potatoes and red beets; both are sure to be highlights. Bookings essential.

ᵀᴼᴾ ᶜʰᵒⁱᶜᵉ ZÜBEYİR OCAKBAŞI   KEBAP $$

Map p236 (☎ 212-293 3951; www.zubeyirocakbasi .com; Bekar Sokak 28; mezes ₺4-6, kebaps ₺10-20; ⊙ noon-1am; Ⓕ Kabataş, then funicular to Taksim) Every morning, the chefs at this popular *ocakbaşı* (grill house) prepare the fresh, top-quality meats to be grilled over their handsome copper-hooded barbecues that night: spicy chicken wings and Adana kebaps, flavoursome ribs, pungent liver kebaps and well-marinated lamb *şış kebap* (roasted skewered meat). Their offerings are famous, so booking a table is essential.

SOFYALI 9   MEYHANE $$

Map p240 (☎ 212-245 0362; Sofyalı Sokak 9, Asmalımescit; mezes ₺2.50-10, mains ₺13-25; ⊙ closed Sun; Ⓕ Karaköy, then funicular to Tünel) Tables are hot property on a Friday or Saturday and no wonder. The food is fresh and tasty, and the atmosphere convivial. Stick to mezes rather than ordering mains: choose cold dishes from the waiter's tray, order hot ones from the menu. The *kalamar* (calamari)

and *Anavut ciğeri* (Albanian fried liver) are delicious.

ENSTİTÜ   MODERN INTERNATIONAL $$

Map p236 (www.istanbulculinary.com; Meşrutiyet Caddesi 59, Tepebaşı; soup ₺8, appetisers ₺8-20, mains ₺13-28, desserts ₺7-8; ⊙ 7.30am-10pm Mon-Fri, 10am-10pm Sat; ☑; Ⓕ Karaköy, then funicular to Tünel) This chic but casual cafe located on one of the city's most fashionable streets would look equally at home in Soho, Seattle or Sydney. Part of the İstanbul Culinary Institute, it offers a limited lunch menu that changes daily and a more-sophisticated dinner menu that makes full use of seasonal products. Prices are a steal considering the quality of the food.

ANTİOCHİA   ANATOLIAN $$

Map p240 (☎ 212-292 1100; www.antiochia concept.com; Minare Sokak 21a, Asmalımescit; mezes ₺8-10, mains ₺13-27; ⊙ lunch Mon-Fri, dinner Mon-Sat; Ⓕ Karaköy, then funicular to Tünel) Dishes from the southeastern city of Antakya (Hatay) are the speciality at this tiny (read cramped) restaurant. Mezes are dominated by wild thyme, pomegranate syrup, olives, walnuts and tangy homemade yoghurt,

START **GALATASARAY LYCÉE**
FINISH **SALT GALATA**
DISTANCE **1.4KM**
DURATION **TWO HOURS**

Neighbourhood Walk
Galatasaray to Galata

Start this walk in front of the
1 Galatasaray Lycée, a prestigious
public school located on the busy corner of
İstiklal and Yeniçarşı Caddesis. Established
in 1868 by Sultan Abdül Aziz, it educates
the sons of İstanbul's elite.

Walking south down İstiklal, you'll pass
the neo-Gothic **2** St Anthony's Cathedral on your left. Built between 1906 and
1911, it is one of two churches fronting the
street in this stretch.

Further south are two of the city's newest
and most exciting gallery spaces – **3** SALT
Beyoğlu and **5** ARTER. Both are housed in
historic buidings that have been imagina-
tively adapted.

Just before ARTER is the **4** Netherlands Consulate General, a handsome
1855 building by the Swiss-born Fossati
Brothers, who designed many buildings for
Sultan Abdülmecit I.

After passing the **6** Russian Consulate, another grand embassy designed
by the Fossati brothers, veer left down
Kumbaracı Caddesi and then into the first
street on your right.

Walk up the hill past **7** Christ Church
and then turn right into one of Beyoğlu's
most interesting shopping streets, Serdar-ı
Ekram Caddesi. Check out its edgy boutiques and consider having a break at bohemian **8** Mavra or chic **9** Le Fumoir.

Continue straight ahead to **10** Galata
Tower and then head down winding Camekan Sokak. You'll eventually come to the
sculptural **11** Camondo Stairs, commissioned and paid for by the famous banking
family of the same name. At the bottom is
Bankalar Caddesi, centre of the city's prosperous banking industry in the 19th century.
It's now home to **12** SALT Galata, where
you can end your walk enjoying a meal in the
rooftop restaurant with its fabulous views of
the Historic Peninsula and Golden Horn.

and the kebaps are equally flavoursome – try the succulent *şiş et* (grilled lamb) or *dürüm* (wrap filled with minced meat, onions and tomatoes).

CHANGA — MODERN INTERNATIONAL $$$

Map p236 (212-249 1348; www.changa-istanbul.com; Sıraselviler Caddesi 47, Taksim; starters ₺25-30, mains ₺35-55; ⊙6pm-1am Mon-Sat Nov-Jun; Kabataş, then funicular to Taksim) A number of eateries in İstanbul attempt fusion cuisine, but few do it well; this sophisticated restaurant is one that does. Most diners opt for the 10-course tasting menu (₺135 per person, minimum two people), but you can also order à la carte. In summer the action moves to the glamorous MüzedeChanga in the Sakıp Sabancı Museum (p155) on the Bosphorus.

MİKLA — MODERN TURKISH $$$

Map p236 (212-293 5656; www.miklarestaurant.com; Marmara Pera Hotel, Meşrutiyet Caddesi 15, Tepebaşı; appetisers ₺25-38, mains ₺51-79; ⊙dinner; Karaköy, then funicular to Tünel) Local celebrity chef Mehmet Gürs is a master of Mod Med, and the Turkish accents on the menu here make his food memorable. Extraordinary views, luxe surrounds and professional service complete the experience. Try the delicious Trakya Kıvırcık lamb dishes, consider a finale of the pistachio and *helva* ice cream and be sure to have a drink at the bar beforehand.

BRASSERIE LA BRISE — FRENCH $$$

Map p236 (212-244 4846; Asmalımescit Sokak 28, Asmalımescit; starters ₺15-30, mains ₺25-52; ⊙lunch & dinner Mon-Fri, dinner Sat; Karaköy, then funicular to Tünel) Hidden in a narrow street near the Pera Palace Hotel, La Brise leaves no Parisienne cliché unexplored, with Piaf on the sound system, mellow lighting in the dining room and a soupçon of attitude on the part of the waiters. The perfectly cooked fillet steak with Béarnaise or pepper sauce comes with wonderfully thick but crisp *pommes frites*.

ASMALI CANIM CİĞERİM — ANATOLIAN $

Map p236 (Minare Sokak 1, Asmalımescit; 5 skewers ₺12; Karaköy, then funicular to Tünel) The name means 'my soul, my liver', and this small place behind the Ali Hoca Türbesi specialises in grilled liver served with herbs, *ezme* (spicy tomato sauce) and grilled vegetables. If you can't bring yourself to eat offal, fear not – you can substitute the liver

with lamb if you so choose. No alcohol, but *ayran* (a yoghurt drink) is the perfect accompaniment.

KAFE ARA — CAFE $$

Map p236 (Tosbağ Sokak 8a, Galatasaray; sandwiches ₺15-20, salads ₺15-23, grills ₺19-24; ⊙7.30am-midnight Mon-Thu, to 1am Fri & Sat, to 10pm Sun; Kabataş, then funicular to Taksim) This casual cafe is named after its owner, legendary local photographer Ara Güler. It occupies a converted garage with tables and chairs spilling out into a wide laneway opposite the Galatasaray Lycée and serves an array of well-priced salads, sandwiches and Turkish staples such as *köfte* (meatballs) and *sigara böreği* (pastries filled with cheese and potato). No alcohol.

ZENCEFİL — VEGETARIAN $

Map p236 (Kurabiye Sokak 8; soup ₺7-9, mains ₺9-17; ⊙10am-11pm Mon-Sat, noon-10pm Sun; ; Kabataş, then funicular to Taksim) We're not surprised that this vegetarian cafe has a loyal following. Its interior is comfortable and stylish, with a glassed courtyard and bright colour scheme, and its food is 100% homemade, fresh and varied. Dishes are available in small and large sizes. 'Zencefil' means 'ginger' in Turkish, and the cafe makes its own ginger beer and ginger ale. You can also order wine by the glass and fresh *limonata* (lemonade) served with Absolut vodka.

ÇOKÇOK — THAI $$$

Map p236 (212-292 6496; www.cokcok.com.tr; Meşrutiyet Caddesi 51, Tepebaşı; starters ₺15-29, salads ₺15-29, mains, ₺15-35; ⊙dinner daily, lunch Tue-Sun) The fragrances of lemongrass, coriander (cilantro) and kaffir lime lure diners into this sleek restaurant on Tepebaşı's main drag. Huge servings of dishes from the classic Thai repertoire go down well with a Tiger or Efes beer. It's one of the best Asian restaurants in the city, so book ahead to be sure of a table.

HACI ABDULLAH — LOKANTA $$$

Map p236 (www.haciabdullah.com.tr; Eski Sakızağacı Caddesi 9a; mezes ₺10.50-23, mains ₺16-42; ⊙noon-10.30pm;) This İstanbul institution (established in 1888) serves a good range of mezes and *hazır yemek* (ready-made food). There's no alcohol, but the range of delicious desserts well and truly compensates. Come for lunch rather than dinner.

BEYOĞLU EATING

GANİ GANİ ŞARK SOFRAS
KEBAPS, PIDE **$$**

Map p236 (Taksim Kuyu Sokak 13; kebaps ₺10-26, pides ₺10-16; ⊙10am-midnight Mon-Thu, to 1am Fri & Sat; ⊠Kabataş then funicular to Taksim) Young Turkish couples love lolling on the traditional Anatolian seating at this friendly eatery. If you'd prefer to keep your shoes on, claim a table and chair on the 1st floor to enjoy excellent kebaps, rich *mantı* (Turkish ravioli) and piping hot pide. No alcohol.

MEDİ ŞARK SOFRASI
KEBAPS **$$**

Map p236 (Küçük Parmak Kapı Sokak 46a; kebaps ₺9-25; ⊠Kabataş, then funicular to Taksim) Another popular *kebapcı* (kebap eatery) off İstiklal, Medi specialises in meat dishes from the southeastern region of Turkey, which are served with the house speciality of *babam ekmek* (my father's bread). It's known for its Adana and *beyti sarma*, which are perfectly accompanied by a glass of frothy *ayran* (no alcohol is served). Seating is Anatolian style.

HELVETİA LOKANTA
LOKANTA **$**

Map p240 (General Yazgan Sokak 8-12, Asmalımescit; soup TL5, portions ₺5-12; ⊙8am-10pm Mon-Sat; ⊠; ⊠Kabataş, then funicular to Tünel) This tiny *lokanta* is popular with locals (particularly of the vegetarian and vegan variety), who pop in here for inexpensive soups, salads and stews that are cooked fresh each day. No alcohol, and cash only.

SARAY MUHALLEBİCİSİ
PUDDING SHOP **$**

Map p236 (www.saraymuhallebicisi.com; İstiklal Caddesi 173; ⊙6am-2am; ⊠Kabataş, then funicular to Taksim) This *muhallebici* (milk pudding shop) has been in business since 1935 and is always packed with locals scratching their heads over which of the 35-odd varieties of pudding to sample. Try the *firin sutlaç*, *aşure* (dried fruit, nut and pulse pudding) or *kazandibi* (slightly burnt chicken-breast pudding). There are branches throughout town, including one opposite the Eminönü ferry docks.

KALLAVİ
MEYHANE **$$$**

Map p236 (☎212-2451213; www.kallavi20.net/en; Kurabiye Sokak 16; set menus incl drinks ₺85; ⊙dinner; ⊠Kabataş, then funicular to Taksim) Those keen to hear some *fasıl* while in town should come to this popular *meyhane* on a Friday or Saturday night. Standard dishes (including plenty of mezes) are accompanied by musicians playing violin, zither and drum. Locals know all of the words, sing along and dance between courses – everyone else hums and looks happy .

LOCAL KNOWLEDGE

MEYHANES

On weekends, locals like to get together with friends and family. And many of these get-togethers occur in *meyhanes* (traditional Turkish taverns).

Meyhanes serve a particular style and range of food. A standard menu will include a lavish array of hot and cold mezes, a limited number of meat kebaps and a selection of whatever fish was fresh and plentiful at the market that morning – all washed down with copious pourings of the local tipple, rakı (aniseed brandy).

Some *meyhanes* rely on their *rakı*-soaked guests to entertain fellow diners with jokes and conversation, but others provide live music. Modern *meyhanes* such as Demeti and Jash (see opposite) in Cihangir sometimes host folk singers or accordion players, but the traditional *meyhane* features a small group of musicians who move from table to table playing *fasıl* music, emotion-charged Turkish folk or pop songs played on traditional instruments. Restaurants such as Feraye and Kallavi in Beyoğlu are known throughout the city for their food-and-*fasıl* combo, and are favourites with large groups, who pay a set charge of between ₺70 and ₺100 to enjoy a generous set menu with either limited or unlimited choices from the bar (limited will be rakı, beer or soft drinks; unlimited means that you could have all or any of these plus local spirits or wine). Guests sing along with the musicians, get up and dance between courses and have a boisterous and boozy time – it's hugely enjoyable to watch and even better if you join in.

Musicians at these places rely on tips to make their living, so if you visit a *meyhane* be sure to tip them (₺10 per person is about right). And when booking, be sure to opt for a Friday or Saturday night when the party vibe is most pronounced.

FERAYE   MEYHANE **$$$**

Map p236 (☎212-244 7472; www.feraye.net; 1st fl, Balo Sokak 1; incl drinks ₺85; ☺dinner Wed-Sat; 🚇Kabataş, then funicular to Taksim) Another popular *meyhane*, Feraye hosts *fasıl* musicians and the occasional solo singer. Everything is authentically *Türk tarzı* (Turkish style).

✗ Çukurcuma & Cihangir

JOURNEY   INTERNATIONAL, CAFE **$$**

Map p240 (www.journeycihangir.com; Akarsu Yokuşu 21a, Cihangir; soups ₺7-9, sandwiches ₺14-19, mains ₺15-39; ☺9am-2am; 🖋; 🚇Kabataş, then funicular to Taksim) This bohemian lounge cafe located in the expat enclave of Cihangir serves a great range of Mediterranean comfort foods, including sandwiches, soups, pizzas and pastas. Most of the dishes use organic produce and there's a decent array of vegetarian options. The crowd is 30-something, the music alternative and the ambience laid-back. Great stuff.

JASH   ANATOLIAN **$$**

Map p236 (☎212-244 3042; www.jashistanbul .com; Cihangir Caddesi 9, Cihangir; mezes ₺8-20, mains ₺20-42; ☺lunch & dinner; 🚇Kabataş, then funicular to Taksim) Armenian specialities such as *topik* (a cold meze made with chickpeas, pistachios, onion, flour, currants, cumin and salt) make an appearance on the menu of this bijou *meyhane* in trendy Cihangir. Come on the weekend, when an accordian player entertains diners and unusual dishes including *harisa* (chicken with a hand-forged wheat and butter sauce) are on offer.

DEMETİ   MEYHANE **$$**

Map p236 (☎212-244 0628; www.demeti.com.tr; Şimşirci Sokak 6, Cihangir; mezes ₺5-20, mains ₺16-25; ☺4pm-2am Mon-Sat; 🚇Kabataş, then funicular to Taksim) This modern *meyhane* has a friendly feel and simple but stylish decor. Reservations are a must if you want one of the four tables on the terrace, which have an unimpeded Bosphorus view. There's occasional live music.

DATLI MAYA   BAKERY **$**

Map p236 (www.datlimaya.com; Türkgücü Caddesi 59, Cihangir; cakes & pastries ₺2-5; ☺8am-10pm; 🚇Kabataş, then funicular to Taksim) Dilara Erbay is an exciting if unpredictable player on the city's culinary scene, and her latest venture, a tiny cafe-bakery located behind the Firuz Ağa Mosque in Cihangir, is as popular as it is fashionable. Her wood-fired oven produces cakes, *lahmacuns* (Arabic pizzas), pides, *böreks* and breads, all of which are enjoyed with glasses of tea dispensed from a battered old samovar.

🍷 DRINKING & NIGHTLIFE

There are hundreds of bars in Beyoğlu. The most popular bar precincts have traditionally been Balo and Sofyalı Sokaks, but the recent ban on outdoor drinking has forced many long-standing and much-loved venues to close. As a result, drinkers are migrating to cafe/ bars and small clubs around the district. Fortunately, the outdoor terraces at Beyoğlu's glamorous rooftop bars remain undisturbed. Note that many of the Beyoğlu clubs close over summer (mid-June–August), when the party crowd moves down to Turkey's southern coasts. We've listed some popular gay bars and clubs; for other options, check the dedicated pages in the monthly Time Out İstanbul (www.istanbulbeatblog .com) magazine.

🍷 Galata & Tophane

TOP CHOICE **TOPHANE NARGİLE CAFES**   NARGİLE CAFE

Map p240 (off Necatibey Caddesi, Tophane; ☺24hr; 🚇Tophane) This atmospheric row of nargile cafes behind the Nusretiye Mosque is always packed with locals enjoying tea, nargile and snacks. Follow your nose to find it – the smell of apple tobacco is incredibly enticing. It's great fun to watch live Süper Lig football matches on the televisions here, as patrons and waiters like to make their allegiances clear.

MAVRA   CAFE

Map p240 (Serdar-ı Ekrem Caddesi 31a, Galata; ☺8am-midnight; 🚇Karaköy, then funicular to Tünel) Serdar-ı Ekrem Caddesi is one of the most interesting streets in Galata, full of ornate 19th-century apartment blocks, avant-garde boutiques and mellow cafes and bars. Mavra is the best of these, offering tasty cheap food and good tea and coffee amid decor that is thrift-shop chic. There's always good music on the turntable here, too.

LE FUMOIR
BAR

Map p240 (www.georges.com; Georges Hotel, Serdar-ı Ekrem Caddesi 24, Galata; ⊘8am-1am; 🚇Karaköy) Oh là là! This atmospheric but small bar in the French restaurant of the same name is an elegant venue for an aperitif or nightcap. It's also a good spot for breakfast, as the French-style pastries and coffee are excellent.

X BAR
BAR

Map p240 (www.xrestaurantbar.com; 7th fl, Sadı Konuralp Caddesi 5, Şişhane; ⊘9am-midnight Sun-Wed, to 4am Thu-Sat) High culture meets serious glamour on the top floor of the İstanbul Foundation for Culture and Arts (İKSV) building. Our meals here haven't been worth their hefty price tags, so we suggest limiting yourself to a sunset aperitif or two – the Golden Horn view is simply extraordinary.

ATÖLYE KULEDIBI
BAR, CAFE

Map p240 (Galata Kulesi Sokak 4, Galata; ⊘10am-midnight Mon-Fri, to 2am Fri & Sat; 🚇Karaköy, then funicular to Tünel) Great music (sometimes live jazz) and a welcoming atmosphere characterise this bohemian place near Galata Tower.

SENSUS WINE BAR
WINE BAR

Map p240 (www.sensuswine.com; Büyük Hendek Sokak 5, Galata; ⊘10am-10pm; 🚇Karaköy, then funicular to Tünel) Set in a stone basement lined with wine bottles, this new bar underneath the Anemon Galata Hotel has a great concept, but needs to work on its customer service. There are close to 300 bottles of local wine to choose from, but when we visited staff were unable or unwilling to offer any wine-related information or drinking suggestions.

🍷 İstiklal & Around

🄣 MİKLA
BAR

Map p236 (www.miklarestaurant.com; Marmara Pera Hotel, Meşrutiyet Caddesi 15, Tepebaşı; ⊘from 6pm Mon-Sat summer only; 🚇Karaköy, then funicular to Tünel) It's worth overlooking the occasional uppity service at this stylish rooftop bar to enjoy what could well be the best view in İstanbul. After a few drinks, consider moving downstairs to eat in the classy restaurant.

🄣 360
BAR

Map p236 (www.360istanbul.com; 8th fl, İstiklal Caddesi 163; ⊘noon-2am Mon-Thu & Sun, 3pm-4am Fri & Sat; 🚇Karaköy, then funicular to Tünel) İstanbul's most famous bar, and deservedly so. If you can score one of the bar stools on the terrace you'll be happy indeed – the view is truly extraordinary. It morphs into a club after midnight on Friday and Saturday, when a cover charge of around ₺40 applies.

🄣 BAYLO
BAR, RESTAURANT

Map p240 (www.baylo.com.tr; Meşrutiyet Caddesi 107a, Tepebaşı; ⊘6.30pm-1am Mon-Thu, to 2.30am Fri & Sat; 🚇Karaköy, then funicular to Tünel) The much anticipated re-opening of the Pera Palace Hotel in the lower section of Asmalımescit has been accompanied by a boom in glamorous bistro-bars in its immediate vicinity. Of these, Baylo is undoubtedly the best. The elegant interior provides a perfect backdrop for the 30-something bankers, architects and other professionals who head here after a busy day at the office.

MANDA BATMAZ
COFFEEHOUSE

Map p236 (Olivia Geçidi 1a, off İstiklal Caddesi; ⊘9.30am-midnight; 🚇Karaköy, then funicular to Tünel) He's been working at this tiny coffeehouse for two decades, so Cemil Pilik really knows his stuff when it comes to making Turkish coffee. The name translates as 'so thick that even a water buffalo won't sink in it', and Cemil's brew is indeed as viscous as it is smooth. You'll find it behind the Barcelona Cafe & Patisserie.

HAZZO PULO ÇAY BAHÇESI
TEA GARDEN

Map p236 (Tarihi Hazzo Pulo Pasaji, off İstiklal Caddesi; ⊘9am-midnight; 🚇Karaköy, then funicular to Tünel) There aren't as many traditional teahouses in Beyoğlu as there are on the Historic Peninsula, so this picturesque cobbled courtyard full of makeshift stools and tables is beloved of local 20-somethings. Order from the waiter and then pay at the small cafe near the narrow arcade entrance. The next-door cafe Grand Boulevard offers more of the same.

OFF PERA CLUB

Map p236 (Gönül Sokak 14a, Asmalımescit; Karaköy, then funicular to Tünel) You'll need to squeeze your way into this tiny club, but once inside your persistence is sure to pay off. The DJs perch on a balcony over the bar and the multi-aged crowd spills out onto the street to smoke and catch its breath. Go on a Tuesday night, when Turkish pop dominates the sound system after midnight.

LEB-İ DERYA BAR

Map p240 (www.lebiderya.com; 6th fl, Kumbaracı Yokuşu 57, Galata; ⊙4pm-2am Mon-Thu, to 3am Fri, 10am-3am Sat, to 2am Sun; Karaköy, then funicular to Tünel) On the top floor of a dishevelled building off İstiklal, Leb-i Derya has wonderful views across to the Old City and down the Bosphorus, meaning that seats on the small outdoor terrace or at the bar are highly prized. There's also food on offer.

LEB-İ DERYA RICHMOND BAR, RESTAURANT

Map p240 (✆212-243 4375; www.lebiderya .com; 6th fl, Richmond Hotel, İstiklal Caddesi 445; ⊙11am-2am Mon-Thu, to 3am Fri & Sat, to 2am Sun; Karaköy, then funicular to Tünel) This sleek younger sister of perennial favourite Leb-i Derya is more restrained and decidedly more chic than her big sis. Fortunately there's no threat of sibling rivalry, as the crowd here is older and more cashed-up. The views from the huge windows are just as fab.

MÜNFERİT BAR

Map p236 (Yeni Çarşı Caddesi 19, Galatasaray; Kabataş, then funicular to Taksim) When this book went to print, this upmarket bar-restaurant designed by the Autoban Design Partnership was the most glamorous watering hole in town. Though the restaurant's take on nouvelle *meyhane* food lacks assurance, the bar is fabulous, serving expertly made cocktails and good wine by the glass to a formidably fashionable crowd.

INDİGO CLUB

Map p236 (www.livingindigo.com; 1st–5th fl, Mısır Apt, 309 Akarsu Sokak, Galatasaray; ⊙10pm-5am Fri & Sat, closed summer; Kabataş, then funicular to Taksim) This is Beyoğlu's electronic music temple and dance-music enthusiasts congregate here on weekends for their energetic kicks. The program spotlights top-notch local and visiting DJs or live acts. Check the website for schedules and cover charges.

LİTERA BAR

Map p236 (www.literarestaurant.com; 5th fl, Yeniçarşı Caddesi 32, Galatasaray; ⊙11am-4am; Karaköy, then funicular to Tünel) Occupying the 5th floor of the handsome building downhill from Galatasaray Meydanı, Litera revels in its extraordinary views of the Old City, Asian side and Bosphorus. It hosts plenty of cultural events, as befits its location in the Goethe Institute building.

NUTERAS BAR, RESTAURANT

Map p236 (www.nupera.com.tr/nuteras; 6th fl, NuPera Bldg, Meşrutiyet Caddesi 67, Tepebaşı; ⊙noon-1am Mon-Thu, to 4am Fri & Sat summer only; Karaköy, then funicular to Tünel) This bar/restaurant attracts a fashionable crowd to the rooftop terrace of the NuPera Building. Its expansive Golden Horn view is spectacular and the after-dinner club scene is trés chic.

DOGZSTAR CLUB

Map p236 (www.dogzstar.com; Kartal Sokak 3, Galatasaray; ⊙closed Sun; Kabataş, then funicular to Taksim) It's a three-storey affair, but the compact size (300 persons max) makes for an acoustic powerhouse. The crowd comprises budding fans or hardcore followers of featured up-and-coming bands or DJs. The owners give the collected (modest) cover charges to performers and also charge reasonable drink prices. Bravo! There's a terrace where clubbers cool off in summer.

URBAN BAR, CAFE

Map p236 (www.urbanbeyoglu.com; Kartal Sokak 6a, Galatasaray; ⊙11am-1am; Kabataş, then funicular to Taksim) A tranquil bolthole in the midst of İstiklal's mayhem, Urban is where the pre-club crowd congregates at night and where many of them can be found kicking back over a coffee during the day. The vaguely Parisienne interior is a clever balance of grunge and glamour.

LOVE DANCE POINT GAY

(www.lovedp.net; Cumhuriyet Caddesi 349, Harbiye; ⊙11.30pm-5am Fri & Sat) Going into its second decade, LDP is easily the most Europhile of the local gay venues, hosting gay musical icons and international circuit parties. Hard-cutting techno is thrown in with gay anthems and Turkish pop. This place attracts the well-travelled and the un-impressionable, as well as some straight hipsters from nearby Nişantaşı.

BEYOĞLU DRINKING & NIGHTLIFE

BÜYÜK LONDRA OTELİ BAR
BAR

Map p236 (Meşrutiyet Caddesi 53, Tepebaşı; ⊙noon-11pm; 🚇Karaköy, then funicular to Tünel) This is a true time-warp experience. We'd guess that the decor of this historic lounge bar has remained untouched for close on a century, and we're pleased to report that the prices haven't hiked up too much during that time.

CLUB 17
GAY

Map p236 (Zambak Sokak 17; ⊙11pm-5am; 🚇Kabataş, then funicular to Taksim) Rent boys outnumber regulars at this narrow bar. At closing time, the crowd spills out into the street to make final hook-up attempts possible. It's quiet during the week but jam-packed late on Friday and Saturday.

BİGUDİ CAFE
GAY

Map p236 (www.bigudiproject.net; terrace fl, Mis Sokak 5; ⊙11pm-4am Fri & Sat; 🚇Kabataş, then funicular to Taksim) The first lesbian-exclusive venue in Turkey, Bigudi is frequented by lipstick lesbians on Saturday nights and is resolutely off limits to non-females. Fridays are open to gay men and the transgendered. To find it, look for the Altin Plak cafe on the ground floor.

ARAF
CLUB

Map p236 (www.araf.com.tr; 5th fl, Balo Sokak 32; ⊙5pm-4am Tue-Sun; 🚇Kabataş, then funicular to Taksim) Grungy English teachers, Erasmus exchange students and Turkish-language students have long claimed this as their favoured destination, listening to world music (including the live in-house gypsy band) and swilling some of the cheapest club beer in the city.

JOLLY JOKER
LIVE MUSIC

Map p236 (www.jjistanbul.com; Balo Sokak 22; ⊙from 10pm Wed-Sat, closed summer; 🚇Kabataş, then funicular to Taksim) The gig-goers among the lively multinational crowd here enjoy the city's best locally brewed beer (the caramel brew) and gravitate towards the upstairs bi-level performance hall, which hosts Turkish rock, alternative and pop outfits. Check the website for schedules and cover charges.

PERLA KALLÂVİ NARGİLE CAFE
NARGILE CAFE

Map p236 (Kallâvi Sokak 2, 4th-6th fl; ⊙10am-2am) Follow the scent of apple tobacco to this nargile cafe occupying the top three floors of an ornate building on İstiklal Caddesi (enter from the side street). It's inevitably full of young people (including plenty of women) enjoying a glass of tea and a bubbling pipe in the welcoming indoor spaces or on the small terrace with its Sea of Marmara views.

🍷 Çukurcuma & Cihangir

TOP CHOICE MİNİMÜZİKHOL
CLUB, LIVE MUSIC

Map p236 (MMH; www.minimuzikhol.com; Soğancı Sokak 7, Cihangir; ⊙Wed-Sat 10pm-late; 🚇Kabataş, then funicular to Taksim) The mothership for inner-city hipsters, MMH is a small, slightly grungy venue near Taksim that hosts live sets by local and international musicians midweek and the best dance party in town on weekends. It's best after 1am.

TOP CHOICE 5 KAT
BAR, RESTAURANT

Map p236 (www.5kat.com; 5th fl, Soğancı Sokak 7, Cihangir; ⊙10am-1am; 🚇Kabataş) This İstanbul institution is a great alternative for those who can't stomach the style overload at Mikla, 360 and the like. In winter, drinks are served in the boudoir-style bar on the fifth floor; in summer, action moves to the outdoor roof terrace. Both have great Bosphorus views.

CAFE SUSAM
CAFE, BAR

Map p236 (Susam Sokak 11, Cihangir; ⊙9am-2am; 🚇Kabataş, then funicular to Kabataş) Susam is the epitome of a great neighbourhood cafe. The expats and arty İstanbullus who call Cihangir home come here to drink good coffee, take advantage of the free wi-fi, snack on sandwiches and drink mean mojitos on weekend evenings.

KİKİ
CLUB, CAFE

Map p236 (www.kiki.com.tr; Sıraselviler Caddesi 42, Cihangir; ⊙closed Sun; 🚇Kabataş, then funicular to Taksim) Cool cafe by day and hip bar-club by night, Kiki has a loyal clientele who enjoy its pizzas, burgers, drinks and music (DJs and live sets). Regulars head to the rear courtyard and budget drinkers appreciate the happy hour, held between 7pm and 9pm from Monday to Thursday (Monday and Wednesay half-price drinks, Tuesday and Thursday free tapas).

SMYRNA
BAR

Map p240 (Akarsu Yokuşu 29, Cihangir; ☺10am-2am Tue-Sun; 🚡Kabataş, then funicular to Taksim) The original boho bar on Cihangir's main entertainment strip, Smyrna has a relaxed atmosphere, retro decor and a self-consciously liter-arty clientele. If you decide to make a night of it here (and many do), there's simple food available.

WHITE MILL
BAR, CAFE

Map p236 (www.whitemillcafe.com; Susam Sokak 13, Cihangir; ☺9.30am-1.30am; 🚡Kabataş, then funicular to Taksim) Forget the hard-edged interior – the draw here is the leafy rear garden, which is a perfect place to while away a lazy summer afternoon or evening. It's particularly popular for weekend brunch. The menu features unadorned globally inspired dishes and good cocktails.

TEK YÖN
GAY

Map p236 (1st fl, Siraselviler Caddesi 63, Taksim; ☺10pm-4am; 🚡Kabataş, then funicular to Taksim) A phenomenal run in the popularity stakes catapulted this originally modest venue to the forefront of İstanbul's gay nightlife, and its sleek premises features the city's largest gay dance floor as well as a garden popular with smokers and cruisers. The core clientele is hirsute and fashion-challenged. Cuddly bears abound.

☆ ENTERTAINMENT

☆ Galata & Tophane

GALATA MEVLEVİİ
MUSEUM
WHIRLING-DERVISH PERFORMANCE

Map p240 (Galata Mevlevihanesi Müzesi; Galipdede Caddesi 15, Tünel; ₺40; ☺performances 4pm Sun; 🚡Karaköy, then funicular to Tünel) The 15th-century *semahane* at this *tekke* is the venue for a *sema* held most Sundays during the year. Tickets are only available on the day of the performance and often sell out – your best bet is to head to the museum and purchase tickets well ahead of the performance (the ticket office opens at 9am).

SALON
LIVE MUSIC

Map p240 (☎212-334 0700; www.saloniksv .com; İstanbul Foundation for Culture & Arts, Nejat Eczacıbaşı Bldg, Sadi Konuralp Caddesi 5, Şişhane; 🚡Karaköy, then funicular to Tünel) This intimate performance space in the İstanbul İKSV building hosts live contemporary music (mainly jazz), lectures and theatrical performances; check the website for program and booking details. Before or after the show, be sure to have a drink at X Bar (p132), in the same building.

NARDİS JAZZ CLUB
JAZZ

Map p240 (☎212-244 6327; www.nardisjazz.com; Kuledibi Sokak 14, Galata; ☺9.30pm-12.30am Mon-Thu, to 1.30am Fri & Sat, closed August; 🚡Karaköy) Named after a Miles Davis track, this intimate venue near the Galata Tower is run by jazz guitarist Önder Focan and his wife Zuhal. Performers include gifted amateurs, local jazz luminaries and visiting international artists. It's small, so you'll need to book if you want a decent table.

☆ İstiklal & Around

🏆 TOP CHOICE BABYLON
LIVE MUSIC, CLUB

Map p240 (www.babylon.com.tr; Şehbender Sokak 3, Asmalımescit; ☺9.30pm-2am Tue-Thu, 10pm-3am Fri & Sat, club closed summer; 🚡Karaköy, then funicular to Tünel) İstanbul's pre-eminent live-music venue has been packing the crowds in since 1999 and shows no sign of losing its allure. The eclectic program often features big-name international music acts, particularly during the festival season. Most of the action occurs in the concert hall, but there's also a lounge with a DJ. Book at Biletix (www.biletix.com) or at the venue's box office.

MUNZUR CAFE & BAR
LIVE MUSIC

Map p236 (www.munzurcafebar.com; Hasnun Galip Sokak, Galatasaray; ☺1pm-4am Tue-Sun, music from 9pm; 🚡Kabataş, then funicular to Taksim) Hasnun Galip Sokak in Galatasaray is home to a number of *Türkü evleri*, Kurdish-owned bars where musicians perform live, emotion-charged *halk meziği* (folk music). The best of these is probably Munzur, which is nearly two decades old and still going strong. It has a great line-up of singers and expert *bağlama* (lute) players. Nearby **Toprak** (Map p236; ☎212-293 4037; www.toprakturkubar.tr.gg/ana-sayfa.htm; Hasnun Galip Sokak, Galatasaray; ☺4pm-4am, show from 10pm) offers more of the same.

BEYOĞLU ENTERTAINMENT

GARAJİSTANBUL CULTURAL CENTRE

Map p236 (☎212-244 4499; www.garajistanbul.org; Kaymakem Reşet Bey Sokak 11a, Galatasaray; 🚊Kabataş, then funicular to Tünel) This performance space occupies a former parking garage in a narrow street behind İstiklal Caddesi and is about as edgy as the city's performance scene gets. It hosts contemporary dance performances, poetry readings, theatrical performances and live jazz.

SHOPPING

Galata & Tophane

TOP CHOICE **DEAR EAST** ARTS & CRAFTS

Map p240 (www.deareast.com; Lüleci Hendek Sokak 35, Tophane; ⏲10.30am-7pm Mon-Sat; 🚊Tophane) Interior designer Emel Güntaş is one of İstanbul's style icons, and this recently opened shop in Tophane is a favourite destination for the city's design mavens. The stock includes cushions (including a new range by fashion designer Rifat Özbek), carpets, kilims (pileless woven rugs), silk scarves, woollen shawls, porcelain and felt crafts. Everything here is artisan-made and absolutely gorgeous. Her next-door store, Hiç, specialises in furniture.

HAMMAM BATHWARE

Map p240 (www.hammam.com.tr; Kule Çıkmazı, Galata; ⏲11am-8pm; 🚊Karaköy) The wonderful smell of naturally scented soap greets shoppers as they enter this small shop hidden in a street in the shadow of Galata Tower. The traditional laurel- and olive-oil soaps on offer are very well priced, as are the attractive cotton and silk *peştemals* (bath towels) and bathrobes.

BAHAR KORÇAN CLOTHING

Map p240 (www.baharkorcan.org; Serdar-ı Ekrem Sokak 9, Galata; ⏲closed Sunday; 🚊Karaköy) Bahar Korçan was in the vanguard of the design community's move into Galata, and her shop with its lofty ceiling, chandeliers and always-arresting window display is one of the most beautiful on Serdar-ı Ekrem Sokak. Her collections are characterised by ultra-feminine designs, whimsical touches and delicate fabrics.

ARZU KAPROL CLOTHING

Map p240 (www.arzukaprol.net; Serdar-ı Ekrem Sokak 22, Galata; 🚊Karaköy) Parisian-trained and lauded throughout Turkey for her exciting designs, Arzu Kaprol's collections of women's clothing and accessories feature in Paris Fashion Week and are stocked by international retailers including Harrods in London. This store showcases her sleek prét-à-porter range.

LÂL HANDICRAFTS

Map p240 (www.lalistanbul.com; Camekan Sokak 4c, Galata; ⏲10.30am-8pm; 🚊Karaköy) Lâl is one of the new breed of handicraft shops in Turkey, selling items such as bags, scarves, clothing and Anatolian lace and braid jewellery made by traditional artisans but featuring a contemporary design aesthetic. The well-priced T-shirts with appliqué decoration are particularly desirable.

İRONİ HOMEWARES

Map p240 (www.ironi.com.tr; Camekan Sokak 4e, Galata; ⏲10.30am-8pm; 🚊Karaköy) Güney İnan's range of silver-plated Turkish-style homewares includes plenty of options for those wanting to take home a souvenir of their trip. The tea sets (tray, glasses with holders, sugar bowls) are extremely attractive, as are the light fittings.

SIR CERAMICS

Map p240 (www.sircini.com; Serdar-i Ekrem Sokak 66, Galata; ⏲closed Sun; 🚊Karaköy, then funicular to Tünel) Ceramics produced in İstanbul can be pricey, but the attractive hand-painted plates, platters, bowls and tiles sold at this small atelier are exceptions to the rule.

İSTANBUL MODERN GIFT SHOP GIFTS

Map p240 (www.istanbulmodern.org; Meclis-i Mebusan Caddesi, Tophane; ⏲10am-6pm Tue, Wed & Fri-Sun, to 8pm Thu; 🚊Tophane) It's often difficult to source well-priced souvenirs and gifts to take home, but this stylish shop in the İstanbul Modern gallery boasts plenty. Check out the niftily designed T-shirts, CDs, stationery, coffee mugs, homewares and jewellery and the cute gifts for kids.

SELDA OKUTAN JEWELLERY

Map p240 (www.seldaokutan.com; Ali Paşa Değirmeni Sokak 10a, Tophane; ⏲closed Sun; 🚊Tophane) Selda Okutan's sculptural pieces featuring tiny naked figures have the local

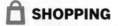

fashion industry all aflutter. Come to her design studio in Tophane to see what all the fuss is about.

İstiklal & Around

LALE PLAK
MUSIC

Map p240 (Galipdede Caddesi 1, Tünel; ⊙9.30am-7.30pm Mon-Sat, 10.30am-7pm Sun; ⊠Karaköy, then funicular to Tünel) This small shop is crammed with CDs, including an excellent selection of Turkish classical, jazz and folk music. It's a popular hang-out for local musicians.

ALİ MUHİDDİN HACI BEKİR
FOOD

Map p236 (www.hacibekir.com.tr; İstiklal Caddesi 83; ⊠Kabataş, then funicular to Taksim Meydanı) The Beyoğlu branch of the famous *lokum* shop.

ARTRIUM
ART, JEWELLERY

Map p240 (www.artrium.com.tr; Tünel Geçidi 7, Tünel; ⊙closed Sun; ⊠Karaköy, then funicular to Tünel) Crammed with antique ceramics, calligraphy, maps, prints and jewellery, this Aladdin's cave of a shop is most notable for the exquisite miniatures by Iranian artist Haydar Hatemi.

BEYOĞLU OLGUNLAŞMA ENSTİTÜSÜ
HANDICRAFTS

Map p236 (www.beyogluolgunlasma.k12.tr; İstiklal Caddesi 28; ⊙9am-5pm Mon-Fri; ⊠Kabataş, then funicular to Taksim) This is the ground-floor retail outlet/gallery of the Beyoğlu Olgunlaşma Enstıtüsü, a textile school where students in their final year of secondary school learn crafts such as felting, embroidery, knitting and lacemaking. It sells well-priced examples of their work, giving them a taste of its commercial possibilities.

ROBINSON CRUSOE
BOOKS

Map p236 (www.rob389.com; İstiklal Caddesi 389; ⊙9am-9.30pm Mon-Sat, 10am-9.30pm Sun; ⊠Karaköy, then funicular to Tünel) There are few more pleasant fates than being marooned here for an hour or so. With its classy decor, good magazine selection and wide range of English-language novels and books about İstanbul, it's one of the best bookshops in the city. There's another

branch specialising in art books on the ground floor of SALT Beyoğlu (p120).

PANDORA
BOOKS

Map p236 (www.pandora.com.tr; Büyük Parmakkapı Sokak 8; ⊙10am-8pm Mon-Wed, 10am-9pm Thu-Sat, 1-8pm Sun; ⊠Kabataş, then funicular to Taksim) This long-standing independent bookshop has a more recent store on the opposite side of the street that is dedicated solely to English-language books. It has great crime-fiction and travel sections, as well as loads of books about Turkey.

TEZGAH ALLEY
CLOTHING

Map p236 (Terkoz Cikmazı; ⊙closed Sun; ⊠Karaköy, then funicular to Tünel) Put your elbows to work fighting your way to the front of the *tezgah* (stalls) in this alleyway off İstiklal Caddesi, which are heaped with T-shirts, jumpers, pants and shirts on offer for under ₺10 per piece. Turkey is a major centre of European clothing manufacture, and the items here are often factory run-ons from designer or high-street-chain orders.

DENİZLER KİTABEVİ
ANTIQUE BOOKS, MAPS & PRINTS

Map p236 (www.denizlerkitabevi.com; İstiklal Caddesi 199a; ⊙9.30am-7.30pm Mon-Sat; ⊠Karaköy, then funicular to Tünel) One of the few interesting shops remaining on İstiklal, Denizler Kitabevi sells old maps, books and prints and also publishes titles on history and navigation.

PAŞABAHÇE
GLASS

Map p236 (www.pasabahce.com; İstiklal Caddesi 314; ⊙10am-8pm; ⊠Karaköy, then funicular to Tünel) Established in 1934, this local firm manufactures excellent glassware from its factory on the Bosphorus. Three floors of glassware, vases and decanters feature and prices are very reasonable. Styles are both traditional and contemporary.

MEPHİSTO
MUSIC

Map p236 (www.mephisto.com.tr; İstiklal Caddesi 125; ⊙9am-midnight; ⊠Kabataş, then funicular to Taksim) If you manage to develop a taste for local music while you're in town, this popular store is the place to indulge it. As well as a huge CD collection of Turkish popular music, there's a select range of Turkish folk, jazz and classical music. It also stocks DVDs and has an upstairs cafe.

BEYOĞLU SHOPPING

İSTANBUL KİTAPÇISI
BOOKS

Map p236 (www.istanbulkitapcisi.com; İstiklal Caddesi 146; ⊙10am-6.45pm Mon-Sat, noon-6.45pm Sun; ⊠Karaköy, then funicular to Tünel) This bookshop is run by the municipality and as a consequence its prices are very reasonable. It stocks some English-language books about İstanbul, and a good range of maps, CDs, postcards and prints.

🏠 Çukurcuma & Cihangir

A LA TURCA
CARPETS, ANTIQUES

Map p236 (www.alaturcahouse.com; Faikpaşa Sokak 4, Çukurcuma; ⊙10.30am-7.30pm Mon-Sat; ⊠Kabataş, then funicular to Taksim) Antique Anatolian kilims and textiles are stacked alongside top-drawer Ottoman antiques in this fabulous shop in Çukurcuma. This is the best area in the city to browse for antiques and curios, and A La Turca is probably the most interesting of its retail outlets. Ring the doorbell to gain entrance.

BERRİN AKYÜZ
CLOTHING

Map p240 (www.berrinakyuz.com; Akarsu Yokuşu Sokak 22, Cihangir; ⊙10.30am-7pm Mon-Sat; ⊠Kabataş, then funicular to Taksim) Local lasses love the reworked vintage clothing on offer at this Cihangir boutique, and no wonder. It's well priced and extremely stylish. There's another branch in Üsküdar.

LEYLA ESKİ EŞYA PAZARLAMA
CLOTHING

Map p236 (Altıpatlar Sokak 6, Çukurcuma; ⊙11am-5.30pm; ⊠Kabataş, then funicular to Taksim) If you love old clothes, you'll adore Leyla Seyhanlı's boutique. Filled to the brim with piles of vintage embroidery and outfits, it's a rummager's delight. It stocks everything from 1950s taffeta party frocks

to silk-embroidery cushion covers that would've been at home in the Dolmabahçe Palace linen cupboard.

MARİPOSA
CLOTHING

Map p236 (Şimşirci Sokak 11a, Cihangir; ⊙10am-8pm Mon-Fri, 11am-8.30pm Sat & Sun; ⊠Kabataş, then funicular to Taksim) Designer Banu One turns out a particularly fetching line in floral frocks at her Cihangir atelier. Fashionistas will adore the fact that she not only makes to order, but also designs and tailors unique ensembles. As well as the dresses, coats and jackets on the racks, the shop sells pretty bedspreads and pillowslips.

LA CAVE WINE SHOP
FOOD & DRINK

Map p236 (La Cave Şarap Evi; www.lacavesarap .com; Sıraselviler Caddesi 109, Cihangir; ⊙10am-9pm; ⊠Kabataş, then funicular to Taksim) Its enormous selection of local and imported wine makes La Cave a good stop for tipplers. The staff can differentiate a chablis from a chardonnay, and though they don't speak much English, they are always happy to give advice on the best Turkish bottles to add to your cellar.

🏃 ACTIVITIES

AĞA HAMAMI
HAMAM

Map p236 (📞212-249 5027; www.agahamami .com; Turnacıbaşı Sokak 48b, Çukurcuma; skin-peeling scrub ₺5, bath ₺30, soap/oil massage ₺5/30; ⊙10am-10pm; ⊠Kabataş, then funicular to Taksim) Dating from 1562, this historic hamam has a low-key ambience and allows communal bathing for both genders, although scrubs and massages are conducted by same-sex masseurs in private spaces. Prices are surprisingly reasonable when compared with the historic hamams in the Old City, but standards of cleanliness could be higher.

Beşiktaş, Ortaköy & Kuruçeşme

Neighbourhood Top Five

1 Getting an insight into the public and private life of one of the last Ottoman sultans, Abdül Mecit I, at his ostentatious creation, **Dolmabahçe Palace** (p141).

2 Partying into the early hours at one of the sybaritic nightclubs on the **Golden Mile**.

3 Indulging in a personalised hamam treatment at the **Four Seasons İstanbul at the Bosphorus** (p145) spa.

4 Tiptoeing through the tulips (and other flowers) in **Yıldız Park** (p142).

5 Enjoying a drink on the terrace of the **Çırağan Palace Kempinski Hotel** (p144).

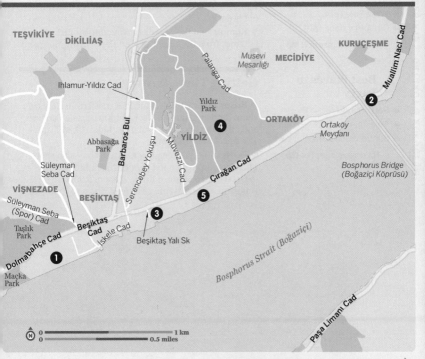

For more detail of this area, see Map p242 and p243 ➡

Lonely Planet's Top Tip

It can be difficult to get past the door staff at the superclubs on the Golden Mile if you're not a celebrity or socialite. If you're keen to party with the glitterati, consider making a booking at one of the club restaurants, which will ensure that you get automatic entrance.

✖ Best Places to Eat

➡ Sıdıka (p143)
➡ Vogue (p143)
➡ Zuma (p143)

For reviews, see p143 ➡

◉ Best Ottoman Palaces

➡ Dolmabahçe Palace (p141)
➡ Yıldız Şale (p142)
➡ Çırağan Palace (p142)

For reviews, see p141 ➡

☆ Best Places to Party

➡ Sortie (p144)
➡ Anjelique (p144)
➡ Supperclub (p144)

For reviews, see p144 ➡

BEŞIKTAŞ, ORTAKÖY & KURUÇEŞME

Exploring Beşiktaş to Kuruçeşme

This part of town has the largest concentration of Ottoman palaces and pavilions in İstanbul, so history and architecture buffs will find it satisfying to spend a day or two exploring. Start by walking to Dolmabahçe Palace from the tram stop at Kabataş, and then walk or bus your way down to Yıldız Park and Çırağan Palace. But be warned that getting back to Kabataş or Taksim by bus or taxi is usually a slow process due to constant traffic jams along Çırağan, Muallim Naci and Kuruçeşme Caddesis.

The waterside suburb of Ortaköy has considerable charm, particularly on warm summer nights when its main square is crowded with locals dining at its waterside restaurants or enjoying an after-dinner coffee and ice cream by the water. It's a good place to kick off an evening of clubbing at the venues along the Golden Mile.

Local Life

➡ **Picnic in the Park** You don't need to organise a portable BBQ and folding furniture to enjoy an al fresco lunch in popular Yıldız Park (p142); although many locals do).

➡ **İskele Idling** Watch the ferries head in and out of dock while lingering in the cafes and bars behind Bahçeşehir University next to the Beşiktaş İskelesi (ferry dock).

➡ **Kumpir** Join the crowds tucking into stuffed potatoes from the stands behind the Ortaköy Mosque.

Getting There & Away

➡ **Buses** Lines 22, 22RE and 25E travel from Kabataş along Çırağan, Muallim Naci and Kuruçeşme Caddesis and on to the Bosphorus suburbs. Lines 40, 40T and 42T travel from Taksim.

➡ **Ferries** Run between Beşiktaş and the Asian shore. There are also commuter services from Eminönü to Ortaköy at 5.50pm, 6.10pm, 6.40pm 6.30pm. Unfortunately no evening services return to Eminönü.

IZZET KERIBAR ©

DOLMABAHÇE PALACE

These days it's fashionable for architects and critics influenced by the less-is-more aesthetic of the Bauhaus masters to sneer at buildings such as Dolmabahçe. Enthusiasts of Ottoman architecture also decry this final flourish of the imperial dynasty, finding that it has more in common with the Paris Opera than with traditional pavilion-style buildings such as Topkapı. But whatever the critics might say, this 19th century imperial residence with its opulent **Selâmlık** (Ceremonial Quarters) and large **Harem** is a clear crowd favourite.

The palace, which is set in well-tended gardens and entered via an ornate imperial gate, is divided into two sections: the over-the-top **Selâmlık** and the slightly more restrained **Harem**. Both are visited on compulsory – and unfortunately rushed – guided tours. The Selâmlık, with its huge chandeliers and crystal staircase made by Baccarat, is the more impressive of the two.

The tourist entrance to the palace is near the ornate **Clock Tower**, built between 1890 and 1894. There's an outdoor cafe near here with premium Bosphorus views and cheap prices (yes, really).

At the end of your tour, make sure that you visit the **Crystal Kiosk**, with its fairytale-like conservatory featuring a crystal fountain and myriad windows, some of them etched. There's even a crystal piano and chair. It's next to the aviary on the street side of the palace.

Note that visitor numbers in the palace are limited to 3000 per day and this ceiling is often reached on weekends and holidays – come mid-week if possible, and even then be prepared to queue (often for a long period and in full sun).

DON'T MISS...

➡ Selâmlık
➡ Harem
➡ Crystal Kiosk

PRACTICALITIES

➡ Dolmabahçe Sarayı
➡ Map p154
➡ www.millisaraylar.gov.tr
➡ Dolmabahçe Caddesi, Beşiktaş
➡ Selâmlık ₺30, Harem ₺20, joint ticket ₺40
➡ ⊘9am-6pm Tue-Wed & Fri-Sun Mar-Sep, until 4pm Oct-Feb
➡ 🚊Kabataş then walk

◉ SIGHTS

DOLMABAHÇE PALACE   PALACE
See p141.

NAVAL MUSEUM   MUSEUM
Map p242 (Deniz Müzesi; www.denizmuzeleri
.tsk.tr; cnr Cezayir & Beşiktaş Caddesis; ⊖Bar-
barossa's tomb 1-5pm Fri; ☐Bahçeşehir Ünv.)
This museum of Turkish naval history focuses on Ottoman maritime power and
the achievements of two great sailors: the
16th-century cartographer Piri Reis and
the admiral of Süleyman the Magnificent's
fleet, Barbaros Heyrettin Paşa (1483–1546),
better known as Barbarossa. The admi-
ral's **tomb** (Barbaros Heyrettin Paşa Türbe; Map
p242), designed by Sinan, is in the square
opposite the museum.

The museum is located on the Bosphorus shore close to the Kadiköy İskele in
Beşiktaş and when this book went to print,
it was closed for a major renovation and extension. When it reopens, an entry charge
will apply.

Outside the museum, dolmuşes (mini-
buses) run up to Taksim Meydanı (Taksim
Square) and to Harbiye, where Turkey's
major military museum, the **Askeri Müze**
(Military Museum; ☑212-233 2720; Vali Konağı
Caddesi; adult/student ₺5/3; ⊖9am-5pm Wed-
Sun), is located. The Ottoman military band
known as the Mehter performs there most
days between 3pm and 4pm.

ÇIRAĞAN PALACE   PALACE
Map p154 (Çırağan Sarayı; Çırağan Caddesi 84,
Ortaköy; ☐Çırağan) Not satisfied with the
architectural exertions of his predeces-
sor at Dolmabahçe, Sultan Abdül Aziz (r
1861–76) built his own grand residence at
Çırağan, only 1.5km away. Here, architect
Nikoğos Balyan, who had also worked on
Dolmabahçe, created an interesting build-
ing melding European neoclassical with
Ottoman and Moorish styles. The palace is
now part of the Çırağan Palace Kempinski
Hotel.

YILDIZ PARK   PARK
Map p242 (Yıldız Parkı; Çırağan Caddesi, Yıldız;
chalet museum adult/child ₺10/5; ⊖chalet museum 9am-4.30pm Tue, Wed & Fri-Sun; ☐Yahya
Efendi) Abdül Hamit II didn't allow himself
to be upstaged by his predecessors, making his architectural mark by adding to the
structures built by earlier sultans in Yıldız

Park. The pretty **şale** (Yıldız Chalet Museum;
☑212-259 4570; admission ₺4, still/video camera
₺6/15; ⊖9.30am-5pm Tue-Wed & Fri-Sun, until
4pm winter), or chalet, that he built here in
1880 originally functioned as a hunting
lodge but was converted to a guesthouse
for visiting foreign dignitaries in 1889. It's
now a museum.

The park itself had begun life as the
imperial hunting reserve for the Çırağan
Sarayı, but after Abdül Hamit built the *şale*
it was planted with rare and exotic trees,
shrubs and flowers and became a huge formal garden. The landscape designer, G Le
Roi, was French.

The park and its various kiosks became
derelict during the early years of the Republic, but in the 1980s it was restored by
the Turkish Touring & Automobile Association (Turing) under lease from the city
government. In 1994 the newly elected city
government declined to renew the lease and
took over operation of the park. Today it's a
pretty, leafy retreat alive with birds, picnicking families and young couples enjoying a
bit of hanky-panky in the bushes. The best
time to visit is in April, when its spring flowers (including thousands of tulips) bloom.

The *şale* is at the top of the hill, enclosed
by a wall. After being expanded and renovated for the use of Kaiser Wilhelm II of
Germany in 1889, it underwent a second
extension in 1898 to accommodate a huge
ceremonial hall. After his imperial guest
departed, the sultan became quite attached
to his 'rustic' creation and decided to live
here himself, forsaking the palaces of Dolmabahçe and Çırağan on the Bosphorus
shore.

Turkish-speaking guides conduct compulsory half-hour tours through the building every 15 minutes on weekends (less
frequently on weekdays). The chalet isn't
as plush as Dolmabahçe, but it's far less
crowded. In fact, on weekdays it's often
empty.

The tour visits a reception hall with
French furniture and an ornate painted
ceiling; the ceremonial hall with its magnificent Hereke carpet; and a series of bed-
rooms, bathrooms and salons.

Around 500m past the turn-off to Yıldız
Şale, you'll come to the **Malta Köşkü** (Yıldız
Parkı), now a restaurant and function cen-
tre. Built in 1870, this was where Abdül
Hamit imprisoned his brother Murat V,
whom he had deposed in 1876. The terrace

here has a view of the Bosphorus and is a pleasant spot for a light lunch, tea or coffee.

If you continue walking past the Malta Köşkü for 10 minutes, you'll arrive at the **Yıldız Porselen Fabrikası** (Yıldız Porcelain Factory; ☑212-260 2370; ⊙9am-3pm). This factory is housed in a wonderful building designed by Italian architect Raimondo D'Aronco, who was to introduce the art nouveau style to İstanbul.

The steep walk uphill from Çırağan Caddesi to the Şale takes 15 to 20 minutes. If you come to the park by taxi, have it take you up the steep slope to the *şale*. A taxi from Taksim Meydanı to the top of the hill should cost around ₺10.

ORTAKÖY MOSQUE   MOSQUE

Map p154 (Ortaköy Camii, Büyük Mecidiye Camii; Ortaköy Meydanı, Ortaköy; ▣Ortaköy) This elegant baroque structure was designed by Nikoğos Balyan, one of the architects of Dolbabahçe Palace, and built for Sultan Abdül Mecit I between 1853 and 1855. With the modern Bosphorus Bridge looming behind it, it now provides a fabulous photo opportunity for those wanting to illustrate İstanbul's 'old meets new' character.

Within the mosque hang several masterful examples of Arabic calligraphy executed by Abdül Mecit, who was an accomplished calligrapher.

The mosque fronts onto Ortaköy Meydanı, the hub of this former fishing village and home to a pretty fountain and waterfront cafes. On weekends, the square and surrounding streets host an unremarkable but popular street market.

EATING

There are plenty of eateries in Beşiktaş and Ortaköy, though few deserve to be singled out for recommendation. Locals tend to gravitate toward the Ortaköy branches of the Kitchenette (p127) and the House Cafe (p127) chains, both of which are packed on weekends.

SIDIKA   TURKISH $$

(☑212-259 7232; www.sidika.com.tr; Şair Nedim Caddesi 38 , Beşiktaş; cold mezes ₺3-14, hot mezes ₺15-20, fish ₺16-18; ⊙5pm-midnight Mon-Sat; ▣Akaretler) Come to this out-of-the-way *meyhane* for simply prepared but absolutely sensational fish and vegetable mezes, best sampled in the mixed cold plate (₺30). Follow with some fried fish, a bowl of pasta or – if it's a Friday – a tasty bowl of fish soup.

VOGUE   INTERNATIONAL $$$

Map p242 (☑212-227 4404; www.istanbuldoors .com; 13th fl, A Blok, BJK Plaza, Spor Caddesi 92, Akaretler; starters ₺25-45, mains ₺28-65; ⊙noon-2am Mon-Sat, 10.30am-2am Sun; ☑; ▣Akaretler) It seems as if Vogue has been around for almost as long as the Republic. In fact this sophisticated bar-restaurant in an office block in Beşiktaş opened just over a decade ago. It's a favourite haunt of the Nişantaşı powerbroker set, who love nothing more than enjoying a drink at the terrace bar before moving into the restaurant for dinner.

ZUMA   JAPANESE $$$

Map p242 (☑212-236 2296; www.zumarestaurant .com; Salhane Sokak 7, Ortaköy; veg mains ₺11-26, fish mains ₺28-65, sushi & sashimi ₺39-89; ⊙lunch & dinner; ☑; ▣Kabataş Lisesi) Good Izakaya-style food and a stunning waterside location makes the local branch of this London favourite a safe bet. It has a bar and lounge on the top floor and a sushi bar and robata grill downstairs.

BANYAN   ASIAN $$$

Map p242 (☑212-259 9060; www.banyanrest aurant.com; 3rd fl, Salhane Sokak 3, Ortaköy; starters ₺12-35, mains ₺36-61; ⊙lunch & dinner; ▣Kabataş Lisesi) The menu here travels around Asia, featuring Thai, Japanese, Vietnamese and Chinese dishes including soups, satays and salads. The food claims to be good for the soul, and you can enjoy it while revelling in the exceptional views of the Ortaköy Mosque and Bosphorus Bridge from the terrace. There's a 15% discount at lunch.

AŞŞK KAHVE   CAFE $$

(Muallim Naci Caddesi 64b, Kuruçeşme; brunch ₺12-30; ⊙closed Mon winter; ☑; ▣Kuruçeşme) The city's glamour set loves this garden cafe to bits, and its weekend brunches are an institution. Go early to snaffle a table by the water and don't forget to have a Botox shot before you go – that way you'll fit in nicely. It's accessed via the stairs behind the Macrocenter.

BEŞIKTAŞ, ORTAKÖY & KURUÇEŞME EATING

DRINKING & NIGHTLIFE

SORTIE CLUB
(☎212-327 8585; www.eksenistanbul.com; Muallim Naci Caddesi 141, Kuruçeşme; cover charge Fri & Sat ₺50, Mon-Thu & Sun free; ⊗summer only; ⊠Şifa Yurdu) Sortie has long vied with Reina for the title of reigning queen of the Golden Mile, nipping at the heels of its rival dowager. It pulls in the city's glamour-pusses and poseurs, all of whom are on the lookout for the odd celebrity guest. If you book at one of the restaurants for dinner, you'll escape the cover charge (but be prepared for a hefty meal cheque).

ANJELIQUE CLUB
Map p242 (☎212-327 2844; www.istanbuldoors.com; Salhane Sokak 10, Ortaköy; no cover charge; ⊗6pm-4am; ⊠Kabataş Lisesi) Occupying a three-storey mansion on the water's edge near Ortaköy Meydanı, this glam venue is a safe bet if you want to have dinner, a few drinks and a dance or two. You can eat Asian or Mediterranean food. Reservations are essential.

REINA CLUB
(☎212-259 5919; www.reina.com.tr; Muallim Naci Caddesi 44, Ortaköy; cover charge Sat & Sun ₺50, Mon-Fri free; ⊗daily summer, Sat & Sun winter; ⊠Ortaköy) According to its website, Reina is where 'foreign heads of state discuss world affairs, business people sign agreements of hundred billions of dollars and world stars visit'. In reality. it's where Turkey's C-list celebrities congregate, the city's nouveaux riches flock and an occasional tourist gets past the doorman to ogle the spectacle. The Bosphorus location is truly extraordinary.

SUPPERCLUB CLUB
(☎212-261 1988; www.supperclub.com; Muallim Naci Caddesi 65; no cover charge; ⊗summer only; ⊠Ortaköy) With an all-white decor and a location close to the Bosphorus, Supperclub has an unmistakable resort feel. Customers lounge or dine in oversized beach beds in lieu of tables and chairs, enjoying the atmospheric lighting, live shows, imported DJ talents and highly creative cuisine.

ÇIRAĞAN PALACE KEMPINSKI HOTEL BAR, CAFE
Map p242 (www.ciragan-palace.com; Çırağan Caddesi 32, Ortaköy; ⊠Çırağan) Nursing a mega-pricey drink or coffee at one of the Çırağan's terrace tables and watching the scene around the city's best swimming pool, which is right on the Bosphorus, lets you sample the lifestyle of the city's rich and famous.

⭐ ENTERTAINMENT

İSTANBUL JAZZ CENTER JAZZ
Map p242 (☎212-327 5050; www.istanbuljazz.com; Salhane Sokak 10, Ortaköy; ⊗from 7pm, live sets 9.30pm & 12.30am Mon-Sat, closed summer; ⊠Kabataş Lisesi) JC's plays regular host to

THE BIG THREE

The Big Three (Üç Büyükler) teams in the national Super League (SüperLig) are Galatasaray (nickname: the Lions), Fenerbahçe (nickname: the Golden Canaries) and Beşiktaş (the Black Eagles). All are based in İstanbul, and locals are extravagantly proud of them. Indeed, when Galatasaray became the first Turkish team to win a UEFA Cup (in 2000), locals went wild with excitement – in many eyes it was probably the most significant event since the Conquest. There are two other teams based in the city: Kasımpaşa SK and İstanbul Büyükşehir Belediyespor.

Eighteen teams from all over Turkey compete from August to May. Each season three move up from the second league into the first and three get demoted. The top team of the first league plays in the UEFA Cup. Matches are usually held on the weekend, often on a Saturday night. Tickets are sold at the stadyum (stadium) on the day of the match, but most fans purchase them ahead of time through Biletix (www.biletix.com). Open seating is affordable; covered seating – which has the best views – can be very pricey.

Although violence at home games is not unknown, most matches are fine. If you're worried, avoid the Galatasaray and Fenerbahçe clashes, as the supporters of these arch-rivals occasionally become overly excited and throw a few punches.

members of the jazz world's who's-who. Its location in the Golden Mile accounts for the steep bill for dinner plus music and drinks.

bathwares. Come here to source items such as boudoir cushion-covers featuring Ottoman rococo prints – they're certain to wow your guests back home.

🛍 SHOPPING

 LOKUM FOOD

(www.lokumistanbul.com; Kuruçeşme Caddesi 19, Kuruçeşme; ⊘9am-7pm Mon-Sat; 🚌Kuruçeşme) *Lokum* (Turkish Delight) is elevated to the status of artwork at this boutique in Kuruçeşme. Owner/creator Zeynep Keyman aims to bring back the delights, flavors, knowledge and beauty of Ottoman-Turkish products such as *lokum, akide* candies (traditional boiled lollies, sometimes made with nuts and dried fruits), cologne water and scented candles. The gorgeous packaging makes for perfect gifts.

HAREMLIQUE HOMEWARES

Map p242 (www.haremlique.com; Şair Nedim Bey Caddesi 11, Beşiktaş; ⊘Mon-Sat; 🚌Akaretler) The shops around the fashionable W Istanbul hotel are some of the most glamorous in the city. Among the international labels that are based here is this local business, which sells top-drawer bed linen and

🏃 ACTIVITIES

FOUR SEASONS ISTANBUL AT
THE BOSPHORUS SPA

Map p242 (☏212-381 4160; www.fourseasons .com/bosphorus; Çırağan Caddesi 28; Beşiktaş; massage €140-250, 30/45min hamam experience €100/150; ⊘9am-9pm; 🚌Bahçeşehir Unv, Çırağan) The spa at this luxury hotel has wow factor in spades. Features include stunning indoor pool area, steam room, spa, sauna and meditation areas. The gorgeous marble hamam is the perfect choice if you're looking for an indulgent – rather than utilitarian – Turkish bath experience, You'll get full-day access to the spa facilities with any treatment.

BOSPHORUS TOURS BOAT TOUR

Map p242 (₺10; ⊘weekdays hourly from 2.20pm, weekends every 20min from 1pm) Every afternoon, ferries leave from the *iskele* behind the Ortaköy Mosque and sail to Anadolu Hisarı and back (approximately one hour).

BEŞİKTAŞ, ORTAKÖY & KURUÇEŞME SHOPPING

Üsküdar

Neighbourhood Top Five

1 Drinking tea at the **Mistanbul Hancı Cafe** (p149) while watching local anglers try their luck in the choppy water of the Bosphorus.

2 Absorbing the decidedly devout atmosphere in the **Atik Valide Mosque** (p148).

3 Admiring the striking modern architecture and magnificent interior decoration of the **Şakirin Mosque** (p148).

4 Heading to nearby **Kadıköy** (p149) for lunch and the best Turkish coffee in the city.

5 Enjoying the ferry trip from Europe to Asia.

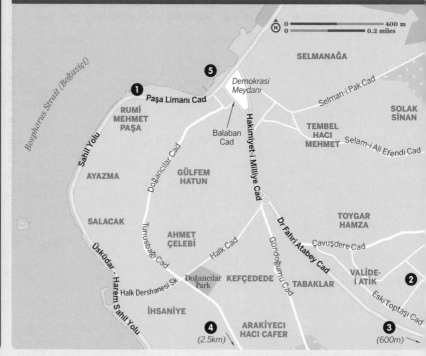

For more detail of this area see Map p245 ➡

Explore: Üsküdar

Üsküdar is a predominantly residential suburb that is best visited midweek, when it is alive with locals shopping in its busy retail strips, gossiping with neighbours on street corners, fishing off the Bosphorus shore and worshipping in its architecturally magnificent mosques. On weekends (especially Sundays) it can be as quiet as the grave.

Located on the Anatolian (Asian) side of the city, it is a short but atmospheric ferry ride from Eminönü and offers a very different – and authentically local – experience to those travellers who choose to spend a morning here and then move on to the nearby suburb of Kadıköy for lunch.

Local Life

➡ **The call to prayer** Üsküdar is a deeply religious suburb, so when the *ezan* (call to prayer) sounds you should expect to see plenty of worshippers rushing to the mosque. The sounds of the *müezzins* calling from the many mosques around the ferry dock is quite magical.

➡ **Waterside promenades** On weekend afternoons, locals love to saunter from the Şemsi Ahmed Paşa Mosque to Salacak or beyond, stopping at *çay bahçesis* (tea gardens) and refreshment kiosks along the way.

Getting There & Away

➡ **Ferry** Frequent passenger ferries travel between Üsküdar, Eminönü and Beşiktaş. Privately operated Dentur and Turyol ferries go to/from Kabataş, Eminönü and Karaköy.

➡ **Bus** Lines 12 and 12A link Üsküdar and Kadıköy. Catch them from the bus station in front of the *iskele* (ferry dock).

Lonely Planet's Top Tip

Females should bring a scarf or shawl to use as a head covering while visiting the mosques, and all visitors should dress appropriately (ie no shorts, short skirts or skimpy tops).

ÜSKÜDAR

✖ Best Places to Eat & Drink

➡ Mistanbul Hancı Cafe (p149)

➡ Çiya Sofrası (p149)

➡ Fazıl Bey (p149)

➡ Kadı Nimet Balıkçılık (p149)

➡ Baylan Pastanesi (p149)

For reviews, see p149 ➡

◉ Best Detour

➡ Kadıköy (p149)

For reviews, see 149 ➡

◉ Best Mosque Architecture

➡ Atik Valide Mosque (p148)

➡ Şakirin Mosque (p148)

➡ Şemsi Ahmed Paşa Mosque (p148)

For reviews, see p148 ➡

⊙ SIGHTS

ATİK VALİDE MOSQUE MOSQUE

Map p245 (Atik Valide Camii; Valide Imaret Sokak; ⊜Üsküdar) This is one of the two great İstanbul mosque complexes designed by Mimar Sinan. Though not as spectacular as the Süleymaniye (p88), it was designed to a similar plan and built in a similarly commanding location. Its extensive *külliye* (includes a now decommissioned hamam on Dr Fahri Atabey Caddesi and, closer to the mosque, an *imaret* (soup kitchen), *medrese* (Islamic school of higher studies), *darüşşifa* (hospital) and *han* (caravanserai).

The mosque was built on Üsküdar's highest hill in 1583 for Valide Sultan Nurbanu, wife of Selim II and mother of Murat III. Nurbanu had been captured by Turks on the Aegean island of Paros when she was 12 years old, ending up as a slave in Topkapı. The poor woman had a lot to bear – first being kidnapped and then taking the fancy of Selim the Sot. But she was his favourite concubine and became a clever player in Ottoman politics. The Kandınlar Sultanatı (Rule of the Women), under which a succession of powerful women influenced the decisions made by their sultan husbands and sons, began with her. Murat adored his mother and on her death commissioned Sinan to build this monument to her.

The mosque is in the neighbourhood of Valide-i Atik, up Hakimiyet-i Milliye and Dr Fahri Atabey Caddesis.

ŞAKİRİN MOSQUE MOSQUE

(cnr Huhkuyusu Caddesi & Dr Burhanettin Üstünel Sokak; ⊜6, 9A, 11P, 11V, 12A, 12C) One of the few architecturally notable modern mosques in İstanbul, this 2009 building was designed by Hüsrev Tayla and its interior was decorated by Zeynep Fadıllıoğlu, best known for her glamorous restaurant and nightclub fit outs. The building itself has a wonderful transparency, but the highlight is the interior, which features a gorgeous turquoise-and-gold mihrab and a magnificent 'dripping glass' chandelier.

The mosque is opposite the Zeynep Kamil Hospital. Take a bus from the *iskele* and alight at the Zeynep Kamil stop, or walk up Dr Fahri Atabey Caddesi from the Atik Valide Mosque and turn right into Nuhkuyusu Caddesi.

ÇİNİLİ MOSQUE MOSQUE

Map p245 (Çinili Camii, Tiled Mosque; Çinili Hamam Sokak; ⊜Üsküdar) Built in 1640, little mosque is fairly unprepossessing from the outside, but the interior is a totally different story. The walls are decorated with gorgeous İznik tiles, the bequest of Mahpeyker Kösem, wife of Sultan Ahmet I and mother of sultans Murat IV and İbrahim I ('İbrahim the Crazy'). It's a 10-minute walk to get here from the Atik Valide Mosque.

ŞEMSİ AHMED PAŞA MOSQUE MOSQUE

Map p245 (Şemsi Paşa Camii, Kuskonmaz Camii; Paşa Limanı Caddesi; ⊜Üsküdar) This charming mosque complex on the waterfront was designed by Mimar Sinan and built in 1580 for one of Süleyman the Magnificent's grand viziers, Şemsi Ahmed Paşa. It is modest in size and decoration, reflecting the fact that its benefactor (whose tomb has an opening into the mosque) only occupied the position of grand vizier for a couple of months.

MİHRİMAH SULTAN MOSQUE MOSQUE

Map p245 (Mihrimah Sultan Camii; Paşa Limanı Caddesi; ⊜Üsküdar) Sometimes called the İskele (Dock) Camii, this mosque was designed by Mimar Sinan for Süleyman the Magnificent's daughter Mihrimah and built between 1547 and 1548. Look out for its attractive ablutions fountain in the traffic island and listen for the *müezzin's* call to prayer if you're in Üsküdar around noon – he has one of the best voices in the city.

YENİ VALİDE MOSQUE MOSQUE

Map p245 (Yeni Valide Camii, New Queen Mother's Mosque; Demokrasi Meydanı; ⊜Üsküdar) Unusual due to the striking 'birdcage' tomb in its overgrown garden, this mosque was built by Sultan Ahmet III between 1708 and 1710 for his mother, Gülnuş Emetullah, who had been the favourite concubine of Mehmet IV. Built late in the period of classical Ottoman architecture, it lacks the architectural distinction of many of Üsküdar's other mosques.

AYAZMA MOSQUE MOSQUE

Map p245 (Mehmet Paşa Değirmeni Sk; ⊜Üsküdar) One of the most prominent sights on the Üsküdar skyline, this baroque-style mosque was built in 1760–61 by Sultan Mustafa III, and is accessed via a courtyard and graceful set of entry stairs.

KADIKÖY

If you feel like eating, drinking or shopping after your explorations in Üsküdar, we recommend that you take a bus or taxi to neighbouring Kadıköy.

Kadıköy's main attraction is a large and wonderfully diverse produce market near the *iskele*. Amid this are two excellent restaurants and two equally excellent cafes.

Known throughout the culinary world, Musa Dağdeviren's **Çiya Sofrası** (www.ciya .com.tr; Güneşlibahçe Sokak 43; portions ₺10-15; ⊙11am-11pm; ▣Kadıköy) showcases dishes from the region surrounding the chef/owner's home city of Gaziantep. While standards in the kitchen seemed to have fallen in recent times, it's still a great place to try Turkish regional specialities. Its next-door **kebapçı** (kebaps ₺15-35) sells a huge variety of tasty meat dishes. Neither sells alcohol.

Locals love **Kadı Nımet Balıkçılık** (🗌216-348 7389; Serasker Caddesi 10a, Kadıköy; mezes ₺6-15, fish mains ₺10-30; ⊙noon-midnight; ▣Kadıköy), a casual place tucked among the fish stalls. It serves some of the freshest seafood in the city and is always busy, so book for dinner. Try the *levrek dolma* (stuffed sea bass meze).

Just down from Kadı Nımet Balıkçılık is **Fazıl Bey** (www.fazilbey.com; Serasker Caddesi 3, Kadıköy; ⊙daily; ▣Kadıköy), a tiny cafe/coffee roastery that has been serving İstanbul's best Turkish coffee since 1923.

Closer to the *iskele*, **Baylan Pastanesi** (🗌216-336 2881; www.baylanpastanesi.com .tr; Muvakkithane Caddesi 9; ⊙7am-10pm; ▣Kadıköy) is known for its excellent espresso coffee, decadent ice-cream sundaes and delicious cakes and pastries (try the *ay çöreği*, a pastry with a walnut, sultana and spice filling).

Turkish Flavours (p124) conducts daily tours of the Spice Market in Eminönü and the produce market here. These include a banquet lunch at Çiya Sofrası.

To get here by bus, take bus 12 or 12A from the bus station in front of the *iskele* (ferry dock). From Kadıköy, ferries travel back to Eminönü and Karaköy.

KIZ KULESİ
TOWER

Map p245 (▣Üsküdar) İstanbul is a maritime city, so it's appropriate that one of its most distinctive landmarks is on the water. In ancient times a predecessor of the current 18th-century structure was used as a toll booth and defence point; the current building has functioned as a lighthouse, quarantine station and restaurant. In 1999 James Bond visited in *The World Is Not Enough*.

The tower is open to the public during the day as a cafe-restaurant. Small boats run from Salacak to the island every 15 minutes from noon to late at night Tuesday to Sunday. Unfortunately, the views from the island aren't great and the tower itself isn't very interesting inside.

EATING & DRINKING

One of the city's most conservative areas, Üsküdar is not the place to come if you're looking for a boozy night on the town. During the day myriad kebab joints and *pastanes* (cake shops) in the street around the ferry terminal do a bustling trade.

MİSTANBUL HANCI CAFE
TEA GARDEN

Map p245 (Sahil Yolu 12; ⊙9am-midnight) The million-dollar location overlooking the water makes this *çay bahçesi* next to the Şemşi Ahmed Paşa Mosque a popular choice. It's a great spot for whiling away an hour or so while admiring the view and monitoring the exertions of the fishermen who congregate here to try their luck in the choppy waters of the Bosphorus.

KANAAT LOKANTASI
LOKANTA $

Map p245 (Selman-i Pak Caddesi 25; portions ₺7-17, kebaps ₺10-15; ⊙6.30am-11pm; ▣Üsküdar) This barnlike place near the *iskele* has been serving up competent *hazır yemek* (ready-made food) since 1933, and is particularly fancied for its desserts, including a house-made ice cream made from sheep's milk and *sahlep* (ground orchid root). Its understated but pleasing decor features framed photographs of old street scenes.

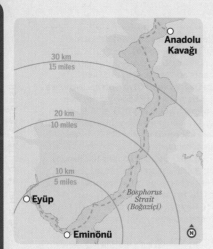

Anadolu
Kavağı

30 km
15 miles

20 km
10 miles

10 km
5 miles

*Bosphorus
Strait
(Boğaziçi)*

Eyüp

Eminönü

Ferry Trips from İstanbul

The Bosphorus p151

Running from the Galata Bridge all the way to the Black Sea (Karadeniz), 32km north, the mighty Bosphorus Strait is İstanbul's major thoroughfare and has been so since classical times.

The Golden Horn p159

This stretch of water to the north of the Galata Bridge offers visitors a glimpse into the suburbs and lifestyles of working-class İstanbul. Get here before it gentrifies.

Princes' Islands p162

A favourite day-trip destination for İstanbullus, the Adalar (Islands) lie in the Sea of Marmara, about 20km southeast of the city. Come here to escape the sensory overload of the big smoke.

The Bosphorus

Explore

The Bosphorus deserves at least one day of your time; two days (one for each shore) is even better.

For the European Shore take the morning cruise from Eminönü, alighting at Sarıyer and working your way back to Kabataş or Taksim by bus, stopping at the Sadberk Hanım Museum, the Sakıp Sabancı Museum, the fortress at Rumeli Hisarı and the waterside suburbs of Bebek and/or Ortaköy on the way.

Take the morning cruise from Eminönü for the Asian Shore, alight at Anadolu Kavağı and work your way back by bus, stopping to visit Hıdiv Kasrı, Küçüksu Kasrı and Beylerbeyi Palace before getting off the bus at Üsküdar and catching a ferry back to Eminönü, Karaköy or Kabataş.

The Best...

➜ **Sight** Beylerbeyi Palace (p152)

➜ **Place to Eat** MüzedeChanga (p158)

➜ **Place to Drink** Sütiş (p159)

Top Tip

If you buy a return ticket on the Bosphorus Cruise, you'll be forced to spend three hours in the tourist-trap village of Anadolu Kavağı. It's much better to buy a one-way ticket and alight at Sarıyer or at Kanlıca and make your way back to town by bus.

Getting There & Away

Ferry Most day trippers take the Uzun Boğaz Turu (Long Bosphorus Tour) operated by Istanbul Şehir Hatları (İstanbul City Routes). The Bosphorus Excursion Ferry travels the entire length of the strait in a 90-minute one-way trip and departs from the ferry dock at Eminönü daily at 10.35am. From April to October there is usually an extra service at 1.35pm, and during summer there is an extra service at noon. A ticket costs ₺25 return (*çift*), ₺15 one way (*tek yön*). The ferry stops at Beşiktaş, Kanlıca, Sarıyer, Rumeli Kavağı and Anadolu Kavağı (the turnaround point). It is not possible to get on and off the ferry at stops along the way using the same ticket.

The ferry returns from Anadolu Kavağı at 3pm (plus 4.15pm from April to October).

From April to October, Istanbul Şehir Hatları also operates a two-hour Kısa Boğaz Turu (Short Bosphorus Tour) that leaves Eminönü daily at 2.30pm. It travels as far as the Fatih Bridge before returning to Eminönü. Tickets cost ₺10.

There are also occasional commuter ferries that cross the Bosphorus. Useful services include Kanlıca to Emirgan (1.05pm, 4.05pm, 5.20pm); Emirgan to Kanlıca and Bebek (4.15pm) and Anadolu Kavağı to Sarıyer (12 ferries a day from 7.15am to 11pm). Note that some of the services are more frequent on Sundays.

Check www.sehirhatlari.com.tr for timetable and fare updates for all services, as these often change.

Another option is to buy a ticket for a cruise on a private excursion boat. Although these only take you as far as Anadolu Hisarı and back (without stopping), the fact that the boats are smaller means that you travel closer to the shoreline and so are able to see a lot more. The entire trip takes about 90 minutes and tickets cost ₺10. Turyol boats leave from the dock on the western side of the Galata Bridge every hour from 11am to 6pm on weekdays and every 45 minutes or so from 11am to 7.15pm on weekends. Boats operated by other companies leave from near the Boğaz İskelesi.

Bus From Sarıyer, lines 25E and 40 head south to Emirgan. From Emirgan, 22, 22RE and 25E head to Kabataş and 40, 40T and 42T go to Taksim. All travel via Rumeli Hisarı, Bebek, Ortaköy, Yıldız and Beşiktaş.

If you decide to catch the ferry to Anadolu Kavağı and make your way back to town by bus, catch line 15A, which leaves from a square straight ahead from the ferry terminal en route to Kavacık Aktarma. Get off at Kanlıca to visit Hıdiv Kasrı or to transfer to lines 15, 15F or 15P, which will take you south to Üsküdar via the Küçüksu stop (for Küçüksu Kasrı) and the Beylerbeyi Sarayı stop (for Beylerbeyi).

All bus tickets and commuter ferry trips cost ₺2 (₺1.75 with an İstanbulkart).

Need to Know

➜ **Area Codes** 📞212 (European shore) and 📞216 (Asian shore)

➜ **Duration** 90 minutes Eminönü to Anadolu Kavağı

➜ **Cost** ₺15 one way, ₺25 return

FERRY TRIPS FROM ISTANBUL THE BOSPHORUS

TOP SIGHTS
BEYLERBEYI PALACE

Every sultan needs a place to escape to, and this 26-room palace was the place for Abdül Aziz I (r 1861–76). The baroque-style building was designed by Sarkis Balyan, brother of Nikoğos (architect of Dolmabahçe), and it delighted both Abdül Aziz and the foreign dignitaries who visited. The palace's last imperial 'guest' was the former sultan Abdül Hamit II, who spent the last years of his life (1913–18) under house arrest here.

The compulsory guided tour whips you past rooms decorated with frescos of maritime scenes, Bohemian crystal chandeliers, Ming vases and sumptuous Hereke carpets. It has a grand Selamlik (ceremonial quarters) and a small but opulent harem. Highlights include the music room with inlaid walnut walls, a sitting room with parquet floors and walls inlaid with ebony and wood, and a dining room with chairs covered in gazelle skin. After the tour, enjoy a glass of tea in the pretty garden cafe.

Unfortunately, the Uzun Boğaz Turu (Long Bosphorus Tour) doesn't stop at Beylerbeyi. You can either visit at another time or alight at the ferry's last stop in Anadolu Kavağı and make your way back here by bus along the Asian shore.

DON'T MISS...

➡ Interior

➡ Bathing Pavilions

➡ Garden Cafe

PRACTICALITIES

➡ Beylerbeyi Sarayı

➡ www.millisaraylar.gov.tr

➡ Abdullah Ağa Caddesi, Beylerbeyi

➡ admission ₺20

➡ ⊙8.30am-4.30pm Tue, Wed & Fri-Sun

➡ 🚢Beylerbeyi Sarayı

⊙ SIGHTS

⊙ Departure Point: Eminönü

Hop onto the boat at the Boğaz İskelesi (Bosphorus Ferry Dock) on the Eminönü quay near the Galata Bridge. It's always a good idea to arrive 30 minutes or so before the scheduled departure time and manoeuvre your way to the front of the queue that builds near the doors leading to the dock. When these open and the boat can be boarded, you'll need to move fast to score a good seat. The best spots are on the sides of the upper deck at the bow.

The Asian shore is to the right side of the ferry as it cruises up the strait, Europe is to the left. When you start your trip, watch out for the small island of Kız Kulesi (p149), just off the Asian shore near Üsküdar. Just before the first stop at Beşiktaş, you'll pass the grandiose Dolmabahçe Palace (p141), built on the European shore of the Bosphorus by Sultan Abdül Mecit between 1843 and 1854.

⊙ Beşiktaş to Kanlıca

After a brief stop at Beşiktaş, Çırağan Palace (p142), once home to Sultan Abdül Aziz and now a luxury hotel, looms up on the left. Next to it is the long yellow building occupied by the prestigious Galatasaray University. On the Asian shore is the Fethi Ahmed Paşa Yalı, a wide white building with a red-tiled roof that was built in the pretty suburb of Kuzguncuk in the late 18th century. The word *yalı* comes from the Greek word for 'coast', and describes the timber summer residences along the Bosphorus built by Ottoman aristocracy and foreign ambassadors in the 17th, 18th and 19th centuries, now all protected by the country's heritage laws. A little further along on your left is the pretty Ortaköy Mosque (p143), its dome and two minarets dwarfed by the adjacent **Bosphorus Bridge**, opened in 1973 on the 50th anniversary of the founding of the Turkish Republic.

Under the bridge on the European shore is the green-and-cream-coloured **Hatice Sultan Yalı** (Map p242), once the home of Sultan Murad V's daughter, Hatice. On the Asian side is the charming Beylerbeyi

Palace (p152) – look for its whimsical marble bathing pavilions on the shore; one was for men, the other for the women of the Harem.

Past the small village of Çengelköy on the Asian side is the imposing **Kuleli Military School** (Çengelköy; ⛴Eminönü-Kavaklar tourist ferry), built in 1860 and immortalised in İrfan Orga's wonderful memoir, *Portrait of a Turkish Family*. Look out for its two 'witch-hat' towers.

Almost opposite Kuleli on the European shore is **Arnavutköy** (Albanian Village), which boasts a number of gabled Ottoman-era wooden houses. On the hill above it are buildings formerly occupied by the American College for Girls. Its most famous alumni was Halide Edib Adıvar, who wrote about the years she spent here in her 1926 work, *The Memoir of Halide Edib*.

Arnavutköy runs straight into the glamorous suburb of **Bebek**, known for its up-market shopping and chic cafe-bars such as Mangerie, Lucca and Kitchenette. It also has the most glamorous Starbucks in the city (right on the water, and with a lovely terrace). Bebek's shops surround a small park and the Ottoman Revivalist–style **Bebek Mosque**; to the east of these is the ferry dock, to the south is the **Egyptian consulate building** (Bebek; ⛴Eminönü-Kavaklar tourist ferry), thought by some critics to be the work of Italian architect Raimondo D'Aronco. This gorgeous art nouveau mini-palace was built for Emine Hanım, mother of the last khedive of Egypt, Abbas Hilmi II. It's the white building with a mansard roof and an ornate wrought-iron fence.

Opposite Bebek on the Asian shore is **Kandilli**, the 'Place of Lamps', named after the lamps that were lit here to warn ships of the particularly treacherous currents at the headland. Among the many *yalıs* here is the huge red **Kont Ostrorog Yalı**, built in the 19th century by Count Leon Ostorog, a Polish adviser to the Ottoman court; French novelist Pierre Loti stayed here when he visited İstanbul in the 1890s. A bit further on, past Kandilli, is the long, white **Kıbrıslı ('Cypriot') Mustafa Emin Paşa Yalı**, which dates from 1760.

Next to the Kıbrıslı are the **Büyük Göksu Deresi** (Great Heavenly Stream) and **Küçük Göksu Deresi** (Small Heavenly Stream), two brooks that descend from the Asian hills into the Bosphorus. Between them is a fertile delta, grassy and shady, which the Ottoman elite thought perfect for picnics. Foreign residents referred to it as 'The Sweet Waters of Asia'.

FERRY TRIPS FROM İSTANBUL THE BOSPHORUS

⊙ TOP SIGHTS
HİDİV KASRI

The Ottomans conquered Egypt in 1517. After surviving a challenge to their rule by the French from 1798 to 1801, they again lost control in 1805, this time to an Albanian-born military commander of the Ottoman army in Egypt called Muhammed Ali, who was given quasi-independence and the title of *hıdiv* (khedive or viceroy) by the sultan.

The Egyptian khedives maintained close ties with the Ottoman Empire and often spent summers in İstanbul. In 1906, Khedive Abbas Hilmi II built himself this palatial art nouveau villa on the most dramatic promontory on the Bosphorus. It became the property of the municipality in the 1930s.

Restored after decades of neglect, the villa now functions as a restaurant and cafe. The building is an architectural gem and the garden is superb, especially during the İstanbul International Tulip Festival in April.

The villa is a 20-minute walk from the ferry dock. Head left (north) up Halide Edip Adivar Caddesi and turn right into the second street (Kafadar Sokak). Turn left into Hacı Muhittin Sokağı and walk up the hill until you come to a fork in the road. Take the left fork and follow the 'Hadiv Kasrı' signs to the villa's car park and garden.

DON'T MISS...

➡ The garden
➡ The entrance lobby
➡ Main dining room

PRACTICALITIES

➡ Khedive's Villa
➡ www.beltur.com.tr
➡ Çubuklu Yolu 32, Çubuklu
➡ admission free
➡ ⊙9am-10pm

If the weather was good, the sultan joined the picnic, and did so in style. Sultan Abdül Mecit's answer to a simple picnic blanket was **Küçüksu Kasrı** (216-332 3303; Küçüksu Caddesi, Beykoz; admission ₺5; 9.30am-4pm Tue, Wed & Fri-Sun; Küçüksu), an ornate hunting lodge built in 1856–7. Earlier sultans had wooden kiosks here, but architect Nikoğos Balyan designed a rococo gem in marble for his monarch. You'll see its ornate cast-iron fence, boat dock and wedding-cake exterior from the ferry.

Close to the Fatih Bridge are the majestic structures of **Rumeli Hisarı** (Fortress of Europe; 212-263 5305; Yahya Kemal Caddesi 42; admission ₺3; 9am-noon & 12.30-4.30pm Thu-Tue; Rumeli Hisarı) and **Anadolu Hisarı** (Fortress of Anatolia). Mehmet the Conqueror had Rumeli Hisarı built in a mere four months in 1452, in preparation for his siege of Byzantine Constantinople. For its location, he chose the narrowest point of the Bosphorus, opposite Anadolu Hisarı, which Sultan Beyazıt I had built in 1391. By doing so, Mehmet was able to control all traffic on the strait, cutting the city off from resupply by sea.

To speed Rumeli Hisarı's completion, Mehmet ordered each of his three viziers to take responsibility for one of the three main towers. If the tower's construction was not completed on schedule, the vizier would pay with his life. Not surprisingly, the work was completed on time. The useful military life of the mighty fortress lasted less than one year. After the conquest of Constantinople, it was used as a glorified Bosphorus tollbooth for a while, then as a barracks, a prison and finally as an open-air theatre.

Within Rumeli Hisarı's walls are parklike grounds, an open-air theatre and the minaret of a ruined mosque. Steep stairs (with no barriers, so beware!) lead up to the ramparts and towers; the views of the Bosphorus are magnificent. Just next to the fortress is a clutch of cafes and restaurants, the most popular of which are Sade Kahve, Nar Cafe and Mama.

The ferry doesn't stop at Rumeli Hisarı; you can either leave the ferry at Kanlıca and catch a taxi across the Fatih Bridge (this will cost around ₺20 including the bridge toll) or you can visit on your way back to town from Sarıyer. Though it's not open as a museum, visitors are free to wander about Anadolu Hisarı's ruined walls.

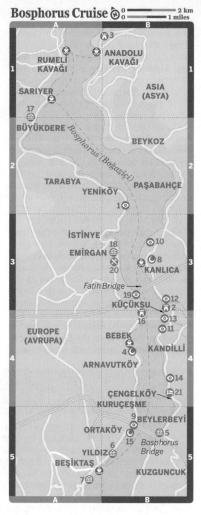

Bosphorus Cruise

There are many architecturally and historically important *yalıs* in and around Anadolu Hisarı. These include the **Köprülü Amcazade Hüseyin Paşa Yalı**, built for one of Mustafa II's grand viziers in 1698 and the oldest *yalı* on the Bosphorus. Next door, the **Zarif Mustafa Paşa Yalı** was built in the early 19th century by the official coffee maker to Sultan Mahmut II. Look for its upstairs salon, which juts out over the water and is supported by unusual curved timber struts.

Almost directly under the **Fatih Bridge** on the European shore is the huge stone **Tophane Müşiri Zeki Paşa Yalı**, a mansion

Bosphorus Cruise

built in the early 20th century for a field marshall in the Ottoman army. Later, it was sold to Sabiha Sultan, daughter of Mehmet VI, the last of the Ottoman sultans, and her husband İmer Faruk Efendi, grandson of Sultan Abdül Aziz. When the sultanate was abolished in 1922, Mehmet walked from this palace onto a British warship, never to return to Turkey.

Past the bridge on the Asian side is **Kanlıca**, the ferry's next stop. This charming village is famous for the rich and delicious yoghurt produced here, which is sold on the ferry and in two cafes on the shady waterfront square. The small **Gâzi İskender Paşa Mosque** in the square dates from 1560 and was designed by Mimar Sinan.

High on a promontory above Kanlıca is Hıdiv Kasrı (p153), a gorgeous art nouveau villa built by the last khedive of Egypt as a summer residence for use during his family's annual visits to İstanbul. You can see its square white tower (often flying a Turkish flag) from the ferry.

◉ Kanlıca to Sarıyer

On the opposite shore is the wealthy suburb of **Emirgan**, home to the impressive **Sakıp Sabancı Museum** (Sakıp Sabancı Müsezi; 🕿212-277 2200; http://muze.sabanciuniv.edu; Sakıp Sabancı Caddesi 42; exhibition admission varies; ⊙10am-6pm Tue, Thu, Fri & Sun, to 10pm Wed & Sat; 🚇Emirgan), which hosts international travelling art exhibitions. Inside the museum grounds is one of İstanbul's most stylish eateries, MüzedeChanga, with an extensive terrace and magnificent Bosphorus views.

On the hill above Emirgan is **Emirgan Woods**, a huge public reserve that is particularly beautiful in April, when it is carpeted with thousands of tulips.

North of Emirgan, there's a ferry dock near the small yacht-lined cove of **İstinye**. Nearby, on a point jutting out from the European shore, is the suburb of **Yeniköy**. This was a favourite summer resort for the Ottomans, as indicated by the cluster of lavish 18th- and 19th-century *yalıs* around the ferry dock. The most notable of these is the frilly white **Ahmed Afif Paşa Yalı**, designed by Alexandre Vallaury, architect of the Pera Palas Hotel in Beyoğlu, and built in the late 19th century.

On the opposite shore is the village of **Paşabahçe**, famous for its glassware factory. A bit further on is the fishing village of **Beykoz**, which has a graceful ablutions fountain, the **İshak Ağa Çeşmesi**, dating from 1746, near the village square. Much of the land along the Bosphorus shore north of **Beykoz** is a military zone.

Originally called Therapia for its healthy climate, the little cove of **Tarabya** on the European shore has been a favourite summer watering place for İstanbul's well-to-do for centuries, though modern developments such as the horrendous multistorey Grand Hotel Tarabya right on the promon-

FERRY TRIPS FROM İSTANBUL THE BOSPHORUS

1. Bosphorus ferry crossing (p151)
Istanbul viewed from the water

2. Rumeli Hisarı and Fatih Bridge (p154)
Built in 1452, Rumeli Hisarı (Fortress of Europe) on the shores of the Bosphorous

3. Princes' Islands (p162)
Fayton (horse-drawn carriage) ride on the car-less Princes' Islands

tory have poisoned much of its charm. For an account of Therapia in its heyday, read Harold Nicolson's 1921 novel *Sweet Waters*. Nicolson, who is best known as Vita Sackville-West's husband, served as the third secretary in the British embassy in Constantinople between 1912 and 1914, the years of the Balkan wars, and clearly knew Therapia well. In the novel, the main character, Eirene, who was based on Vita, spent her summers here.

North of the village are some of the old summer embassies of foreign powers. When the heat and fear of disease increased in the warm months, foreign ambassadors would retire to palatial residences, complete with lush gardens, on this shore. The region for such embassy residences extended north to the village of **Büyükdere**, also notable for its churches and the **Sadberk Hanım Museum** (☎212-242 3813; www.sadberkhanim muzesi.org.tr; Piyasa Caddesi 27-29; adult/student ₺7/₺2; ⊙10am-5pm Thu-Tue). Named after the wife of the late Vehbi Koç, founder of Turkey's foremost commercial empire, the museum is housed in a graceful old *yalı* and is a showcase for her extraordinary private collection of antiquities and Ottoman heirlooms. This includes İznik and Kütahya ceramics, Ottoman silk textiles and needlework, and an exquisite collection of diadems from the Mycenaean, Archaic and Classical periods. To get here, alight from the ferry at Sarıyer and walk left (south) from the ferry dock for approximately 10 minutes.

The residents of **Sarıyer**, the next village up from Büyükdere on the European shore, have traditionally made a living by fishing, and the area around the ferry terminal (the next stop) is full of fish restaurants.

⊙ Sarıyer to Anadolu Kavaği

From Sarıyer, it's only a short trip to **Rumeli Kavağı**, a sleepy place where the only excitement comes courtesy of the arrival and departure of the ferry. To the south of the town is the shrine of the Muslim saint **Telli Baba**, reputed to be able to find suitable husbands for young women who pray there.

Anadolu Kavağı, on the opposite shore, is where the Long Bosphorus Tour finishes its journey. Once a fishing village, its local economy now relies on the tourism trade and its main square is full of mediocre fish restaurants and their touts.

Perched above the village are the ruins of **Anadolu Kavağı Kalesi** (Yoros Kalesi; Anadolu Kavağı; ⛴Eminönü-Kavaklar tourist ferry), a medieval castle that originally had eight massive towers in its walls. Built by the Byzantines, it was restored and reinforced by the Genoese in 1350, and later by the Ottomans. Unfortunately the castle is in such a serious state of disrepair that it has been fenced so that noone can enter and enjoy its spectacular Black Sea views. As a result, we suggest giving the steep 25-minute walk up here a miss.

✖ EATING & DRINKING

TOP CHOICE MÜZEDECHANGA   MODERN TURKISH $$$
(☎212-323 0901; www.changa-istanbul.com; Sakıp Sabancı Müzesi, Sakıp Sabancı Caddesi 42, Emirgan; starters ₺18-29; mains ₺37-49; ⊙10.30am-1am Tue-Sun) Operated by Changa, one of the city's top restaurants, this venue in the Sakıp Sabancı Museum has a terrace with Bosphorus views, an ultrastylish interior fit out and a delicious menu. It's extremely popular for weekend lunch or brunch. If you don't feel like visiting the museum, door staff will waive the entry fee and point you towards the restaurant.

MAMA   ITALIAN $$
(www.mamapizzeria.com; Baltalimanı Caddesi 4, Rumeli Hisarı; pizzas ₺16-33, pastas ₺18-29; ⊙10am-11.30pm Mon-Sat, from 9am Sun; ☐22, 22RE, 25E from Kabataş, 40, 40T, 42T from Taksim) The resort decor and wide range of Italian dishes will make you feel as if you're relaxing in a trattoria on the Amalfi Coast rather than here in İstanbul. Great pizzas and pastas, a good range of drinks (including excellent fresh *limonata*), lavish Sunday brunch choices and a kids' menu all make Mama as loved as its namesake.

SUMAHAN ON
THE WATER   CAFE, RESTAURANT $$$
(www.sumahan.com; Sumahan on the Water, Kuleli Caddesi 51, Çengelköy; mezes ₺14-15, mains ₺30-38; ⊙lunch & dinner; ☐15, 15F, 15H, 15ÇK, 15M, 15N, 15P, 15ŞN, 15Y from Üsküdar) The grassed waterside terrace at this boutique hotel is an idyllic place to while away the afternoon hours. Ferries, fishing boats and private launches will pass as you sit in the sun enjoying well-prepared Turkish dishes and a glass of wine or a good

Italian-style coffee. You'll find it north of the *iskele* (ferry dock); the entrance is via the hotel foyer.

SÜTİŞ
CAFE $

(Sakıp Sabancı Caddesi 1, Emirgan; ☺6am-1am; ☐22, 22RE, 25E from Kabataş, 40, 40T,42T from Taksim) The Bosphorus branch of this popular chain has an expansive and extremely comfortable terrace overlooking the water. It's known for serving all-day breakfasts and milk-based puddings – we recommend the *simit* (sesame-encrusted bread ring) with honey and *kaymak* (clotted cream). Watching the valet-parking ritual on weekends is hilarious.

LUCCA
BAR, CAFE

(☑212-257 1255; www.luccastyle.com; Cevdetpaşa Caddesi 51b, Bebek; ☐22, 22RE, 25E from Kabataş, 40, 40T, 42T from Taksım) Glam young things flock here on Friday and Saturday nights to see and be seen, but the mood is more relaxed during the week. Food choices are global, the caffe latte reigns supreme during the day and cocktails claim the spotlight at night.

The Golden Horn

Explore

You can explore the Golden Horn (Haliç) in half a day by boarding the ferry in Eminönü, alighting once at either the Rahmi M Koç Müzesi or the Eyüp Sultan Mosque and then reboarding a ferry for the return trip.

If you have a full day, you could visit both of these sights or head to Aynalıkavak Kasrı after visiting the Rahmi M Koç Müzesi. Another good option is to alight at Ayvansaray and follow our walking tour along the historic land walls, visit the Kariye Müzesi and then make your way back to Eminönü by the return ferry or by bus.

The Best...
⇒ **Sight** Rahmi M Koç Museum
⇒ **Entertainment** Sunday jazz at Tamirane (p161)
⇒ **Place to Drink** Pierre Loti Cafe (p112)

TOP SIGHTS
RAHMI M KOÇ MUSEUM

This splendid museum is dedicated to the history of transport, industry and communications in Turkey. Its collection of artefacts from İstanbul's industrial past is highly eclectic, giving the impression of being a grab-bag of cool stuff collected over the decades or donated to the museum by individuals, organisations or companies who didn't know what else to do with it. This might sound like we're damning the museum with faint praise, but this is far from the case – in fact, we highly recommend a visit, particularly if you are travelling with children.

The museum is in two parts: a new building on the Golden Horn side of the road and a superbly restored and converted Byzantine stone building opposite. The exhibits concerned with forms of transport are particularly fascinating: you can sit in a classic car; take a cruise on a restored 1936 steam tug; enter the cabin of a Douglas DC-3 Dakota; board a 1944 US naval submarine; or take a short trip on a working narrow-gauge railway.

Excellent interpretive panels in Turkish and English are provided. There's also a cafe right on the waterfront.

DON'T MISS...
⇒ Sultan Abdul Aziz's railway carriage
⇒ 1961 Amphicar (half car, half boat)
⇒ Re-created olive-oil factory

PRACTICALITIES
⇒ Rahmi M Koç Müzesi
⇒ www.rmk-museum.org.tr
⇒ Hasköy Caddesi 5, Hasköy
⇒ adult/child ₺6/3
⇒ ☺10am-5pm Mon-Fri, to 6pm/8pm Sat & Sun winter/summer
⇒ ☐47 from Eminönü, 54HT from Taksim, ☐Hasköy

Golden Horn Cruise

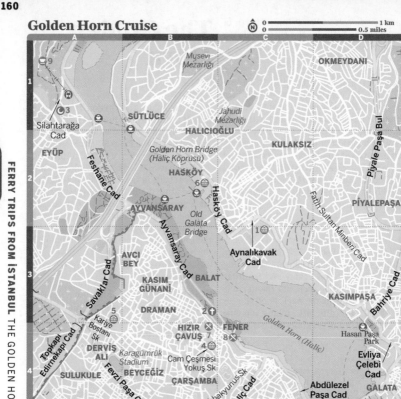

Top Tip

If visiting the Eyüp Sultan Mosque, dress appropriately (no short or skimpy skirts and tops). Females should bring a scarf or shawl to use as a head covering.

Getting There & Away

Ferry Golden Horn ferries leave Eminönü every hour from 10.45am to 7.45pm; the last ferry returns to Eminönü from Eyüp at 7.45pm. The ferry trip takes 35 minutes and costs ₺2 per leg (₺1.75 if you use an İstanbulkart). Check www.sehirhatlari .com.tr for timetable and fare updates.

Bus If you wish to return from Eyüp by bus rather than ferry, buses 36CE, 44B and 99 travel from outside the ferry stop at Eyüp via Balat and Fener to Eminönü. Bus 39 travels to Beyazıt via Edirnekapı, allowing you to stop and visit the Kariye Museum on your way back.

Golden Horn Cruise

To return to Taksim from Hasköy or Sütluce by bus, take bus 54HT. For Eminönü, take bus 47.

All bus tickets cost ₺2 (₺1.75 if you use an İstanbulkart).

Need to Know

→ **Area Code** 212
→ **Duration** Ferry 35 minutes one way
→ **Cost** ₺2

◉ SIGHTS

◉ Departure Point: Eminönü

These ferries start in Üsküdar on the Asian side before taking on most of their passengers at the Haliç İskelesi (Golden Horn Ferry Dock) on the western side of the Galata Bridge at Eminönü. The ferry dock is behind a car park next to the Storks building. The ferry then passes underneath the Atatürk Bridge and stops at Kasımpaşa on the opposite side of the Golden Horn. This area is where the Ottoman imperial naval yards were located, and some of the original building stock is still evident.

◉ Kasımpaşa to Hasköy

As the ferry makes its way to the next stop, Hasköy, you can see the fascinating Western District suburbs of Fener and Balat on the western (left) shore. Both are covered in detail in the Western Districts section of this book (p102).

Fener is the traditional home of the city's Greek population, and although few Greeks are resident these days, a number of important Greek Orthodox sites remain. The prominent red-brick building on the hill is the **Greek Lycée of the Fener** (Megali School or Great School), the oldest house of learning in İstanbul. The school has been housed in Fener since before the Conquest – the present building dates from 1881. Sadly it currently has a total enrolment of only 50 students.

The Gothic Revival church building you can see in the waterside park is the Church of St Stephen of the Bulgars (p109).

The next suburb, **Balat**, was once home to a large proportion of İstanbul's Jewish population but is now crowded with migrants from the east of the country.

Passing the derelict remains of the original Galata Bridge on its way, the ferry then docks at Hasköy. In the Ottoman period,

this part of the city was home to a naval shipyard and a sultan's hunting ground. Today, it has two sights of interest to visitors, the Rahmi M Koç Museum (p159), which is located directly to the left of the ferry stop (Hasköy İskelesi); and **Aynalıkavak Kasrı** (www.millisaraylar.gov.tr; Kasımpaşa-Hasköy Caddesi, Hasköy; admission ₺5; ☺9am-4pm Tue, Wed & Fri-Sun), a short walk away. This ornate 18th-century imperial hunting pavilion is set in extensive grounds and now houses a collection of historic musical instruments. To get there, walk southeast (right) along Hasköy Caddesi, veer left into Aynalıkavak Caddesi and then right into Kasimpaşa-Hasköy Caddesi.

◉ Hasköy to Sütlüce

The ferry's next stop is at **Ayvansaray** on the opposite shore. From here, you can visit the Kariye Museum (Chora Church; p104) or walk along the historic city walls.

From Ayvansaray, the ferry crosses to **Sütlüce** and then returns to the western shore to terminate at **Eyüp**. This conservative suburb is built around the Eyüp Sultan Mosque (p110), one of the most important religious sites in Turkey. After visiting the complex, many visitors head north up the hill to enjoy a glass of tea and the wonderful views on offer at the Pierre Loti Café.

✕ EATING & DRINKING

Köfteci Arnavut (p110), Tarihi Haliç Işkembecisi (p110) and Pierre Loti Café (p112) provide tasty eating and drinking options.

☆ ENTERTAINMENT

TAMİRANE JAZZ
(www.tamirane.com; Bilgi Üniversitesi, Kazım Karabekir Caddesi, Eyüp; sandwiches ₺14-20, pastas ₺15-25; ☺9.30am-11pm Mon-Thu, 9.30am-2am Fri, 10am-2am Sat, 10am-9pm Sun; ▣36T, 47, 47C, 47E, 47N from Sütluce, 44B from Eyüp) This self-described 'avant-garde café-restaurant and music venue for urban explorers' is located in the grounds of the privately run Bilgi Üniversitesi. A huge warehouse-style space with an outdoor terrace, it is best known for its Sunday-afternoon live-jazz sessions, which kick off at 3pm.

Princes' Islands

Explore

This is a great day trip, particularly as the ferry ride is so enjoyable. If you manage to catch an early ferry, you will be able to spend the morning on Heybeliada and the afternoon on Büyükada (or vice versa).

The islands are busiest in summer and ferries can be unpleasantly crowded on weekends at this time; consider visiting midweek instead. In winter many hotels, restaurants and shops close for the season.

The Best...

➡ **Sight** Haghia Triada Monastery, Heybeliada

➡ **Place to Eat** Heyamola Ada Lokantası (p164), Heybeliada

➡ **Place to Drink** Yücetepe Kır Gazinosu Restaurant (p164), Büyükada

Top Tip

One of the wonderful things about the Princes' Islands is that they have no cars. Be sure to enjoy a *fayton* (horse-drawn carriage) ride while you're here.

Getting There & Away

Ferry At least eight ferries run to the islands each day from 6.50am to 7.40pm (midnight mid-June to mid-September), departing from the Adalar İskelesi (ferry dock) at Kabataş. The most useful departure times for day trippers are 10.40am and noon (8.30am, 9.30am, 10.30am and 11.30am mid-June to mid-September). On summer weekends, board the vessel and grab a seat at least half an hour before departure time unless you want to stand the whole way. The trip costs ₺4 (₺3 with an İstanbulkart) to the islands and the same for each leg between the islands and for the return trip. To be safe, check the timetable at www.sehirhatlari.com.tr, as the schedule often changes.

Ferries return to İstanbul every two hours or so. The last ferry of the day leaves Büyükada at 8pm and Heybeliada at 8.15pm (10.40pm and 10.55pm mid-June to mid-September).

Need to Know

➡ **Area Code** ☏216

➡ **Location** 20km southeast of İstanbul

➡ **Duration** 80 minutes to Heybeliada, 95 minutes to Büyükada

◉ SIGHTS

◉ Departure Point: Kabataş

After boarding, try to find a seat on the right side of the ferry so that you can view the various islands as the ferry approaches them.

Heading towards the Sea of Marmara, passengers are treated to fine views of Topkapı Palace, Aya Sofya and the Blue Mosque on the right and Kız Kulesi, Haydarpaşa Railway Station and the distinctive minaret-style clock towers of Marmara University on the left. After a fire in 2011 and its decommissioning as a rail hub, Haydarpaşa Railway Station was placed on the World Monument Fund's international watch list of endangered buildings. The future of this landmark building, which opened in 1909, was unknown at the time of writing and many locals were concerned that it would undergo unsympathetic conversion into a hotel and shopping mall.

After a quick stop at Kadıköy, the ferry makes its way to the first island in the group, Kınalıada. This leg takes 30 minutes. After that, it's another 15 minutes to the island of Burgazada and another 15 minutes again to Heybeliada, the second-largest and perhaps the most charming of the islands.

◉ Heybeliada

Heybeliada (Heybeli for short and Halki in Greek) is popular with day trippers, who come here on weekends to walk in the pine groves and swim from the tiny (but crowded) beaches. The island's major landmark is the hilltop **Haghia Triada Monastery** (☏216-351 8563; ⊘open daily, appointments essential; ▣Heybeliada), which is perched above a picturesque line of poplar trees in a spot that has been occupied by a Greek monastery since Byzantine times. The current monastery buildings date from 1844 and housed a Greek Orthodox theological school until 1971, when it was closed on the government's orders. The Ecumenical Patriarchate of Constantinople is waging an ongoing campaign to have it reopened. The monastery has a small church with an ornate altar and an internationally renowned library, which is home to many old and rare manuscripts. To visit the library, you'll need to gain special permission from the abbot, Metropolitan Elpidophoros. A *fayton* will charge ₺25 to bring you here from the centre of town.

The delightful walk from the *iskele* (ferry dock) up to the Merit Halki Palace hotel at the top of Refah Şehitleri Caddesi passes a host of large wooden villas set in lovingly tended gardens. Many laneways and streets lead to a picnic spot and lookout points. To find the hotel, turn right as you leave the ferry and head past the waterfront restaurants and cafes to the plaza with the Atatürk statue. From here walk up İşgüzar Sokak, veering right until you hit Refah Şehitleri Caddesi. If you don't feel like walking up to the hotel (it's uphill but not too steep), you can hire a bicycle (₺5 per hour, ₺15 per day) from one of the shops in the main street or a *fayton* to take you around the island. A 25-minute tour *(küçük turu)* costs ₺40 and a one-hour tour *(büyük turu)* costs ₺50; the *fayton* stand is behind the Atatürk statue. Some visitors spend the day by the **pool** (weekdays/weekends ₺40/60) at the Merit Halki Palace, which is a good idea, as the waters around the island aren't very clean. Towels and chaise longues are supplied, and there's a pleasant terrace restaurant for meals or drinks.

◉ Büyükada

The largest island in the group, Büyükada (Great Island), is impressive when viewed from the ferry, with gingerbread villas climbing up the slopes of the hill and the bulbous twin cupolas of the Splendid Otel providing an unmistakable landmark.

The **ferry terminal** is an attractive building in the Ottoman Revival style; it dates from 1899. Inside there's a pleasant tile-decorated cafe with an outdoor terrace.

The island's main drawcard is the **Greek Orthodox Monastery of St George**, located in the 'saddle' between Büyükada's two highest hills. To walk here, head from the ferry to the clock tower in İskele Meydanı (Dock Square). The shopping district (with cheap eateries) is left along Recep Koç Sokak. Bear right onto 23 Nisan Caddesi, then head along Çankaya Caddesi up the hill to the monastery; when you come to a fork in the road, veer right. The walk, which takes at least one hour, takes you past a long progression of impressive wooden villas set in gardens. About a quarter of the way up on the left is the Büyükada Kültür Evi, a charming spot where you can enjoy a tea or coffee in a garden setting. After 40 minutes or so you will reach a reserve called 'Luna Park' by the locals. The monastery is a 25-minute walk up an extremely steep hill from here. As you ascend, you'll sometimes see pieces of cloth tied to the branches of trees along the path – each represents a prayer, most made by female supplicants visiting the monastery to pray for a child.

There's not a lot to see at the monastery. A small and gaudy church is the only building of note, but there are fabulous

---

SLEEPING ON THE PRINCES' ISLANDS

You'll need to book ahead if you want to stay overnight in summer. Both of the recommendations below are open year-round.

➡ **Merit Halki Palace** (📞216-351 0025; www.halkipalacehotel.com; Refah Şehitleri Caddesi 94; s €80-180, d €125-320; @🛜🏊) This old-fashioned place commands wonderful water views and has comfortable though chintzy rooms equipped with ceiling fans. There's a large pool and two terraces where meals can be enjoyed.

➡ **Gala Hotel** (📞216-382 2223; www.galahotelbuyukada.com; Çankaya Caddesi 3, Büyükada; d €95-130; ❄@🛜) There are 11 rooms in this recently restored timber mansion; deluxe and superior rooms are preferable to the standard option, which is cramped.

panoramic views from the terrace, as well as the pleasant Yücetepe Kır Gazinosu restaurant. From its tables you will be able to see all the way to İstanbul and the nearby islands of Yassıada and Sivriada.

The new **Museum of the Princes' Islands** (Adalar Müzesi Hangar Müze Alanı; www .adalarmuzesi.org; Aya Nikola Mevkii; admission ₺5, Wed free; ⊗9am-6pm Tue-Sun, to 4pm winter) is also worth a visit, with exhibits covering local lifestyle, famous residents, food etc. It's hard to locate, so it's best to take a *fayton* (₺20).

Bicycles are available for rent in several of the town's shops (₺5 per hour, ₺15 per day), and shops on the market street can provide picnic supplies. The *fayton* stand is to the left of the clock tower. Hire one for a long tour of the town, hills and shore (one hour, ₺50) or a shorter tour of the town (₺40). It costs ₺20 to be taken to Luna Park.

✕ EATING & DRINKING

TOP CHOICE HEYAMOLA ADA LOKANTASI
TURKISH $$

(Mavi Marmara Yalı Caddesi 30b, Heybeliada; mezes ₺5-21, mains ₺15-30, set brunch ₺25; ⊗lunch & dinner Mon-Fri, brunch & dinner Sat & Sun, closed Mon Nov-Apr; 🛳Heybeliada) Until recently there were few decent places to eat on the islands. Fortunately, Basir Seving remedied that situation by opening this restaurant opposite the İDO dock. Heyamola wows customers with a huge array of mezes (try the baked saganaki cheese), delicious fish mains (order *mezgit* if it's on offer) and an interesting and affordable wine list featuring plenty of boutique labels.

BÜYÜKADA KÜLTÜR EVİ
CAFE $

(Çankaya Caddesi 21, Büyükada; sandwiches ₺8-14, grills ₺16; ⊗daily Apr-Oct, Sat & Sun only Nov-Mar) Occupying a villa dating from 1878, this garden cafe serves breakfast, lunch and dinner in its terraced garden. Service can be desultory and the food's not up to much, but it's an undeniably pretty setting and a great spot for a morning glass of tea or a late-afternoon beer.

YÜCETEPE KIR GAZİNOSU RESTAURANT
TURKISH $

(www.yucetepe.com; Monastery of St George, Büyükada; mezes ₺5-8, mains ₺12-15; ⊗daily Apr-Oct, Sat & Sun only Nov-Mar) At the very top of the hill where the Monastery of St George is located, this simple place has benches and chairs on a terrace overlooking the sea and İstanbul. Dishes are simple but good – the *köfte* (meatball) is particularly tasty. You can also enjoy a beer or glass of tea here.

🛏 Sleeping

Every accommodation style is available in İstanbul. You can live like a sultan in a world-class luxury hotel, doss in a hostel dorm or settle into a stylish boutique establishment. The secret is to choose the neighbourhood that best suits your interests, and then look for accommodation that will suit your style and budget – there are loads of options to choose from.

Accommodation Trends

Despite what certain members of the EU may think, İstanbul is a European city and accommodation styles and prices here are similar to those in most major European capitals. Recent trends have seen customers moving away from the small midrange and budget hotels that dominate Sultanahmet towards pricier boutique and designer choices that have been opening in Beyoğlu. Many of these are suite or apartment hotels offer Nespresso machines, iPod docks, French toiletries and other trappings of the international designer lifestyle.

Accommodation Styles

The boutique and suite hotels in Beyoğlu and along the Bosphorus are hip rather than historic, even though many of them occupy handsome 19th-century apartment blocks or mansions. Most have been fitted out by architects versed in international modernism, and have interiors that would suit Stockholm, Sydney or a host of other cities as much as they do İstanbul. In most of Sultanahmet's hotels, the decor is different. These places are often owned and run by locals who are originally from the east of the country and have a resolutely Anatolian aesthetic – you'll see lots of carpets and kilims, silk bedspreads and *nazar boncuks* (the blue glass beads that Turks believe protect against the evil eye). That said, there are a number of Sultanahmet hotels that seem to have melded the best of both worlds, delivering quietly elegant interiors with Anatolian or Ottoman flourishes. We've recommended many of these in this book.

Rates & Reservations

Hotels here are busy, so you should book your room as far in advance as possible, particularly if you are visiting during the high season (Easter–May, September–October and Christmas/New Year). Recent years have seen significant fluctuations in tourist numbers in İstanbul, so most hotels now use yield management systems when setting their rates. This means that in quiet times prices can drop dramatically (sometimes by as much as 50%) and in busy times they can skyrocket. As a result, you should treat our prices as a guide only – it is possible that the price you are quoted will be quite different. Note that most hotels in İstanbul set their prices in euros or US$, and we have listed them as such here.

SLEEPING

NEED TO KNOW

Price Guide
We use the following coding to indicate the high-season price per night of an en suite double room with breakfast:

€	under €70
€€	€70 to €180
€€€	over €180

Tax
Value-Added Tax of 8% is added to all hotel bills. This is usually included in the price quoted when you book.

Airport Transfers
Most hotels will provide a free airport transfer from Atatürk International Airport if you stay three nights or more.

Discounts
Many hotels offer a discount of between 5% and 10% for cash payments. Room rates in the low season (November–Easter excluding Christmas and New Year) are usually discounted; the prices we have provided in each review range from the low-season rate to the high-season rate.

Breakfast
Breakfast is almost always included in the room rate. A standard Turkish breakfast buffet includes fresh bread, jams, yoghurt, sheep's milk cheese, boiled eggs, olives, tomatoes, cucumber and tea or coffee. Often cakes and *böreks* (filled pastries) are added to the mix.

Lonely Planet's Top Choices

Hotel Ibrahim Pasha (p168) Contemporary style with Ottoman overtones; overlooks the Blue Mosque.

Sumahan on the Water (p171) A romantic escape with blissful Bosphorus views.

Witt Istanbul Hotel (p171) Sleek suite rooms in bohemian Cihangir.

Hotel Empress Zoe (p168) This atmospheric boutique choice near Aya Sofya perfectly balances charm and comfort.

Beş Oda (p171) Affordable style and a friendly vibe in the avant-garde enclave of Galata.

Best by Budget

€
Marmara Guesthouse (p168)
Hotel Peninsula (p170)

€€
Sirkeci Konak (p168)
Hotel Uyan İstanbul (p169)

€€€
Four Seasons Istanbul at the Bosphorus (p172)
TomTom Suites (p171)

Best Suite Hotels
Galateia Residence (p171)
Serdar-ı Ekrem 59 (p172)
Ansen Suites (p172)

Best for Families/ Kids
Sirkeci Konak (p168)
Emine Sultan Hotel (p170)
Four Seasons Istanbul at the Bosphorus (p172)

Best Roof Terraces
Hotel Nomade (p169)
Agora Life Hotel (p170)
TomTom Suites (p171)
Marmara Pera (p172)
And Hotel (p171)
Hotel Alp (p169)

Best In-House Spas or Hamams
Four Seasons Istanbul at the Bosphorus (p172)
Sirkeci Konak (p168)
Pera Palace Hotel (p172)
Radisson Blu Bosphorus Hotel (p173)

Best In-House Restaurants
Ottoman Hotel Imperial (p168)
And Hotel (p171)
Marmara Pera (p172)
Four Seasons Istanbul at the Bosphorus (p172)

Best Entertainment Programs
Sirkeci Konak (p168)
Neorion Hotel (p169)
Metropolis Hostel (p170)
Bahaus Hostel (p170)

Best Ottoman-Influenced Decor
Acra Hotel (p168)
Ottoman Hotel Imperial (p168)
Neorion Hotel (p169)
Erten Konak (p169)
Ayasofya Konakları (p168)

Where to Stay

Neighbourhood	For	Against
Sultanahmet & Around	This is the heart of the historic peninsula, so hotels in this area are close to most of the city's important monuments and museums. There's a handy tram service that runs from Sultanahmet over the Galata Bridge to Beyoğlu.	Carpet touts can be annoying, but the biggest drawback is the lack of decent places to eat and drink.
Beyoğlu	Buzzing, bohemian Beyoğlu has the best wining, dining, clubbing and shopping in the city. It also has the greatest concentration of boutique hotels, suite hotels and apartment rentals in the city. A convenient tram service connects it with the historic peninsula and a metro links it with ritzy shopping, commercial and residential suburbs to its northeast.	Lots of bars and nightclubs mean that the streets around İstiklal Caddesi and in Cihangir can be noisy.
Beşiktaş, Ortaköy & Kuruçeşme	Scattered along the Bosphorus shoreline, these suburbs offer spectacular water views, the greatest concentration of five-star hotels and a good array of upmarket nightclubs and eateries.	Traffic along the Bosphorus access roads is always congested, so making your way by bus or taxi (the only options other than private car) is painfully slow; buses are often uncomfortably crowded.
The Bosphorus	The Bosphorus villages aren't as frenetic as the rest of the city, so the boutique hotels found here offer relatively tranquil surrounds. Rooms and restaurants overlooking the water are romantic, and there's something quite magical about hopping aboard hotel launches to criss-cross the Bosphorus between Asia and Europe.	The distance from the historic peninsula is considerable, so the trip back to your hotel can be tiring after a full day of sightseeing. Also, eating and drinking choices around the hotels here can be limited.

SLEEPING

🛏 Sultanahmet & Around

TOP CHOICE HOTEL IBRAHIM PASHA
BOUTIQUE HOTEL $$

(☎212-518 0394; www.ibrahimpasha.com; Terzihane Sokak 7; r standard €99-195, deluxe €139-265; ❄@🖧; 🚇Sultanahmet) Located just off the Hippodrome, this exemplary designer hotel successfully combines Ottoman style with contemporary decor, and is notable for its high levels of service. All of the rooms are gorgeous but some are small – opt for a deluxe one if possible. We love the comfortable lounge and the terrace bar with its knockout views of the Blue Mosque.

TOP CHOICE HOTEL EMPRESS ZOE
BOUTIQUE HOTEL $$

(☎212-518 2504; www.emzoe.com; Akbıyık Caddesi 4, Cankurtaran; s €70-90, d €105-160, ste €135-300; ❄🖧; 🚇Sultanahmet) Named after the feisty Byzantine Empress whose portrait is in Aya Sofya, this fabulous place is the prototype for most of Sultanahmet's boutique hotels but is unique in that it is constantly being changed and improved. Its garden suites are particularly enticing, overlooking a gorgeous flower-filled courtyard where breakfast is served in warm weather. The terrace bar has great views.

TOP CHOICE SIRKECI KONAK
HOTEL $$

(☎212-528 4344; www.sirkecikonak.com; Taya Hatun Sokak 5, Sirkeci; d standard €155-185, superior & deluxe €170-270; ❄@🖧🏊; 🚇Gülhane) The owners of this terrific hotel overlooking Gülhane Park know what keeps guests happy – rooms are impeccably clean, well sized and loaded with amenities. It has a restaurant, a roof terrace, an indoor pool and a hamam. Top marks go to the incredibly helpful staff and the complimentary entertainment program, which includes cooking classes, walking tours and afternoon teas.

SARI KONAK HOTEL
BOUTIQUE HOTEL $$

(☎212-638 6258; www.istanbulhotelsarikonak. com; Mimar Mehmet Ağa Caddesi 42-46, Cankurtaran; r €69-179, ste €129-279; ❄@🖧; 🚇Sultanahmet) This is a truly classy joint. The deluxe rooms are spacious and beautifully decorated, the superior rooms are nearly as nice, and standard rooms, though small, are very attractive. Guests (mostly American) enjoy relaxing on the roof terrace with its Sea of Marmara and Blue Mosque views, but can also take advantage of the comfortable lounge and courtyard downstairs.

MARMARA GUESTHOUSE
PENSION $

(☎212-638 3638; www.marmaraguesthouse .com; Terbıyık Sokak 15, Cankurtaran; s €30-65, d €40-70, f €60-100; ❄@; 🚇Sultanahmet) There are plenty of family-run pensions in Sultanahmet, but few can claim the Marmara's levels of cleanliness and comfort. Manager Elif Aytekin and her family go out of their way to make guests feel welcome, offering plenty of advice and serving a delicious breakfast on the vine-covered, sea-facing roof terrace. Rooms have comfortable beds and double-glazed windows.

ACRA HOTEL
HOTEL $$

(☎212-458 9410; www.acrahotel.com; Amiral Tafdil Sokak 15, Cankurtaran; s €60-145, d €70-160, f €115-250; ❄@🖧; 🚇Sultanahmet) Most of the small hotels in Sultanahmet fit the same pleasant if unexciting mould, but the Acra offers something different. Large rooms with an elegant Ottoman-influenced decor feature lovely marble bathrooms, spacious wardrobes and comfortable beds. There's no roof terrace, but the extraordinary breakfast room-cum-Byzantine archeological site compensates, as does free afternoon tea in the foyer.

OTTOMAN HOTEL IMPERIAL
HOTEL $$

(☎212-513 6150; www.ottomanhotelimperial .com; Caferiye Sokak 6; s €99-159, d standard €109-179, superior €139-259; ❄@🖧; 🚇Sultanahmet) This four-star hotel is in a wonderfully quiet location just outside the Topkapı Palace walls. Its large and comfortable rooms have plenty of amenities and are decorated with Ottoman-style objets d'art – opt for one with an Aya Sofya view or one in the rear annexe. No roof terrace, but the excellent Matbah (p76) restaurant is based here.

AYASOFYA KONAKLARI
BOUTIQUE HOTEL $$$

(☎212-513 3660; www.ayasofyakonaklari.com; Soğukçeşme Sokak; s €96-140, d €136-200, ste €280-500; ❄@🖧; 🚇Sultanahmet) If you're keen to play out Ottoman fantasies, come here. A row of wooden houses occupying an entire cobbled street abutting Topkapı Palace, Ayasofya Konakları is about as authentic as the Ottoman boutique hotel comes and it's picturesque to boot. The 63 rooms are charmingly decorated and breakfast is served in a glass conservatory complete with chandeliers.

HOTEL UYAN İSTANBUL HOTEL $$
(☑212-518 9255; www.uyanhotel.com; Utangaç Sokak 25, Cankurtaran; s €50-60, d standard €79-99, deluxe €95-150; ❄@🖵) The Uyan's elegant decor nods towards the Ottoman style, but never goes over the top – everyone will feel comfortable here. The breakfast spread is generous. Rooms are comfortable and attractive, with a good range of amenities.

HOTEL NOMADE BOUTIQUE HOTEL $$
(☑212-513 8172; www.hotelnomade.com; Ticarethane Sokak 15; s €85, d €100-120; ❄) Designer style and budget pricing don't often go together, but the Nomade bucks the trend. Just a few steps off busy Divan Yolu, it offers simple rooms that some guests find too small – book a superior version if possible. Everyone loves the roof-terrace bar (smack-bang in front of Aya Sofya), and the hip foyer.

DERSAADET HOTEL HOTEL $$
(☑212-458 0760; www.dersaadethotel.com; Kapıağası Sokak 5; s €70-105, d €80-145, ste €140-280; ❄🖵; 🚇Sultanahmet) Roughly translated, the Turkish word 'Dersaadet' means 'Place of Happiness' – and you will indeed be happy if you stay here. The interior of this painstakingly restored Ottoman wooden house features exquisitely painted ceilings and custom-designed wooden furniture throughout. Rooms, which have four-star amenities, are extremely comfortable and there's a roof terrace with Sea of Marmara and Blue Mosque views.

HOTEL ALP HOTEL $$
(☑212-517 7067; www.alpguesthouse.com; Adliye Sokak 4, Cankurtaran; s €35-60, d €55-80, f €80-110; ❄@🖵; 🚇Sultanahmet) The Alp lives up to its location in Sultanahmet's premier small-hotel enclave, offering a range of attractive, well-priced rooms. Bathrooms are small but very clean, and there are plenty of amenities. The roof terrace is one of the best in this area, with great sea views and comfortable indoor and outdoor seating.

ERTEN KONAK HOTEL $$
(☑212-458 5000; www.ertenkonak.com; Akbıyık Değirmeni Sokak, Cankurtaran; garden r €60-80, deluxe r €70-100, executive r €80-140; ❄🖵; 🚇Sultanahmet) Lovers of antiques and collectables will enjoy staying in this historic wooden *konak* (mansion), which has been completely rebuilt in recent years. Public areas are full of objects d'art and all 16 rooms are attractively decorated. Garden rooms are cramped – opt for an executive room if possible. No roof terrace, but the glassed winter garden compensates.

NEORION HOTEL HOTEL $$
(☑212-527 9090; www.neorionhotel.com; Orhaniye Caddesi 14, Sirkeci; d standard €155-185, superior & deluxe €170-270; ❄@🖵❄; 🚇Sirkeci) This recent addition to the Sirkeci Group's hotel portfolio offers the comfortable, well-appointed rooms and high-level customer care that the group's properties are known for. The 'Modern Ottoman' decor here is attractive, the roof terrace has spectacular views, and there's a health club with small pool, jacuzzi, sauna and two hamams. Everyone loves the free early-evening meze buffet.

HOTEL ŞEBNEM HOTEL $$
(☑212-517 6623; www.sebnemhotel.net; Adliye Sokak 1, Cankurtaran; s €40-70, d €50-100, f €70-120; ❄@🖵; 🚇Sultanahmet) Simplicity is the rule at the Şebnem, and it works a treat. Rooms have wooden floors, good bathrooms and comfortable beds with crisp white linen. The large terrace upstairs has views over the Sea of Marmara (as do the more expensive double rooms), and two downstairs rooms have a private courtyard garden.

SARUHAN HOTEL HOTEL $
(☑212-458 7608; www.saruhanhotel.com; Cinci Meydanı Sokak 34, Kadırga; s €25-65, d €35-70, f €60-100; ❄@🖵; 🚇Çemberlitaş) Hitherto bereft of hotels, the quiet residential pocket of Kadırga is inching its way into the limelight courtesy of impressive family-run operations like this one. The Saruhan offers 17 comfortable and well-equipped rooms and a lovely terrace with a sea view. It's a 20-minute walk to the sights in Sultanahmet and a shorter (but steep) walk to the Grand Bazaar.

SULTANS ROYAL HOTEL HOTEL $$
(☑212-517 1307; www.sultansroyalhotel.com; Mustafa Paşa Sokak 29, Küçük Ayasofya; s €40-90, d €45-95, ste €65-140; ❄@🖵; 🚇Sultanahmet) Restrained but elegant decor and quietly efficient service are the hallmarks of this recently opened hotel in the peaceful

Küçük Ayasofya neighbourhood. The 16 rooms feature wooden floorboards covered by rugs, ceilings with hand-painted decoration, comfortable beds and plenty of amenities. Unfortunately, there's no roof terrace.

TAN HOTEL
HOTEL $$

(📞212-520 9130; www.tanhotel.com; Dr Emin Paşa Sokak 20; s €65-115, d €70-125, ste €90-159; ✴@🛜; 🚇Sultanahmet) This well-run hotel off Divan Yolu is notable for its convenient location and its excellent customer service. Rooms are large, with spacious bathrooms (all have tubs), and the lavish breakfast buffet includes freshly squeezed orange juice and eggs cooked to order. The roof terrace sports views of the Blue Mosque and the Sea of Marmara.

EMINE SULTAN HOTEL
HOTEL $$

(📞212-458 4666; www.eminesultanhotel.com; Kapıağası Sokak 6, Cankurtaran; s €75-85, d €105-120; ✴@🛜; 🚇Sultanahmet) Solo female travellers and families will feel particularly at home here because manager Özen Dalgın is as friendly as she is efficient, and the rest of the staff follow her lead. Rooms have a pretty cream-and-pink decor and some have sea views. A delicious breakfast is served in the upstairs breakfast room, which overlooks the Sea of Marmara.

HOTEL PENINSULA
HOTEL $

(📞212-458 6850; www.hotelpeninsula.com; Adliye Sokak 6, Cankurtaran; s €30-50, d €40-65, f €90-120; ✴@🛜; 🚇Sultanahmet) Hallmarks here are friendly staff, comfortable rooms and bargain prices. It has a terrace with sea views and hammocks, and a breakfast room with outdoor tables. Basement rooms are dark, but have reduced prices. The same owners operate the slightly more expensive and comfortable **Grand Peninsula** (📞212-458 7710; www.grandpeninsulahotel.com; Cetinkaya Sokak 3, Cankurtaran; s €35-60, d €45-80; ✴@🛜), a few streets away.

HANEDAN HOTEL
HOTEL $

(📞212-516 4869; www.hanedanhotel.com; Adliye Sokak 3, Cankurtaran; s €30-50, d €45-65, f €75-100; ✴@🛜; 🚇Sultanahmet) The 11 rooms at this cheap, clean and comfortable choice feature lino floors, lace curtains and small white marble bathrooms. One large and two interconnected rooms are perfect for families, and the pleasant roof terrace overlooks the sea and Aya Sofya.

AGORA LIFE HOTEL
HOTEL $$$

(📞212-526 1181; www.agoralifehotel.com; Cağoloğlu Hamamı Sokak 6, Cağoloğlu; s €69-129, d €79-209, ste €199-259; ✴@🛜) Opened in 2010, this hotel in a quiet cul-de-sac around the corner from the Cağaloğlu Hamamı isn't aiming for hip hotel status, instead focusing on service and quiet elegance as its signatures. There are plenty of amenities in the rooms, and the rooftop terrace has a simply extraordinary view. Opt for one of the deluxe or suite rooms if possible.

METROPOLIS HOSTEL
HOSTEL $

(📞212-518 1822; www.metropolishostel.com; Terbıyık Sokak 24, Cankurtaran; dm €13-18, s without bathroom €30-44, d €45-75, without bathroom €30-48; ✴@🛜; 🚇Sultanahmet) Located in a quiet street far enough away from noisy Akbıyık Caddesi that a good night's sleep is assured, this friendly place offers a mix of dorms and rooms – all with comfortable beds and private lockers. Showers and toilets are clean but in limited supply. Guests love the rooftop terrace with its sea views and enjoy the busy entertainment program.

CHEERS HOSTEL
HOSTEL $

(📞212-526 0200; www.cheershostel.com; Zeynep Sultan Camii Sokak 21; dm €15-20, d €60-75, tr €90-105; ✴@🛜; 🚇Gülhane) This friendly place has lovely dorms that are worlds away from the impersonal barracks-like spaces so often seen in hostels. Bright and airy, they feature wooden floorboards, rugs, lockers and comfortable beds; most have air-con. Bathrooms are clean and plentiful. It's a great choice in winter because the cosy rooftop bar has an open fire.

BAHAUS HOSTEL
HOSTEL $

(📞212-638 6534; www.bahaushostelistanbul .com; Bayram Fırını Sokak 11, Cankurtaran; dm €11-19, d €25-30, without bathroom €20-25; @🛜; 🚇Sultanahmet) There's no design-driven minimalism at this Bauhaus. A small and slightly chaotic operation, it stands in stark and welcome contrast to the huge institutional-style hostels found on nearby Akbıyık Caddesi. Dorms (some female-only with bathroom) have curtained bunks with good mattresses; those upstairs are nicest. Top marks go to the plentiful bathrooms, entertainment program and rooftop terrace bar.

BOSPHORUS NIGHTS

If you're in İstanbul to relax rather than indulge in an orgy of sightseeing, you should consider staying in one of a growing number of glam boutique hotels in the Bosphorus suburbs. Most of these are housed in painstakingly restored *yalıs* (waterside timber mansion), have chic fitouts and offer excellent restaurants. They're a long way from the sights of Sultanahmet and the entertainment district of Beyoğlu, but are perfect places for a romantic retreat. Our two favourites are the elegant **Sumahan on the Water** (216-422 8000; www.sumahan.com; Kuleli Caddesi 51, Çengelköy; r €175-325, ste €225-615; ❋@🛜; 🚌15. 15F & 15P from Üsküdar) and the stylish **A'jia** (216-413 9300; www.ajiahotel.com; Cubuklı Caddesi 27, Kanlıca; r €150-320, ste €300-470; ❋@🛜; 🚤Kanlıca, 🚌15, 15F, 15P from Üskudar). Both are located on the Asian side of the strait and have waterside terraces, in-house bar/restaurants and hotel launches to transport guests across the water; Sumahan also has a hamam.

MOTIF APARTMENTS APARTMENT **$$**
(212-458 7702; www.motifapart.com; Yeni Saraçhane Sokak 10, Cankurtaran; apt €60-150; ❋🛜; 🚇Sultanahmet) Apartments are relatively hard to find in Sultanahmet, so this recently opened place is most welcome. Three good-sized rooms (one on each floor) have a bed, sofa bed and kitchenette, making them a good choice for families of three or – at a pinch – four. The top-floor apartment has a sea view and there's a small communal roof terrace.

AND HOTEL HOTEL **$$**
(212-512 0207; www.andhotel.com; Yerebatan Caddesi 36; s €79-99, d €99-109; ❋@🛜; 🚇Sultanahmet) We've included this resolutely old-fashioned place (imagine ivory wallpaper and floral carpets) for three reasons: it's wonderfully located opposite Aya Sofya; the Cihannüma restaurant (p76) on its top floor is one of the best in Sultanahmet; and its prices are remarkably reasonable. You could do a lot worse.

🛏 Beyoğlu

TOP CHOICE WITT ISTANBUL
HOTEL BOUTIQUE HOTEL **$$$**
(212-293 1500; www.wittistanbul.com; Defterdar Yokuşu 26; ste €160-390; ❋@🛜; 🚇Tophane) Showcasing nearly as many designer features as an issue of *Monocle* magazine, this stylish apartment hotel in the trendy suburb of Cihangir has 18 suites with fully equipped kitchenettes, seating areas, CD/DVD players, iPod docks, Nespresso machines, king-sized beds and huge bathrooms. Penthouse and Sea View suites have

fabulous views. The hotel is conveniently located near the Tophane tram stop.

TOP CHOICE BEŞ ODA BOUTIQUE HOTEL **$$**
(212-252 7501; www.5oda.com; Şahkulu Bostan Sokak 16, Galata; ste €85-150; ❋@🛜; 🚇Karaköy, then funicular to Tünel) The name means 'Five Rooms', and that's exactly what this stylish and friendly suite hotel in bohemian Galata is offering. A great deal of thought has gone into the design here – each suite has an equipped kitchenette, lounge area, custom-designed furniture, large bed with good reading lights, black-out curtains, and windows that open to let in fresh air.

TOMTOM SUITES BOUTIQUE HOTEL **$$$**
(212-292 4949; www.tomtomsuites.com; Tomtom Kaptan Sokak 18; ste €185-720; 🚇Karaköy, then funicular to Tünel) We're more than happy to beat the drum about this suite hotel occupying a former Franciscan nunnery off İstiklal Caddesi. Its contemporary decor is understated but elegant, with particularly impressive bathrooms, and each suite is beautifully appointed. There's also a rooftop bar/restaurant with fantastic views

GALATEIA RESIDENCE APARTMENT **$$$**
(212-245 3032; www.galateiaresidence.com; Şahkulu Bostan Sokak 9, Galata; 2-/3-bed apt €140-270, 4-/5-bed apt €170-360; ❋🛜; 🚇Karaköy, then funicular to Tünel) Galateia's 13 attractive and very comfortable apartments opened in 2009 and are wearing well. Housed in two adjacent 19th-century buildings, they are perfect for families or for those on business. Good work-desks, large beds, well-equipped kitchens, home-entertainment systems and ample wardrobe space offer all the comforts

APARTMENT LIVING

We all daydream about packing our bags and escaping to live in another country at some stage in our lives. In İstanbul, it's easy to hire an apartment and do just that for a week or two.

There's a rapidly proliferating number of short-term apartment rentals on offer here, all of which are furnished and most of which come with amenities such as wi-fi, washing machines and weekly maid service. Many are located in historic apartment blocks and offer spectacular views – just remember that the usual trade-off for this is a steep flight of stairs.

The following companies are worth investigating; most have three- or four-day minimum rental periods:

1001 Nites (www.1001nites.com; Sultanahmet apt for 2 people per night €100, Çukurcuma apt for 4 people 120€, 10% discount for weekly stays) Reasonably new outfit run by a charming American and her Turkish business partner. Locations in Sultanahmet, Gümüşsuyu, Çukurcuma and Cihangir.

Istanbul Apartments (☑0212-249 5065; www.istanbulapt.com; d €70-80, tr €85-95, q €110-120; ✶@) Run by an urbane Turkish couple, with properties in Cihangir, Tarlabası and off İstiklal.

İstanbul Holiday Apartments (☑212-251 8530; www.istanbulholidayapartments.com; apt per night €115-260, minimum stay 3 or 7 nights; ✶) Run by an American and with locations as diverse as Sultanahmet, Galata and Gümüşsuyu.

Manzara Istanbul (☑212-252 4660; www.manzara-istanbul.com/en; Serdar-ı Ekrem Sokak 14, Galata; per night €55-190; ✶🔓) A huge operation run by a Turkish/German architect. Locations are mainly in Galata, Cihangir and Kabataş.

---

of home, sometimes with extraordinary views. A four-night minimum stay applies.

SERDAR-I EKREM 59 — BOUTIQUE HOTEL $$$

(☑212-243 3575; www.serdar-iekrem59.com; Serdar-ı Ekrem Sokak 59, Galata; apt €120-205; 🔓Karaköy) Cleverly retaining its old-world charm while at the same time introducing an impressive range of modern amenities, this five-storey building offers one stylish apartment on each floor. Each has a bedroom, bathroom, living room and kitchenette; the top one has a spectacular view. The location on Galata's most atmospheric street couldn't be better.

MARMARA PERA — HOTEL $$$

(☑212-251 4646; www.themarmarahotels.com; Meşrutiyet Caddesi 1, Tepebaşı; r €107-269, ste €238-458; ✶@🔓✶; 🔓Karaköy, then funicular to Tünel) A great location in the midst of Beyoğlu's major entertainment enclave makes this high-rise modern hotel an excellent choice. Added extras include a health club, a tiny outdoor pool and the Mikla (p129) rooftop bar and restaurant. It's worth paying extra for a room with a sea view.

ANEMON GALATA — HOTEL $$

(☑212-293 2343; www.anemonhotels.com; cnr Galata Kulesi Sokak & Büyük Hendek Sokak, Galata; s US$140-210, d US$160-230, ste US$225-270; ✶@; 🔓Karaköy) Located on the attractive square surrounding Galata Tower, this wooden building dates from 1842 but has been completely rebuilt inside. Rooms are elegantly decorated and well equipped; some have water views (ask for 405) There's a rooftop bar/restaurant with great views and the atmospheric Sensus Wine Bar (p132) is in the basement.

PERA PALACE HOTEL — HISTORIC HOTEL $$$

(☑212-377 4000; www.perapalace.com; Meşrutiyet Caddesi 52 , Tepebaşı; r €205-325, ste €350-2600; ✶@🔓; 🔓Karaköy, then funicular to Tünel) Rarely has a reopening engendered as much anticipation as this one. The hotel's €23 million restoration was completed in 2010 and locals have flocked here to see the result. Rooms have been given a luxurious facelift, and although most are cramped, the sumptuous breakfast buffet and extensive facilities (restaurants, spa, gym) compensate. Don't bother paying extra for a Golden Horn view.

WORLD HOUSE HOSTEL HOSTEL $

(212-293 5520; www.worldhouseistanbul .com; Galipdede Caddesi 85, Galata; dm €10-18, d €45-55; @ ; Karaköy, then funicular to Tünel) Hostels in İstanbul are usually impersonal hulks with jungle-like atmospheres, but World House is reasonably small and very friendly. Best of all is its location close to Beyoğlu's entertainment strips but not too far from the sights in Sultanahmet. There are large and small dorms (one shower for every six beds), but none are female-only. Internet costs TL3 per hour.

ANSEN SUITES BOUTIQUE HOTEL $$$

(212-245 8808; www.ansensuites.com; Meşrutiyet Caddesi 70, Asmalımescit; ste €129-289; @ ; Karaköy, then funicular to Tünel) The Asmalımescit neighbourhood has become extremely fashionable in recent times, something that the Ansen's owners anticipated when they restored this historic five-storey building in 2003. Suites are large and exceptionally well set up, with work desk, satellite TV and lovely bathroom; some also have an equipped kitchenette and Golden Horn view. There's a popular Italian restaurant on the ground floor.

CHAMBERS OF THE BOHEME HOSTEL $

(212-251 0931; www.hostelsistanbul.net; Küçük Parmak Kapı Sokak 13 , Taksim; dm €14-20, f €100; @ ; Kabataş, then funicular to Taksim) Despite its name, this popular hostel isn't a bit pretentious. A friendly vibe prevails, but the location is very noisy – bring earplugs or prepare to party throughout the night.

Beşiktaş & Ortaköy

FOUR SEASONS ISTANBUL
AT THE BOSPHORUS LUXURY HOTEL $$$

(212-381 4000; www.fourseasons.com/bos phorus; Çırağan Caddesi 28; s €370-540, d €400-570, ste €600-18,000; @ ; Bahçeşehir University or Çırağan) One of two Four Seasons choices in İstanbul, this hotel incorporates an Ottoman building known as the Atik Paşa Konak. Service here is exemplary, rooms are luxurious and the setting on the Bosphorus is truly magical. Add to this an excellent spa, a restaurant, a terrace bar/cafe and a huge outdoor pool overlooking the Bosphorus and you are left with an unbeatable package.

HOUSE HOTEL BOUTIQUE HOTEL $$$

(212-244 3400; www.thehousehotel.com; Salhane Sokak 1, Ortaköy; r €200-250, ste €260-820; ; Kabataş Lisesi) This handsome 19th century building presides over Ortaköy's main square and has balconies fronting the Bosphorus. Recently converted into a 26-room hotel by the people behind the wildly successful House Cafes (one of which is on the ground floor), the hotel offers fabulous suites and less-impressive (because cramped) 'superior' rooms; all can be noisy at night. There are other branches in Nişantaşı (great) and Galatasaray (so-so).

RADISSON BLU BOSPHORUS
HOTEL HOTEL $$$

(212-310 1500; www.radissonsas.com; Çırağan Caddesi 46, Ortaköy; r €230-320, ste €560-1045; @ ; Kabataş Lisesi) Located on the 'Golden Mile' of nightclubs, the Radisson offers 120 well-sized rooms, some of which have Bosphorus views and all of which share the modern style that the hotel chain is known for. It has a spa and wellness centre on site (no pool, though) as well as a branch of the London-based Japanese restaurant, Zuma (p143).

SLEEPING BEŞIKTAŞ & ORTAKÖY

Understand İstanbul

İstanbul Today

This meeting point of East and West has rarely been so full of confidence and hope for the future. In its guise as Constantinople the city was powerful and mysterious, but as the 21st century gets into gear, modern İstanbul is revelling in unprecedented growth and prosperity. It's also getting larger – the official population is 14 million, but most locals think that 20 million is a more accurate estimate, leading to huge problems with urban sprawl and inadequate infrastructure.

Best in Music

Mercan Dede A major name on the international World Music scene, Dede's distinctive Sufi-electronic techno-fusion is showcased in his albums *Sayahatname* (2001), *Nar* (2002), *Sufi Traveller* (2004) and *Nefes* (2007).

İlhan Erşahin The Turkish-American jazz saxophonist is a big name in both New York, where he resides, and İstanbul, where he regularly plays at venues such as Babylon in Beyoğlu with the Istanbul Sessions ensemble. Their most recent album is *Night Rider* (2012).

Fazıl Say The internationally renowned pianist and composer has innumerable compositions and recordings to his credit, including the 2009–10 *İstanbul Symphony*.

Baba Zulu A local alternative outfit with a unique psychedelic sound combining traditional Turkish instruments, electronica, reggae and dub. Their most-recent album is *Gecekondu* (2010).

Sezen Aksu The queen of Turkish pop; *Optum* (2011) was her first international release.

Too Many Tourists?

Tourism has boomed here over the last decade. Turkey is now the sixth-most-visited tourism destination in the world, and İstanbul's role as a 2010 European Capital of Culture focused the international spotlight on the city, firming up its position as the country's number-one destination for visitors. At present, the city hosts nearly eight million visitors per year, and while this brings prosperity, it also brings challenges. Chief among these are the detrimental effects that crowds can have on the physical condition of ancient monuments. Internationally significant sites such as Aya Sofya and Topkapı Palace host three million visitors per year, and this makes it very hard for museum authorities to maintain the buildings properly. Some experts, including Dr İlber Ortaylı, president of Topkapı, think that the only solution is to limit visitor admissions to the major monuments.

Infrastructure Upgrades

The constantly growing population has placed a huge strain on the city's transport system, which is ageing and in constant need of expansion. Fortunately, the local authorities and Ankara anticipated this problem and in 2005 commenced works on the Marmaray project, one of the major transportation infrastructure projects in the world at present. It involves upgrading and extending the city's 76km-long railway system, building an underwater railway link between the European and Asian suburbs, and integrating the new railway lines with other city transport options. Construction has been slowed by constant archaeological discoveries (always a possibility in a city this ancient), meaning the project isn't expected to be complete until June 2015, when it will make getting around the city a breeze.

Heritage Initiatives

The city's starring role as a European Capital of Culture in 2010 led to a massive program of heritage restoration in the Old City that is still underway. Great monuments such as the imperial mosques have been given loving restorations, as have historically significant but hitherto neglected Byzantine monuments. Once a regular nominee on the World Monuments Fund's list of endangered buildings, İstanbul has well and truly lifted its game when it comes to heritage protection, and visitors to the city benefit as a result. The most exciting of these restorations is undoubtedly that of Aya Sofya, which was completed in 2012.

An Exciting Cultural Landscape

In recent years the city's big banks, business dynasties and universities have built and endowed an array of cutting-edge museums and cultural centres, many of which have been designed by local architectural practices with growing international reputations. These institutions host programs and exhibitions of visual and performance art, and are nurturing a new and exciting generation of Turkish arts practitioners. Complementing this activity is the city's festival circuit, which is growing in size and status and is now one of the busiest in Europe.

Unfortunately, many of the city's cultural luminaries have fallen foul of the country's restrictive laws against insulting the nation and its religion. Writers Orhan Pamuk, Elif Şafak and Perihan Mağden have all been charged in the past, and composer and pianist Fazıl Say is due to stand trial in October 2012.

And Some Dodgy Developments

The city's skyline is in many ways its signature, but in the past decade some modern – and mind-blowingly ugly – developments have been added to it. In order to accommodate this 'urban regeneration' some residents – a good percentage of whom, critics have noted, are members of minority social groups – have been forcibly removed from their homes. Local environmental and heritage activists are quick to point out that many of the developments are being built by developers with strong ties to the ruling AKP party.

İSTANBUL TODAY

if İstanbul were 100 people

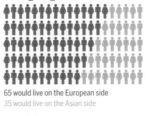

65 would live on the European side
35 would live on the Asian side

religion
(% of population)

   • 1

Sunni Muslim   Alevi Muslim   Non-Muslim (Christian, Jewish)

population per sq km

ISTANBUL   TURKEY

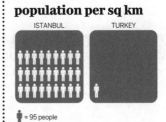

≈ 95 people

History

İstanbul has a history that has been turbulent and triumphant in equal parts. In its guises of Byzantium and Constantinople it was ruled by Greeks, Romans and their descendants, many of whom left their stamp on the city's built heritage. After its incarnation as İstanbul, it functioned as the capital of the world's most powerful empire and benefited from the riches associated with this. Ruled by a succession of powerful emperors, sultans and politicians, its politics have given us the descriptor 'Byzantine' and its patrons have endowed it with a legacy of buildings and artefacts that certainly bring history to life.

BYZANTIUM

Legend tells us that the city of Byzantium was founded around 667 BC by a group of colonists from Megara, northwest of Athens. It was named after their leader, Byzas.

The new colony quickly prospered, largely due to its ability to levy tolls and harbour fees on ships passing through the Bosphorus, then as now an important waterway. A thriving marketplace was established and the inhabitants lived on traded goods and the abundant fish stocks in the surrounding waters.

In 512 BC Darius, emperor of Persia, captured the city during his campaign against the Scythians. Following the retreat of the Persians in 478 BC, the town came under the influence and protection of Athens and joined the Athenian League. Though a turbulent relationship, it stayed under Athenian rule until 355 BC, when it gained independence.

By the end of the Hellenistic period, Byzantium had formed an alliance with the Roman Empire. It retained its status as a free state, and kept this even after being officially incorporated into the Roman Empire in AD 79 by Vespasian. Life was relatively uneventful until the city's leaders made a big mistake: they picked the wrong side in a Roman war of succession following the death of the Emperor Pertinax in AD 193. When Septimius Severus emerged victorious over his rival Pescennius Niger, he mounted a three-year siege of the city, eventually massacring Byzantium's citizens, razing its walls and burning it to the ground. Ancient Byzantium was no more.

TIMELINE	1000 BC	667 BC	512 BC
	Thracian tribes found the settlements of Lygos and Semistra; Plinius mentions the founding of Semistra in his histories and traces of Lygos remain near Seraglio Point.	Legend tells us that Byzas, a citizen of the city of Megara, northwest of Athens, travels up the Bosphorus and founds Byzantium on the site of Lygos.	The army of the Persian emperor Darius captures the city; after the Persians' retreat in 478 BC, Byzantium chooses to join the Athenian League for protection.

The new emperor was aware of the city's important strategic position, and he soon set about rebuilding it. He pardoned the remaining citizens and built a circuit of walls enclosing a city twice the size of its predecessor. The Hippodrome was built by Severus, as was a colonnaded way that followed the present path of Divan Yolu. Severus named his new city Augusta Antonina and it was subsequently ruled by a succession of emperors, including the great Diocletian (r 284–305).

CONSTANTINOPLE

Diocletian had decreed that after his retirement, the government of the Roman Empire should be overseen by co-emperors Galerius in the east (Augusta Antonina) and Constantine in the west (Rome). This resulted in a civil war, which was won by Constantine in AD 324 when he defeated Licinius, Galerius' successor, at Chrysopolis (the present-day suburb of Üsküdar).

With his victory, Constantine (r 324–37) became sole emperor of a reunited empire. He also became the first Christian emperor, though he didn't formally convert until he was on his deathbed. To solidify his power he summoned the First Ecumenical Council at Nicaea (İznik) in 325, which established the precedent of the emperor's supremacy in church affairs.

Constantine also decided to move the capital of the empire to the shores of the Bosphorus, where he had forged his great victory and where the line between the Eastern and Western divisions of the Empire had previously been drawn. He built a new, wider circle of walls around the site of Byzantium and laid out a magnificent city within. The Hippodrome was extended and a forum was built on the crest of the second hill, near today's Nuruosmaniye Mosque. The city was dedicated on 11 May 330 as New Rome, but soon came to be called Constantinople.

Constantine died in 337, just seven years after the dedication of his new capital. His empire was divided up between his three sons: Constantius, Constantien and Constans. Constantinople was part of Constantius' share. His power base was greatly increased in 353 when he overthrew both of his brothers and brought the empire under his sole control.

Constantius died in 361 and was succeeded by his cousin Julian. Emperor Jovian was next, succeeded by Valens (of aqueduct fame).

The city continued to grow under the rule of the emperors. Theodosius I ('the Great'; r 378–95) had a forum built on the present site of Beyazıt Meydanı (Beyazıt Square) and erected the Obelisk of

The name İstanbul probably derives from 'eis ten polin' (Greek for 'to the city'). Though the Turks kept the name Constantinople after the Conquest, they also used other names, including İstanbul and Dersaadet (City of Peace and/or Happiness). The city's name was officially changed to İstanbul by Atatürk in the early republican years.

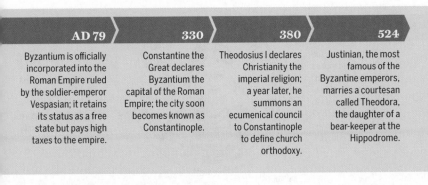

AD 79	330	380	524
Byzantium is officially incorporated into the Roman Empire ruled by the soldier-emperor Vespasian; it retains its status as a free state but pays high taxes to the empire.	Constantine the Great declares Byzantium the capital of the Roman Empire; the city soon becomes known as Constantinople.	Theodosius I declares Christianity the imperial religion; a year later, he summons an ecumenical council to Constantinople to define church orthodoxy.	Justinian, the most famous of the Byzantine emperors, marries a courtesan called Theodora, the daughter of a bear-keeper at the Hippodrome.

POWERS BEHIND THE THRONE

Many powerful women have featured in İstanbul's imperial history. Our favourites are the following:

Theodora

The wife of Justinian, Theodora (500–548) was the daughter of a bear-keeper at the Hippodrome and had been a courtesan before she married. She subsequently became extremely devout and endowed a number of churches in the city. Justinian was devoted to her and she was widely acknowledged by contemporary historians to be the true power behind the throne. During her time as consort, she established homes for ex-prostitutes, granted women more rights in divorce cases, allowed women to own and inherit property, and enacted the death penalty for rape.

Zoe

Our favourite of all the empresses, feisty Zoe (978–1050) was 50 years old and supposedly a virgin when her dying father, Constantine VIII, insisted she marry the aged Romanus III Argyrus. Romanus had in fact been happily married for 40 years but neither Zoe nor her father were going to let that get in their way, threatening him with blinding if he didn't consent. When Constantine died, Romanus was crowned emperor and Zoe empress. Finding married life a tad dull, Zoe took as her lover the much younger Michael the Paphlagonian. After Romanus mysteriously drowned in his bath in 1034, Zoe quickly married her virile companion, who joined her on the throne as Michael IV. Eight years later, after Michael died from an illness contracted while on campaign, Zoe and her sister Theodora ruled as empresses in their own right. At the age of 64 Zoe was married again, this time to an eminent senator, Constantine IX Monomachus, who eventually outlived her.

Roxelana

The wife of Süleyman the Magnificent, Hürrem Sultan (1506–1558) was more commonly known as Roxelana. She was beautiful, clever and a thoroughly nasty piece of work. Though allowed four legal wives and as many concubines as he could support by Islamic law, Süleyman was devoted to Roxelana alone and ended up marrying her. Secure in her position, she mastered the art of palace intrigue and behind-the-scenes manipulation, even convincing the sultan to have İbrahim Paşa, Süleyman's lifelong companion and devoted grand vizier, strangled when he objected to her influence. Unfortunately, she also made sure that her drunken son, Selim the Sot, would succeed to the throne by having the able heir apparent, Prince Mustafa, strangled.

527

Justinian takes the throne and makes Theodora joint ruler; his introduction of heavy taxes leads to the Nika riots of 532 and half of the city is destroyed.

565

Justinian dies; his lasting memorial is the church of Hagia Sophia (Aya Sofya), which was to be the centre of Eastern Orthodox Christianity for many centuries.

Justinian I

Theodosius at the Hippodrome. His grandson Emperor Theodosius II (r 408–50), threatened by the forces of Attila the Hun, ordered that an even wider, more formidable circle of walls be built around the city. Encircling all seven hills of the city, the walls were completed in 413, only to be brought down by a series of earthquakes in 447. They were hastily rebuilt in a mere two months – the rapid approach of Attila and the Huns acting as a powerful stimulus. The Theodosian walls successfully held out invaders for the next 757 years and still stand today, though they are in an increasingly dilapidated state of repair.

Theodosius died in 450 and was succeeded by a string of emperors, including the most famous of all Byzantine emperors, Justinian the Great. A former soldier, he and his great general Belisarius reconquered Anatolia, the Balkans, Egypt, Italy and North Africa. They also successfully put down the Nika riots of 532, killing 30,000 of the rioters in the Hippodrome in the process.

Three years before taking the throne, Justinian had married Theodora, a strong-willed former courtesan who is credited with having great influence over her husband. Together, they further embellished Constantinople with great buildings, including SS Sergius and Bacchus, now known as Küçük (Little) Aya Sofya, Hagia Eirene (Aya İrini) and Hagia Sophia (Aya Sofya), which was completed in 537.

From 565 to 1025, a succession of warrior emperors kept invaders such as the Persians and the Avars at bay. Though the foreign armies often managed to get as far as Chalcedon (the present-day suburb of Kadıköy), none were able to breach Theodosius' land walls. The Arab armies of the nascent Islamic empire tried in 669, 674, 678 and 717-18, each time in vain.

In 1071 Emperor Romanus IV Diogenes (r 1068–1071) led his army to eastern Anatolia to do battle with the Seljuk Turks, who had been forced out of Central Asia by the encroaching Mongols. However, at Manzikert (Malazgirt) the Byzantines were disastrously defeated, the emperor captured and imprisoned, and the former Byzantine heartland of Anatolia thus thrown open to Turkish invasion and settlement. Soon the Seljuks had built a thriving empire of their own in central Anatolia, with their capital first at Nicaea and later at Konya.

As Turkish power was consolidated to the east of Constantinople, the power of Venice – always a maritime and commercial rival to Constantinople – grew in the West. This coincided with the launch of the First Crusade and the arrival in Constantinople of the first of the Crusaders in 1096. Soldiers of the Second Crusade passed through the city in 1146

620	717	1204	1261
Heraclius I (r 610–41) changes the official language of the eastern empire from Latin to Greek, inaugurating what we now refer to as The Byzantine Empire.	Leo III, a Syrian, becomes emperor after deposing Theodosius III; he introduces edicts against the worship of images, ushering in the age of iconoclasm.	Enrico Dandolo, Doge of Venice, leads the crusaders of the Fourth Crusade in a defeat of Constantinople; they sack the city and steal many of its treasures.	Constantinople is recaptured by Michael VIII Palaeologus, a Byzantine aristocrat in exile who had risen to become co-emperor of Nicaea; the Byzantine Empire is restored.

during the reign of Manuel I, son of John Comnenus II 'the Good' and his empress, Eirene, both of whose mosaic portraits can be seen in the gallery at Aya Sofya.

In 1204, soldiers of the Fourth Crusade led by Enrico Dandolo, Doge of Venice, attacked and ransacked the city. They then ruled it with an ally, Count Baldwin of Flanders, until 1261, when soldiers under Michael VIII Palaeologus, a Byzantine aristocrat in exile who had risen to become co-emperor of Nicaea, successfully re-captured it. The Byzantine Empire was restored.

Stella Duffy's *Theodora: Actress. Empress. Whore.* (2010) is a rollicking biographical novel about the Byzantine empress.

İSTANBUL

Two decades after Michael reclaimed Constantinople, a Turkish warlord named Ertuğrul died in the village of Söğüt near Nicaea. He left his son Osman, who was known as Gazi (Warrior for the Faith), a small territory. Osman's followers became known in the Empire as Osmanlıs and in the West as the Ottomans.

Osman died in 1324 and was succeeded by his son Orhan. In 1326 Orhan captured Bursa, made it his capital and took the title of sultan. A victory at Nicaea followed, after which he sent his forces further afield, conquering Ankara to the east and Thrace to the west. His son Murat I (r 1362–89) took Adrianople (Edirne) in 1371.

Murat's son Beyazıt (r 1389–1402) unsuccessfully laid siege to Constantinople in 1394, then defeated a Crusader army 100,000 strong on the Danube in 1396. Though temporarily checked by the armies of Tamerlane and a nasty war of succession between Beyazıt's four sons that was eventually won by Mehmet I (r 1413–21), the Ottomans continued to grow in power and size. By 1440 the Ottoman armies under Murat II (r 1421–51) had taken Thessalonica, unsuccessfully laid siege to Constantinople and Belgrade, and battled Christian armies for Transylvania. It was at this point in history that Mehmet II 'The Conqueror' (r 1451–81) came to power and vowed to attain the ultimate prize – Constantinople.

In four short months, Mehmet oversaw the building of Rumeli Hisarı (the great fortress on the European side of the Bosphorus) and also repaired Anadolu Hisarı, built on the Asian shore half a century earlier by his great-grandfather Beyazıt I. Together these fortresses controlled the strait's narrowest point.

The Byzantines had closed the mouth of the Golden Horn with a heavy chain to prevent Ottoman boats from sailing in and attacking the city walls on the northern side. Not to be thwarted, Mehmet marshalled his boats at a cove (where Dolmabahçe Palace now stands) and had

1432	1453	1520
Mehmet II, son of the Ottoman sultan Murad II, is born in Edirne; he succeeds his father as sultan twice – once in 1444 and then permanently in 1451.	Mehmet's army takes İstanbul and he assumes power in the city becoming known as Fatih, 'The Conqueror'; he dies in 1481 and is succeeded by his son Beyazıt II.	Beyazıt's grandson Süleyman, who would come to be known as 'The Magnificent', ascends to the throne and soon builds a reputation for his military conquests.

Fall of Constantinople

them transported overland by night on rollers, up the valley (present site of the Hilton Hotel) and down the other side into the Golden Horn at Kasımpaşa. Catching the Byzantine defenders by surprise, he soon had the Golden Horn under control.

The last great obstacle was provided by the city's mighty walls. No matter how heavily Mehmet's cannons battered them, the Byzantines rebuilt the walls by night and, come daybreak, the impetuous young sultan would find himself back where he'd started. Finally, he received a proposal from a Hungarian cannon founder called Urban who had come to help the Byzantine emperor defend Christendom against the infidels. Finding that the Byzantine emperor had no money, Urban was quick to discard his religious convictions and instead offered to make Mehmet the most enormous cannon ever seen. Mehmet gladly accepted and the mighty cannon breached the western walls, allowing the Ottomans into the city. On 28 May 1453 the final attack began and by the evening of the 29th the Turks were in complete control of the city. The last Byzantine emperor, Constantine XI Palaiologos, died fighting on the walls.

Seeing himself as the successor to great emperors such as Constantine and Justinian, the 21-year-old conqueror at once began to rebuild and repopulate the city. Aya Sofya was converted to a mosque; a new mosque, the Fatih (Conqueror) Camii, was built on the fourth hill; and the Eski Saray (Old Palace) was constructed on the third hill, followed by a new palace on Sarayburnu a few years later. The city walls were repaired and a new fortress, Yedikule, was built. İstanbul, as it began to be known, became the new administrative, commercial and cultural centre of the ever-growing Ottoman Empire.

Under Mehmet's rule, Greeks who had fled the city were encouraged to return and an imperial decree calling for resettlement was issued; Muslims, Jews and Christians all took up his offer and were promised the right to worship as they pleased. The Genoese, who had fought with the Byzantines, were pardoned and allowed to stay in Galata, though the fortifications that surrounded their settlement were torn down. Only Galata Tower was allowed to stand.

Mehmet died in 1481 and was succeeded by Beyazıt II (r 1481–1512), who was ousted by his son, the ruthless Selim the Grim (r 1512–20), famed for executing seven grand viziers and numerous relatives during his relatively short reign.

The building boom that Mehmet kicked off was continued by his successors, with Süleyman the Magnificent (r 1520–66) and his architect Mimar Sinan being responsible for an enormous amount of construction. The city was endowed with buildings commissioned by the sultan

Great Reads

Byzantium (Judith Herrin; 2007)

Constantinople (Philip Mansel; 1995)

Inside the Seraglio (John Freely; 1999)

Istanbul: The Imperial City (John Freely; 1996)

A Short History of Byzantium (John Julian Norwich; 1997)

Strolling through Istanbul (John Freely & Hilary Sumner-Boyd; 1972)

1556	1729	1839	1853-56
Süleyman dies while on a military campaign in Hungary; his son Selim II assumes the throne and becomes known as 'The Sot' for obvious reasons.	A huge fire sweeps through the city, destroying 400 houses and 140 mosques and causing 1000 deaths.	Mahmut II implements the Tanzimat reforms, which integrate non-Muslims and non-Turks into Ottoman society through civil liberties and regulations.	The Ottoman empire fights in the Crimean War against Russia; Florence Nightingale arrives at the Selimiye Army Barracks near Üsküdar to nurse the wounded.

and his family, court and grand viziers; these include the city's largest and grandest mosque, the Süleymaniye (1550). Later sultans built mosques and a series of palaces along the Bosphorus, among them Dolmabahçe.

However, what had been the most civilised city on earth in the time of Süleyman eventually declined along with the Ottoman Empire, and by the 19th century İstanbul had lost much of its former glory. Nevertheless, it continued to be the 'Paris of the East' and, to affirm this, the first great international luxury express train, the famous Orient Express, connected İstanbul and the French capital in 1883.

The post-WWI campaign by Mustafa Kemal (Atatürk) for national salvation and independence was directed from Ankara and after the Republic was founded, the new government was set up in that city. Robbed of its status as the capital of a vast empire, İstanbul lost much of its wealth and atmosphere. The city's streets and neighbourhoods decayed, its infrastructure was neither maintained nor improved and virtually no economic development occurred.

> Although he was instrumental in moving the capital of Turkey from İstanbul to Ankara, Atatürk loved the city and spent much of his time here. He kept a set of apartments in Dolmabahçe Palace and died there on 10 November 1938.

THE RECENT PAST

Under the presidency of economist Turgut Özal, the 1980s saw a free-market-led economic and tourism boom in Turkey and its major city. Özal's government also presided over a great increase in urbanisation, with trainloads of peasants from eastern Anatolia making their way to İstanbul in search of jobs in the booming industrial sector. The city's infrastructure couldn't cope back then and is still catching up, despite three decades of large-scale municipal works being undertaken.

The municipal elections of March 1994 were a shock to the political establishment, with the upstart religious-right Refah Partisi (Welfare Party) winning elections across the country. Its victory was seen in part as a protest vote against the corruption, ineffective policies and tedious political wrangles of the traditional parties. In İstanbul Refah was led by Recep Tayyip Erdoğan (b 1954), a proudly Islamist candidate. He vowed to modernise infrastructure and restore the city to its former glory.

In the national elections of December 1996, Refah polled more votes than any other party (23%), and eventually formed a government vowing moderation and honesty. Emboldened by political power, Prime Minister Necmettin Erbakan and other Refah politicians tested the boundaries of Turkey's traditional secularism, alarming the powerful National Security Council, the most visible symbol of the centrist military establishment's role as the caretaker of secularism and democracy.

1914	1915	1922	1923
The government enters WWI; the Bosphorus and Dardenelles are closed to shipping, leading to the Allies' decision to attack Gallipoli.	Many prominent members of the city's 164,000-strong Armenian population have their property confiscated and are deported from the city.	The Turkish Grand National Assembly abolishes the Ottoman sultanate; the last sultan, Mehmet VI, leaves the country on a British warship.	The Grand National Assembly relocates the nation's capital from İstanbul to Ankara; shortly afterward, it proclaims the Turkish Republic.

In 1997 the council announced that Refah had flouted the constitutional ban on religion in politics and warned that the government should resign or face a military coup. Bowing to the inevitable, Erbakan did as the council wished. In İstanbul, Mayor Erdoğan was ousted by the secularist forces in the national government in late 1998.

National elections in April 1999 brought in a coalition government led by Bülent Ecevit's left-wing Democratic Left Party. After years under the conservative right of the Refah Partisi, the election result heralded a shift towards European-style social democracy, something highlighted by the country's successful bid to be accepted as a candidate for membership of the European Union.

Unfortunately for the new government, there was a spectacular collapse of the Turkish economy in 2001, leading to its electoral defeat in 2002. The victorious party was the moderate Adalet ve Kalkınma Partisi (Justice and Development Party, AKP), led by phoenix-like Recep Tayyip Erdoğan who – despite continuing tensions with military hard-liners – has run an increasingly stable and prosperous Turkey ever since. In İstanbul, candidates from the AKP have been elected into power in most municipalities, including the powerful Fatih Municipality, which includes Eminönü. The current AKP-endorsed mayor of İstanbul, Kadir Topbaş (b 1945) is one of Erdoğan's former advisors and a former mayor of the Beyoğlu municipality.

1925	1942	2006	2011
The Republican government bans Dervish orders; many of the city's historic *tekkes* (Dervish lodges) are demolished.	A wealth tax is introduced on affluent citizens. Ethnic minorities are taxed at a higher rate than Muslims; many are bankrupted and forced to leave the city.	İstanbul successfully bids to become a European Capital of Culture for 2010, and launches an ambitious program of heritage restoration and cultural development.	The ruling soft-Islamist Justice & Development Party (AKP), led by İstanbul-born Prime Minister Recep Tayyip Erdoğan, wins a third term in government.

Architecture

Byzantine Architecture

The city spent 1123 years as a Christian metropolis and there are a surprising number of structures surviving from this era.

When Mehmet the Conqueror descended on İstanbul in 1453 many churches were converted into mosques; despite the minarets, you can usually tell a church-cum-mosque by the distinctive red bricks that are characteristic of all Byzantine churches.

During Justinian's reign (r 527–65), architects were encouraged to surpass each other's achievements when it came to utilising the domed, Roman-influenced basilica form. **Aya Sofya** (p46) is the supreme example of this.

Early Byzantine basilica design used a centralised polygonal plan with supporting walls and a dome set on top, inside rectangular external walls. The lovely **Little Aya Sofya** (p72; Küçük Aya Sofya Camii), built around 530, is an example. Later, a mixed basilica and centralised polygonal plan developed. This was the foundation for church design from the 11th century until the Conquest and many Ottoman mosques were inspired by it. The **Monastery of Christ Pantokrator** (p94) is a good example.

The Byzantines also had a yen for building fortifications. The greatest of these is the still-standing land wall. Constructed in the 5th century by order of Emperor Theodosius II, it was 20km long and protected the city during multiple sieges until it was finally breached in 1453.

Constantine the Great, the first Byzantine Emperor, named his city 'New Rome'. And like Rome it was characterised by great public works such as the stone **aqueduct** (p93) built by Emperor Valens between 368 and 378. The aqueduct fed a series of huge cisterns built across the city, including the **Basilica Cistern** (p68).

Like Rome, the city was built on seven hills and to a grid pattern that included ceremonial thoroughfares such as Divan Yolu and major public spaces such as the **Hippodrome** (p70).

Clockwise from top
1. Little Aya Sofya (p72) 2. Carved Medusa head, Basilica Cistern (p68)

Ottoman Architecture

After the Conquest, the sultans wasted no time in putting their architectural stamp on the city. Mehmet didn't even wait until he had the city under his control, building the monumental Rumeli Hisarı (p154) on the Bosphorus.

Once in the city, Mehmet kicked off a centuries-long Ottoman building spree, constructing a number of buildings including a mosque on the fourth hill. After these he started work on the most famous Ottoman building of all: **Topkapı Palace** (p53).

Mehmet had a penchant for palaces, but his great-grandson, Süleyman the Magnificent, was more of a mosque man. With his court architect, Mimar Sinan, he built the greatest of the city's Ottoman imperial mosques. Sinan's prototype mosque form has a forecourt with a *şadırvan* (ablutions fountain) and domed arcades on three sides. On the fourth side is the mosque, with a two-storey porch. The main prayer hall is covered by a central dome surrounded by smaller domes and semidomes. There was usually one minaret, though imperial mosques had either two or four; and one imperial mosque, the later **Blue Mosque** (p64), has six.

Each imperial mosque had a *külliye* (mosque complex) clustered around it. This was a philanthropic complex including a *medrese* (Islamic school of higher studies), hamam, *darüşşifa* (hospital), *imaret* (soup kitchen), *kütüphane* (library) and cemetery with *türbes* (tombs). Over time, many of these *külliyes* were demolished; fortunately, many of the buildings in the magnificent **Süleymaniye** (p88) and **Atik Valide** (p148) complexes are intact.

Later sultans continued Mehmet's palace-building craze. No palace would rival Topkapı, but Sultan Abdül Mecit I tried his best with the grandiose

....

Clockwise from top left
1. Rumeli Hisari (p154) 2. Blue Mosque (p64)
3. Dolmabahçe Palace (p141)

Dolmabahçe Palace (p141) and Abdül Aziz I built the extravagant **Çırağan Palace** (p142) and **Beylerbeyi Palace** (p152). These and other buildings of the era have been collectively dubbed 'Turkish baroque'.

These mosques and palaces dominate the landscape and skyline of the city, but there are other quintessentially Ottoman buildings: the hamam and the Ottoman timber house. Hamams were usually built as part of a *külliye,* and provided an important point of social contact as well as facilities for ablutions. Architecturally significant hamams include the **Ayasofya Hürrem Sultan Hamamı** (p81), the **Çemberlitaş Hamamı** (p101) and the **Cağaloğlu Hamamı** (p82). All are still functioning.

Wealthy Ottomans and foreign diplomats built many *yalıs* (waterside timber mansions) along the shores of the **Bosphorus**; city equivalents were sometimes set in a garden but were usually part of a crowded, urban streetscape. Unfortunately, not too many of these houses survive, a result of the fires that regularly raced through the Ottoman city.

THE GREAT SINAN

None of today's star architects come close to having the influence over a city that Mimar Koca Sinan had over Constantinople during his 50-year career.

Born in 1497, Sinan was a recruit to the *devşirme*, the annual intake of Christian youths into the janizaries. He became a Muslim (as all such recruits did) and eventually took up a post as a military engineer in the corps. Süleyman the Magnificent appointed him the chief of the imperial architects in 1538.

Sinan designed a total of 321 buildings, 85 of which are still standing in İstanbul. He died in 1588 and is buried in a self-designed *türbe* (tomb) located in one of the corners of the Süleymaniye Mosque, the building that many believe to be his greatest work.

Ottoman Revivalism & Modernism

In the late 19th and early 20th centuries, architects created a blend of European architecture alongside Turkish baroque, with some concessions to classic Ottoman style. This style has been dubbed 'Ottoman Revivalism' or First National Architecture. Its main proponents were architects Vedat Tek (1873–1942) and Kemalettin Bey (1870–1927). Tek is best known for his Central Post Office (p205) in Sirkeci (1909) and Haydarpaşa İskelesi (ferry dock, 1915–17). Kemalettin Bey's Bebek Mosque (p153; 1913) and Fourth Vakıf Han (1912–26), a bank building in Eminönü that now houses the Legacy Ottoman Hotel, are his best-known works.

During the same period, art nouveau hit the city. Raimondo D'Aronco, an Italian architect, designed a number of elegant buildings, including the gorgeous but sadly dilapidated **Botter House** on İstiklal Caddesi (p115).

When Atatürk proclaimed Ankara the capital of the Republic, İstanbul lost much of its glamour and investment capital. Modernism was played out on the new canvas of Ankara, while İstanbul's dalliances went little further than the **İstanbul City Hall** in Fatih, designed by Nevzat Erol and built in 1953; the **İstanbul Hilton Hotel**, designed by SOM and Sedad Hakkı Eldem and built in 1952; the **Atatürk Library** in Gümüşsuyu, also by Eldem; and the much-maligned **Atatürk Cultural Centre** by Hayati Tabanlıoğlu, built from 1956 to 1957 and currently undergoing a major renovation.

Recent notable architecture in the city includes 2009 **Şakirin Mosque** (p148), and **Kanyon** – a mixed residential, office and shopping development in Levent designed by the LA-based Jerde Partnership with local architects Tabanlıoğlu Partnership. The nearby **Loft Gardens** residential complex and **İstanbul Sapphire** tower, both by Tabanlıoğlu Partnership, are also noteworthy.

Many art museums and cultural centres around town feature impressive new wings or inspired architectural conversions of industrial or commercial spaces. The best of these are **İstanbul Modern** (p116), by Tabanlıoğlu Partnership; **SALT Galata** (p117), by Mimarlar Tasarım; the **Sakıp Sabancı Museum** (p155), by Savaş, Erkel and Çırakoğlu; the new **Naval Museum** (p142) in Beşiktaş, by Mehmet Kütükçüoğlu, and **santralistanbul** in Sütluce on the Golden Horn, by Emre Arolat, Nevzat Sayın and Han Tümertekin.

When this book went to print, UK-based architect Zaha Hadid had just been commissioned to design a new art museum on the Golden Horn for a branch of the Sabancı family. Other high-profile international names are sure to follow in her footsteps.

Clockwise from top left
1. İstanbul Modern (p116) 2. Botter House on İstiklal Caddesi (p115) 3. Hüsrev Tayla's Şakirin Mosque (p148)

İstanbul on Page & Screen

İSTANBUL IN PRINT

Turkey has a rich but relatively young literary tradition. Its brightest stars tend to be based in İstanbul and are greatly revered throughout the country. Many are being translated into English, which is great news for people wanting to do some background reading before travelling here.

Literary Heritage

Under the sultans, literature was really a form of religious devotion. Ottoman poets, borrowing from the great Arabic and Persian traditions, wrote sensual love poems of attraction, longing, fulfilment and ecstasy in the search for union with God.

By the late 19th century the influence of Western literature began to be felt. This was the time of the Tanzimat political and social reforms initiated by Sultan Abdül Mecit, and in İstanbul a literary movement was established that became known as 'Tanzimat Literature'.

This movement was responsible for the first serious attacks on the ponderous cadences of Ottoman courtly prose and poetry, but it wasn't until the foundation of the republic that the death knell of this form of literature finally rang. Atatürk decreed that the Turkish language should be purified of Arabic and Persian borrowings, and that in the future the nation's literature should be created using the new Latin-based Turkish alphabet. Major figures in the new literary movement (dubbed 'National Literature') included poet Yahya Kemal Beyatli and novelist Halide Edib Adıvar.

Lord Byron spent two months in Constantinople in 1810 and wrote about the city in his satiric poem *Don Juan*.

Though not part of the National Literature movement, İrfan Orga (1908–70) is probably the most famous Turkish literary figure of the 20th century. His 1950 masterpiece *Portrait of a Turkish Family* is his memoir of growing up in İstanbul at the start of the century and is among the best writing about the city ever published.

Politician and novelist Ahmet Hamdi Tanipar (1901–62) wrote *A Mind at Peace* in 1949. Set in the city at the beginning of WWII, it is beloved by many Turks.

Halide Edib Adıvar

A writer and vocal leader of the emerging women's emancipation movement in Turkey, Halide Edib Adıvar (1884–1964) was an ally of Atatürk and a leading figure in the War of Independence. Her 1926 autobiography, *Memoir of Halide Edib*, recounts her privileged upbringing in Beşiktaş and Üsküdar, progressive education at the American College for Girls in Arnavutköy and subsequent marriage to a noted mathematician, who humiliated her by taking a second wife. After leaving him, she joined the Nationalists, remarried, worked closely with Atatürk and wrote a popular history of the War of Independence called *The Turkish Ordeal* (1928). In later years she worked as a university lecturer, wrote over 20 novels – the most famous of which was probably the 1938 work *Thewn and His Daughter* – and had a brief stint as a member of parliament. A fictionalised account of the early part of this fascinating woman's life can be found in *Halide's Gift*, an enjoyable novel by American writer Frances Kazan.

Contemporary Novelists

The second half of the 20th century saw a raft of İstanbul-based writers and poets being published locally and internationally. Many were socialists, communists or outspoken critics of the government, and spent long and repeated periods in jail. The two most famous were Nâzım Hikmet (1902–63), whose masterwork is the five-volume collection of lyric and epic poetry entitled *Human Landscapes from My Country;* and Yaşar Kemal (b 1923), whose best-known work is *Mehmed, My Hawk.* Two of his novels – *The Birds Are Also Gone* and *The Sea-Crossed Fisherman* – are set in İstanbul.

Another local novelist whose work is worth seeking out include O Z Livaneli (b 1946), author of the 2003 bestseller *Bliss* (*Mutluluk,* in Turkish). Set in a rural village in southeastern Turkey, in İstanbul and on the Aegean coast, it deals with weighty issues such as honour killing and was made into a film in 2007.

High-profile writer Elif Şafak was born in Strasbourg in 1971 to Turkish parents and now lives in İstanbul; she writes in both Turkish and English. Her best-known novels are *The Flea Palace* (2002), *The Saint of Incipient Insanities* (2004), *The Bastard of İstanbul* (2006) and *The Forty Rules of Love* (2010). Her most recent work is *Honour* (2012).

Through Foreign Eyes

Foreign novelists have long tried to capture the magic and mystery of İstanbul in their work. One of the earliest to do so was French novelist Pierre Loti (1850–1923), whose romantic novel *Aziyadé*, written in

In his 2007 book *The Bridge*, Dutch writer Geert Mak paints the Galata Bridge and its denizens (including anglers and street vendors) as being a microcosm of modern Turkey. Though prematurely dated, it's still a fascinating read.

ORHAN PAMUK

When the much-fêted Orhan Pamuk (born 1952) was awarded the 2006 Nobel Prize in Literature, the international cultural sector was largely unsurprised. The writing of the İstanbul-born, now US-based, novelist had already attracted its fair share of critical accolades, including the IMPAC Dublin Literary Award, *The Independent* newspaper's Foreign Fiction Award of the Month and every local literary prize on offer.

In their citation, the Nobel judges said that in his 'quest for the melancholic soul of his native city' (ie İstanbul), Pamuk had 'discovered new symbols for the clash and interlacing of culture'. The only voices heard to criticise their judgment hailed from Turkey. Like Elif Şafak, Pamuk had been charged with 'insulting Turkishness' under Article 301 of the Turkish Criminal Code (the charges were dropped in early 2006), and some local commentators alleged that in his case the Nobel Prize was awarded for political (ie freedom of speech) reasons rather than purely on the merit of his literary oeuvre.

Pamuk has written eight novels to date. His first, *Cevdet Bey & His Sons* (1982), is a dynastic saga of the İstanbul bourgeoisie. It was followed by *The Silent House* (1983), *The White Castle* (1985) and *The Black Book* (1990). The latter was made into a film (*Gizli Yuz*) by director Omer Kavur in 1992. After this came *The New Life* (1995), *My Name is Red* (1998), and *Snow* (2002). His most recent novel is *The Museum of Innocence* (2009), a moving story of love and loss set in İstanbul circa 1975. In 2005, he published a memoir, *İstanbul: Memories of a City*, about the city he loves so well.

In 2012, Pamuk opened the Museum of Innocence (p121), his conceptual art project occupying an entire house in Cihangir. It was inspired by his novel of the same name.

THE DARK SIDE OF THE CITY

İstanbul features as the setting for some great crime novels. If you're a fan of the genre, you may like to read or see the following:

➧ **The Inspector İkmen Novels** Barbara Nadel investigates the city's underbelly in a suitably gripping style. Whether they're set in Balat or Beyoğlu, her books are always evocative and well researched. Start with *Belshazzar's Daughter* (1999).

➧ **The Yashim the Ottoman Investigator Novels** Jason Goodwin writes historical crime novels with a protagonist who is a eunuch attached to the Ottoman court. Titles in the series include *The Janissary Tree* (2006) and *An Evil Eye* (2011).

➧ **Murder on the Orient Express** Hercule Poirot puts ze leetle grey cells to good use on the famous train in this 1934 novel by Agatha Christie. It was made into a film by Sidney Lumet in 1974 and features a few opening shots of İstanbul.

➧ **The Kamil Paşa Novels** These historical crime novel by Jenny White feature a magistrate in one of the new Ottoman secular courts. Titles include *The Sultan's Seal* (2006), *The Abyssinian Proof* (2009) and *The Winter Thief* (2010).

➧ **Island Crimes** Lawrence Goodman's series of comic mystery novels set on the Princes' Islands includes *Sweet Confusion on the Princes' Islands*, *Sour Grapes on the Princes' Islands*, *A Grain of Salt on the Princes' Islands* and *Something Bitter on the Princes' Islands*.

➧ **The Hop-Çıkı-Yaya Novels** Mehmet Murat Somer's series of gay crime novels features a transvestite amateur sleuth. Titles include *The Prophet Murders* (2008), *The Kiss Murders* (2009) and *The Gigolo Murders* (2009).

➧ **The Kati Hirschel Murder Mysteries** Written in Turkish and (badly) translated into English, these novels by Esmahan Aykol feature a German amateur sleuth who owns a bookshop in Galata. Titles include *Hotel Bosphorus* (2011).

1879, introduced Europe to Loti's almond-eyed Turkish lover and to the mysterious and all-pervasive attractions of the city itself.

After Loti, writers such as Harold Nicolson set popular stories in the city. Nicholson's 1921 novel *Sweet Waters* is a moving love story cum political thriller set in İstanbul during the Balkan Wars. Nicholson, who was based here as a diplomat, based the novel's main character on his wife, Vita Sackville-West.

Graham Greene's 1932 thriller *Stamboul Train* focuses on a group of passengers travelling between Ostend and İstanbul on the Orient Express. It was filmed in 1934 as *Orient Express*.

Historical novels set here include *The Rage of the Vulture* (Barry Unsworth; 1982), *The Stone Woman* (Tariq Ali; 2001), *The Calligrapher's Night* (Yasmine Ghata; 2006), and *The Dark Angel* (Mika Waltari; 1952). Young readers will enjoy *The Oracle of Stamboul* (Michael David Lukas; 2011).

Although best known as Pamuk's English translator and John Freely's daughter, Maureen Freely is also a writer of fiction. In her 2007 novel *Enlightenment* she writes about truth, repression and the personal and political risks of becoming enmeshed in a foreign culture.

Alan Drew's 2008 novel *Gardens of Water* follows the lives of two families in the aftermath of the devastating earthquake that struck western Turkey (including İstanbul's outskirts) in 1999.

CINEMA

Turks have taken to cinema-going with alacrity over recent decades, and the local industry has gone from strength to strength. Local directors, many of whom are based in İstanbul, are now fixtures on the international festival circuit.

Local Stories

Oddly enough, few masterpieces of Turkish cinema have been set in İstanbul. Acclaimed directors including Metin Erksan, Yılmaz Güney and Erdan Kıral tended to set the social-realist films they made in the 1960s, '70s and '80s in the villages of central or eastern Anatolia.

All this started to change in the 1990s, when many critical and popular hits were set in the city. Notable among these were the films of Zeki Demirkubuz, Omer Kavur, Yeşim Ustaoğlu, Mustafa Altıoklar and Yavuz Turgul.

Contemporary directors of note include Ferzan Özpetek, who has a growing number of Turkish/Italian co-productions to his credit. His 1996 film *Hamam*, set in İstanbul, was a big hit on the international festival circuit and is particularly noteworthy for addressing the hitherto hidden issue of homosexuality in Turkish society.

Nuri Bilge Ceylan's 2003 film *Distant* received a rapturous response from critics and audiences alike when it was released, winning the Jury Prize at the Cannes Film Festival among other accolades. Set in İstanbul, this story of two cousins who are both alienated from society is in the bleak but visually beautiful tradition of Yılmaz Güney's films. Ceylan's 2006 film *Climates* and 2008 film *Three Monkeys* are also set in the city.

Yavuz Turgul's 2005 film *Lovelorn* is the story of idealist Nazim, who returns home to İstanbul after teaching for 15 years in a remote village in eastern Turkey and starts a doomed relationship with a single mother who works in a sleazy bar. It's particularly notable for the soundtrack by Tamer Çıray, which features the voice of Aynur Doğan.

Kutluğ Ataman's 2005 film *2 Girls* and Reha Erdem's 2008 film *My Only Sunshine* are both dramas in which the city provides an evocative backdrop.

Turkish-German director Fatih Akın received rave reviews and a screenwriting prize at Cannes for his 2007 film *The Edge of Heaven*, parts of which are set in İstanbul. His 2005 documentary about the Istanbul music scene – *Crossing the Bridge: The Sound of Istanbul* – was instrumental in raising the Turkish music industry's profile internationally.

Through Foreign Eyes

Many of the foreign-made films set here have been thrillers. These include James Negulesco's *The Mask of Dimitrios* (1944), a spy flick based on an Eric Ambler novel; and three James Bond films: *From Russia with Love* (1974), *The World Is Not Enough* (1999) and *Skyfall* (2012).

Other films to look out for are Jacques Vierne's 1961 film *Tintin and the Golden Fleece*; Alan Parker's 1978 hit *Midnight Express*; and Jules Dassin's 1964 crime spoof, *Topkapi*, which was based on the Eric Ambler 1962 novel *In the Light of Day*.

Greek director Tassos Boulmetis set part of his popular 2003 arthouse film *A Touch of Spice* here.

Travelogues

Constantinople (Edmondo De Amici; 1878)

Constantinople in 1890 (Pierre Loti; 1892)

The Innocents Abroad (Mark Twain; 1869)

The Turkish Embassy Letters (Lady Mary Wortley Montagu; 1837)

Clamour over Galata Tower, Aya Sofya's dome, the minarets of the Blue Mosque and the roof of Topkapı Palace while playing the popular PS3/X-Box 360 video game *Assassin's Creed: Revelations*, which is set in Constantinople in 1511.

Survival Guide

Transport

GETTING TO İSTANBUL

As it's the national capital in all but name, getting to İstanbul is easy. There are two international airports and two *otogars* (bus stations) from which international services arrive and depart. At the time of research international rail connections were few and far between, but this situation may change when upgrades to rail lines throughout the country are completed.

Flights, tours and rail tickets can be booked at www .lonelyplanet.com/bookings.

Atatürk International Airport

The city's main airport, **Atatürk International Airport** (IST, Atatürk Havalimanı; ☑212-463 3000; www.ataturk airport.com), is in Yeşilköy, 23km west of Sultanahmet.

The international terminal (Dış Hatlar) is polished and organised. Close by, the domestic terminal (İç Hatlar) is smaller but no less efficient.

There are car-hire desks, exchange offices, stands of mobile-phone companies, a 24-hour pharmacy, ATMs and a PTT (post office) at the international arrivals area. There is also a **Tourist Information Desk** (☑212-465 3451; International Arrivals Hall, Atatürk International Airport; ☺9am-10pm) supplying maps, advice and brochures. A 24-hour supermarket is located on the walkway to the metro. The 24-hour **left-luggage service** (☑212-465 3442; ☺24hr) charges ₺18 to ₺25 per suitcase per 24 hours; you'll find the booth to your right as you exit customs.

One of the few annoying things about Atatürk airport is that travellers must pay to use a trolley on either side of immigration. You can pay in lira (₺1) or euros (€1), which you get back when you return the trolley.

Taxi

A taxi from the airport costs around ₺40 to Sultanahmet, ₺50 to Taksim Meydanı (Taksim Square) and ₺70 to Kadıköy.

Metro & Tram

There's an efficient metro service from the airport to Zeytinburnu, from where it's easy to connect with the tram to Sultanahmet, Eminönü and Kabataş. From Kabataş, there's a funicular to Taksim Meydanı.

The metro station is on the lower ground floor beneath the international departures hall – follow the 'Metro/Subway' signs down the escalators and through the underground walkway. A token costs a mere ₺2 and services depart every 10 minutes or so from 5.40am until 1.40am. When you get off the metro, the

---

CLIMATE CHANGE & TRAVEL

Every form of transport that relies on carbon-based fuel generates CO_2, the main cause of human-induced climate change. Modern travel is dependent on aeroplanes, which might use less fuel per kilometre per person than most cars but travel much greater distances. The altitude at which aircraft emit gases (including CO_2) and particles also contributes to their climate change impact. Many websites offer 'carbon calculators' that allow people to estimate the carbon emissions generated by their journey and, for those who wish to do so, to offset the impact of the greenhouse gases emitted with contributions to portfolios of climate-friendly initiatives throughout the world. Lonely Planet offsets the carbon footprint of all staff and author travel.

tram platform is right in front of you. You'll need to buy another token (₺2) to pass through the turnstiles. The entire trip from the airport takes around 50 to 60 minutes to Sultanahmet, 60 to 70 minutes to Eminönü and 85 to 95 minutes to Taksim.

Airport Bus

If you are staying in Beyoğlu, the **Havataş** (☎212-444 0487; www.havas.com.tr) airport bus from Atatürk International Airport is even more convenient. This departs from outside the arrivals hall. Buses leave every 30 minutes between 4am and 1am; the trip takes between 40 minutes and one hour, depending on traffic. Tickets cost ₺10 and the bus stops in front of the Turkish Airlines (THY) office on Cumhuriyet Caddesi, just off Taksim Meydanı. Note that signage on the buses and at stops sometimes reads 'Havaş' rather than 'Havataş'.

A public bus service (no 96T) travels from a stop next to the Havataş buses outside the arrivals hall and travels to Taksim Meydanı, but to travel on this passengers must have an İstanbulkart (travelcard) and these are not available at the airport.

Hotel Shuttle

Many hotels will provide a free pick-up service from Atatürk airport if you stay with them for three nights or more. There are also a number of cheap (but very slow) shuttle-bus services from hotels to the airport for your return trip. Check details with your hotel.

Sabiha Gökçen International Airport

The city's second international airport, **Sabiha Gökçen International Airport** (SAW, Sabiha Gökçen

---

Havalimanı; ☎216-588 8888; www.sgairport.com), is at Pendik/Kurtköy on the Asian side of the city. It's popular with low-cost airlines.

There are ATMs, car-hire and accommodation-booking desks, exchange bureaux, a mini-market, a left-luggage office and a PTT in the international arrivals hall.

Taxi

Taxis from this airport to the city are expensive. To Taksim you'll be looking at around ₺90. To Sultanahmet you'll be looking at around ₺120.

Airport Bus

The **Havataş** (☎212-444 0487; www.havas.com.tr) airport bus travels from the airport to Taksim Meydanı between 5am and midnight; after midnight there are shuttle

services 30 minutes after every flight arrival. Tickets cost ₺12 and the trip takes approximately 90 minutes. If you're heading towards the Old City, you'll then need to take the funicular to Kabataş and the tram from Kabataş to Sultanahmet.

A public bus service (no E10) goes from the airport to Kadıköy, from where ferries travel to Eminönü. Another bus (E3) goes to Levent, from where it's possible to transfer to a metro heading to Taksim Meydanı. Unfortunately, passengers must have an İstanbulkart (travel card) to travel on these services, and these are not available at the airport.

Hotel Shuttle

Hotels rarely provide free pick-up services from Sabiha Gökçen. Shuttle-bus services from hotels to the airport for return trips are infrequent – check details with your hotel. The trip can take up to two hours, so allow plenty of time.

Boat

Cruise ships arrive at the **Karaköy International Maritime Passenger Terminal** (☎212-249 5776), near the Galata Bridge.

Bus

The **Büyük İstanbul Otogarı** (Big İstanbul Bus Station; ☎212-658 0505; www.otogaristanbul.com) is the city's main bus station for both intercity and international routes. Called simply the *otogar* (bus station), it's in the western district of Bayrampaşa, just south of the expressway and about 10km west of Sultanahmet. There's an ATM here and a few cafes. The metro service from Aksaray stops here (Otogar stop) on its way from the airport; you can catch this to Aksaray and then connect with a tram to Sultanahmet. If you're going to Beyoğlu, bus 830 leaves from the centre of the *otogar* every 15 minutes between 5.50am and 8.45pm and takes approximately one hour to reach Taksim Meydanı. Bus 910 leaves for Eminönü every 15 to 25 minutes between 6am and 8.45pm; the trip takes approximately 50 minutes. Both trips cost ₺2. A taxi will cost approximately ₺30 to Sultanahmet, ₺35 to Taksim.

There's a smaller bus station on the Asian shore of the Bosphorus at Harem, south of Üsküdar and north of Haydarpaşa train station. If you're arriving in İstanbul by bus from anywhere on the Anatolian side of Turkey, it's always quicker to get out at Harem and take the car ferry to Sirkeci/Eminönü

(₺2; every 30 minutes from 7am to 10.30pm); if you stay on the bus until the *otogar*, you'll add at least an hour to your journey. If you're going the other way, you may want to catch your bus here, instead of at the *otogar*; if your destination is serviced by frequent buses (eg Ankara or Antalya) you should have no trouble arriving at the Harem *otogar* and buying a ticket on the spot; if there are fewer services (eg Cappadocia) you should reserve your ticket by calling the bus line ahead of time, requesting that you board at Harem instead of the Büyük *otogarı*.

Train

At the time of our research, only one international service – the daily Bosfor/Balkan Ekspresi between İstanbul and Bucharest, Sofia and Belgrade – was operating in and out of İstanbul. Check **Turkish State Railways** (TCDD; www.tcdd.gov.tr) for details.

Services from İstanbul to cities within Turkey were also severely curtailed, largely due to an extensive upgrade to the rail link between it and Ankara. When this line reopens in 2014, it will feature high-speed trains that will depart from a new railway hub in Üsküdar, on the Asian shore.

PUBLIC TRANSPORT OPERATORS

İstanbul Elektrik Tramvay ve Tünel (İETT, Istanbul Electricity, Tramway and Tunnel General Management; www.iett.gov.tr) is responsible for running public buses, funiculars and historic trams in the city. Its website has useful timetable and route information in Turkish and English. Metro and tram services are run by **İstanbul Ulaşım** (www.istanbul-ulasim.com.tr), ferry services are run by **İstanbul Şehir Hatları** (İstanbul City Routes; www.sehirhatlari.com.tr), and seabus and fast ferry services are operated by **İstanbul Deniz Otobüsleri** (İDO; ☎212-444 4436; www.ido.com.tr).

GETTING AROUND İSTANBUL

Public transport options are cheap, plentiful and efficient. This is fortunate, as traffic congestion is a growing problem and driving here can be stressful and time-consuming.

Tram

An excellent *tramvay* (tramway) service runs from Bağcılar, in the city's west, to Zeytinburnu (where it connects with the metro from the airport) and on to Sultanahmet and Eminönü. It then crosses the Galata Bridge to Karaköy (to connect with the Tünel) and Kabataş (to connect with the funicular to Taksim Meydanı). In the future, it will be extended from Kabataş to the ferry dock at Beşiktaş. Services run every five minutes from 6am to midnight. The fare is ₺2; *jetons* (ticket tokens) are available from machines on every tram stop. Travel cards can be used.

Ferry

The most enjoyable way to get around town is by ferry. Crossing between the Asian and European shores, up and down the Golden Horn and Bosphorus, and over to the Princes' Islands, these vessels are as efficient as they are popular with locals. **İstanbul Şehir Hatları** (İstanbul City Routes; www .sehirhatlari.com.tr) has fare and timetable information or you can pick up a printed timetable at an *iskelesi* (ferry dock).

On the European side, the major ferry docks are at the mouth of the Golden Horn (Eminönü and Karaköy), at Beşiktaş and next to the tram stop at Kabataş, 2km past the Galata Bridge.

The ferries run to two annual timetables: winter (mid-September to May) and summer (June to mid-September). Tickets are cheap (usually ₺2) and it's possible to use an İstanbulkart on most routes.

There are also *deniz otobüsü* (seabus) and *hızlı feribot* (fast ferry) services, but these ply routes that are of less interest to the traveller and are also more expensive than the conventional ferries. The most useful of these routes are Bostancı–Karaköy–Eminönü, Yenikapı–Bandırma (for İzmir), Sarayburnu–Avşa, Sirkeci–Harem, Kadıköy–Kabataş–Sariyer and Kabataş–Princes' Islands–Bostancı. For more information, check **İstanbul Deniz Otobüsleri** (İDO; ☎212-444 4436; www.ido.com.tr).

Taxi

İstanbul is full of yellow taxis. Some drivers are lunatics, others are con artists; most are neither. If you're caught with the first category and you're about to go into meltdown, say '*yavaş!*' (careful/slow down!). Drivers in the second of these categories – the con artists – tend to prey on tourists. All taxis have digital meters and must run them, but some of these drivers ask for a flat fare, or pretend the meter doesn't work so they can gouge you at the end of the trip. The

best way to counter this is to tell them no meter, no ride.

Taxi fares are very reasonable, and rates are the same during both day and night. It costs around ₺15 to travel between Beyoğlu and Sultanahmet.

Few taxis have seatbelts. If you catch a taxi over either of the Bosphorus Bridges, it is your responsibility to cover the toll. The driver will add this to your fare.

Metro

An efficient metro service connects Aksaray with the airport, stopping at 15 stations, including the *otogar*, along the way. Trains leave every 10 minutes or so from 5.40am to 1.40am. There are plans to extend the service to Yenikapı. Tickets cost ₺2 and İstanbulkarts can be used.

Another line connects Şişhane, near Tünel Meydanı in Beyoğlu, and Hacıosman, northeast of Taksim. Unfortunately, it's not possible to travel between the two points in one trip – one metro runs between Şişhane and Taksim Meydanı; another runs between Taksim and Hacıosman, stopping at nine

stations along the way. The full trip takes around one hour. Services run every five minutes or so from 6.15am to midnight. Tickets cost ₺2 and İstanbulkarts can be used.

Works are currently underway to extend the Taksim-Şişhane route over the Golden Horn via a new metro bridge and under the Old City to Yenikapı via stops at Unkapanı and Şehzadebaşı. It will then connect with the metro to Aksaray and with a transport tunnel being built under the Bosphorus as part of the Marmaray project. This tunnel will include a metro connection between Yenikapı, Sirkeci, Üsküdar and Söğütlüçeşme. Other works underway include construction of a 16-stop metro line running between Kadıköy and Kartal on the Asian side of town.

Funicular & Cable-Car

There are two funiculars (*funiküleri*) and two cablecars (*teleferic*) in the city.

An antique funicular called the Tünel carries passengers

THE MARMARAY PROJECT

Marmaray (www.marmaray.com) is an ambitious public transport project aimed at relieving İstanbul's serious traffic congestion. Its name comes from combining the name of the Sea of Marmara, which lies just south of the project site, with *ray*, the Turkish word for rail.

The project will see the Halkali–Sirkeci rail line, which runs alongside the historical peninsula's coastline, going underground at Yedikule and travelling to a huge underground transport hub at Yenikapı before continuing to Sirkeci and then on to a 5km tunnel being built under the Bosphorus. This will link the historical peninsula with another new underground transport hub in Üsküdar on the Asian side of the city. From there, the rail line will return to ground level at Söğütlüçeşme, 2km east of Kadıköy, where it will connect with the Gebze Anatolian rail line.

The project's original completion date was to be 2010, but important archaeological finds made during excavation works have slowed the process down. These include the site of a Byzantine harbour complete with wooden boats at Yenikapı and an ancient port and bazaar at Üsküdar. It's now hoped that the project will be completed in June 2015.

bus (*otobüs*) or on the electronic display at its front.

İstanbul Elektrik Tramvay ve Tünel (İETT, Istanbul Electricity, Tramway and Tunnel General Management; www.iett.gov.tr) buses are operated by the city. You must have a ticket (usually ₺2) before boarding. Buy these from the white booths near major stops and bus, tram and metro stations, or from some nearby shops for a small mark-up (look for 'İETT *otobüs bileti satılır*'). You can also use an İstanbulkart and save some money. Private buses regulated by the city called Özel Halk Otobüsü often run the same routes; these accept cash (pay the conductor) and some accept İstanbulkarts.

Dolmuş

A dolmuş is a shared minibus; it waits at a specified departure point until it has a full complement of passengers (in Turkish, dolmuş means full), then follows a fixed route to its destination. Destinations are displayed in the window of the dolmuş. Passengers flag down the driver to get on and indicate to the driver when they want to get off, usually by saying '*inecek var!*' (someone wants to get out!). Fares vary (pay on board) but are usually the same as municipal buses. Dolmuşes are almost as comfortable as taxis, run later into the night in many instances and often ply routes that buses and other forms of transport don't service.

between Karaköy, at the base of the Galata Bridge (Galata Köprüsü), to Tünel Meydanı, the southwestern end of İstiklal Caddesi. A fare costs ₺1.40.

The second funicular carries passengers from Kabataş – at the end of the tramline – to Taksim Meydanı in Taksim, where it connects to the metro. It runs every day between 6.10am and 12.50am and a fare costs ₺2.

A cable-car runs between the waterside at Eyüp to the Pierre Loti Café (₺2). Another travels between Maçka (near Taksim) downhill to the İstanbul Technical University in Taşkışla, but is of little use to travellers.

All are short trips and İstanbulkarts can be used.

Bus

The bus system in İstanbul is extremely efficient, though traffic congestion in the city means that bus trips can be very long. The introduction of Metrobüs lines (where buses are given dedicated traffic lanes) aims to relieve this problem, but these tend to service residential suburbs out of the city centre and are thus of limited benefit to travellers. The major bus stands are at Taksim Meydanıq, Beşiktaş, Kabataş, Eminönü, Kadıköy and Üsküdar, and most services run between 6.30am and 9pm. Destinations and main stops on city bus routes are shown on a sign on the right (kerb) side of the

Directory A–Z

Business Hours

Opening hours vary wildly across businesses and services in İstanbul. The following is a very general guide:

Post offices & banks 8.30am–noon, 1.30pm–5.30pm Monday–Friday

Shops 9am–7pm Monday–Saturday

Restaurants & cafes Breakfast 7.30am–10.30am, lunch noon–2.30pm, dinner 7.30pm–10pm

Bars Afternoon to early morning

Nightclubs 10pm till late

Customs Regulations

İstanbul's Atatürk International Airport uses the red and green channel system, randomly spot-checking passengers' luggage. You're allowed to import the following without paying duty:

Alcohol 1L of spirits, 2L of wine

Tobacco 600 cigarettes

Food 2kg of coffee, tea, chocolate or sugar products

Currency No limit

Other goods No more than €1500, but this varies by nationality

Note that it's illegal to take antiquities out of the country. Check www.gumruk.gov.tr for more information.

Electricity

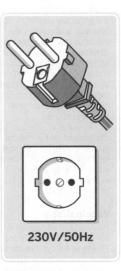

230V/50Hz

230V/50Hz

Emergency

Ambulance (☎112)

Fire (☎110)

Police (☎155)

Tourism Police (☎212-527 4503)

Gay & Lesbian Travellers

Homosexuality isn't illegal in Turkey, but neither is it officially legal. There's a generally ambivalent attitude towards it among the general population, although there are sporadic reports of violence towards gay people and conservative İstanbullus frown upon open displays of affection between persons of the same sex.

The monthly *Time Out İstanbul* magazine includes gay and lesbian listings.

Useful websites include the following:

IstanbulGay.com Handy guide to the gay, lesbian and transgendered scenes in the city. It includes plenty of information about gay-friendly clubs, bars and hotels.

Lambda (☎212-245 7068; www.lambdaistanbul.org; 2nd fl, Tel Sokak 2; ⏰3-8pm Sat & Sun) Turkish branch of the international Gay, Lesbian, Bisexual and

Transgender Liberation Group. It's based in Beyoğlu.

Pride Travel Agency
(📞212-527 0671; www.travel agencyturkey.com; 2nd fl, İncili Çavuş Sokak 33) Well-regarded gay-owned and gay-run travel agency specialising in booking accommodation and tours for gay travellers.

Health

Food & Water

Standards of food hygiene are generally high in İstanbul, and visitors experience few food-related illnesses. To be safe, treat street food with caution and if you dine in a *lokanta* (restaurant serving ready-made food) make sure you choose dishes that look hot and freshly prepared.

Tap water in İstanbul is chlorinated, but is still not guaranteed to be safe (many locals don't drink it). Spring water is cheap and sold everywhere in 0.33L, 1.5L and 3L plastic bottles.

Vaccinations

You won't need special inoculations before entering Turkey unless you're coming from an endemic or epidemic area. However, do discuss your requirements with a doctor. Consider typhoid fever and hepatitis A and B vaccinations if you plan to travel off the beaten track in Turkey; also make sure that your tetanus/diphtheria and polio vaccinations are up to date (boosters are necessary every 10 years).

Internet Access

As is the case elsewhere in Europe, the proliferation of personal communications devices has led to internet cafes becoming a dying breed. Wi-fi connections are ubiquitous in hotels and hostels, and common in chain cafes and fast-food joints.

An **@**icon is used to indicated accommodation that provides an internet station or laptops for guest use. A 🕿 icon is included if wi-fi access is offered.

If using a local computer, you may have to use a Turkish keyboard. When doing so, be aware that Turkish has two 'i's: the familiar dotted 'i' and the less familiar dotless 'ı'. Unfortunately the one in the usual place is the dotless 'ı' on a Turkish keyboard; you will need to make sure you use the correct dotted 'i' when typing in a web or email address. To create the @ symbol, hold down the 'q' and the right-hand ALT keys at the same time.

Legal Matters

➡ The age of consent in Turkey is 18 – as is the legal age for voting, driving and drinking.

➡ Technically, you should carry your passport at all times. Many travellers choose to carry a photocopy and leave the actual document in their hotel safe.

➡ It is illegal to take antiquities out of the country.

➡ In recent years, local politics has become increasingly socially conservative. This has manifested itself in a number of ways, including a ban on outdoor drinking in the Beyoğlu Belediyesi (Beyoğlu local government area) and a police crackdown on gay venues across the city, especially gay hamams and spas, which are regularly accused of breaching public decency laws. If you visit one of these, there is a chance that you could be caught up in a police raid.

Media

There are print and online English-language editions of the daily **Hürriyet Daily News** (www.hurriyetdailynews .com) and **Today's Zaman** (www.todayszaman.com) newspapers. A printed English-language edition of the monthly **Time Out İstanbul** (www.istanbulbeatblog.com) magazine is available. The online edition of **The Guide İstanbul** (www.theguide istanbul.com), an advertising-driven listings magazine, is more useful than its printed counterpart.

Medical Services

Turkey doesn't have reciprocal health-care arrangements with other countries, so having travel insurance is highly advisable.

For minor problems, it's customary to ask at a *eczane* (chemist/pharmacy) for advice. Many pharmacists speak English and will prescribe treatment on the spot. Drugs requiring a prescription in Western countries are often sold over the counter (except for the most dangerous or addictive ones) and will often be cheaper too. Make sure that you know the generic name of your medicine; the commercial name may not be the same in Turkey.

Most doctors in Turkey speak English and half of all the physicians in İstanbul are women. If a woman visits a male doctor, it's customary for her to have a companion present during any physical examination or treatment.

Though they are expensive, it's probably easiest to visit one of the private hospitals listed here if you need medical care when in İstanbul. Their standard of care is generally quite high and you will have no trouble finding staff who speak

English. Both accept credit-card payments and charge around ₺200 for a standard consultation.

Universal Taksim Alman Hastanesi (Universal German Hospital; ☎212-293 2150; www.uhg.com.tr; Sıraselviler Caddesi 119; ☺8.30am-6pm Mon-Fri, 8.30am-5pm Sat) Emergency, eye, dental and paediatric clinics.

Vehbi Koç American Hospital (Amerikan Hastenesi; ☎212-444 3777 ext 9, 212-311 2000; www .americanhospitalistanbul .org/ENG; Güzelbahçe Sokak 20, Nişantaşı; ☺24hr emergency department)

Money

We have cited prices for most hotels and organised tours in euros to reflect the reality on the ground; similarly in rare instances we've cited prices in US dollars. All other prices given are in ₺.

ATMs

ATMs (cashpoints) are everywhere in İstanbul. Virtually all of them offer instructions in English, French and German and will pay out Turkish liras when you insert your bank debit (cash) card. They will also pay cash advances on Visa and MasterCard. The limit on cash withdrawals is generally ₺600 to ₺800 per day, though this varies from bank to bank.

Changing Money

The 24-hour *döviz bürosus* (exchange bureaux) in the arrivals halls of the international airports usually offer competitive rates.

US dollars and euros are easily changed at exchange bureaux. They are sometimes accepted in carpet shops and hotels.

Turkish liras are fully convertible, so there is no black market.

Credit Cards

Most hotels, car-rental agencies, shops, pharmacies, entertainment venues and restaurants will accept Visa and MasterCard; Amex isn't as widely accepted as the others and Diner's is often not accepted. Inexpensive eateries usually accept cash only.

Post

Post offices are known as PTTs (peh-teh-teh; *Posta, Telefon, Telegraf*) and have black-and-yellow signs.

İstanbul's **Central Post Office** (Merkez Postane; Büyük Postane Caddesi) is several blocks southwest of Sirkeci train station.

The *yurtdışı* slot is for mail to foreign countries, *yurtiçi* is for mail to other Turkish cities, and *şehiriçi* is for mail within İstanbul.

Mail delivery is fairly reliable. For more information on PTT services go to www.ptt.gov.tr.

Public Holidays

Banks, offices and government services close for the day on the following secular public holidays:

New Year's Day 1 January

National Sovereignty & Children's Day 23 April

May Day 1 May

Atatürk Commemoration & Youth Day 19 May

Victory Day 30 August

Republic Day 29 October

Religious festivals are celebrated according to the Muslim lunar Hejira calendar; two of these festivals (Şeker Bayramı and Kurban Bayramı) are also public holidays. Şeker Bayramı is a three-day festival at the end of Ramazan, and Kurban Bayramı, the most important religious holiday of the year, is a four-day festival which date changes each year. During these festivals, banks and offices are closed and hotels, buses, trains and planes are heavily booked.

Though most restaurants and cafes open to serve non-Muslims during the holy month of Ramazan (called Ramadan in other countries), it's polite to avoid ostentatious public smoking, eating and drinking during this period.

Safe Travel

Pedestrian Safety

As a pedestrian, always give way to vehicles; the sovereignty of the pedestrian is recognised in law but not out on the street.

Racial Discrimination

Turkey is not ethnically diverse. This means that travellers who are Asian or black stand out as being different and can be treated unacceptably as a consequence. As well as harassment, there have been isolated incidents of violence towards black travellers, allegedly at the hands of individual members of the police force.

Theft & Robbery

Theft is not generally a big problem and robbery (mugging) is comparatively rare, but don't let İstanbul's relative safety lull you. Take normal precautions. Areas to be particularly careful in include Aksaray/Laleli (the city's red-light district), the Grand Bazaar (pickpocket central), and the streets off İstiklal Caddesi in Beyoğlu.

Telephone

If you are in European İstanbul and wish to call a number in Asian İstanbul, you must dial 0, followed by 216. If you are in Asian İstanbul and wish to call a number in European İstanbul use 0 followed by 212. Do not use a prefix (that is, don't use the 0 or 212/6) if you are calling a number on the same shore.

Country code 90

European İstanbul 212

Asian İstanbul 216

Code to make an intercity call 0 + local code

International Access Code 00

Directory Inquiries 118

International Operator 115

Mobile/Cell Phones

Mobile reception is excellent in İstanbul.

All mobile numbers start with a four-figure code beginning with ☑05.

There are three networks: **Turkcell** (www.turkcell.com .tr), **Vodafone** (www.vodafone .com.tr) and **Avea** (www.avea .com.tr), all of which offer prepaid SIM cards (*kontürlü SIM karts*) that are handy for travellers. These cost ₺25 (including ₺5 credit) or ₺35 (including ₺20 credit) and can be topped up with credit.

Turkey uses the standard GSM network operating on 900MHz or 1800MHz (so not all US and Canadian phones work here).

To use a local SIM in a phone you've bought from home, you'll need to register the phone. To do this, have your passport with you when you buy a SIM card and ask the dealer to register both the SIM and the phone. Unfortunately, the registration can take days to be approved.

If you buy a local SIM card and use it in your mobile from home without registering the phone, the network will detect and bar it within a week or two.

If you purchase a phone in Turkey, you won't need to register it. Just put in the SIM card and ask the dealer to organise the activation for you. You may need to show your passport. The account should activate within an hour or two.

There are plenty of shops selling phones in the streets opposite the Sirkeci Railway Station. Starting models cost around ₺100.

Time

İstanbul time is East European Time, two hours ahead of Coordinated Universal Time (UTC, alias GMT), except in the warm months, when clocks are turned ahead one hour. Daylight-saving (summer) time usually begins at 1am on the last Sunday in March and ends at 2am on the last Sunday in October.

Turks use the 24-hour clock.

Tourist Information

The **Ministry of Culture & Tourism** (www.turizm.gov.tr) currently operates four tourist information offices or booths in the city; a fifth is

scheduled to open at some stage in the future inside the Atatürk Cultural Centre on Taksim Meydanı (Taksim Square). Frankly, none of them are particularly helpful.

Tourist Information Desk – Atatürk Airport (☑212-465 3451; International Arrivals Hall, Atatürk International Airport; ◷9am-10pm)

Tourist Information Office – Karaköy (Karaköy International Passenger Terminal, Kemankeş Caddesi, Karaköy ; ◷9.30am-5pm Mon-Sat)

Tourist Information Office – Sirkeci Railway Station (☑212-511 5888; Sirkeci Station, Ankara Caddesi, Sirkeci; ◷9.30am-6pm mid-Apr–Sep, 9am-5.30pm Oct–mid-Apr)

Tourist Information Office – Sultanahmet (☑212-518 8754; Hippodrome, Sultanahmet; ◷9.30am-6pm mid-Apr–Sep, 9am-5.30pm Oct–mid-Apr; ◪Sultanahmet)

Travellers with Disabilities

İstanbul can be challenging for mobility-impaired travellers. Roads are potholed and pavements are often crooked and cracked. Fortunately, the city is attempting to rectify this.

Government-run museums are free of charge for disabled visitors and many have wheelchair access. Airlines and most four- and five-star hotels have wheelchair access and at least one room set up for disabled guests. All public transport is free for the disabled, and the metro and tram can be accessed by people in wheelchairs.

Visas

At the time of research, nationals of the following countries (among others) could enter Turkey for up to three months with only a valid passport (no visa required): Denmark, Finland, France, Germany, Greece, Italy, Israel, Japan, New Zealand, Sweden and Switzerland.

Nationals of the following countries (among others) could enter for up to three months upon purchase of a visa sticker at their point of arrival (ie not at an embassy in advance): Australia, Canada, Ireland, Netherlands, Spain, UK and USA.

Nationals of Russia and many Eastern European and Central Asian countries could enter for up to one or two months upon purchase of a visa sticker at their point of arrival.

Nationals of other countries including China and India needed to organise visas in their home countries. These were available for one-month stays.

Your passport must have at least three months' validity remaining, or you may not be admitted into Turkey. If you arrive at Atatürk International Airport, get your visa from the booth to the right of the 'Other Nationalities'

counter in the customs hall before you go through immigration. You can pay in Turkish lira, euros or US dollars; customs officials sometimes insist on correct change. An ATM dispensing Turkish liras is next to the counter, but it's not always working. The fees change, but at the time of research Australians, Americans, Britons and most other nationalities paid €15 (US$20); for some reason Canadians paid €45 (US$60). See the website of the **Ministry of Foreign Affairs** (www.mfa.gov.tr) for the latest information.

Visa Extensions

There are single- and multiple-entry visas. Single-entry visas are valid for one or three months from the day of entry; multiple-entry visas are valid for three-month blocks during a one-year period. Depending on your nationality, you may be able to extend your visa. Most visitors wanting to extend their stay for a few months avoid bureaucratic tedium by taking a quick overnight trip to Greece (Thessaloniki or

Rhodes), returning to Turkey the next day with a new three-month stamp in their passports.

Women Travellers

Travelling in İstanbul as a female is easy and enjoyable provided you follow some simple guidelines. Tailor your behaviour and your clothing to your surroundings – outfits that are appropriate for neighbourhoods such as Beyoğlu and along the Bosphorus (skimpy tops, tight jeans etc) are not appropriate in conservative suburbs such as Üsküdar, for instance.

It's a good idea to sit in the back seat of a taxi or dolmuş rather than next to the driver. If approached by a Turkish man in circumstances that upset you, try saying *Ayıp!* (ah-*yuhp*), which means 'Shame on you!'

You'll have no trouble finding tampons, sanitary napkins and condoms in pharmacies and supermarkets in İstanbul. Bring a shawl to cover your head when visiting mosques.

Language

Turkish belongs to the Ural-Altaic language family. It's the official language of Turkey and northern Cyprus, and has approximately 70 million speakers worldwide.

Pronouncing Turkish is pretty simple for English speakers as most Turkish sounds are also found in English. If you read our coloured pronunciation guides as if they were English, you should be understood just fine. Note that the symbol ew represents the sound 'ee' pronounced with rounded lips (as in 'few'), and that the symbol uh is pronounced like the 'a' in 'ago'. The Turkish r is always rolled and v is pronounced a little softer than in English.

Word stress is quite light in Turkish – in our pronunciation guides the stressed syllables are in italics.

BASICS

Hello.
Merhaba. — mer·ha·ba

Goodbye.
Hoşçakal. — hosh·cha·kal
(said by person leaving)
Güle güle. — gew·le gew·le
(said by person staying)

Yes.
Evet. — e·vet

No.
Hayır. — ha·yuhr

Excuse me.
Bakar mısınız. — ba·kar muh·suh·nuhz

WANT MORE?
....
For in-depth language information and handy phrases, check out Lonely Planet's *Turkish Phrasebook*. You'll find it at **shop.lonelyplanet.com**, or you can buy Lonely Planet's iPhone phrasebooks at the Apple App Store.

Sorry.
Özür dilerim. — er·zewr dee·le·reem

Please.
Lütfen. — lewt·fen

Thank you.
Teşekkür ederim. — te·shek·kewr e·de·reem

You're welcome.
Birşey değil. — beer·shay de·eel

How are you?
Nasılsınız? — na·suhl·suh·nuhz

Fine, and you?
İyiyim, ya siz? — ee·yee·yeem ya seez

What's your name?
Adınız nedir? — a·duh·nuhz ne·deer

My name is ...
Benim adım ... — be·neem a·duhm ...

Do you speak English?
İngilizce — een·gee·leez·je
konuşuyor — ko·noo·shoo·yor
musunuz? — moo·soo·nooz

I understand.
Anlıyorum. — an·luh·yo·room

I don't understand.
Anlamıyorum. — an·la·muh·yo·room

ACCOMMODATION

Where can I find a ...?	Nerede ... bulabilirim?	ne·re·de ... boo·la·bee·lee·reem
campsite	kamp yeri	kamp ye·ree
guesthouse	misafirhane	mee·sa·feer·ha·ne
hotel	otel	o·tel
pension	pansiyon	pan·see·yon
youth hostel	gençlik hosteli	gench·leek hos·te·lee

How much is it per night/person?
Geceliği/Kişi — ge·je·lee·ee/kee·shee
başına ne kadar? — ba·shuh·na ne ka·dar

Is breakfast included?
Kahvaltı dahil mi?   kah·val·*tuh* da·*heel* mee

Do you have a ...?	... odanız var mı?	... o·da·*nuz* var muh
single room	Tek kişilik	tek kee·shee·*leek*
double room	İki kişilik	ee·*kee* kee·shee·*leek*
air conditioning	klima	*klee*·ma
bathroom	banyo	*ban*·yo
window	pencere	*pen*·je·re

DIRECTIONS

Where is ...?
... nerede?   ... *ne*·re·de

What's the address?
Adresi nedir?   ad·re·*see* ne·*deer*

Could you write it down, please?
Lütfen yazar mısınız?   *lewt*·fen ya·*zar* muh·suh·*nuhz*

Can you show me (on the map)?
Bana (haritada) gösterebilir misiniz?   ba·*na* (ha·ree·ta·*da*) gers·te·re·bee·leer mee·seen·*neez*

It's straight ahead.
Tam karşıda.   tam kar·shuh·*da*

at the traffic lights
trafik ışıklarından   tra·*feek* uh·shuhk·la·ruhn·*dan*

at the corner	köşeden	ker·she·*den*
behind	arkasında	ar·ka·suhn·*da*
far (from)	uzak	oo·*zak*
in front of	önünde	er·newn·*de*
near (to)	yakınında	ya·kuh·nuhn·*da*
opposite	karşısında	kar·shuh·suhn·*da*
Turn left.	Sola dön.	so·*la* dern
Turn right.	Sağa dön.	sa·*a* dern

EATING & DRINKING

What would you recommend?
Ne tavsiye edersiniz?   ne tav·see·*ye* e·*der*·see·neez

What's in that dish?
Bu yemekte neler var?   boo ye·mek·*te* ne·ler var

I don't eat ...
... yemiyorum.   ... ye·mee·yo·room

Cheers!
Şerefe!   she·re·*fe*

That was delicious!
Nefisti!   ne·*fees*·tee

The bill/check, please.
Hesap lütfen.   he·*sap* lewt·fen

KEY PATTERNS

To get by in Turkish, mix and match these simple patterns with words of your choice:

When's (the next bus)?
(Sonraki otobüs) ne zaman?   (son·ra·*kee* o·to·*bews*) ne za·*man*

Where's (the market)?
(Pazar yeri) nerede?   (pa·zar ye·*ree*) ne·re·de

Where can I (buy a ticket)?
Nereden (bilet alabilirim)?   ne·re·den (bee·*let* a·*la*·bee·lee·reem)

I have (a reservation).
(Rezervasyonum) var.   (re·zer·vas·yo·*noom*) var

Do you have (a map)?
(Haritanız) var mı?   (ha·ree·ta·*nuhz*) var muh

Is there (a toilet)?
(Tuvalet) var mı?   (too·va·*let*) var muh

I'd like (the menu).
(Menüyü) istiyorum.   (me·new·*yew*) ees·*tee*·yo·room

I want to (make a call).
(Bir görüşme yapmak) istiyorum.   (beer ger·rewsh·*me* yap·*mak*) ees·*tee*·yo·room

Do I have to (declare this)?
(Bunu beyan etmem) gerekli mi?   (boo·*noo* be·*yan* et·*mem*) ge·rek·*lee* mee

I need (assistance).
(Yardıma) ihtiyacım var.   (yar·duh·*ma*) eeh·tee·ya·*juhm* var

I'd like a table for ...	... bir masa ayırtmak istiyorum.	... beer ma·*sa* a·yuhrt·*mak* ees·*tee*·yo·room
(eight) o'clock	Saat (sekiz) için	sa·*at* (se·*keez*) ee·*cheen*
(two) people	(İki) kişilik	(ee·*kee*) kee·shee·*leek*

Key Words

appetisers	mezeler	me·ze·*ler*
bottle	şişe	shee·*she*
bowl	kase	ka·*se*
breakfast	kahvaltı	kah·val·*tuh*
(too) cold	(çok) soğuk	(chok) so·*ook*
cup	fincan	feen·*jan*
delicatessen	şarküteri	shar·kew·te·ree
dinner	akşam yemeği	ak·sham ye·me·ee
dish	yemek	ye·*mek*

food	yiyecek	yee·ye·jek
fork	çatal	cha·tal
glass	bardak	bar·dak
grocery	bakkal	bak·kal
halal	helal	he·lal
highchair	mama sandalyesi	ma·ma san·dal·ye·see
hot (warm)	sıcak	suh·jak
knife	bıçak	buh·chak
kosher	koşer	ko·sher
lunch	öğle yemeği	er·le ye·me·ee
main courses	ana yemekler	a·na ye·mek·ler
market	pazar	pa·zar
menu	yemek listesi	ye·mek lees·te·see
plate	tabak	ta·bak
restaurant	restoran	res·to·ran
spicy	acı	a·juh
spoon	kaşık	ka·shuhk
vegetarian	vejeteryan	ve·zhe·ter·yan

Meat & Fish

anchovy	hamsi	ham·see
beef	sığır eti	suh·uhr e·tee
calamari	kalamares	ka·la·ma·res
chicken	piliç/ tavuk	pee·leech/ ta·vook
fish	balık	ba·luhk
lamb	kuzu	koo·zoo
liver	ciğer	jee·er
mussels	midye	meed·ye
pork	domuz eti	do·mooz e·tee
veal	dana eti	da·na e·tee

Fruit & Vegetables

apple	elma	el·ma
apricot	kayısı	ka·yuh·suh
banana	muz	mooz
capsicum	biber	bee·ber
carrot	havuç	ha·vooch
cucumber	salatalık	sa·la·ta·luhk
fruit	meyve	may·ve
grape	üzüm	ew·zewm
melon	kavun	ka·voon
olive	zeytin	zay·teen
onion	soğan	so·an
orange	portakal	por·ta·kal

peach	şeftali	shef·ta·lee
potato	patates	pa·ta·tes
spinach	ıspanak	uhs·pa·nak
tomato	domates	do·ma·tes
watermelon	karpuz	kar·pooz

Other

bread	ekmek	ek·mek
cheese	peynir	pay·neer
egg	yumurta	yoo·moor·ta
honey	bal	bal
ice	buz	booz
pepper	kara biber	ka·ra bee·ber
rice	pirinç/ pilav	pee·reench/ pee·lav
salt	tuz	tooz
soup	çorba	chor·ba
sugar	şeker	she·ker
Turkish delight	lokum	lo·koom

Drinks

beer	bira	bee·ra
coffee	kahve	kah·ve
(orange) juice	(portakal) suyu	(por·ta·kal) soo·yoo)
milk	süt	sewt
mineral water	maden suyu	ma·den soo·yoo
soft drink	alkolsüz içecek	al·kol·sewz ee·che·jek
tea	çay	chai
water	su	soo
wine	şarap	sha·rap
yoghurt	yoğurt	yo·oort

Signs	
Açık	Open
Bay	Male
Bayan	Female
Çıkışı	Exit
Giriş	Entrance
Kapalı	Closed
Sigara Içilmez	No Smoking
Tuvaletler	Toilets
Yasak	Prohibited

Question Words

How?	*Nasıl?*	na-*seel*
What?	*Ne?*	ne
When?	*Ne zaman?*	ne za-*man*
Where?	*Nerede?*	ne-re-de
Which?	*Hangi?*	han-*gee*
Who?	*Kim?*	keem
Why?	*Neden?*	ne-den

EMERGENCIES

Help!
İmdat!   eem-dat

I'm lost.
Kayboldum.   kai-bol-*doom*

Leave me alone!
Git başımdan!   geet ba-shuhm-*dan*

There's been an accident.
Bir kaza oldu.   beer ka-za ol-*doo*

Can I use your phone?
Telefonunuzu   te-le-fo-noo-noo-*zoo*
kullanabilir miyim?   kool-la-*na*-bee-leer mee-*yeem*

Call a doctor!
Doktor çağırın!   dok-*tor* cha-uh-ruhn

Call the police!
Polis çağırın!   po-*lees* cha-uh-ruhn

I'm ill.
Hastayım.   has-*ta*-yuhm

It hurts here.
Burası ağrıyor.   boo-ra-*suh* a-*ruh*-yor

I'm allergic to (nuts).
(Çerezlere)   (che-rez-le-*re*)
alerjim var.   a-ler-*zheem* var

SHOPPING & SERVICES

I'd like to buy ...
... almak istiyorum.   ... al-*mak* ees-*tee*-yo-room

I'm just looking.
Sadece bakıyorum.   sa-de-je ba-*kuh*-yo-room

May I look at it?
Bakabilir miyim?   ba-*ka*-bee-leer mee-*yeem*

The quality isn't good.
Kalitesi iyi değil.   ka-lee-te-*see* ee-*yee* de-*eel*

How much is it?
Ne kadar?   ne ka-*dar*

It's too expensive.
Bu çok pahalı.   boo chok pa-ha-*luh*

Do you have something cheaper?
Daha ucuz birşey   da-*ha* oo-*jooz* beer-*shay*
var mı?   var muh

There's a mistake in the bill.
Hesapta bir   he-sap-*ta* beer
yanlışlık var.   yan-luhsh-*luhk* var

ATM	*bankamatik*	ban-ka-ma-*teek*
credit card	*kredi kartı*	kre-dee kar-*tuh*
post office	*postane*	pos-*ta*-ne
signature	*imza*	eem-*za*
tourist office	*turizm*	too-*reezm*
	bürosu	bew-ro-*soo*

TIME & DATES

What time is it?   *Saat kaç?*   sa-*at* kach
It's (10) o'clock.   *Saat (on).*   sa-*at* (on)
Half past (10).   *(On) buçuk.*   (on) boo-*chook*

in the morning	*öğleden evvel*	er-le-*den* ev-*vel*
in the afternoon	*öğleden sonra*	er-le-*den* son-ra
in the evening	*akşam*	ak-*sham*
yesterday	*dün*	dewn
today	*bugün*	boo-*gewn*
tomorrow	*yarın*	ya-*ruhn*

Monday	*Pazartesi*	pa-zar-te-see
Tuesday	*Salı*	sa-*luh*
Wednesday	*Çarşamba*	char-sham-ba
Thursday	*Perşembe*	per-shem-be
Friday	*Cuma*	joo-*ma*
Saturday	*Cumartesi*	joo-mar-te-see
Sunday	*Pazar*	pa-zar

January	*Ocak*	o-*jak*
February	*Şubat*	shoo-*bat*
March	*Mart*	mart
April	*Nisan*	nee-*san*
May	*Mayıs*	ma-*yuhs*
June	*Haziran*	ha-zee-ran
July	*Temmuz*	tem-*mooz*
August	*Ağustos*	a-oos-*tos*
September	*Eylül*	ay-*lewl*
October	*Ekim*	e-*keem*
November	*Kasım*	ka-*suhm*
December	*Aralık*	a-ra-*luhk*

TRANSPORT

Public Transport

At what time does the ... leave/arrive?	*... ne zaman kalkacak/ varır?*	... ne za-*man* kal-ka-*jak*/ va-*ruhr*
boat	*Vapur*	va-*poor*
bus	*Otobüs*	o-to-*bews*
plane	*Uçak*	oo-*chak*
train	*Tren*	tren

Numbers

1	*bir*	beer
2	*iki*	ee·*kee*
3	*üç*	ewch
4	*dört*	dert
5	*beş*	besh
6	*altı*	al·*tuh*
7	*yedi*	ye·*dee*
8	*sekiz*	se·*keez*
9	*dokuz*	do·*kooz*
10	*on*	on
20	*yirmi*	yeer·*mee*
30	*otuz*	o·*tooz*
40	*kırk*	kuhrk
50	*elli*	el·*lee*
60	*altmış*	alt·*muhsh*
70	*yetmiş*	et·*meesh*
80	*seksen*	sek·*sen*
90	*doksan*	dok·*san*
100	*yüz*	yewz
1000	*bin*	been

Does it stop at (Maltepe)?
(Maltepe'de) (*mal*·te·pe·de)
durur mu? doo·*roor* moo

What's the next stop?
Sonraki durak son·ra·*kee* doo·*rak*
hangisi? han·gee·*see*

Please tell me when we get to (Beşiktaş).
(Beşiktaş'a) (be·*sheek*·ta·sha)
vardığımızda var·duh·uh·muhz·*da*
lütfen bana *lewt*·fen ba·*na*
söyleyin. say·le·yeen

I'd like to get off at (Kadıköy).
(Kadıköy'de) inmek (ka·*duh*·kay·de) een·*mek*
istiyorum. ees·*tee*·yo·room

I'd like a ...	*(Bostancı'ya)*	(bos·*tan*·juh·ya)
ticket to	*... bir bilet*	*... beer* bee·*let*
(Bostancı).	*lütfen.*	*lewt*·fen
1st-class	*Birinci mevki*	bee·*reen*·jee mev·*kee*
2nd-class	*İkinci mevki*	ee·*keen*·jee mev·*kee*
one-way	*Gidiş*	gee·*deesh*
return	*Gidiş-dönüş*	gee·*deesh*·der·*newsh*
first	*ilk*	eelk
last	*son*	son
next	*geleçek*	ge·le·*jek*

I'd like a/an ... seat.	*... bir yer istiyorum.*	*... beer* yer ees·*tee*·yo·room
aisle	*Koridor tarafında*	ko·ree·*dor* ta·ra·fuhn·*da*
window	*Cam kenarı*	jam ke·na·*ruh*
cancelled	*iptal edildi*	eep·*tal* e·deel·*dee*
delayed	*ertelendi*	er·te·len·*dee*
platform	*peron*	pe·*ron*
ticket office	*bilet gişesi*	bee·*let* gee·she·*see*
timetable	*tarife*	ta·ree·*fe*
train station	*istasyon*	ees·tas·*yon*

Driving & Cycling

I'd like to hire a ...	*Bir ... kiralamak istiyorum.*	*beer* ... kee·ra·la·*mak* ees·*tee*·yo·room
4WD	*dört çeker*	dert che·*ker*
bicycle	*bisiklet*	bee·seek·*let*
car	*araba*	a·ra·*ba*
motorcycle	*motosiklet*	mo·to·seek·*let*
bike shop	*bisikletçi*	bee·seek·let·*chee*
child seat	*çocuk koltuğu*	cho·*jook* kol·*too*·oo
diesel	*dizel*	dee·*zel*
helmet	*kask*	kask
mechanic	*araba tamircisi*	a·ra·*ba* ta·meer·jee·*see*
petrol/gas	*benzin*	ben·*zeen*
service station	*benzin istasyonu*	ben·*zeen* ees·tas·yo·*noo*

Is this the road to (Taksim)?
(Taksim'e) giden (tak·see·me) gee·*den*
yol bu mu? yol boo moo

(How long) Can I park here?
Buraya (ne kadar boo·ra·*ya* (ne ka·*dar*
süre) park sew·*re*) park
edebilirim? e·de·bee·*lee*·reem

The car/motorbike has broken down (at Osmanbey).
Arabam/ a·ra·*bam*/
Motosikletim mo·to·seek·le·*teem*
(Osmanbey'de) (os·*man*·bay·de)
bozuldu. bo·*zool*·doo

I have a flat tyre.
Lastiğim patladı. las·tee·*eem* pat·la·*duh*

I've run out of petrol.
Benzinim bitti. ben·zee·*neem* beet·tee

GLOSSARY

Below are some useful Turkish words and abbreviations:

ada(lar) – island

arasta – row of shops near a mosque

Asya – Asian İstanbul

Avrupa – European İstanbul

bahçe(si) – garden

bey – 'Mr'; follows the name

boğaz – strait

bulvar(ı) – often abbreviated to 'bul'; boulevard or avenue

caddesi – often abbreviated to 'cad'; street

cami(i)– mosque

çarşı(sı) – market, bazaar

çay bahçesi – tea garden

çeşme – spring, fountain

deniz – sea

deniz otobüsü – catamaran; sea bus

dervish – member of the Mevlevi Muslim brotherhood

dolmuş – shared taxi (or minibus)

döviz bürosu – currency-exchange office

eczane – chemist/pharmacy

eski – old (thing, not person)

ezan – the Muslim call to prayers; also *azan*

fasıl – energetic folk music played in *meyhanes* (taverns)

fayton – horse-drawn carriage

feribot – ferry

hamam(ı) – Turkish steam bath

han – traditional name for a caravanserai

hastanesi – hospital

hısar(ı) – fortress or citadel

imam – prayer leader; Muslim cleric; teacher

iskele(si) – landing place, wharf, quay

kadın – wife

kale(si) – fortress, citadel

kapı(sı) – door, gate

karagöz – shadow-puppet theatre

KDV – *katma de er vergisi*; value-added tax (VAT)

kebapçı – place selling kebaps

keyif – relaxation

kilim – pileless woven run

konak, konağı – mansion, government headquarters

köprü – bridge

köy(ü) – village

külliye – mosque complex

kuru temizleme – dry cleaning

mahfil – high, elaborate chair

Maşallah – Wonder of God! (said in admiration or to avert the evil eye)

medrese –Islamic school of higher studies

merkez postane – central post office

meydan(ı) – public square, open place

mihrab – niche in a mosque indicating the direction of Mecca

mimber – pulpit in a mosque

minaret – mosque tower from which Muslims are called to prayer

müezzin – the official who sings the *ezan*

müze(si) – museum

nargile – water pipe

oda(sı) – room

otel(ı) – hotel

otobus – bus

otogar – bus station

Ottoman – of or pertaining to the Ottoman Empire, which lasted from the end of the 13th century to the end of WWI

padişah – Ottoman emperor, sultan

paşa – general, governor

pazar(ı) – weekly market, bazaar

PTT – Posta, Telefon, Teleğraf; post, telephone and telegraph office

Ramazan – Islamic holy month of fasting (Ramadan)

şadırvan – fountain where Muslims perform ritual ablutions

saray(ı) – palace

sebil – fountain

şehir – city; municipal area

selamlık – public/male quarters of a traditional household

Seljuk – of or pertaining to the Seljuk Turks, who in the 11th to 13th centuries created the first Turkish state to rule Anatolia

sema – dervish ceremony

semahane – hall where whirling-dervish ceremony is performed

sokak, sokağı – often abbreviated to 'sk' or 'sok'; street or lane

Sufi – Muslim mystic, member of a mystic (dervish) brotherhood

sultan – sovereign

tarikat – a Sufic order

tavla – backgammon

TC – Türkiye Cumhuriyeti (Turkish Republic); designates an official office or organisation

tekke – dervish lodge

tramvay – tram

tuğra – sultan's monogram, imperial signature

türbe – tomb

ücretsiz servis – free service

valide sultan – queen mother

vezir – vizier (minister) in the Ottoman government

yalı – waterside timber mansion

yeni – new

yıldız – star

yol(u) – road, way

MENU DECODER

General Terms

acı – spicy

afıyet olsun – bon appétit

aile salonu – family room; for couples, families and women in a Turkish restaurant

akşam yemeği – dinner

ana yemekler – main courses

bakkal – grocery store

balık restoran – fish restaurant

bardak – glass

bıçak – knife

börekçi – place selling pastries

büfe – snack bar

buz – ice

çatal – fork

dolma – vegetables stuffed with rice and/or meat

etyemez/vejeteryan – vegetarian

fasulyeci – restaurant serving cooked beans

fincan – cup

garson – waiter/waitress

hazır yemek lokanta – casual restaurant serving ready-made-food

helal – halal

hesap – the bill

içmek – drink

İngilizce menu – menu in English

kaşık – spoon

kase/tas – bowl

kahvaltı – breakfast

kebapci – kebap restaurant

köfteci – köfte restaurant

koşer – kosher

lokanta – abbreviation of *hazır yemek lokanta*

mama sandalyesi – highchair

menu – menu

meyhane – tavern

meze – small dishes eaten at the start of a meal; similar to hors d'ouevres

ocakbaşı – fireside kebap restaurant

öğle yemeği – lunch

pastane – cake shop

pazar – market

peçete – napkin

pidecisi – pizza restaurant

porsiyon – portion, helping

restoran – restaurant

sade – plain

şarküteri – delicatessen

şerefe! – cheers!

servis ücreti – service charge

sıcak – hot; warm

şişe – bottle

tabak – plate

uç – tip

yarım porsiyon – half porsiyon

yemek – eat; dish

zeytinyağlı – food cooked in olive oil

Staples

ayva – quince

bal – honey

balık – fish

beyaz peynir – salty white cheese similar to fetta

biber – bell pepper

ceviz – walnut

ciğer – liver

çilek – strawberry

çorba – soup

dana eti – veal

domates – tomato

ekmek – bread

elma – apple

enginar – artichoke

erik – plum

et – meat

et suyu – meat stock

fıstık – pistachio

hamsi – anchovy

havuç – carrot

incir – fig

ıspanak – spinach

kalamar – calamari

kalkan – turbot

kara/toz biber – black/white pepper

karpuz – watermelon

kaşar peyniri – cheddar-like sheep's milk cheese

kavun – melon

kayısı – apricot

kestane – chestnuts

kiraz – cherry

kuzu – lamb

levrek – sea bass

limon – lemon

lüfer – bluefish

mantar – mushroom

meyve – fruit

midye – mussels

muz – banana

pastırma – pressed beef preserved in garlic and spices

patates – potato

patlıcan – eggplant

peynir – cheese

pirinç/pilav – rice

portakal – orange

salata – salad

salatalık – cucumber

sebze – vegetables

şeftali – peach

şeker – sugar

sığır eti – beef

simit – sesame-encrusted bread ring

soğan – onion

tavuk/piliç – chicken

taze fasulye – green beans

tuz – salt

un – flour

uskumru – mackerel

üzüm – grape

vişne – sour cherry, morello

yumurta – egg

zeytin – olive

Popular Dishes

MEZE

acılı ezme – spicy tomato and onion paste

ançüez – salted or pickled anchovy

barbunya piliki – red-bean salad

beyaz peynir – white cheese from sheep or goat

çacık – yoghurt dip with garlic and mint

çerkez tavuğu – Circassian chicken; made with chicken, bread, walnuts, salt and garlic

enginar – cooked artichoke

fasulye pilaki – white beans cooked with tomato paste and garlic

fava salatası – mashed broad-bean salad

haydari – yoghurt dip with roasted eggplant and garlic

humus – chickpea dip with sesame oil, lemon and spices

imam bayıldı – literally 'the imam fainted'; eggplant, onion, tomato and peppers slow-cooked in olive oil

kalamar tava – fried calamari

lakerda –strongly flavoured salted kingfish salad

midye dolma – stuffed mussels

muhammara – dip of walnuts, bread, tahini, olive oil and lemon juice; also known as *acuka* or *civizli biber*

patlıcan kızartması – fried aubergines with tomatoes

piyaz – white-bean salad

Rus salatası – Russian salad

semizotu salatası – green purslane with yoghurt and garlic

sigara böreği – deep-fried cigar-shaped pastries filled with white cheese

turşu – pickled vegetables

yaprak sarma/yaprak dolması – vine leaves stuffed with rice, herbs and pine nuts

yeşil fasulye – green beans

KEBAPS (KEBABS) & KÖFTE

Adana kebap – a spicy version of şiş köfte

alinazik – eggplant puree with yoghurt and ground *köfte*

beyti sarma – spicy ground meat baked in a thin layer of bread and served with yoghurt

çiğ köfte – raw ground-lamb mixed with pounded bulgur, onion, spices and pepper

döner kebap – compressed meat (usually lamb) cooked on a revolving upright skewer and thinly sliced

fıstıklı kebap – minced lamb studded with pistachios

içli köfte – meatballs rolled in bulgar and fried

İskender (Bursa) kebap – döner lamb served on crumbled pide with yoghurt, topped with tomato and butter sauces

ızgara köfte – grilled meatballs

karışık ızgara – mixed grilled lamb

kebap – meat grilled on a skewer

köfte – meatballs

patlıcan kebap – cubed or minced lamb grilled with aubergine

pirzola – lamb cutlet

şiş kebap – small pieces of lamb grilled on a skewer

şiş köfte – meatballs wrapped around a flat skewer and barbecued

tavuk şiş – small chicken pieces grilled on a skewer

testi kebap – small pieces of lamb or chicken in sauce that is slow-cooked in a sealed terracotta pot

tokat kebap – lamb cubes grilled with potato, tomato, aubergine and garlic

Urfa kebap – a mild version of the Adana kebap served with lots of onion and black pepper

Other Dishes

Arnavut çiğeri – Albanian-style spicy fried liver

balık ekmek – sandwich of grilled fish and salad

börek – sweet or savoury filled pastry

çoban salatası – salad of tomatoes, cucumber, onion and pepper

gözleme – filled savoury pancake

hünkâr beğendi – literally 'sultan's delight'; lamb or beef stew served on a mound of rich eggplant puree

iç pilav – rice with onions, nuts and currants

işkembe çorbası – tripe soup

kısır – bulgar salad

kokoreç – seasoned, grilled lamb/mutton intestines

kuru fasulye – haricot beans cooked in a spicy tomato sauce

lahmacun – thin and crispy Arabic-style pizza

mantı – Turkish ravioli stuffed with beef mince and topped with yoghurt, garlic, tomato and butter

menemen – breakfast eggs cooked with tomatoes, peppers and white cheese

mercimek çorbası – lentil soup

pide – Turkish-style pizza

su böreği – lasagne-like layered pastry laced with white cheese and parsley

sucuk – spicy beef sausage

tavuk kavurma – roast chicken

Drinks & Desserts

Amerikan kahvesi – instant coffee

aşure – dried fruit, nut and pulse pudding

ayran – drink made with yoghurt and salt

baklava – layered filo pastry with honey or sugar syrup; sometimes made with nuts

beyaz şarap – white wine

bira – beer

bitki çay – herbal tea

çay – tea

dondurma – ice-cream

elma çay – apple tea, predominantly a tourist drink

fırın sütlaç – rice pudding

helva – sweet prepared with sesame oil, cereals and honey or sugar syrup

kadayıf – dough soaked in syrup and topped with a layer of kaymak (clotted cream)

kahve – coffee

kırmızı şarap – red wine

kiraz suyu – cherry juice

kola – cola-flavoured soft drink

künefe – shredded-wheat pastry with pistachios, honey and sugar syrup

limonata – lemonade

lokum – Turkish delight

maden suyu – mineral water

mahallebi – sweet rice-flour and milk pudding

meyve suyu – fruit juice

rakı – strong aniseed-flavoured liquor

sahlep – hot drink made with crushed tapioca-root extract

şalgam suyu – sour turnip juice

şarap – wine

su – water

süt – milk

(taze) nar suyu – (fresh) pomegranate juice

(taze) portakal suyu – (fresh) orange juice

Türk kahvesi – Turkish coffee

...az şekerli – with a little sugar

...çok şekerli – with a lot of sugar

...orta şekerli – with medium sugar

...şekersiz – no sugar

Behind the Scenes

SEND US YOUR FEEDBACK

We love to hear from travellers – your comments keep us on our toes and help make our books better. Our well-travelled team reads every word on what you loved or loathed about this book. Although we cannot reply individually to postal submissions, we always guarantee that your feedback goes straight to the appropriate authors, in time for the next edition. Each person who sends us information is thanked in the next edition – and the most useful submissions are rewarded with a selection of digital PDF chapters.

Visit **lonelyplanet.com/contact** to submit your updates and suggestions or to ask for help. Our award-winning website also features inspirational travel stories, news and discussions.

Note: We may edit, reproduce and incorporate your comments in Lonely Planet products such as guidebooks, websites and digital products, so let us know if you don't want your comments reproduced or your name acknowledged. For a copy of our privacy policy visit lonelyplanet.com/privacy.

OUR READERS

Many thanks to the travellers who used the last edition and wrote to us with helpful hints, useful advice and interesting anecdotes:

A Claire Allen, **B** Leila Badsha, Kim Browne, Ceyda Bulat, Andy Bundell, **C** Janet Cater, **D** Gabriella Dembitz, Nick Dillen, Ernest Djan, Stefan Durwael, Margrit Dutt, **F** Stefano Fontana, **G** Stephanie Gessner, Tugrul Gokce, Mustafa Gokhan Bulut, Patrick Gourley, Bulent Guzelkan, **H** Anthony Hartnett, Chris Harvey, **I** Laura Iseppi De Filippis, **K** Miha Kolner, Irma Kreiten, Nelleke Kruijs Voorberge, **M** Sheila Miller, Beatrice Milmor, **P** Florencia Peña, Johan Poels, **Q** Edgar F. Quiñonesmorales, **R** Hugh Rosenbaum, Ronan Royer, **S** Stephen Sharpe, Ayse Slevogt, Karin Sluiter, Alex Sutcliffe, **T** Françoise Terzian, Sunil Thakar, Anemone Thomas, Victoria Thomson, **U** Serhat Uzunel, **V** Bernard Vixseboxse, Kate Vyborny, **W** Rl Watson, Stefan Weck, Teresa Wong, **Y** Tahir Yasin, Huseyin Yilmaz

AUTHOR THANKS

Virginia Maxwell

Many thanks to Pat Yale, Faruk Boyacı, Tahir Karabaş, Eveline Zoutendijk, George Grundy, Saffet Tonguç, Demet Sabancı Çetindoğan, Ercan Tanrıvermiş, Ann Nevans, Tina Nevans, Jennifer Gaudet, Özlem Tuna, Shellie Corman, Mehmet Umur, Emel Güntaş, Tuna Mersinli, Halûk Dursun, İnci Döndaş, İlber Ortayli, Selin Rozanes, Ansel Mullins, Megan Clark, Atilla Tuna, Elif Aytekin and the many locals who shared their knowledge and love of the city with me.

ACKNOWLEDGMENTS

Illustrations p46-7, p48-9 by Javier Zarracina.

Cover photograph: Yeni Mosque, İstanbul, Turkey; Murat Ayranci/Photolibrary ©.

THIS BOOK

This 7th edition of Lonely Planet's *İstanbul* guidebook was researched and written by Virginia Maxwell. The previous three editions were also written by Virginia. This guidebook was commissioned in Lonely Planet's London office, and produced by the following:

Commissioning Editor Clifton Wilkinson

Coordinating Editors Tasmin Waby, Simon Williamson

Coordinating Cartographer Jeff Cameron

Coordinating Layout Designer Clara Monitto

Managing Editor Brigitte Ellemor

Senior Editors Andi Jones, Catherine Naghten

Managing Cartographers Anita Banh, Adrian Persoglia

Managing Layout Designer Jane Hart

Assisting Editors Elizabeth Jones, Helen Koehne, Anne Mason

Cover Research Naomi Parker

Internal Image Research Aude Vauconsant

Language Content Branislava Vladisavljevic

Thanks to Dan Austin, Ryan Evans, Tobias Gattineau, Asha Ioculari, Jouve India, Charlotte Orr, Trent Paton, Raphael Richards, Averil Robertson, Fiona Siseman, Lieu Thi Pham, Samantha Tyson, Gerard Walker, Danny Williams

Index

See also separate subindexes for:

✗ **EATING P221**

🍺 **DRINKING & NIGHTLIFE P222**

☆ **ENTERTAINMENT P223**

🛍 **SHOPPING P223**

🏃 **SPORTS & ACTIVITIES P223**

🛏 **SLEEPING P223**

🍴 EATING

İstanbul Maps

Map Legend

Sights

- Beach
- Buddhist
- Castle
- Christian
- Hindu
- Islamic
- Jewish
- Monument
- Museum/Gallery
- Ruin
- Winery/Vineyard
- Zoo
- Other Sight

Eating

- Eating

Drinking & Nightlife

- Drinking & Nightlife
- Cafe

Entertainment

- Entertainment

Shopping

- Shopping

Sleeping

- Sleeping
- Camping

Sports & Activities

- Diving/Snorkelling
- Canoeing/Kayaking
- Skiing
- Surfing
- Swimming/Pool
- Walking
- Windsurfing
- Other Sports & Activities

Information

- Post Office
- Tourist Information

Transport

- Airport
- Border Crossing
- Bus
- Cable Car/Funicular
- Cycling
- Ferry
- Monorail
- Parking
- S-Bahn
- Taxi
- Train/Railway
- Tram
- Tube Station
- U-Bahn
- Underground Train Station
- Other Transport

Routes

- Tollway
- Freeway
- Primary
- Secondary
- Tertiary
- Lane
- Unsealed Road
- Plaza/Mall
- Steps
- Tunnel
- Pedestrian Overpass
- Walking Tour
- Walking Tour Detour
- Path

Boundaries

- International
- State/Province
- Disputed
- Regional/Suburb
- Marine Park
- Cliff
- Wall

Geographic

- Hut/Shelter
- Lighthouse
- Lookout
- Mountain/Volcano
- Oasis
- Park
- Pass
- Picnic Area
- Waterfall

Hydrography

- River/Creek
- Intermittent River
- Swamp/Mangrove
- Reef
- Canal
- Water
- Dry/Salt/Intermittent Lake
- Glacier

Areas

- Beach/Desert
- Cemetery (Christian)
- Cemetery (Other)
- Park/Forest
- Sportsground
- Sight (Building)
- Top Sight (Building)

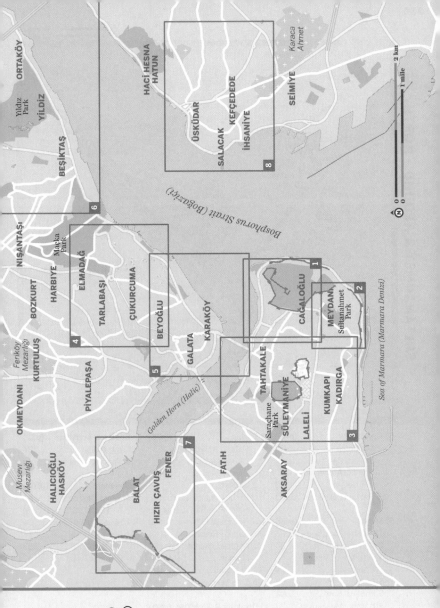

MAP INDEX

ORTAKÖY

YILDIZ

Yıldız
Park

BEŞİKTAŞ

NİŞANTAŞI

Maçka
Park

ELMADAĞ

HARBIYE

BOZKURT

TARLABAŞI

ÇUKURCUMA

KURTULUŞ

Feriköy
Mezarlığı

PIYALEPAŞA

BEYOĞLU

GALATA

KARAKÖY

OKMEYDANI

HALICIOĞLU
HASKÖY

Mûsevi
Mezarlığı

Golden Horn (Haliç)

BALAT

HIZIR ÇAVUŞ

FENER

FATIH

AKSARAY

LALELI

SÜLEYMANİYE

Saraçhane
Park

TAHTAKALE

KUMKAPI

KADIRGA

CAĞALOĞLU

MEYDANI

Sultanahmet
Park

Bosphorus Strait (Boğaziçi)

HACI HESNA
HATUN

ÜSKÜDAR

SALACAK

KEÇEDEDE

İHSANİYE

SEİMİYE

Karaca
Ahmet

Sea of Marmara (Marmara Denizi)

0   1 mile

0   2 km

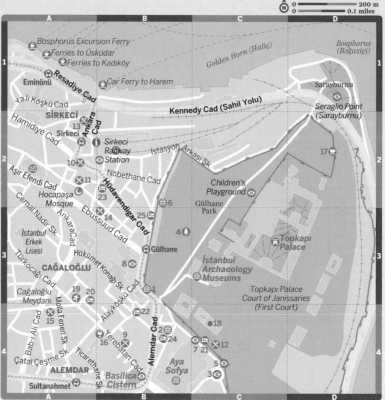

SULTANAHMET & AROUND - SOUTH *Map on p232*

Key on p231

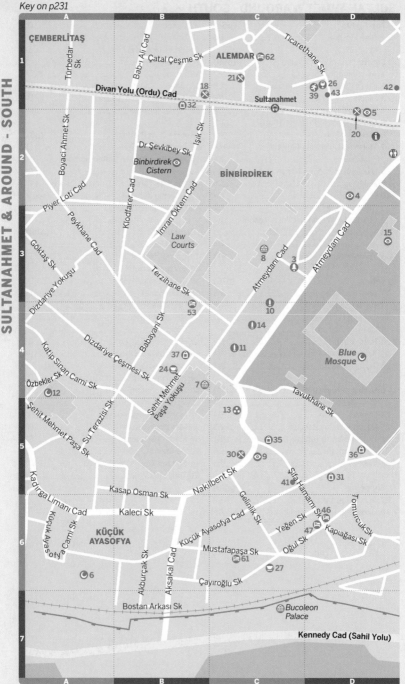

ÇEMBERLİTAŞ

Türbedar Sk

Bab-ı Ali Cad

Çatal Çeşme Sk

ALEMDAR 62

Ticarethane Sk

21

18

Divan Yolu (Ordu) Cad

32

Sultanahmet

39 26 43

42

20 5

Boyaci Ahmet Sk

Dr Şevkibey Sk

Işık Sk

Binbirdirek Cistern

BİNBİRDİREK

4

Piyer Loti Cad

Klodfarer Cad

İmran Öktem Cad

15

Pelyhane Cad

Law Courts

8

Atmeydanı Cad

3

Göktaş Sk

Dizdariye Yokuşu

Terzihane Sk

Atmeydanı Cad

Babayan Sk

53

10

Katip Sinan Cami Sk

Dizdariye Çeşmesi Sk

37

24

14

11

Blue Mosque

Özbekler Sk

12

Su Terazisi Sk

Şehit Mehmet Paşa Yokuşu

7

Tavukhane Sk

Şehit Mehmet Paşa Sk

13

35

36

30

9

Kadırga Limanı Cad

Kasap Osman Sk

Nakilbent Sk

41

31

Küçük Ayasofya Cami Sk

Kaleci Sk

Küçük Ayasofya Cad

Gelinik Sk

Sifa Hamamı Sk

46

47

Kapıağası Sk

Tomrucuk Sk

KÜÇÜK AYASOFYA

Akburçak Sk

Aksakal Cad

Mustafapaşa Sk

Yeğen Sk

Oğul Sk

61

6

Çayıroğlu Sk

27

Bostan Arkası Sk

Bucoleon Palace

Kennedy Cad (Sahil Yolu)

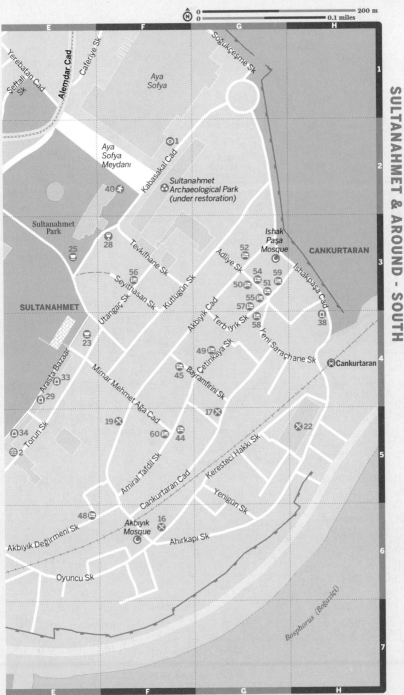

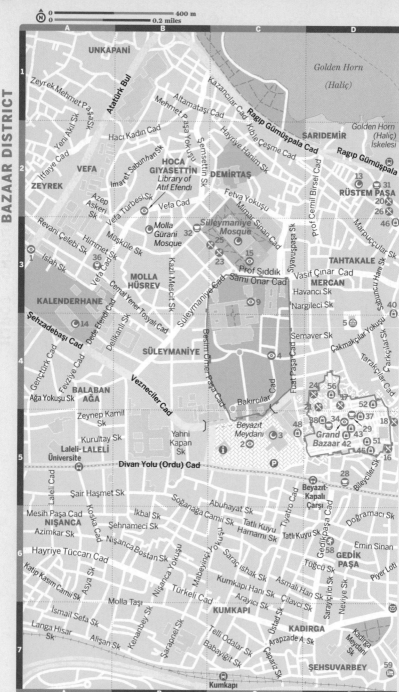

0
0
400 m
0.2 miles

UNKAPANI

Golden Horn
(Haliç)

Zeyrek Mehmet Paşa Sk

Atatürk Bul

Kazancılar Cad

Ragıp Gümüşpala Cad

SARIDEMİR

Golden Horn
(Haliç)
İskelesi

Altamataşı Cad

Mehmet Paşa Yokuşu

Hacı Kadın Cad

Kıble Çeşme Cad

Ragıp Gümüşpala

Yeni Akıl Sk

İtfaiye Cad

Şemsettin Sk

Hayriye Hanım Sk

13

31

VEFA

HOCA
GIYASETTİN
Library of
Atıf Efendı

DEMİRTAŞ

RÜSTEM PAŞA

20

ZEYREK

Imaret Sabunhan Sk

Fetva Yokuşu

26

Azep
Askeri
Sk

Vefa Türbesi Sk

Vefa Cad

Mimar Sinan Cad

Prof Cemil Birsel Cad

46

Revanî Çelebi Sk

Himmet Sk

Molla
Gürani
Mosque

Süleymaniye
Mosque

32

25

Marpuççular Sk

Müşküle Sk

TAHTAKALE

1

İslah Sk

36

MOLLA
HÜSREV

15

Siyavuşpaşa Sk

Vasıf Çınar Cad

MERCAN

Vefa Cad

Kazlı Mescit Sk

23

Prof Şıddık
Sami Onar Cad

Havancı Sk

40

KALENDERHANE

Cemal Yener Tosyalı Cad

Süleymaniye Cad

9

Nargileci Sk

5

Çakmakçılar Yokuşu

Sabuncu Han Cad

Dede Efendi Cad

14

Semaver Sk

Tarakçılar Cad

Şehzadebaşı Cad

Delikanlı Sk

4

Fuat Paşa Cad

Çakmakçılar Yokuşu

SÜLEYMANİYE

Besim Ömer Paşa Cad

Gençtürk Cad

Feyziye Cad

Vezneciler Cad

24

56

BALABAN
AĞA

47

Ağa Yokuşu Sk

Bakırcılar

21

52

Zeynep Kamil
Sk

38

34

37

Kurultay Sk

Yahni
Kapan
Sk

Beyazıt
Meydanı

3

48

Grand
Bazaar 42

29

18

LALELİ
Üniversite

2

43

51

Laleli-
Üniversite

Divan Yolu (Ordu) Cad

45

16

Laleli Cad

28

Şair Haşmet Sk

Beyazıt-
Kapalı
Çarşı

Bileyciler Sk

Mesih Paşa Cad

Abuhayat Sk

Tiyatro Cad

Doğramacı Sk

NİŞANCA

İkbal Sk

Soğanağa Camii Sk

Tatlı Kuyu
Hamamı Sk

Tatlı Kuyu

Gedik Paşa Cad

Emin Sinan

Azimkar Sk

Şehnameci Sk

GEDİK
PAŞA

Hayriye Tüccarı Cad

Nişanca Bostan Sk

58

Piyer Loti

Katip Kasım Camii Sk

Asya Sk

Koska Cad

Nişanca Yokuşu

Mabeyinci Yok

Saraç İshak Sk

Asmalı Han Sk

Tüğcü Sk

Sarayiçi Sk

Neviye Sk

İsmail Sefa Sk

Molla Taşı

Türkeli Cad

Kumkapı Hanı Sk

Çilavci Sk

Arayıcı Sk

KUMKAPI

Langa Hisar
Sk

Alişan Sk

Kenanbey Sk

Saraç Sk

Telli Odalar Sk

Babayiğit Sk

Arapzade A. Sk

Ustad Sk

KADIRGA

Çaparız Sk

Kadırga
Meydanı
Sk

ŞEHSUVARBEY

59

Kumkapı

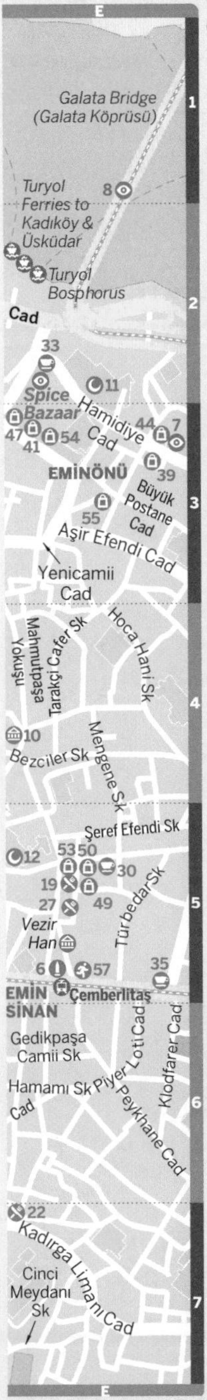

BAZAAR DISTRICT

Galata Bridge
(Galata Köprüsü)

Turyol
Ferries to
Kadıköy &
Üsküdar

Turyol
Bosphorus

Cad

33

Spice
Bazaar
47 41 54 Cad
EMİNÖNÜ

Hamidiye Cad
44
7
39
Büyük
Postane
Cad

55

Aşir Efendi Cad

Yenicamii
Cad

Mahmutpaşa
Yokuşu

Tarakçı Cafer Sk

Hoca Hanı Sk

10

Bezciler Sk

Mengene Sk

Şeref Efendi Sk

12
53 50
30
19
27
49

Türbedar Sk

Vezir
Hanı

6
57
35

EMİN
SİNAN

Çemberlitaş

Gedikpaşa
Camii Sk

Piyer Loti Cad

Klodfarer Cad

Hamamı Sk

Peykhane Cad

Cad

22

Kadırga Limanı Cad

Cinci
Meydanı
Sk

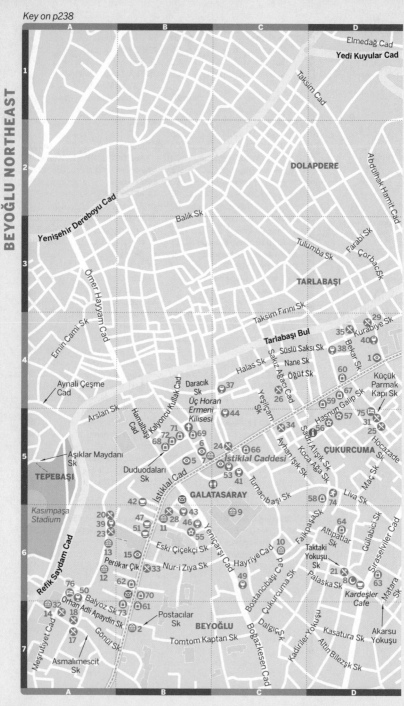

BEYOĞLU NORTHEAST

Elmedağ Cad
Yedi Kuyular Cad

Taksim Cad

Abdülhak Hamit Cad

DOLAPDERE

Yenişehir Dereboyu Cad

Balık Sk

Farabi Sk
Çorbacı Sk
Tulumba Sk

Ömer Hayyam Cad

TARLABAŞI

Emin Cami Sk

Taksim Fırını Sk

Tarlabaşı Bul

29
35 Kurabiye Sk
40
38 Bekar Sk

Süslü Saksı Sk
Halas Sk
Sakiz Ağacı Cad
Nane Sk
Öğüt Sk

Aynali Çeşme
Cad

1

Daracık
Sk 37
26 60

Küçük
Parmak
Kapı Sk

Arslan Sk

Hamalbaşı Cad
Kalyoncu Kullak Cad

Üç Horan
Ermeni
Kilisesi

Yeşilçam Sk
67
59 57 75

Hasnun Galip Sk
31
25

44
34
56
ÇUKURCUMA

71
69
68 72

Sakıt Ali Işık Sk
Koca Ağa Sk

Hocazade

6 24
5 7 66
İstiklal Caddesi

Duduodaları
Sk

Aşıklar Maydanı
Sk

TEPEBAŞI

Ayhan Işık Sk
Koca Ağa Sk

53
41

Turnacıbaşı Sk

Kasımpaşa
Stadium

42
GALATASARAY

58 74

Liva Sk

Gülllabici Sk

İstiklal Cad

43
9

64

20 28
47 46
39 51 11 55
23

Eski Çiçekçi Sk
Yeniçarşı Cad

Falakpaşa Sk
Altıpatlar
Sk

Sıraselviler Cad

Refik Saydam Cad

13

HayriyeCad

10

Taktaki
Yokuşu
Sk
21
8

15

Perükar Çik 33
12

Nur-i Ziya Sk

49

Bostancıbaşı Cad
Çukurcuma Cad

Palaska Sk
63

Matara Sk

Kardeşler
Cafe

Akarsu
Yokuşu

76 50
32
14 18
17

62
70
73 61

BEYOĞLU

Balyoz Sk
Orhan Adli Apaydin Sk

Postacılar
Sk

Dalgıç Sk

Kadiriler Yokuşu

Kasatura Sk

Altın Bilez Sk

Gönül Sk

2

Tomtom Kaptan Sk

Boğazkesen Cad

Meşrutiyet Cad

Asmalımescit
Sk

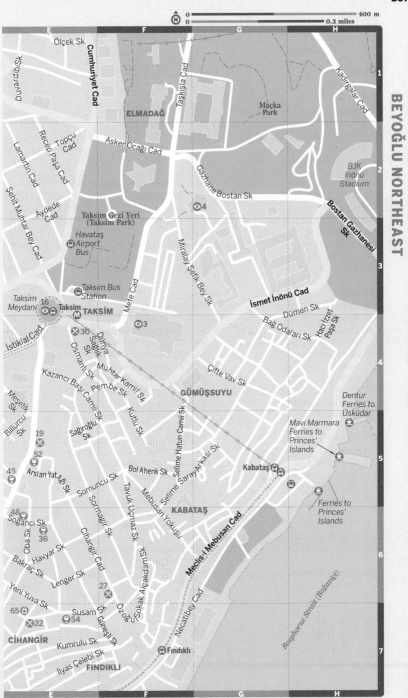

0 — 400 m
0 — 0.2 miles

Ölçek Sk

Duvardıbı Sk

Cumhuriyet Cad

Taşkışla Cad

ELMADAĞ

Maçka Park

Kadırgalar Cad

Recep Paşa Cad

Topçu Cad

Asker Ocağı Cad

BJK İnönü Stadium

Lamartin Cad

Aydede Cad

Şehit Muhtar Bey Cad

Gazhane Bostan Sk

Bostan Gazhanesi Sk

Taksim Gezi Yeri (Taksim Park)

4

Havataş Airport Bus

Miralay Şefik Bey Sk

Mete Cad

İsmet İnönü Cad

Taksim Bus Station

Taksim Meydanı 16

Taksim TAKSİM

Dümen Sk

Bağ Odaları Sk

Hacı İzzet Paşa Sk

İstiklal Cad

30

Dünya Sağlık Sk

3

Osmanlı Sk

Muhtar Kamil Sk

Çifte Vav Sk

GÜMÜŞSUYU

Kazancı Başı Camii Sk

Pembe Sk

Meşelik Sk

Billurcu Sk

19

Sağıroğlu Sk

Kutlu Sk

Selime Hatun Camii Sk

Dentur Ferries to Üsküdar

Mavi Marmara Ferries to Princes' Islands

52

45

Arslan Yatağı Sk

Bol Ahenk Sk

Saray Arkası Sk

Kabataş

Somuncu Sk

Sormagir Sk

Tavuk Uçmaz Sk

Mebusan Yokuşu

KABATAŞ

Ferries to Princes' Islands

48

Soğancı Sk

36

Oba Sk

Çukurcuma Cad

Changir Cad

Meclis-i Mebusan Cad

Havyar Sk

Bakraç Sk

Lenger Sk

27

Yeni Yuva Sk

65

22

Susam Sk

54

Özoğ

Sokak Alçakdam Sk

Güneşli Sk

Necatibey Cad

Bosphorus Strait (Boğaziçi)

CİHANGİR

Kumrulu Sk

Fındıklı

İlyas Çelebi Sk

FINDIKLI

BEYOĞLU - NORTHEAST *Map on p236*

BEYOĞLU - SOUTHWEST *Map on p240*

◉ **Top Sights**	**(p116)**
İstanbul Modern	F3

◎ **Sights**	**(p117)**
1 Arab Mosque	B4
2 Azapkapı Sokollu Mehmet Paşa Camii	A4
3 Botter House	C2
4 Christ Church	D3
5 Depo	E3
6 Galata Mevlevi Museum	C2
7 Galata Tower	C4
8 Jewish Museum of Turkey	C5
9 Kasa Galeri	C4
10 Museum of Innocence	E1
11 Patisserie Lebon	C2
12 SALT Galata	C4
13 Schneidertempel Art Center	C4

✖ **Eating**	**(p124)**
14 Antiochia	C2
15 Asmalı Cavit	C1
Ca' d'Oro	(see 12)
16 Fasuli Lokantaları	F3
17 Fürreyya Galata Balıkçısı	C3
18 Galata House	C4
19 Galata Konak Patisserie Cafe	C4
20 Güney Restaurant	C3
21 Helvetia Lokanta	C2
22 İstanbul Modern Cafe/Restaurant	F3
23 Journey	F1
24 Karaköy Güllüoğlu	D5
25 Karaköy Lokantası	E4
26 Kiva Han	C3
27 Lokanta Maya	E4
28 Namlı	D5
29 Sofyalı 9	C2
30 The House Café	C2

◗ **Drinking & Nightlife**	**(p131)**
31 Atölye Kuledıbı	C4
32 Baylo	C2

33 Cafe Gündoğdu	C4
34 Le Fumoir	D3
35 Leb-i Derya	D2
36 Leb-i Derya Richmond	D2
37 Mavra	D3
38 Sensus Wine Bar	C3
39 Smyrna	F1
40 Tophane Nargile Cafes	F3
41 Waterfront Çay Bahçesis	H2
42 X Bar	B2

☺ **Entertainment**	**(p135)**
43 Babylon	C2
Galata Mevlevi Museum	(see 6)
44 Nardis Jazz Club	C4
Salon	(see 42)

⬡ **Shopping**	**(p136)**
45 Artrium	C2
46 Arzu Kaprol	C3
47 Bahar Korçan	C3
48 Berrin Akyüz	G1
49 Dear East	D3
50 Hammam	C4
51 İroni	C4
52 İstanbul Modern Gift Shop	F3
53 Lâl	C4
54 Lale Plak	C2
55 Selda Okutan	E4
56 SIR	D2

⬛ **Sleeping**	**(p171)**
Anemon Galata	(see 38)
57 Ansen Suites	C2
58 Beş Oda	D2
59 Galateia Residence	D2
60 Manzara Istanbul	C3
61 Serdar-ı Ekrem 59	D2
62 TomTom Suites	D1
63 Witt Istanbul Hotel	F2
64 World House Hostel	C3

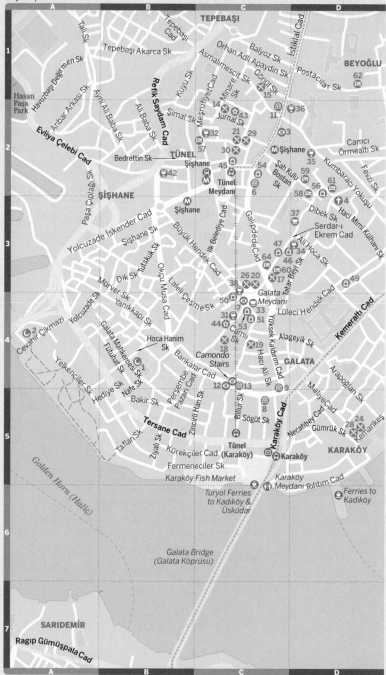

BEYOĞLU SOUTHWEST

TEPEBAŞI

BEYOĞLU

Tepebaşı Cad
Tepebaşı Akarca Sk
Talı Sk

Hasan Paşa Park
Havuzbaşı Değirmen Sk
Anbar Arkası Sk
Ayni Ali Baba Sk
Ali Baba Sk

Evliya Çelebi Cad

Kuyu Sk
Refik Saydam Cad
Şimal Sk
Mesrutiyet Cad
Minare Sk
Orhan Adli Apaydin Sk
Balyoz Sk
İstiklal Cad
Postacılar Sk
Asmalimescit Sk
Gönül Sk
Jurnal Sk

62

ŞİŞHANE

Bedrettin Sk
TÜNEL
Şişhane
42

Camcı Örmealtı Sk
Şah Kulu Bostan Sk
Şişhane
Kumbaracı Yokuşu
Fevzi Sk
35
59
61
56
58
Haci Mimi Külhani Sk

TÜNEL Meydanı
6
54
Dibek Sk
Serdar-ı Ekrem Cad
Ali Hoca Sk
37

Şişhane

Yolcuzade İskender Cad
Şişhane Sk
Büyük Hendek Cad
İlk Belediye Cad
Galipdede Cad
47
64
34
46
17
Tatar Beyi Sk
60
49

Dik Sk
Tutsluk Sk
Okçu Musa Cad
Laleli Çeşme Sk
Mürver Sk
Yanikkapi Sk
38
26 20
50
7
Galata Meydanı
Lüleci Hendek Cad
Kemeralti Cad

Cevahir Çıkmazı
Yolcuzade Cad
Galata Mahkemesi Sk
Fütuhat Sk
2
31
44
53
33
51
Camli
18
Hoca Hanim Sk
19
Alageyik Sk
GALATA
Arapoğlan Sk

Yelkenciler Sk
Hediye Sk
Nafe Sk
Bakir Sk
1
Camondo Stairs
Bankalar Cad
Haci Ali Sk
Yüksek Kaldirim Cad
Maliye Cad

Taflan Sk
Zivali Sk
Perşembe Pazari Cad
Zincirli Han Sk
12
13
9
Necatibey Cad
Gümrük Sk
28
24
Kemankeş

Tersane Cad
8
Birlik Sk
Söğüt Sk
Karaköy Cad
KARAKÖY

Kürekçiler Cad
Tünel (Karaköy)
Karaköy
Fermeneciler Sk
Karaköy Fish Market
Karaköy Meydanı
Rihtim Cad
Ferries to Kadıköy

Golden Horn (Haliç)

Turyol Ferries to Kadıköy & Üsküdar

Galata Bridge (Galata Köprüsü)

SARIDEMİR
Ragıp Gümüşpala Cad

A B C D

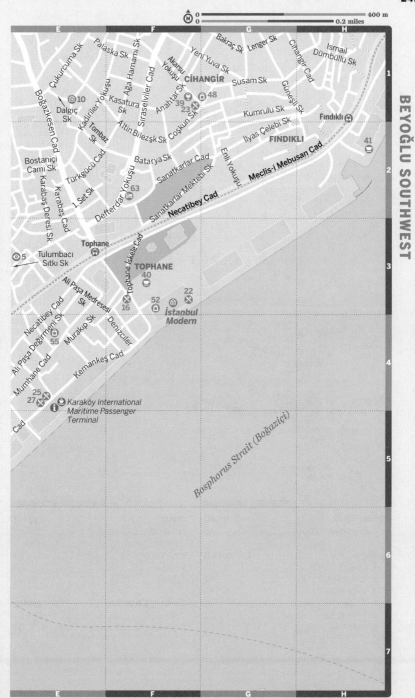

0 400 m
0 0.2 miles

Bakraç Sk
Lenger Sk
Çukurcuma Sk
Palaska Sk
Ağa Hamamı Sk
Kasatura Sk
Sıraselviler Cad
Akarsu Yokuşu
Yeni Yuva Sk
Ismail Dümbüllü Sk
CİHANGİR
Susam Sk
Cihangir Cad
Boğazkesen Cad
Dalgıç Sk
10
Kadiriler Yokuşu
Anahtar Sk
39
48
23
Güneşli Sk
Altın Bilezik Sk
Coşkun Sk
Kumrulu Sk
Fındıklı
Tombaz Sk
Türkgücü Cad
Batarya Sk
İlyas Çelebi Sk
FINDIKLI
41
Bostancı Cami Sk
Karabaş Deresi Sk
Karabaş Cad
Sanatkarlar Cad
Enli Yokuşu
Meclis-i Mebusan Cad
1 Set Sk
Defterdar Yokuşu
63
Sanatkarlar Mektebi Sk
Necatibey Cad
Tophane
Tulumbacı Sıtkı Sk
5
Tophane İskele Cad
TOPHANE
40
Ali Paşa Medresesi Sk
Ali Paşa Değirmeni Sk
16
22
Necatibey Cad
52
İstanbul Modern
Murakıp Sk
Denizciler
55
Mumhane Cad
Kemankeş Cad
25
27
Karaköy International Maritime Passenger Terminal
Cad

Bosphorus Strait (Boğaziçi)

BEŞİKTAŞ ORTAKÖY

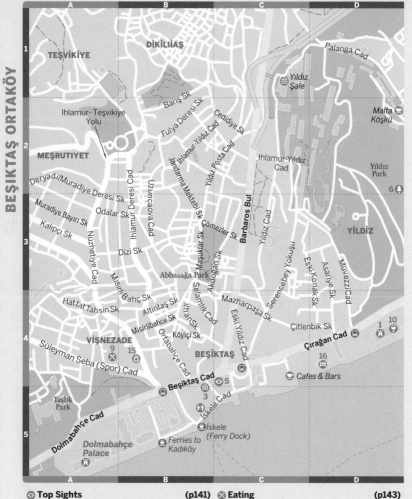

BEŞİKTAŞ ORTAKÖY

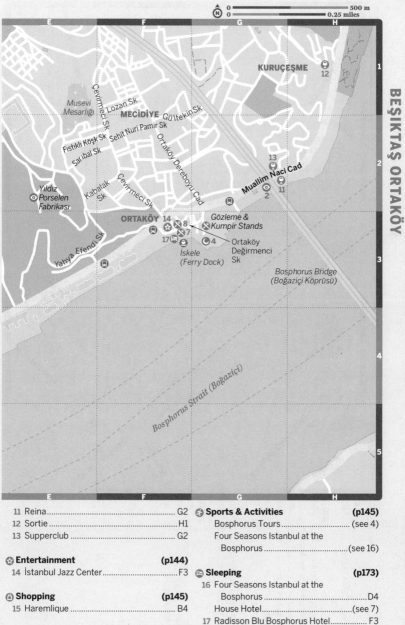

244

WESTERN DISTRICTS

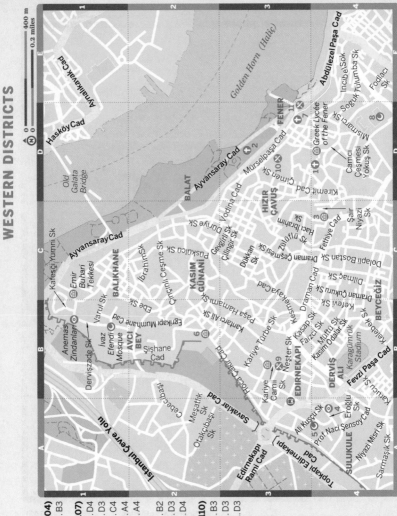

ÜSKÜDAR

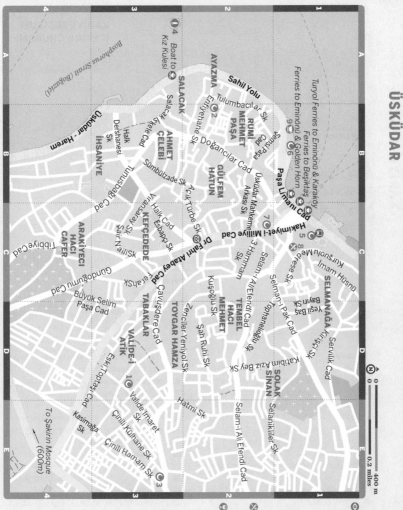

0 400 m
0 0.2 miles

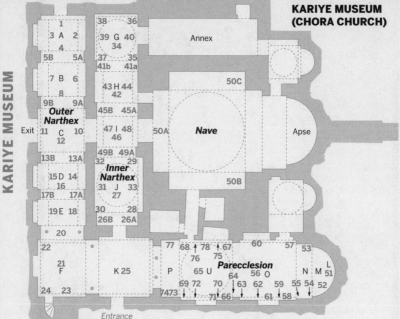

KARIYE MUSEUM (CHORA CHURCH)

KARIYE MUSEUM

Annex

50C

Outer
Narthex

Exit

Nave

Apse

Inner
Narthex

50A

50B

Parecclesion

Entrance

⊙ **Mosaics**

1 The voyage of the Virgin to Bethlehem & the dream of Joseph

2 The census held for the enrolment for taxation & registration of Mary & Joseph in the presence of Cyrenius, Governor of Syria

3 Jesus going with Mary & Joseph to Jerusalem

4 Remains of mosaics – Jesus among the doctors in the temple

5A St Trachos

5B St Andronikus

6 The birth of Jesus

7 The return of the Virgin Mary with Jesus

8 The attempts of Satan to deceive Jesus

9A St Georgios

9B St Demetrius

10 Jesus & the inscription 'the dwelling-place of the living'

11 The prayer of the Virgin & the attendant angels

12 The wedding at Cana & the miracles

13A Depiction of the saints

13B Depiction of the saints

14 The Magi on their way to Jerusalem riding on horseback & the three Magi in audience with King Herod

15 Elizabeth & John the Baptist running away from a pursuing soldier

16 Remains of mosaics

17A Depiction of the saints

17B Depiction of the saints

18 The scene of King Herod's investigation & a guard standing

19 The mourning mothers

20 No mosaics left

21 A decorative medallion

22 The meeting of Jesus with the Samaritan woman at the well

23 The healing of a paralysed person by Jesus

24 King Herod giving the order for the massacre of the innocents & the execution thereof

25 Remains of mosaics

26A The healing by Jesus of a young man with an injured arm

26B The healing by Jesus of leprous man

27 Twenty-four of the early ancestors of Jesus (Genealogy of Christ)

28 The healing by Jesus of a woman asking for the restoration of her health

29 The healing by Jesus of the mother-in-law of St Peter

30 The healing by Jesus of a deaf person

31 Dispersion of good health by Jesus to the people

32 The healing by Jesus of two blind men

33 The Khalke Jesus & the praying Virgin

34 The Virgin & the Child Jesus

35 Joachim in the mountains praying to have a child

36 No mosaics left

37 The breaking of the good news of the birth of Jesus to Mary – The Annunciation

38 The chief priest Zacchariah judging the Virgin

39 Mary & Joseph bidding each other farewell

40 The breaking of the good news of the birth of Mary to Anne

41A The meeting of Anne & Joachim

41B Joseph bringing the Virgin into his house

42 Mary in the arms of Anne & Joachim & the blessing by the priests

43 Giving of the stick with young shoots indicating Joseph as Mary's fiancé

44 The birth of the Virgin Mary

45A The first seven steps of the Virgin & below, St Peter

45B The prayer of the chief priest Zacchariah in front of the 12 sticks

46 The presentation of Mary (age three) to the temple by her parents

47 The Virgin taking the skeins of wool to weave the veil for the temple

48 Theodore Metochites presenting a small model of the church to Jesus

49A The feeding of the Virgin by an angel & below, St Peter

49B Remains of mosaics – Directives given to the Virgin at the temple

50A The Assumption of the Virgin

50B Mary & the Child Jesus

50C Jesus in a standing posture, holding the Bible in his hand

◉ **Frescoes**

51 The Anastasis

52 The Church Fathers

53 The raising (resurrection) of the widow's son)

54 The healing of the daughter of Jairus

55 The Virgin Elousa

56 The Last Judgment

57 Abraham & the beggar Lazarus on his lap

58 St George

59 Rich man burning in Hell's fire

60 Those entering Heaven & the Angel Seraphim with the semi-nude good thief.

61 Depiction of Andronikus II & his family & the inscription & depiction above of Makarios Tornikes & his wife Eugenia

62 The Bearing of the Ark of the Covenant

63 St Demetrius

64 St Theodore Tiro

65 Mary & Child Jesus with the 12 attending angels

66 Four Gospel Writers (Hymnographers): St Cosmos

67 Four Gospel Writers (Hymnographers): St John of Damascene

68 Four Gospel Writers (Hymnographers): St Theophanes

69 Four Gospel Writers (Hymnographers): St Joseph

70 St Theodore Stratelates

71 King Solomon & the Israelites

72 Placement into the temple of the Ark of the Covenant

73 The combat of an angel with the Asurians in the outskirts of Jerusalem.

74 St Procopios, St Sabas Stratelates

75 Moses in the bushes

76 Jacob's ladder & the angels

77 Aaron & his sons carrying votive offerings, in front of the altar

78 St Samonas & guiras

Our Story

A beat-up old car, a few dollars in the pocket and a sense of adventure. In 1972 that's all Tony and Maureen Wheeler needed for the trip of a lifetime – across Europe and Asia overland to Australia. It took several months, and at the end – broke but inspired – they sat at their kitchen table writing and stapling together their first travel guide, *Across Asia on the Cheap*. Within a week they'd sold 1500 copies. Lonely Planet was born.

Today, Lonely Planet has offices in Melbourne, London and Oakland, with more than 600 staff and writers. We share Tony's belief that 'a great guidebook should do three things: inform, educate and amuse'.

Our Writer

Virginia Maxwell

Although based in Australia, Virginia spends much of her year researching guidebooks in the Mediterranean countries. Of these, Turkey is unquestionably her favourite. As well as working on the previous three editions of this city guide, she is also the author of Lonely Planet's *İstanbul* pocket guide and the İstanbul chapter of Lonely Planet's *Turkey* guide, and she writes about the city for a host of international magazines and websites. Virginia usually travels with partner Peter and son Max, who have grown to love Turkey as much as she does.

Read more about Virginia at:
lonelyplanet.com/members/virginiamaxell

Published by Lonely Planet Publications Pty Ltd
ABN 36 005 607 983
7th edition – February 2013
ISBN 978 1 74179 961 3
© Lonely Planet 2013   Photographs © as indicated 2013
10 9 8 7 6 5 4 3 2
Printed in China

Although the authors and Lonely Planet have taken all reasonable care in preparing this book, we make no warranty about the accuracy or completeness of its content and, to the maximum extent permitted, disclaim all liability arising from its use.